A Certain Style

Jacqueline Kent was born and lives in Sydney. Originally trained as a journalist and broadcaster for the ABC, she has since 1975 worked as an editor of fiction and non-fiction for most of Australia's major publishers. She is also the author of two general social histories and six books of fiction for young adults. She won the National Biography Award in 2002 for *A Certain Style*.

ALSO BY JACQUELINE KENT

NON-FICTION

Out of the Bakelite Box: The Heyday of Australian Radio
In the Half Light: Life as a Child in Australia 1900–1970

YOUNG ADULT FICTION

Angel Claws I Love You
Bad Behaviour (with Joanne Horniman)

A Certain Style

Beatrice Davis
a literary life

JACQUELINE KENT

PENGUIN BOOKS

Penguin Books

Published by the Penguin Group
Penguin Books Australia Ltd
250 Camberwell Road, Camberwell, Victoria 3124, Australia
Penguin Books Ltd
80 Strand, London WC2R 0RL, England
Penguin Putnam Inc.
375 Hudson Street, New York, New York 10014, USA
Penguin Books Canada Limited
10 Alcorn Avenue, Toronto, Ontario, Canada M4V 3B2
Penguin Books (NZ) Ltd
Cnr Rosedale and Airborne Roads, Albany, Auckland, New Zealand
Penguin Books (South Africa) (Pty) Ltd
24 Sturdee Avenue, Rosebank, Johannesburg 2196, South Africa
Penguin Books India (P) Ltd
11, Community Centre, Panchsheel Park, New Delhi 110 017, India

First published by Penguin Books Australia 2001
First published in paperback 2002

1 3 5 7 9 10 8 6 4 2

Cover design by Susannah Low, Penguin Design Studio
Text design by John Canty, Penguin Design Studio
Front cover photographs by Bill Davis (left) and Desmond Woolley (centre)
Typeset in 11/14.5pt Bembo by Post Pre-press Group, Brisbane, Queensland
Printed and bound in Australia by McPherson's Printing Group,
Maryborough, Victoria

National Library of Australia
Cataloguing-in-Publication data:

Kent, Jacqueline.
A certain style: Beatrice Davis, a literary life.

Bibliography.
Includes index.
ISBN 0 143 00067 5.

1. Davis, Beatrice, 1909–1992. 2. Women editors – Australia – Biography. 3.
Book editors – Australia – Biography. 4. Women publishers – Australia –
Biography. 5. Angus & Robertson – History. 6. Publishers and publishing –
Australia – History – 20th century. I. Title.

070.5092

This project has been assisted by the Commonwealth Government through the
Australia Council, its arts funding and advisory body.

For my father
Lance Albert Kent
(1917–1997)

CONTENTS

PART 3
1945–1960   89 Castlereagh Street

PART 4
1960–1973   221 George Street

PART 5
1973–1992   Folly Point and Hunters Hill

Introduction

On a cold July evening in 1980 a small elegant woman climbed the wooden staircase to the first floor of the Kirribilli Neighbourhood Centre on the north side of Sydney Harbour, almost under the bridge. She moved slowly, clutching the rail – the stairs were steep, she was seventy-one and a lifetime of cigarette smoking had made her wheezy – pausing for breath only when she reached the top landing. From behind a half-open door she heard the murmuring voices of about forty young women who were waiting for her to speak to them. Most were in their twenties or thirties, young enough to be her daughters. In one sense that is exactly who we were.

We were book editors. Most of us worked for the Australian branches of the American- and British-based publishers who had dominated the local publishing scene since the early 1970s. Like book editors the world over, we were mainly middle-class women with university degrees. Almost none of us had started our working lives as editors – we were former teachers, librarians, university tutors, researchers – and we all knew we would have been much better paid if we had stayed in our original jobs.

Yet we had turned our backs on other, more lucrative jobs because we wanted to work with books. Most of us found seductive the idea of engaging with the minds and imaginations of writers. And whatever our problems with schedules or costs, ridiculous deadlines, impossible authors or execrably written texts flung together to catch a market, we still enjoyed turning a manuscript from a pile of paper to a finished book, and seeing 'our' books in bookshops and on library shelves, knowing that – maybe – they would not have been as good without us.

We had come out on this midwinter night because the speaker we were about to hear knew more about the craft of editing than anyone else in Australia. She was legendary, and for many of us she had been a role model from the day we started in publishing. It was this woman, Beatrice Davis, who had written: 'Nothing quite equals the surprised by joy feeling when an editor comes upon a writer, previously unknown, who shows signs of the creative imagination that is so rare, so hard to define, so immediately recognisable.'

We knew that Beatrice Davis was the bridge spanning modern Australian literature from Miles Franklin to Tim Winton. She had been with Angus and Robertson for thirty-six years, from 1937 until 1973, and was now the Sydney editor for Thomas Nelson. She had been much more than a polisher of other people's prose. In the early 1940s, with Douglas Stewart, she had founded *Australian Poetry* and *Coast to Coast,* ground-breaking anthologies which presented the work of an emerging generation of Australian writers, among them Judith Wright, A.D. Hope, Dal Stivens and Judah Waten, and which continued to publish outstanding poetry and prose for more than thirty years.

She had been a friend to dozens of Australian poets and novelists, including Thea Astley, Hal Porter, Xavier Herbert, Douglas Stewart and Ruth Park. As a judge of the Miles Franklin Award from its inception in 1957 she had influenced public perception of what was best in Australian fiction. She had trained a generation of editors to follow her. Douglas Stewart had written about her: 'As much as anyone else, and more than most, she kept Australian literature alive for more than a quarter of a century.' She had been made an MBE in 1965, Bookman of the Year in 1976, and was shortly to be made an AM. We also knew that Beatrice Davis had been dismissed from Angus and Robertson in 1973, at the age of sixty-four, a casualty of the company's takeover by Gordon Barton's IPEC. Richard Walsh, who had fired the bullet, was still excoriated seven years later. Some of us were eagerly indignant on Beatrice's behalf, ready to consider her a martyr to the feminist cause.

In her dress of fine blue wool, stockings and black high-heeled shoes, with immaculately waved grey hair, discreet makeup and elegant jewellery, Beatrice seemed to belong in the old Queen's Club, a place of antique furniture and gleaming mirrors. Barbara Ker Wilson, a former colleague of Beatrice's at Angus and Robertson, introduced her, speaking with enthusiasm of Beatrice's achievements and honours. Some of us noticed Beatrice give her a swift, quizzical glance: *Darling, let's not overdo it.* A minute later she began to speak. Her hands, we noticed, were empty: her skill and experience in public speaking evidently transcended the use of notes. 'I have been asked to speak to you about the role of the editor,' she began in a low-pitched voice, her vowels rounded in the cultivated Australian speech of an earlier era. 'And although I can see that this audience consists mainly of women, I shall throughout refer to the editor as *he*.' She paused and looked around the room, her chin raised.

The few editors who had worked with Beatrice smiled at each other. They knew her dislike of inclusive language, her distaste for the distortions she considered feminism had imposed on the language of Fowler and the *Oxford English Dictionary*. But others frowned and folded their arms. If Beatrice noticed this evidence of resistance, she gave no sign. 'I shall begin by saying that editing should never be obvious,' she continued evenly. 'The author's voice is sacrosanct, and the editor must always remember that the book does not belong to him, but to the author.'

Beatrice was echoing the words of Maxwell Perkins – the legendary US editor of Thomas Wolfe, F. Scott Fitzgerald and Ernest Hemingway – who had once observed that in the end an editor can get out of an author only what that author has in him. Yet as Beatrice continued – 'The editor should . . .' 'The editor must . . .' 'It is the editor's responsibility to . . .' – some of us felt uneasy. We knew Beatrice was condensing almost fifty years of her professional life into half an hour, but she seemed to be speaking to us not as colleagues but as students, laying down the law: in effect, ordering us to be submissive. We found difficulty in believing that a woman with such a strong personality, someone so much in control, even bossy, was quite as deferential to her authors as she was telling us to be.

When the time came for questions from the audience, an editor in her early thirties challenged Beatrice on her attitude to inclusive language. Looking irritated, Beatrice invoked traditional English grammar in support of her position, her snappy tone making it clear that she considered the subject closed. The editor was ready to continue the argument, but the feeling of the meeting was against her: it seemed the height of bad manners to wrangle with such a distinguished guest.

For some years after this, I met Beatrice Davis at various literary events; we acknowledged each other, but never really had a conversation. Then in 1983 my first book, a history of Australian radio, was published. Not long afterwards Beatrice greeted me with: 'I believe you've written a book, dear.' When I admitted this, gratified that she had noticed, her reply was: 'You are an editor. Editors do not write books.' I felt that I had been slapped on the wrist.

A few years afterwards we had a more interesting encounter. It was October 1987 and I was coming to the end of a dreadful year. Kenneth Cook, the author of *Wake in Fright* whom I had married in January, had died of a heart attack three months later and I was still raw. Beatrice came up to me and said crisply, 'I'm sorry about your husband, dear.' I was touched and thanked her. 'Yes,' she added, 'it's really difficult when you have to bury them, isn't it?'

Them? How many men did she mean, for heaven's sake? There was something about the blunt tactlessness of her comment that I found, and still do, oddly endearing, perhaps because it was so unexpected. For the first time I realised that Beatrice's genteel, ladylike persona was only part of her story. Later I discovered that she was famous for her forthright comments to, and about, authors. 'Go to bed with Xavier Herbert?' she said to his biographer. 'No. He never stopped talking long enough.' (She was lying.) I also learned that Beatrice had cut quite a swathe through the male literary community, though her comment to me suggested that she considered men expendable.

When Beatrice left Angus and Robertson, about eighty of her authors – some of whom had been the subject of her blunt remarks – put together a book of tributes to her. Their words give a softer picture of the acerbic woman I was beginning to know. Thea Astley, whom Beatrice had discovered and whose first novel, *Girl With a Monkey*, A&R published in 1958, said that her first editor had always been 'a helpful friend who has the capacity to advise without hurt, to correct without making the author feel ashamed or inadequate'. Others commented on Beatrice's elegant appearance, the time and care she put into training a new generation of editors, her thoughtfulness, the sensitive sympathy and practical help she gave to many writers. Granted that critical comment is unlikely to be found in this kind of informal *Festschrift*, the genuine affection that Beatrice inspired among writers of poetry, fiction, children's books and non-fiction was still striking.

After Beatrice retired in the late 1980s, several people suggested she write her memoirs. She refused, adding revealingly, 'Most of the authors are (or have been when alive) my friends. How *could* I expose them?'

It was a tease on her part, but Beatrice would never have written a tell-all memoir: such a book would destroy the unspoken compact between author and editor. Neither tells the other's secrets. Authors often give their editors information they do not want to be made public; editors don't gossip about their authors to the wider world – or usually not until the author is dead (as in the case of Xavier Herbert). Beatrice might also have been reluctant to tell readers what their favourite authors were 'really' like, having long since learned to shrug off appalling authorial behaviour as the price to be paid for a good book.

But she was not entirely indifferent to the claims of posterity. In 1977 she allowed herself to be interviewed for the archives of the National Library of Australia, the tape of which is entirely without revealing comment about her authors or herself. She also co-operated with Anthony Barker, a friend and former colleague at Angus and Robertson, in a 47-page biographical study published by The Victorian Society of Editors. *One of the First and One of the Finest: Beatrice Davis, Book Editor*, which appeared in 1991, is full of fascinating glimpses into Beatrice's life at Angus and Robertson. Former prime minister Billy Hughes struggles up the stairs to her attic office crying, 'Where is she? Where's the woman I'd leave home for?' Beatrice drinks with her authors in her studio in lower George Street, throws herself into her job after the death of her husband Frederick Bridges. It's an admirable study, undoubtedly constrained by the fact that Beatrice was still alive and that she and Anthony Barker were friends.

Beatrice Davis died on 24 May 1992, aged eighty-three. 'A publisher's editor,' wrote Kylie Tennant in 1973, 'has to be a cross between Man O' War and Pardon the Son of Regret, with a heart that nothing can break.' Beatrice might not have enjoyed being compared to a couple of racehorses, but she might have liked Tennant's assertion that she had stamina and staying power. She lived during – indeed, presided over – a time of great change in Australian publishing, guiding the careers of many of our best-known authors. Her position as a literary taste-maker remained unchallenged for many years. She was a 'career woman' at a time when such a creature was relatively rare. She was also a complex and contradictory character.

Beatrice spent most of her time editing non-fiction and other work she called 'roast and boil prose', but she always preferred to work on fiction. Most of the authors whose stories are told here are writers of novels or short stories. These are also the writers with whom she had most empathy, and her relationship with them often illuminates their personalities as well as Beatrice's own. Beatrice also had long-standing and close friendships with imaginative writers in other categories – poets, writers of literary non-fiction, children's authors – and where their stories illustrate Beatrice's work practice or give fresh insight into writing and publishing, they too have been included. A strictly chronological approach to the writing of this book proved problematic: like all professional editors, Beatrice worked on several manuscripts at once, and her relationships with authors varied in duration and intensity. To avoid confusion, *A Certain Style* has been organised by theme along broadly chronological lines – tracing the whole history of Beatrice's involvement with a particular author, for example. A list giving the dates and major works of key writers will be found at the end of this book.

In one way, researching the life and times of Beatrice Davis has been relatively easy because she lived in Sydney and was known to so many people who still live there. But it has been unexpectedly difficult to enter her world, to see things as she did, because so much of her Sydney no longer exists. Especially since the early 1960s, most of the solidly Victorian maritime city she knew has been pulled down and smashed. Number 89 Castlereagh Street, the former livery stables where the wonderfully cavernous Angus and Robertson bookshop stood for eighty years and where Beatrice edited manuscripts in an attic office the size of a sentry box, is now the site of the Centrepoint Tower; at the former entrance stands an automatic teller machine. At 213B George Street, the raffish and tumbledown terrace where as a young woman Beatrice flouted family convention by renting a room on her own, is a blank-faced office block. There are many other differences: trams have vanished from the city's streets to be replaced by bellowing traffic; most of the old arcades with their hatters, dressmakers, palmists and beauticians have gone; people walk faster, unimpeded by melting asphalt pavements, potholes, street photographers. Look up from Circular Quay as Beatrice did and you see not the Eiffel-like AWA Tower, once the tallest building in the city, but massively looming and largely anonymous office buildings. The winds off the harbour dodge round canyons and pinnacles of glass and concrete.

The publishing industry has greatly changed, too. In Beatrice's day many employees of the bookshop, publishing company and printery that comprised Angus and Robertson began work with 'the auld Firm' as boys and stayed until they were in their eighties. (Men only, of course: for many years women were expected to leave when they married.) Systems established at the turn of the century were unchanged sixty years later; estimates of print runs were sometimes given by production staff or printers likely to remember how many copies of a similar book had been printed ten, twenty, even forty years before. This kind of 'race memory' is almost incredible in these days of accountants and computer projections. The idea of attending regular lunchtime lectures on

printing techniques by a craftsman typographer, as Beatrice's staff did
during the 1950s, is unknown to today's book editors, wrestling with too
many manuscripts and too little time. Back then 'deadline' still had its
original 1868 meaning of 'a line drawn round a military prison, beyond
which a prisoner may be shot down' (*Shorter Oxford English Dictionary*,
1947 edition). It now seems almost beyond belief that in Beatrice's
heyday a manuscript was given all the time, care and attention the editor
thought it required. In its lack of urgency about scheduling, its painstaking and careful devotion to the written word, Angus and Robertson
was more like an old-fashioned university arts department than a
modern commercial publishing company.

Most of Beatrice's career coincided with a time when people kept
in touch by letter; the telephone was used for essential communication
only. (Beatrice was notorious for abruptly ending telephone conversations.) Tucked away in manila folders in various Australian libraries are
hundreds of pages with 'BD' in the top left-hand corner – copies of letters Beatrice wrote to her authors over almost forty years. Some are
formal, others friendly, irritated, waspish, thoughtful or delighted: all are
written with clarity, economy and precision. It is in these letters, as well
as in comments, explanations and anecdotes given by her family, friends,
authors and colleagues, that Beatrice is to be found.

A richly layered, sometimes contradictory picture emerges. A petite
woman in her thirties sits in her tiny office calmly making tiny red-ink
marks on a manuscript, her handwriting so delicate that Miles Franklin
once told her it should be played on a piano. At an Admiralty House
reception held by the governor-general Sir Paul Hasluck, she grows
impatient with the company of the other women after dinner and,
fortified by a couple of red wines, begins playing classical music on the
piano in the corner. At a meeting of the English Association she quietly
steers one belligerent writer away from another. Long known as a hostess, she is so nervous on hearing Douglas Stewart describe the virtues
of wild duck that she drops her main course – roast duck – on the floor.
Horrified to hear the children's writer Joan Phipson announce that she
doesn't possess a copy of *Brewer's Dictionary of Phrase and Fable*, she sends
her one immediately. She makes love on the flat roof of her house; she

appears in a Norman Lindsay engraving wearing nothing but an exotic headdress.

There are some surprising glimpses of authors, too. A fascinated Hal Porter, driving Eve Langley around Gippsland, hears her address a young boy as Oscar Wilde. At lunch with Beatrice at the Australia Hotel, Xavier Herbert talks so long and loudly about himself that it is too late to eat. Ernestine Hill sends exotic shells discovered by deep-sea divers near Broome. Douglas Stewart has a long and joky correspondence with her ('Dear Miss Davis, Are you fond of poetry?' . . . 'PS: I had a tooth out last week. Would you like it?').

Though there is no shortage of material by and about her, in another way Beatrice is not easy to find. By temperament and upbringing she was a reserved, even secretive person, giving very little of herself away. Sometimes her sense of privacy and gentlewoman's manners exasperated her more rumbustious authors. 'Have you ever seen her spitting?' Xavier Herbert once asked Hal Porter. 'I guess not. She has wonderful self-control. I think she smashes things only after one is out of earshot.' If Beatrice ever indulged in smashing plates, glasses or furniture, she undoubtedly waited until she was alone. Her frustrations with authors and colleagues at Angus and Robertson, her griefs, bereavements, disappointments – these she rarely confided to anyone. 'It's all too boring,' she would say. An A&R colleague observed that there were times when she didn't think Beatrice had tear ducts.

But like most people, Beatrice found it impossible to behave with perfect restraint all the time. Particularly after what she called 'a tiny piece of whisky', or a larger piece of red wine, she was apt to let her guard drop and become quite outspoken, sometimes with disconcerting results. She wasn't alone in this, of course – Australian literary life has always more or less floated on a sea of alcohol – but the change that drink made to Beatrice's usually calm and discreet behaviour was dramatic. She could switch from being charming and attentive to grumpy, sarcastic, even downright rude, capable of telling certain writers that in her opinion they couldn't write for nuts.

Fortunately, she had a more valuable, consoling means of emotional release than alcohol. 'Music has always been the art to which I have been most devoted and most disinterestedly dedicated – an art in which I should have loved to excel, but an art in which I could never have made a living,' she wrote to one of her authors. In her childhood she had wanted to be a composer or a concert pianist. For years she studied the piano, giving up only when she knew her ambitions would never be realised. But she continued to play for her own pleasure and that of her friends.

Beatrice Davis was a very attractive woman, small with a trim figure, clear classical features, a delicate complexion and deep-blue eyes. She always dressed well – for many years a dressmaker made most of her clothes – and was particularly admired for her stylish, audacious hats. Her combination of elegance, charm, intelligence, wit, professionalism and beauty made many men go weak at the knees. And an influential woman with these qualities is certain to be gossiped about.

There were many rumours about Beatrice's private life. Until she was well into her seventies she knew how to make herself appealing to men, and undoubtedly had many lovers. (The journalist Elizabeth Riddell once commented that she invariably saw Beatrice on the arm of some well-preserved military gentleman or other.) It was said that a male author stood no chance of having his novel accepted by A&R unless he went to bed with Beatrice. She was also said to be bisexual. Australian literary circles have always compensated for being small by the intensity of their gossip, and the reason these stories flourished – because Beatrice was enigmatic as well as influential – is at least as interesting as the stories themselves.

Beatrice's friend Hal Porter once shrewdly remarked that 'the Lady Beatrice has always been attracted to the devil in the basement'. All her life Beatrice, no slave to convention herself, was drawn to people who lived on the edge, including many writers. Though she had a gracious house on the fringe of Sydney Harbour and was apparently the epitome of middle-class respectability, Beatrice was a complex person, sometimes displaying Anglophile gentility, even pretension, at other times uninhibitedly doing as she pleased without apparently giving a damn for anyone's opinion. The novelist D'Arcy Niland summed her up the first time he met her, saying to his wife Ruth Park, 'There goes a gentlewoman . . . and she's a little beaut, too!' And so she was.

PART I
1909–1937

Bendigo and Sydney

Little Sweetheart

Beatrice Davis was not a sentimental woman, nor did she feel strongly connected to her childhood. Yet among her possessions found after her death was a small, loose-leaf book with a dark cover, like a child's first photograph album. It does not hold family photographs, though the subjects are clearly Australian: the women in their long Edwardian dresses with high necklines and tight sleeves, and the dark-suited men in stiff collars and hats are frozen against wide streets lined with gum trees and scored with the tracks of horse-drawn vehicles – streets that probably dwindle to tracks before vanishing into scrubby bush.

Presiding over these hot and dusty thoroughfares are public buildings whose stern façades, urns and cornucopias, elaborate porticoes and Corinthian pillars recall the banks and town halls of nineteenth-century English provincial cities. These edifices insist that this is a town of substance, of great prosperity, despite being thousands of miles from Home. The last photograph in the album, taken from a hilltop with the town stretched out below, shows the source of this affluence: the gracious bungalows, churches and solid public buildings are punctuated by chimney stacks and the skeletal headframes of mines. This is Bendigo, Victoria, founded on the richest gold-bearing reef in the world.

Beatrice was born here in 1909. Her great-grandfather Joseph Davis, a gunsmith by profession who had been one of England's biggest military suppliers, had come to this rough mining settlement with his family in 1852 under shady circumstances – he apparently owed money to the Board of Ordnance. He was evidently a well-educated man with an inquiring and lively mind and a judicious way with words. A rationalist by nature, he came down solidly on the side of science, dismissing the study of theology as fit only for the weak-minded. Joseph's interest in science and lack of it in religion were inherited by Beatrice, who studied chemistry at university and who, according to a colleague at Angus and Robertson, had 'no religious sense at all'.

Joseph's son William, Beatrice's grandfather, carved out a solid, steady career as a banker. He set up business in the small town of Kilmore and in 1875 became manager of the Colonial Bank of Australasia in nearby Bendigo, where he remained for the rest of his life. William was an important citizen; his portraits show a steady-eyed, bewhiskered man with a long Victorian chin and an expression of unrelenting rectitude. He held civic offices appropriate to a pillar of the community, being a board member of the Benevolent Asylum, a justice of the peace and treasurer of the local fire brigade. William Davis was also keenly interested in the arts, an enthusiastic amateur actor and member of the Bendigo Shakespearean Society who also gave regular public lectures on the works of Charles Dickens.

His wife matched him artistically and intellectually. Ellen Hayes belonged to a lively Irish family of independent and enterprising women. She was a teacher by profession, running her own school for several years. Like her granddaughter Beatrice, she was also musical, with a special interest in the piano. Ellen and William Davis lived in a large and pleasant house in Quarry Hill, Bendigo, and owned property in other parts of the town. Ellen gave up teaching to raise her family of three boys and two girls. Their third son, Charles Herbert Davis, born in 1872, was Beatrice's father.

Educated in Bendigo, Charles was articled to a local lawyer when he left school at seventeen, completed the University of Melbourne's articled clerks' course, and was admitted to practise as a solicitor in 1895. He opened his own practice in the Bendigo Arcade, Pall Mall, the centrally located lawyers' precinct. Charles was a 'deliberative, calm and invariably courteous' man, a keen reader with a large library.¹ He inherited musical talent from his mother, playing the piano and having a pleasant tenor voice, and he also wrote poetry, some of which he set to music as parlour songs for voice and piano (with such titles as 'Twilight' and 'A Rose'). He also composed more technically ambitious works, including a sonata for piano and cello.

Charles liked a well-organised, disciplined life and was attracted to the army as well as to the law. In his early twenties he was commissioned into an infantry battalion of the Victorian Defence Forces – he became a good friend of John Monash, who was later commander of the Australian forces in France in World War I – and was promoted to captain four years later, in 1900. The following year, at very short notice, he commanded the guard of honour at the opening of Australia's first parliament, in Melbourne on 9 May 1901 in the presence of the Duke of York and Cornwall (later King George V). By 1910 he was Lieutenant-Colonel Davis, commanding Bendigo's 2nd Battalion.

Good-looking in a solidly English way, from a prosperous family, and with a steady income, an interest in music and literature, and a part-time career as a dashing soldier, Charles Davis could fairly be considered a good catch, but by thirty he was still unmarried. And then in 1905 he met Emily Beatrice Deloitte.

Emily came from a Sydney family with great style and pride of lineage and relatively little money. Her grandfather William Salmon Deloitte, the son of a French aristocrat forced to flee to England during the revolution of 1789, had come to Australia in 1838, settled in Sydney, married Bessie Maria Marley and set up in business as W.S. Deloitte & Co., Merchants. His business fortunes were erratic, but he maintained a steady presence in the colony, becoming justice of the peace for the City of Sydney and an original member of the Australian Club. He and his family lived in a large and beautiful house in Wharf Road, Snails Bay (now Birchgrove).

William and Bessie had seven sons and six daughters, brought up according to the rules of the time. The boys were encouraged to study for professions; their sisters stayed at home, played the piano or did needlework and waited for suitable young men to marry them. Bessie never left her room before luncheon and had to be waited upon constantly (if she wanted to sit up late at night, one of her children was expected to stay up with her). But beneath this leisured façade lay unpalatable reality: the Deloittes were often short of money. A stroke left William paralysed for the last nine years of his life and his eldest son, also William, suffered a disabling spinal injury. The other sons had to find what work they could to help keep the large family. The youngest, Marmaduke, who became Emily's father, was forced to leave school at fourteen to help the family finances.

Marmaduke became an insurance broker and married Emma Millett, a young woman with family connections in Bendigo. Marmaduke and Emma had five daughters: Mary, Phyllis, Emily Beatrice, and twins Brenda and Enid. The two most closely involved in Beatrice's story are Emily, who became her mother, and Enid, her aunt.

Marmaduke and his family lived next door to 'Wyoming', a splen-did house owned by Marmaduke's brother Quarton.[2] Quarton Deloitte, who was considered the best-dressed man in Sydney, lived there with his wife, two uniformed maids, and a resident gardener whose job was to tend the lawns that sloped gently down to Sydney Harbour. Quarton's standards were exacting – he once stormed into David Jones demanding that a pair of corsets be removed from a window display – and he domi-nated his youngest brother. He seems also to have given Marmaduke's family some financial support; at any rate Emma was obliged to go through the household accounts with her brother-in-law once a month, and woe betide her if she had been extravagant or made a mistake.

Later, Marmaduke, his wife and daughters moved farther up Wharf Road to number 17, a large house named 'Ianthena'. It had six bed-rooms, an anteroom and drawing rooms, a conservatory, and a bathroom with a modern gas bath-heater. Governesses gave the Deloitte girls a rudimentary education suitable for young ladies, the most important part of which was music. The sisters all learned to play the piano and violin; when anyone from the large network of Deloitte cousins came to visit, the dining-room carpet would be rolled back for dancing and the girls took turns to play.

It was from this household that Emily Beatrice Deloitte, a pretty 23-year-old with no intellectual interests, trained to do nothing but play the piano beautifully, went to visit her mother's brother Edwin in Bendigo and met Charles Davis.

He was immediately attracted to her; she was young, very sweet, and they both loved music. Emily returned to 'Ianthena' with an engagement ring. After the customary two-year interval, she and Charles were married on 25 April 1907 at St John's Church, Snails Bay, and Emily went to live with him in Bendigo. She was twenty-five, Charles thirty-four.

Charles and Emily Davis settled in a wide-verandahed bungalow named 'Huddersfield' at 40 Lilac Street, Bendigo, some distance from the centre of town. The house probably belonged to Charles's parents. Emily must have been dismayed: though pleasant with a shady garden, it was a far cry from 'Ianthena' or 'Wyoming'. She had been used to a household full of noise and company – the visits of relatives, picnics and night fishing on the harbour, chatting to her friends on the porch while someone practised scales or arpeggios upstairs. Now from her front verandah she surveyed not the sparkling harbour but mile after mile of flat, grey-green bush, its quiet broken only by the rhythmic thumping of mining machinery.

Nor did she feel entirely comfortable with her clever, bookish new family. The Davises enjoyed debating everything from the nature of the universe to the current political situation: Emily, no great reader, was unable to join in. Her Irish mother-in-law no doubt looked sharply at this pretty young woman who had never had to earn her own living, did not know how to run a house and had no intellectual interests apart from music. Charles spent little time at home. He was running his law practice, involved in the army, and an active member of several local organisations, including the Art Gallery Committee and the Benevolent Society. His young wife was not entirely starved for company – when Charles was otherwise occupied she had her uncle's family, her sister Phyllis came for long visits and there were Charles's friends – but time probably hung heavily on her hands. She and Charles started a family soon after their marriage. Their first child, John Deloitte, was born early in 1908, their daughter Beatrice Deloitte on 28 January 1909.

As a child Beatrice was always called Trix or Trixie – a common diminutive of Beatrice – to distinguish her from her mother, who was always known as Beatrice rather than Emily.[3] Beatrice never much liked Trix: from her early twenties she insisted on her full name. Years later, when an author asked whether she might call her Bea, she snapped, 'You certainly may not!'

Beatrice was a beautiful child, with big blue eyes and curly hair, but despite her angelic appearance she was apparently not the archetypal sweet little girl. There are no family photographs of her clutching favourite dolls; instead there she is, aged about six, laughing, barefoot, in a pretty white dress, playing horses with her brother. (Given Beatrice's later relationships with men, it is probably significant that she is holding the reins while John plays the horse.) She and John were inseparable. Once they ganged up against a local minister of whom they did not approve: when he came to visit they put weed killer into his horse's feed, causing the animal to become very sick and almost die. John and Beatrice were horrified and guilty, but never confessed.

When Beatrice was six her younger brother Charles Deloitte, always known as Del, was born. It soon became clear that Beatrice and her two brothers were very different characters. John was calm, quiet and patient, a contrast to the quick, astute Beatrice. She didn't always win her arguments with him: he knew how to deal with her occasionally dictatorial manner. Del was a carefree soul with a sunny disposition and wicked sense of humour. Though they fought occasionally, the three Davis children remained close all their lives.

Their mother apparently spent little time with them; indeed, Emily's attitude to domestic matters, including children, verged on the regal. Her marriage certificate might describe her occupation as 'home duties' but she carried out few of these, preferring to escape into music whenever possible. Her sharp-eyed daughter – never her greatest fan – was wont to say that the pinnacle of her mother's ambition was to play the piano and look decorative. She was able to do both because Charles's income and social position allowed for hired help, and most of the work around the home was done by Maria Richardson, known as Bobs. A young woman from Bendigo, Bobs had worked as a maid or housekeeper for Charles's father and knew the family well. Little Beatrice loved Bobs, and was closer to her than to her own mother.

However, from her earliest years the most important person in Beatrice's life was her father. She was apparently closer in temperament to the Davises than to the Deloittes, though her musical talent, which she showed very early, came from both sides of the family. Her mother was probably her first piano teacher. Charles Davis doted on Beatrice, his 'little sweetheart', and she adored him. When he went away to war, she took one of his boots to bed with her.

Like so many other towns across Australia, Bendigo reacted quickly to the declaration of war in August 1914. The first local recruits were accepted for the Australian Expeditionary Force less than two weeks later, and a rally was held at the Royal Princess Theatre with stirring lectures on the subject of patriotism. (This was much better publicised than a town hall lecture the following evening by Sir Ernest Rutherford on the subject of radium – a substance, he said, with enormous possibilities.) The first contingent of volunteers from the Bendigo district left on 7 September.

Though he had been actively engaged in drilling new recruits on the parade ground at Epsom racecourse about five kilometres from town, Lieutenant-Colonel Charles Davis did not go overseas with them. He was appointed senior assistant censor, which meant working in Melbourne, then he became cable censor and finally chief censor. He did not go to war until mid-1916, when he became commander of the 38th Battalion of the AIF, formed mainly from local Bendigo volunteers. Charles Davis must have hated having to leave Bendigo for the battlefields of France. He was in his forties – old for a soldier – with a wife and three children, the youngest still a baby; it was already apparent that the war would not end quickly, and he had no idea when he would return.

Charles and Emily decided that she and the children would live with her parents in Sydney until the war was over, when they would come back to Bendigo and Charles would resume his legal practice. Emily's family were no longer living in 'Ianthena'; the implacable Quarton Deloitte had quarrelled with them over his niece Phyllis's engagement, and life in Wharf Road had become so uncomfortable that Marmaduke

and his family let 'Ianthena' and fled to the north side of the harbour, to
Neutral Bay. By the time Charles was ready to embark for the front,
Marmaduke, Emma, Brenda and Enid were living in 'Lynton', 42 Ben
Boyd Road, where Emily and the children would join them. (The two
eldest Deloitte daughters, Phyllis and Mary, had already married and left
home.)

Neutral Bay, a tuck of Sydney Harbour originally named by
Governor Arthur Phillip as an anchorage for foreign ships until their
credentials could be determined, was then by no means the fashionable
suburb it later became. In 1916, years before completion of the Sydney
Harbour Bridge, it was connected to the city only by ferry, and a steam
tram grumbled up the steep, winding road from the wharf to a small
cluster of shops in Military Road at the top of the ridge. Neutral Bay was
a suburb of camphor laurel trees, small houses of cheap sandstone and
rickety weatherboard, with a scattering of grander residences. 'Lynton'
in Ben Boyd Road, about halfway up the hill to Military Road, was a
modest bungalow and, with five adults and three children, it was a tight
squeeze. Beatrice, John and Del slept on the balcony with their Aunt
Enid. John and Beatrice, who had recently started school, walked to
the Neutral Bay Superior Primary School about five minutes away,
where the poet Mary Gilmore, whom Beatrice would know in years to
come, had been a teacher in the 1890s.

Brenda and Enid spent their time knitting socks for the troops, as
well as organising and performing in fundraising concerts and concert
parties at the army camps. Brenda was the family star, playing piano,
violin and cello for the Amateur Orchestral Society and the Philhar-
monic Society; Enid also played piano and violin. With three musicians
in the family including her mother, young Beatrice was unlikely to get
away with skimping on piano practice. In the evenings everybody sat
around the large dining table – lit by a single hanging gas lamp to save
money – reading, writing letters or sewing, or doing homework.

As in every Australian household affected by the war, the arrival of
the post was the highlight of the day. There was a strict Deloitte routine about mail. Outgoing letters were always placed on the hall table for
Marmaduke to post. When the postman came, all letters received had to

be taken to Emma, Beatrice's Granny Deloitte. If she was out, they were put on the hall table to await her return. Her daughters were actually expected to read their letters aloud to their mother – even their personal ones. (Brenda got around this by having her sweetheart's letters sent to a friend.)

Emily must have suffered agonies to see an envelope addressed to her 'c/- Mrs Deloitte' in Charles's writing, knowing she wouldn't be able to read it until her mother came home. But as the casualty lists grew longer, the mere sight of an envelope in Charles's regular, looping hand was a great relief. Charles wrote to his wife regularly and sent weekly postcards to each of his children, which they proudly pasted into albums. For Beatrice's eighth birthday in January 1917 he sent a dozen lace handkerchiefs from France. Emily had the children photographed professionally and Charles carried this photograph, as well as a rather severe portrait of Emily, in a soft leather wallet throughout the war.

He wrote from Armentières, Ploegsteert Wood, Passchendaele, Ypres, the Somme. He was afraid that Emily would worry herself sick – 'you know what a worried little person you are' – and took delight in his children's progress, telling his wife that 'Trixie thinks she writes better than Jack'. He did not mention the relentless crump of the guns, or mud so deep that men, mules and packhorses stumbling into shell-holes sank and died of suffocation, or the bitter cold that within minutes turned a mug of hot tea into brown ice.

Most particularly he did not write about what he was doing: training eager, undisciplined young soldiers to be night commando raiders. It was one of the war's most perilous and difficult jobs. Parties of 650 armed men, some carrying mats and portable bridges, would run in a kilometre-wide front, under incessant fire from German guns, rockets and shells, across No Man's Land into the enemy trenches, where they fought hand to hand with grenades and rifle fire. The casualties were often appalling.

After masterminding an important and highly successful raid at Houplines, Charles Davis was awarded the Distinguished Service Order on 6 June 1917, the day before his forty-fifth birthday. (The DSO is given for sustained valour and leadership, not as the result of only one action.)

He was also mentioned in dispatches three times. His letters home made light of this; recognition, though gratifying, meant little against what was happening to some of the men he had known in Bendigo. 'Our men found the body of one of our officers,' he wrote to Emily on 17 October 1917, after Passchendaele. '[Morrison] . . . must have wandered back and been killed by a shell. He leaves a young wife in Bendigo and a little child whom he has never seen.'

By the end of that dreadful year, Charles was bone weary of the mud, blood and slaughter. 'My darling girl, I'm sick of the war, so deadly sick of it that I should give anything to have a good excuse to return,' he wrote on 3 December. 'But what can I do? . . . I must carry out my job as others are doing . . . How I miss the time I should have had with bubs [Del].' He had gone to the front a robust man but now his health had deteriorated, his lungs damaged and weakened by mustard gas. 'I think I'm getting too old for this game,' he wrote to his wife. General Monash had recommended him as brigade commander, but nothing seemed to be happening. The war was not yet over, and like other Australian officers he was disheartened that the 1917 referendum had rejected conscription. 'I suppose we must look forward to gradual extinction, one division after another,' he wrote gloomily.

Promotion did come: in May 1918 Charles Davis was made colonel and sent to command the AIF base at Le Havre. He spent the closing months of the war as an administrator, and after the Armistice on 11 November took charge of the Australian General Base Depot, helping move the 100 000 Australian soldiers across the Channel to England for repatriation. 'I have never felt that I will not return to you,' he wrote to Emily, though this certainty must have faltered many times. Charles knew how lucky he was. He had survived for two years, even with gas-damaged lungs, when officers in the trenches often lasted only a matter of weeks. The war was officially over, leaving him free to consider what to do next. He longed for the security of Bendigo, where he and the family had been comfortable and happy; perhaps he would replant the wattle trees in the garden, which he was sure had been ruined by the tenants.

But this was mere nostalgia, for Charles did not believe he could ever settle in Bendigo again. Too much had been changed by the war: so many men he had trained, some he had known all his life, were never coming back. Perhaps he could try a new career, even at his age; being a solicitor in a country town seemed so restricting in the new world that was surely coming. He considered finding a partner to run his law practice, moving to Melbourne and going into business with his adjutant, a man named Marks. Meanwhile Emily was naturally longing to see him again. In January 1919, almost as soon as the seas had been declared safe, she took ship for London, leaving the children behind in the care of their grandparents.

Grandpa and Granny Deloitte were the nominal rulers of 'Lynton', but Enid ran the house. Having spent her life at home since her education finished at fourteen, she looked after the accounts, did most of the shopping and cooking, organised family events and parties (her twin Brenda was seriously pursuing a musical career). A bundle of practical energy, she had wanted to be a nurse, an idea that horrified Marmaduke. 'You have a father to keep you,' he said. However, though she lacked the fine-boned beauty of her sisters and had the disadvantage of being almost completely deaf, Enid was hardly the stereotypical downtrodden spinster aunt. With very little to spend on clothes or luxuries, she always managed to look elegant and stylish – and her deafness had never prevented her from studying music, which she loved.

It was Enid, in her mid-twenties when Beatrice first knew her, who gave her niece and nephews the bread-and-butter mothering that all children need and that Emily had never really given. From her Aunt Enid, her surrogate mother, Beatrice learned valuable lessons in the feminine arts: how to cook, the rudiments of dressmaking, the art of dressing with elegance and style on little money. Aunt and niece formed a bond that remained strong for the rest of their lives.

Charles and Emily Davis returned to Australia in October 1919. As an honoured and decorated soldier – the king had conferred the CBE on him earlier that year – Charles was given an official welcome to Sydney. After more than three years without her father, the ten-year-old Beatrice was thrilled to see him again. In his homecoming photograph she stands very straight and proud, holding his arm proprietorially. Charles Davis looks old enough to be her grandfather.

The family moved from 'Lynton' to 'Noailles', a small house at 29 Yeo Street, still within walking distance of Neutral Bay primary school. Now Charles had to make up his mind about his future career. He allowed himself to abandon the idea of moving to Melbourne, probably dissuaded by Emily and her parents on the grounds that all her friends and family were in Sydney and the children were happily settled at school. He was already being considered for the position of Victoria's police commissioner, which the Deloittes did not consider a suitable job.

So Charles, tired and ill, in his late forties and with a growing family, had to make a new beginning in a city whose business networks were unfamiliar to him. He did throw in his lot with his former adjutant and became the Sydney representative of Marks & Co., selling luxury goods, including perfume, probably on a retainer or commission basis. The decision was an unhappy one. Charles no longer had the two institutions that had always sustained him – the law and the army. At first he must have welcomed the change in career, especially after the horrors of the war, but the life of a salesman was awkward and disappointing for a man whose professional life had always been bound and defined by rules and procedures. Charles did not enjoy having to convince largely indifferent strangers that they needed the goods he had to sell, becoming in some measure a supplicant instead of a figure of authority whose judgement was respected.

He found solace in his wife and children, and was particularly close to his daughter. Beatrice was now a dark-haired and fine-boned girl, quick-minded and clever. She had discovered books, but as her mother and brother John were not great readers, she discussed her reading mainly with her father. A few months after her eleventh birthday Charles gave her a copy of *The 38th Battalion* by Eric Fairey, published by the *Bendigo Advertiser*. Most returned soldiers were very reluctant to tell their families about what they had endured, so this gift from a father to his young daughter is an intriguing one, which must have strengthened the bond between them. (If he gave copies to his sons too, the books have not survived.)

In 1921, when she was twelve, Beatrice started at North Sydney Girls' High. She quickly moved to the top classes, where she remained throughout her school career. High-school education at the time was heavily dependent on lists and rote learning: the rivers of New South Wales, Latin and French irregular verbs, the rules of English grammar, formulas in chemistry, tables, large slabs of Shakespeare and poetry, mainly from the nineteenth century. English, maths and French were compulsory, history was the story of the kings and queens of England. What had happened in Australia – wool, wheat, sheep, the dotted-line outback journeys of explorers – was considered second-rate and dull.

A cool, quiet and self-contained girl, apparently free of the need to be liked by everybody, Beatrice was never one of the most popular in her class and her friends remained a small and carefully chosen group. A close friend was Heather Sherrie, later assistant librarian at Sydney's Mitchell Library: it was partly because of Heather and her father, a journalist, that Beatrice developed her interest in literature. She read the usual English classic writers – Austen, Dickens, Hardy, Wordsworth, Browning, Keats, Tennyson – but Mr Sherrie liked 'modern writers' at a time when Eliot usually meant George, not T.S. He and his daughter probably introduced Beatrice to Yeats, Forster, perhaps even Virginia Woolf, a writer Beatrice admired all her life. English and literature were synonymous: books by contemporary Australian authors such as A.B. Paterson, Henry Lawson, Steele Rudd, C.J. Dennis, Norman Lindsay – most of them published or sold by an eager, black-bearded Scotsman named George Robertson from his city bookshop at 89 Castlereagh Street – were scarcely taken seriously. The idea that anything written by Australians might be worthy of academic study, capable of being ranged with the English poets, seemed absurd.

Beatrice was also continuing her musical education, studying piano and violin at the Sydney Conservatorium of Music, as her Aunt Brenda had done. At one stage, possibly to emulate her father, she wanted to write music, though she kept this ambition to herself. Women just weren't composers in those days.

Then, shortly before she turned fourteen, in December 1922, her father became ill with headaches and fever. He gradually grew worse and when he began to bleed from the gums, a sign of acute typhoid fever, a frightened Emily had him admitted to North Shore Hospital. Typhoid was serious but curable; however, Charles's illness seems to have been wrongly diagnosed and treated. He improved briefly, but he knew he was dying. On 11 January 1923 he was dead, at the age of fifty.

It had all happened so quickly and the family was devastated. Emily, shocked, became more remote than ever, unable to console herself, let alone her children. For Beatrice, the death of her adored father was a loss beyond words. This first grief of her life drove the highly intelligent, self-possessed young girl further within herself. Deloitte good manners dictated that grief should be private, to be battled alone, and it was probably from this point in her life that Beatrice learned to present a stoic front to the world.

Children who keep their feelings to themselves are often better able to help other people than to confide their own problems: maybe Beatrice found some relief in looking after John, Del and her mother. Perhaps not. Her relationship with her mother, which had never been close – possibly because of competition for her father's affection – grew worse after Charles's death. Beatrice never thought her mother did her duty as a soldier's wife; during the war, she said, Emily should have stayed in Bendigo, comforting the families of Charles's men, not running home to her own family at the first opportunity.

Her father's death had one other significant effect on Beatrice. From her mid-twenties she was attracted to men who were much older than she. The last lover of her life was a lawyer/soldier who, in World War II, had been awarded the same military medals as Charles Davis.

The Family Intellectual
Becomes an Editor

Beatrice never intended to follow the example of the Deloitte women, finishing her education early, studying music and looking after her mother while she waited for a husband. Even if she had wanted to do such a thing, the family couldn't afford it. Besides, this was the 1920s, not the 1890s, and bright girls were being educated to have jobs. In 1925 Beatrice sat for the Leaving Certificate and did well: honours in chemistry, As in English and maths I, and Bs in Latin, French, history and maths II. The first woman in her family to be eligible for university, she decided to study Arts.

However, Emily had only Charles's army pension, the invested capital from the sale of the Bendigo house, and some money from the estate of her father Marmaduke (who had died in 1923, the same year as Charles). With three students to support – John was studying at Hawkesbury Agricultural College, Del was about to go to secondary school – she had to live frugally, and she could not afford to send her daughter to university. For this reason alone Beatrice applied for a teachers' college scholarship, which paid fees and a small living allowance. She would study for her Diploma of Education after finishing her Arts degree, and would then become a secondary-school teacher.

The University of Sydney, founded in 1850 and the oldest in Australia, saw itself as the Antipodean Oxbridge. Even its motto, *Sidere mens eadem mutato* ('the same spirit under changed stars'), was a reassuring sign that, even though the place was at the bottom of the known world, British intellectual traditions would be maintained. One of these, fortunately changing, was that higher education was the province of men. During the war Sir Mungo MacCallum, professor of English literature, had begun his lectures with the word 'Gentlemen', while he glared at the small number of women present. When Beatrice started, only about 15 per cent of the student body consisted of women, most of whom, like Beatrice, were studying Arts.

Beatrice was far too adventurous to stay behind female barriers. At seventeen she was developing her own style, making and wearing classic jackets and fitted coats and skirts that showed off her neat 'pocket Venus' figure. She put on her new clothes, swept her dark hair up into a knot at the back of her head and made sure she was noticed by the men in law and medicine. Most of them found irresistible her combination of elegance, prettiness, cool self-possession, intelligence and wit, and she was considered great fun. While she was at university she was engaged three times. Why these engagements came to nothing is unknown, but nobody's heart seems to have been broken. Certainly Beatrice's was not. She was having the time of her life.

Emily viewed her daughter's free and easy behaviour with suspicion. The Deloitte family followed Victorian rules of behaviour: even after the war Granny Deloitte had insisted on chaperoning Brenda and Enid to dances, despite their horrified pleas. In the same spirit, Emily once accompanied Beatrice and her current beau to an art exhibition. Beatrice told her mother exactly what she thought about this – she was probably supported by her aunts – and Emily never did it again. Beatrice continued to juggle concerts and parties and sport (she played university hockey) with the occasional lecture, as well as piano lessons at the conservatorium with the eminent teacher Winifred Burstyn. She had given up the idea of being a composer, but still thought of a career as a concert pianist.

With all this activity, as well as being the belle of the university, Beatrice could be rather full of herself. Once fourteen-year-old Del encountered her at a bus stop chatting vivaciously in French to a young man who was evidently a lecturer. '*Ah*,' said Beatrice to her companion in her best patronising Parisian accent, '*je vous présente mon petit frère, Charles.*' Del bowed gravely, clicked his heels together and said, '*Pomme de terre.*'

Beatrice did manage to do some study. At the end of her first year she passed in English, French and Latin, with a distinction in chemistry. Her second year was less successful. She passed in English, philosophy and chemistry but failed French and had to sit for the exam again. She passed her final exams, majoring in English and French and gaining her Bachelor of Arts degree in 1928.

Having taken the teachers' college shilling, Beatrice was now expected to do her diploma and become a teacher. But after some practice teaching she had discovered she loathed classrooms and children, and pleaded with the university registrar to release her from her contract. He agreed on condition that she repaid three years' worth of tuition fees, amounting to several hundred pounds.

This was awkward, and both sides of Beatrice's family had quite a lot to say about it. Her Davis aunts could not understand why Beatrice was turning her back on one of women's few respectable career opportunities.[1] Emily's view was more basic: here was her ungrateful daughter not only turning down a steady and secure job and refusing to help with the family finances, but selfishly saddling them with a huge debt. How *could* she?

Beatrice and her mother argued bitterly for weeks. A less determined young woman might have given in to family pressure, but not Beatrice. Her resolve was the more remarkable because she had no idea what she was going to do. Already she realised she was not quite good enough to be a professional musician, and the idea of teaching music horrified her. That left librarianship, the other major career possibility for female Arts graduates, which did not appeal either. In the end, Beatrice wore the family down and was allowed to have her way. The money was found somehow, the Education Department eventually repaid.

It was now 1929 and Beatrice was twenty, with a new Bachelor of Arts degree and no marketable skills. There was only one acceptable way for her to earn a living: as a secretary. Miss Hale's Business

College in Margaret Street in the city offered a full course in typing, short-hand, bookkeeping and business principles. As it was beyond the family's means, Beatrice enrolled to study only basic typing and shorthand.

At the end of three carefree years at university she found herself behind a school desk again, with a group of girls younger than she. Typing she picked up very easily and she had no trouble with the lines, pothooks and squiggles of Pitman's phonetic shorthand. After only three weeks she asked to be promoted to the speed class, but this was a little too fast for Miss Hale, who refused. Beatrice decided she didn't need to stay at the college: office skills could be practised at home. She left and continued to study alone, taking down and transcribing the words of announcers on the family crystal set.[2]

Perhaps through university contacts – Beatrice kept in touch with the University of Sydney all her life – she heard of a vacancy for a sten-ographer at the French Trade Commission. The salary was a very low two pounds a week, but at least it was an income. Beatrice put on her best suit and hat, brushed up her French and, no doubt charmingly equivocal about her experience as a shorthand typist, talked her way into the job. It meant taking down and transcribing letters in French – more of a challenge than she had expected. With ingenuity and the help of an excellent memory, she worked out a way of adapting the stolidly British Pitman's to the liquid French vowel sounds.

Despite the low salary, Beatrice quite enjoyed the job. The Trade Commission was a hotbed of intrigue and she quickly made her name as the most discreet person on the staff, able to be relied on to keep other people's secrets. This involved handling delicate situations – that is, keep-ing spouses and lovers ignorant of each other's existence. By now Beatrice probably had a few secrets of her own to keep as well.

She was still playing the piano. In the late 1920s and early 1930s amateur music making was very popular, and most Sydney suburbs had music clubs. There were several in Neutral Bay, and Beatrice belonged to one in Bannerman Street. There she met Mervyn Archdall, an ebul-lient doctor in his late forties who was the assistant editor of the *Medical Journal of Australia*. He had a fine tenor voice and they often teamed in duets. Dr Archdall was very taken with the pretty and talented Miss

Davis, aged twenty-one, and was pleased to discover that they took the same ferry to work.

One morning in 1930, after Beatrice had been working at the French Trade Commission for about a year, Dr Archdall told her that his secretary was leaving. Beatrice asked, 'What do you pay her?' When he said £3 10s a week – half as much again as her salary at the Trade Commission – Beatrice swiftly said, 'I'll take the job.' It was one of the most important decisions she ever made.

The *Medical Journal of Australia* was produced and printed in a solid, rather forbidding brick building in Arundel Street, Glebe, on the high side of Parramatta Road opposite the university. Established in 1914, the magazine was an Anglo-Australian hybrid, another example of Britannia ruling Australia's waves. Though all the material in it was Australian, its publisher was the British Medical Association; the Australian Medical Association did not yet exist. The journal went to the 2000 Australian members of the BMA.

Beatrice got the job – she later said Archdall praised her appearance, saying she was 'very neat about the stockings'. Shortly after she started as his secretary, the journal's editor, Dr Henry Armit, died and Archdall took his place. Beatrice was now not only Archdall's secretary but his editorial assistant. She stayed in the job for the next seven years.

It was a very busy office. With only a manual typewriter, Beatrice and Archdall were responsible for bringing out a weekly magazine of never fewer than thirty pages. The copy, much of it handwritten, consisted of reports of medical and scientific meetings, analyses of medical politics, abstracts, case commentaries, summaries of medical literature, original scientific articles – three or four per issue – obituaries, book reviews and letters to the editor. Whatever was not supplied Archdall or Beatrice had to write. They selected and edited the material, chose the layouts, read and checked proofs: they did almost everything.

Beatrice quickly discovered that her boss was brilliant at his job. Though married, Archdall had no children and always joked that the *MJA* was his baby. Punctilious about grammar and punctuation, he taught his editorial assistant how to write abstracts and short book reviews – very useful when she came to assess manuscripts later.

He was also an exact proofreader. Beatrice, whose education in science had taught her the importance of precision, could hardly have had a better teacher of the skills on which her career would depend.

However, she found that Mervyn Archdall could be very demanding. A short man with reddish-brown hair and prominent ears, he was part Irish, part German and explosively emotional. He suffered from various nervous complaints, particularly asthma, and stammered so badly that when he was agitated his jaw jammed up and he could hardly speak. He would flare into an instant rage and then, like a furious child, he was difficult to pacify. Beatrice soon learned to read his moods. If all was well, he was likely to greet her as she approached the building by waving an exuberant leg out the window; if he was depressed his gloom would envelop her as soon as she stepped into the office. Beatrice's way of handling him was to remain very calm and keep out of his way until he recovered his equilibrium.

Archdall was also a man with firm views about etiquette, some of which dated from the nineteenth century. He considered it an intolerable impertinence to be on first-name terms with anyone he had known for less than ten years – Beatrice was always Miss Davis – and he corrected anyone who addressed him simply as Doctor instead of Dr Archdall, as Doctor was a title, not his name. He also firmly believed that men who wore suede shoes were cads. When a colleague came to visit him with these offending objects on his feet, Archdall announced to Beatrice that the man must never, *never* come into the office again. Beatrice accepted all this calmly. Archdall's insistence on rules of proper behaviour might even have reminded her of Granny Deloitte.

Beatrice and Archdall formed one of those quasi-family alliances that people often do when they work closely together. Both being keen on music, they frequently discussed concerts they had heard on the wireless, and Archdall lent Beatrice gramophone records. Though he generally represented the teacher/father and Beatrice the student/daughter, the roles could be reversed; Beatrice knew more about books and literature than he did. Archdall supplied them both with boxes of Craven A cigarettes during the day – Beatrice had started smoking as soon as she could afford it – and after work they occasionally went to the Hotel Sydney near Central railway station for a sherry. They slipped into a private language of their own: 'Shall we be excessive this morning?' meant 'Shall we have cake or biscuits for morning tea?' If Archdall vehemently assured Beatrice, as he often did, that he was a blighted being and that woe was him, she was likely to reply, 'You're a poor sad thing, docky-docky.'

Now that Beatrice had a stimulating, relatively well-paid job and was learning new skills, as well as maintaining a strenuous social life, she began to feel restless. The time had come, she decided, to leave home. But where could she go? The Sydney of the 1930s offered little accommodation for single women of good family. There were boarding houses, usually tenanted by single men and women middle-aged or older, but they had a rather threadbare reputation and lacked privacy. Beatrice could, however, rent her own place. Down by Circular Quay among the sailors' pubs, crouching at the foot of the almost completed Harbour Bridge, were many old buildings, some warehouses, others former offices of shipping companies dating from the days of sail. These had been cheaply fitted up as rental accommodation, warrens of variously sized rooms with tenants ranging from ships' chandlers to artists and writers. The rent was low, the area close to the city and only a tram ride away from the office. But for Beatrice the real attraction was its air of bohemia. It might be only ten minutes across the harbour by ferry, but George Street was a long way from Neutral Bay.

Shortly after starting work, Beatrice moved to 213B Lower George Street, in a row of three-storeyed terraces belonging to the Harbour Trust.[3] Her room was a large, ground-floor studio at the end of a long corridor with a grimy window. She furnished it in best post-student style, with a cushion-covered divan bed, some books in a bookcase, a gramophone and a stack of records, and her piano. Cooking was done on a gas ring in an odd little corner cupboard. The bathroom, which she shared with two or three other tenants, was halfway along the corridor.

Now, for the first time, Beatrice had her own living space. She could come home from work or from a piano lesson at the conservatorium up the hill, kick her shoes off and just be alone to play music or to study German (for a while she took lessons one night a week). Her neighbours, the painters Rah Fizelle and Grace Crowley, often dropped in and introduced her to other artists in the area. She met the young short-story writer Dal Stivens and gave a pre-wedding party in her room for him and his first wife Mary, and she and Dal remained warm friends. She kept in touch with friends from university, and fellow musical students from the conservatorium. Her brothers came to see her; John visited from Narrabri, where he had now settled with his new wife. Another addition to her circle, one who became a lifelong friend, was Vincentia Boddam-Whetham, a former kindergarten teacher who came to work in the *MJA* office in 1936.

Some evenings after work Beatrice would make dinner for six or seven people. She had developed a great flair for cooking and cut recipes out of the Sunday papers (not from the *Women's Weekly*, which she didn't read). Everyone drank sherry: spirits were expensive and Australian wine was considered rotgut, usually known as 'fourpenny dark'. There was a great deal of talk, laughter and music, and after the ferries and trains had stopped running Beatrice would make up beds on the floor for those who stayed over.

Through her work at the *MJA*, which often included attending medical conferences and taking notes for a report in the journal, Beatrice made many medical contacts. After a few years she became friendly with a young doctor and agreed to marry him. She later said that neither of them was particularly serious, but this might have been her rationale for what happened one day late in 1933 when her fiancé took her to visit a friend of his in hospital, a fellow doctor who was suffering from tuberculosis.

In his mid-forties and therefore twenty years older than Beatrice, Frederick Bridges had been medical superintendent of Prince Alfred Hospital, though more recently he had been working as a GP in the northern suburb of Chatswood. However, he seems to have considered his medical career as something of a sideline. In his youth he had wanted to be an actor, but his businessman father had hated the idea. Frederick dutifully studied medicine and did well, but he never much enjoyed medical practice. His friends were not anaesthetists or pathologists but writers, artists, musicians. He knocked around with some of the *Bulletin* people, such as Norman and Percy Lindsay and Hugh McCrae.

One of his oldest friends, Dick Jeune, was rumoured to have been a gun-runner or a pirate.

Though Frederick was generally well liked, his reputation in Sydney's conservative medical circles was equivocal. He was too fond of artistic types for his medical colleagues' liking, and he was also divorced. He had married young, but after several years his wife had left him for another doctor, taking their two sons with her. Frederick had not seen them for ten or twelve years, not since Peter, the elder, was seven or eight years old.

Frederick Bridges was of middle height, rather stocky with a bull-like neck, thinning light-brown hair and brown eyes; the young Vincentia Boddam-Whetham, who had definite views about male attractiveness, considered him ugly. But Beatrice was attracted to him from the moment they met. They had a great deal in common: tastes in books, an interest in French, which Frederick read and spoke fluently, and a love of music – every Christmas Day he presented a program of light classics on radio station 2UW. He knew how to make Beatrice laugh and he was someone she could talk to, the kind of companion she had not found before. Beatrice had had many beaux but her heart had not been engaged. This, she knew, was different.

Her current fiancé, who knew nothing about this, was quite happy for Frederick to squire Beatrice around when he was busy, so he was disconcerted when she decided to break their engagement.[4] By 1934 Beatrice and Frederick were spending a great deal of time together.

Mervyn Archdall was aware that his friend Frederick Bridges knew Beatrice, but he was far too busy with the journal to concern himself with her private life. Archdall was also moonlighting, editing technical, medical and scientific manuscripts for an old friend, Walter Cousins, the publishing manager of Angus and Robertson. After a while this extra editing became too much even for the ferociously energetic Archdall, who began passing some of the work over to his editorial assistant.

And so Beatrice began her career as a book editor. She really enjoyed the detailed work of manuscript editing – it was so much more satisfying to work on books than short journal articles, abstracts and book reviews. She was also coming to the conclusion that she did not want to spend the rest of her life at the *Medical Journal of Australia*. Six years of being the indispensable Miss Davis had become repetitive and stressful, and she felt that she had learned all the *MJA* had to teach her.

She wondered whether there were any opportunities at Angus and Robertson. She knew and liked Walter Cousins, who had also taken a shine to her, and she was quickly acquiring a reputation as a painstaking, efficient and dependable editor. One day she decided to ask Cousins for a job but he told her that the company did not need a full-time editor on staff.

Beatrice bided her time. Early in 1937 Cousins went on an extended holiday and Bill Kirwan, the manager of Halstead Press (the printing company that Angus and Robertson also owned) temporarily took over. Beatrice asked Kirwan the same question she had asked Cousins. 'When can you start?' asked Kirwan.

But he was only offering her work as a proofreader and manuscript checker at Halstead Press. Beatrice would work for Halstead until four-thirty every afternoon and would then spend an hour working in A&R's bookshop. Bill Kirwan assured her that if Walter Cousins could find nothing for her at A&R when he returned, there was plenty of work at Halstead. Beatrice now had a new job and the chance of a new career. 'I'm never going to make my own clothes again!' she told Vincentia with glee.

Nor was this the only major change in her life at the time. Early in 1937 she agreed to marry Frederick Bridges. To many of her friends it seemed a quixotic decision. Frederick Bridges was much older, regarded as *déclassé* and by no means rich. He didn't want more children, having two already. Most alarming of all, he suffered from open tuberculosis – a cavity in the lung – which was not only incurable but could be infectious. Why would Beatrice, intelligent, accomplished, beautiful Beatrice, who could surely have any man she wanted, throw away the possibility of a comfortable life and a family of her own?

But for Beatrice it was a logical decision. For her, marriage meant neither children nor respectability. For the first time she had found a companion who shared her interests, who possessed her quickness of mind, who made her laugh. Being witty and ironical rather than jovial herself, she enjoyed Frederick's sense of the ridiculous. He was daring and unconventional in ways she was not: once, very early in the morning after a boozy party, he collected all the empty bottles and stacked them outside the house of the Anglican Archbishop of Sydney. Frederick Bridges was buoyant and light of spirit, fun to be with; he knew interesting people and he encouraged Beatrice to break away and find a new career for herself. And – possibly this was what made him irresistible – despite all his sophistication, he needed her to look after him. Vincentia Boddam-Whetham was in no doubt that theirs was a love match.

The biggest problem was Mervyn Archdall. Knowing what an autocrat he was, Beatrice could guess what he would say when she told him that not only was she marrying one of his old friends, but – even worse – she had taken another job. She put off telling him until she was about to start at A&R. Archdall's reaction was even worse than she had anticipated: he flew into a passionate rage. She was ungrateful and treacherous, he shouted, she had betrayed him. How could she do this to him? She must leave immediately! The depth of his fury does suggest that his relationship with Beatrice went beyond their work together.

Beatrice, shaken, left the *MJA* as soon as she could. But Mervyn Archdall continued to behave like a jealous lover. When a few years later Vincentia married Dr Douglas Anderson, she knew she could invite either Archdall or Beatrice to her wedding but not both. Archdall never forgave Beatrice and never spoke to her again.[5]

PART 2
1937–1945

Our Miss Davis

Counter, Desk and Bench:
The Story of Angus and Robertson

When Beatrice joined Angus and Robertson in 1937 the company consisted of three parts: the bookshop, the publishing company and the printery, Halstead Press. Of these, the most profitable was the bookshop; sprawling across a city block at 89–95 Castlereagh Street, opposite David Jones, it was a landmark for book lovers throughout Australia. With its varied departments – fiction and general, theology, military, children's, history, hobbies, biography – wooden counters piled with new books in their crisp jackets, and the seductive and pervasive scents of fresh paper and printer's ink, the bookshop was a magical place. Angus and Robertson sold second-hand as well as new books, and also boasted a small and select rare-book department and the Sydney Book Club, a large circulating library that provided an essential resource in the days before free municipal libraries (not gazetted in New South Wales until 1944). At one time the bookshop had also held a small art gallery, run by Captain de Groot of the New Guard, the horseman who had prematurely sabre-slashed the ribbon at the 1932 opening of the Sydney Harbour Bridge. The basement was a warehouse where spare copies were stored, and it was also the headquarters of the mail-order department, where books were wrapped and dispatched to all parts of Australia.

At the back of the ground floor shallow wooden steps led up to a mezzanine level where the cashiers sat, intercepting the metal cylinders on a pulley system that whizzed money and dockets up from the shop floor and sent them down again with change. Above the mezzanine were more wooden stairs to the first floor, with the accounts department and publishing offices, and beyond that was a staircase that led to a few cupboardlike spare rooms known as the attic.

Beatrice would certainly have been told the bookshop's folklore. Some employees remembered the day in April 1895 when a sallow, beaky solicitor in his thirties came in with a sheaf of verses he had written for the *Bulletin* under the name of 'The Banjo'. *The Man from Snowy River and Other Verses* became A&R's first great publishing success and Andrew Barton Paterson, who took his pseudonym from the name of a horse, Australia's best-selling poet. Paterson's friendly rival Henry Lawson, who died in 1922, was the subject of many stories. Tall, with a mop of dark hair, a hook nose and brilliant, lively dark eyes, Lawson was usually the worse for wine. One day a disgusted woman customer in the art book section asked who 'that dreadful man' was. When told, she approached Lawson for his autograph. With a flourish, he picked up the nearest ten-guinea art book, ripped out the title page, signed it and handed it to the customer. After that, according to legend, Lawson was paid ten shillings a week to keep out of the bookshop.

The black-bearded, genial and autocratic ghost of George Robertson, who had died four years before Beatrice joined the company, presided over the whole of Angus and Robertson. Some of the older hands, men who had started working in the bookshop as boys, still remembered his partner David Mackenzie Angus, the pale, red-headed Scot with troublesome lungs who had seen the bookshop prosper and the publishing company get on its feet, only to die in his forties fifteen years later, in 1901.

Robertson, always known within the company as G.R., was a combination of hardheaded bookseller, fastidious connoisseur and pirate; he even looked like a buccaneer. The son of a Scots clergyman who came to Australia from England at the age of twenty-two and who named Halstead Press for his Essex birthplace, George Robertson developed a passion for Australiana and collected rare and valuable books, pamphlets, prints, maritime charts, explorers' journals, early watercolours, and grammars of Aboriginal, Maori and Pacific Island languages. His friend and chief rival was David Scott Mitchell, a reclusive figure who used his inherited wealth to indulge his taste for rare books, maps and manuscripts. At Robertson's suggestion, Mitchell offered his collection to the New South Wales state government, who – predictably – dithered about whether to accept it. An exasperated Robertson managed to persuade the government to house Mitchell's collection in the separate wing of the new library they were building in Macquarie Street, and it became known as the Mitchell Library.

Robertson always considered that his 'boss business' was selling books, old or new. But he was a restless man and found the idea of publishing his own books immensely appealing. In the late 1880s he chanced his arm with two volumes of poetry – *A Crown of Wattle* by H. Peden Steel and *Sun and Cloud on River and Sea* by 'Ishmael Dare', the pseudonym of the writer and reviewer Arthur W. Jose. The results encouraged him to continue, though he still thought of publishing as a sideline. Then came the huge success in 1895 of A.B. Paterson's *The Man from Snowy River and Other Verses* and Henry Lawson's book of verse *In the Days When the World Was Wide and Other Verses*, and his short-story collection *While the Billy Boils*, both published in 1896. They convinced Robertson that books about the bush could make money.

The bush verse of Barcroft Boake, 'John O'Brien' (the pseudonym of Father Patrick Hartigan) and Will Ogilvie swelled the A&R coffers, but Robertson also published more innovative poetry. One of the 'modern' poets he encouraged almost became part of the firm. Christopher Brennan edited manuscripts for A&R when he needed the money, though even in dire financial straits he retained an air of *noblesse oblige*. He would go to the second-hand books counter, choose several volumes, drop them into his capacious bag and say, 'Charge them to me.' He did not have an account at the bookshop, but the staff knew he was under G.R.'s protection.

In A&R's early years poetry was a strong and steady seller. *Songs of a Campaign* (1917), war verse by Gallipoli veteran Leon Gellert, sold 7000 copies in its first printing; Zora Cross's passionate *Songs of Love and Life* (1917) went through several editions. (When asked to illustrate it, Norman Lindsay, seldom a sound man on the subject of sex, declined, saying that women couldn't write love poetry because 'All love poetry comes from the connection of the spinal column and the productive apparatus, and it is a notorious fact that God did not connect the two in women.') But the real runaway success, second only to *The Man from Snowy River*, was C.J. Dennis's *The Sentimental Bloke* (1916). Not only did it sell 125 000 copies very quickly, but it was adapted for the stage and in 1919 became a famous silent movie, directed by Raymond Longford and starring Arthur Tauchert and Lottie Lyell.

A&R also published novels, starting with the very popular *Teens: A Story of Australian Schoolgirls* (1897) by *Bulletin* journalist Louise Mack. But one novel G.R. wanted to publish escaped him. In 1899 a nineteen-year-old girl sent him a manuscript she described as 'merely a few pictures of Australian life'. The author – whose style scarcely changed throughout the rest of her long writing life – was Stella Maria Sarah Miles Franklin, and she called her novel *My Brilliant (?) Career*. A&R turned the novel down; it was published, with a recommendation from Henry Lawson and without the question mark, by Blackwoods of London, and it made Miles Franklin's name. Robertson blamed its rejection on an underling who was running the publishing department during the boss's absence. G.R. and Miles Franklin later became good friends, though he mourned the loss of *My Brilliant Career* ever afterwards.

Robertson did have a priggish streak: once Norman Lindsay, irritated because A&R turned down his proposal for a book of pen drawings of female nudes, described him as 'a black Calvinist'. Katharine Susannah Prichard might have agreed. In 1928 Robertson rejected her novel *Coonardoo*, the first in which a relationship between an Aboriginal girl and a white man was presented as more than physical, on the grounds that A&R had done their fair share of showing the world the hardships and 'sordidness' of Australian life. A whiff of Caledonian puritanism continued to permeate A&R even after G.R.'s departure.

Publishing books for children presented none of these problems. In 1916 Norman Lindsay told G.R. he was writing and illustrating one featuring 'a good feed'. G.R. wanted it to be about 'native bears', but Lindsay protested that drawing nothing but koalas was boring. He compromised with one named Bunyip Bluegum, added a lot of other characters, including a crotchety pudding, and the result was *The Magic Pudding*, published in 1918. The same year came May Gibbs's *Snugglepot and Cuddlepie*. An astute businesswoman, Gibbs parlayed her drawings and stories of the Australian bush into comic strips, baby books and bookmarks. She and A&R did very well out of her gumnut babies.

Despite such classics, George Robertson's greatest legacy as a publisher was probably his non-fiction. Here his pursuit of the profit motive was less keen: he believed that if a particular book was needed, it should be published, regardless of its money-making potential. It was a view – bound up with a need to put something back, to contribute to Australian culture – that became a cornerstone of A&R's publishing ethos. In 1912 G.R. decided to publish Australia's first encyclopedia. The first volume, edited by Arthur W. Jose, was delayed by the war and other factors and did not appear until 1925; the second volume came out the following year. The whole thing, originally budgeted at about £7000, finally cost £30 000.

Undaunted, Robertson continued to publish monumental Australian works. The twelve-volume *Official History of Australia in the War of 1914–18*, under the general editorship of C.E.W. Bean, began appearing in 1921. The entire project, into which Angus and Robertson sank thousands of pounds, was not finished until 1942, and it still stands as our most complete military history. Bean's descriptions of the Gallipoli campaign helped to articulate the Anzac legend.

A&R's early books of social history and observation proved enduringly popular, including Bean's two classics *On the Wool Track* (1910) and *The 'Dreadnought' of the Darling* (1911), and Mary Gilmore's *Old Days, Old Ways* (1934), which reinstated women to the outback where Bean had almost ignored them. Natural history also sold well, one of the best-known titles being *What Bird Is That?* by Neville Cayley, first published in 1931 and still in print.

G.R. took a keen interest in the editing of A&R's books; he and his deputy Fred Shenstone did much of the detailed work. In 1918 he wrote C.J. Dennis a twelve-page letter with suggestions for altering his book of verse *Backblock Ballads and Other Verses*, and he read every proof of *The Australian Encyclopedia*, worked through each of the three thousand columns of print with Arthur Jose and made many last-minute corrections. But G.R. also used an editorial machete when it suited. In 1916 he sent Jose the galleys for Banjo Paterson's short-story collection *Three Elephant Power and Other Stories*, advising the editor to 'Hack it about just as if its author was dead, instead of being in Egypt. I'll say I did it.'[1] Paterson wasn't the only author to be given this treatment: Robertson, Jose and David McKee Wright all happily tinkered with Henry Lawson's verse. Indeed, 'improving' Lawson became something of an A&R sport for a while. If Lawson complained, G.R. took out a sovereign and put it on the desk between them. For the sake of having the coin change pockets, Lawson gave in.[2]

G.R.'s chief outside literary and editorial adviser was Thomas G. Tucker, emeritus professor of classical and comparative philology at the University of Melbourne. Robertson called his work 'tuckering', which makes it sound like a form of stonemasonry. Tucker was a champion of clear, basic English, a man who disapproved of fanciness in any form. Good writing was still considered inseparable from standard English; several A&R editors strongly disliked what they considered excessive Australianness. Fred Shenstone wanted the characters in *The Sentimental Bloke* to have all their aspirates and final 'g's neatly in place, but C.J. Dennis patiently pointed out that they were not educated people: 'I might mention that towards the end the Bloke's grammar improves a little on account of better associations,' he added.[3]

Some writers objected to other aspects of A&R's editing: Banjo Paterson, normally a fairly compliant author, complained about Jose's habit of scattering punctuation about the landscape of his manuscripts. Jose does seem to have been an over-enthusiastic user of brackets and dashes: H.B. Gullett objected to their use in his volume of the *Official History of Australia in the War of 1914–18*. A London cartoon by David Low shows Robertson at the top of a tower hauling up a rope ladder while a group of authors below shake fists and sticks at him. Perhaps they were protesting about the work of Jose, Tucker, et al.

George Robertson died in August 1933, aged seventy-three. In his *Sydney Morning Herald* obituary published on 29 August, C.E.W. Bean said that Robertson had wanted to give Australian books an honoured place on the shelves of every great library in the world. He was also determined that every book he produced would be 'fit to stand beside works of the sort produced by any country in the world – in style, matter and appearance, inside and out, reading, printing and binding'. Being a Scot with a reverence for learning, Robertson believed that producing and selling books was crucial to a civilised society. A bookshop, he said, should be the centre of culture for every town in the nation. Bean thought it a pity that Australia had not awarded Robertson any particular recognition of his efforts on behalf of Australian literature, education and culture.

Robertson was survived by his second wife, Eva Ducat, and two daughters and a son by his first marriage.[4] Importantly for the future of Angus and Robertson, his daughter married John Alexander Ferguson (1881–1969), who as Mr Justice Ferguson compiled the massive *Bibliography of Australia*. Their son, George Adie Ferguson, who joined A&R as a young man, played a leading role in the firm's story in years to come.

'That Woman'

From the time Beatrice arrived at Angus and Robertson she must have heard a great deal about G.R. from those who had known him personally. The publishing director, Walter Cousins, had been at A&R since 1901; A.A. Ritchie, later chairman of directors, started in 1909. Bill Kirwan, head of Halstead Press and Beatrice's first employer, had joined A&R as a boy, probably about the turn of the century; Ernie Williams, who ran the bookshop, in 1914. The record for the longest unbroken service belonged to Sid McCure, who came in 1892 and retired sixty-two years later, in 1954. All revered the memory of their former boss. Robertson had been dead four years when Beatrice joined, but at times of uncertainty or crisis, the question was still: What would G.R. have done?

Beatrice's first job in the bookshop meant coming to terms with Hedley Jeffries, the chief buyer of fiction and general. Jeffries, who guarded his department jealously, had joined the company as a young man in the 1920s and bookselling was his life. Rather pink and fond of eau de cologne, he had a huge and admiring fan club consisting mostly of older women; the writer and actor Dulcie Deamer and her friends would sweep into the shop, make a beeline for him and hang on his every word. He often quoted G.R.'s dictum that you didn't simply sell a customer the book they requested, you always tried them with several others, and he was expert at sending customers away with three books when they had thought they only wanted one. So brilliant a salesman was he that his orders for the bookshop often influenced print runs for some British publishers. Beatrice always had a healthy respect for Jeffries's expertise as a bookseller, though she found his swishy, supercilious style not much to her taste.

From behind her counter Beatrice must have seen many of G.R.'s authors cross the bookshop on their way to visit Walter Cousins on the first floor. Banjo Paterson, now an old man (he would die in 1941) was one; another was Mary Gilmore, one of Angus and Robertson's great supporters. Hugh McCrae, Norman Lindsay, May Gibbs and Louise Mack were all greeted by the staff as old friends. Ion Idriess (always called Jack) had used A&R's premises as his office for years. His tales of wild Australia had been extremely successful ever since *Madman's Island* in 1927, and he felt entitled to the privilege. A&R's publicity portrayed him as a romantic adventurer out of Rider Haggard: 'He has crisscrossed the continent from east to west, from north to south, while his tracks among the wild places of Cape York Peninsula on the east coast are legion . . .' A true professional with no great pretensions to literary merit, Idriess wrote more than fifty books, publishing at least one a year for more than thirty years. On average he sold about 35 000 copies of each title – impressive numbers, particularly during the Depression. His greatest success was probably *Prospecting for Gold* (1931), which sold more than 300 000 copies: many men 'on the wallaby' bought it hoping it would give them a way of making a living. Day after day at his desk on the mezzanine floor Idriess busily covered sheets of quarto paper with his large schoolboy scrawl, handing them to a typist when he had finished. He was very keen to autograph copies of his books – so keen that George Ferguson joked that future antiquarian booksellers' catalogues would have entries that ran 'Idriess, Ion L., unsigned, scarce'.

Like most companies of its time, Angus and Robertson was run by men. All the executives were male, women were subordinates. They worked in the bookshop, in the accounts department, as secretaries and clerical assistants. The most influential woman in the company was Rebecca Wiley, a tiny, soft-voiced autocrat in steel-rimmed spectacles who ran the mailing department. The company's first woman employee, Wiley started as a clerk in 1894, became switchboard operator and cashier and then secretary and confidante to G.R., to whom she was devoted; when his first wife died it was thought she might become the second Mrs Robertson. She was the company's unofficial historian, keeping detailed diaries and voluminous books of newspaper cuttings, and she had known Walter Cousins and most of the other Angus and Robertson executives since they started as boys.

Rebecca Wiley was in charge of the female clerical staff, and what she said went. Her girls were not permitted to wear scarves or jewellery, and she put a sign in the washroom forbidding the use of lipstick. She once sent a young girl home to scrub off rouge. Every Thursday morning the women lined up to receive their small brown pay packets from Rebecca Wiley's hands and were expected to say, 'Thank you, Miss Wiley,' as if their salaries came directly from her.[1]

Beatrice, mainly employed as a proofreader, had relatively little to do with Rebecca Wiley, who retired about a year after Beatrice joined A&R. The technology for preparing books had not changed since the invention of the Linotype machine in 1884. Solid lines of type were cast from brass dies, or matrices, automatically selected by operating a keyboard. This type, known as hot metal, was arranged in long, shallow trays called galleys, from which an impression was taken and transferred to long strips of paper. These strips, which had to be checked and corrected against the original manuscript before being made up into pages, were called galley proofs.

Beatrice worked with Grace George, known as Georgie, the head proofreader, who had been with A&R for at least thirty years. Georgie supervised the company's readers and copyholders (whose job was to read the text aloud while the reader corrected the proofs), all of whom were women. Originally Rebecca Wiley's clerical assistant, Georgie had been taught to read proofs by George Robertson. It was she who most often asked, 'What would G.R. have done?'

Georgie had a sharp eye. Her proofreaders not only read for typographical errors in galleys, but they were expected to check dates, facts, style and references. If any A&R book had more than three typographical errors, Georgie would be the first to ask questions. At the same time she was very protective of 'her girls'; whenever Ion Idriess made flirtatious comments on his proofs, or Frank Clune littered his with ribald jokes, she reminded them severely that her proofreaders were impressionable young women. As diminutive as Rebecca Wiley, she sat in a huge sagging armchair stuffed with cushions that threatened to overwhelm her, smoked incessantly and was famous for having the untidiest desk at Angus and Robertson. Always on the telephone, she rather enjoyed whipping up a crisis that only she could deal with. Despite this apparent sense of urgency, her attitude to deadlines was lackadaisical: manuscripts were read when she thought they should be, and not before. Georgie and her staff worked on the top floor of 89 Castlereagh Street, though they later moved to Arnold Place, off Oxford Street, Darlinghurst.

Not long after Beatrice started at Angus and Robertson, Walter Cousins decided that she should be more than a proofreader and bookshop assistant and that the company needed a staff editor after all. Beatrice therefore became Angus and Robertson's first full-time book editor and almost certainly the first in Australia. Her pleasure in her new job must have faded the moment she saw her office, a tiny cubbyhole and former storeroom at the top of the stairs to the attic, boiling hot in summer and freezing in winter. It had a small high window looking onto a stairwell and just enough room for Beatrice, a desk and a set of bookshelves. With heat provided by an ancient heater in winter and the only exit to the floors below via a wooden staircase, Beatrice's office made a mockery of fire regulations – and it never improved in all the years she was there.

The appointment of a woman as the only staff editor, when previously all editing had been done by men, was revolutionary. But, though Cousins, Kirwan and the other men knew that Beatrice was better educated, better read and probably more intelligent than most of them, they did not treat her as a professional equal. Walter Cousins held regular meetings to discuss manuscripts and make publishing recommendations, attended by staff from the bookshop and Halstead Press, as well as one or two of the freelance editors. Beatrice was not invited.

In her early days, just being an editor could be stressful enough. One of the first manuscripts Beatrice had to tackle was an enormous tailoring manual. It was an appalling job. The author, an ancient former tailor in a dusty suit and bowler hat, presented his work as a series of pink pages gummed together; if the manuscript was dropped everything unfolded like a concertina. There were also dozens of unnumbered, hand-drawn diagrams that had to be decoded, arranged in order, captioned and inserted into the text. As she struggled with ways of taking crotch measurements for ladies' jodhpurs, Beatrice felt like giving up altogether.[2]

She took a little while to become familiar with Australian authors. One of her first letters, addressed to 'Mr Miles Franklin', began 'Dear Sir', but from the beginning she enjoyed reading and reporting on unsolicited manuscripts. Her work at the *Medical Journal of Australia* had developed a talent for precise summary, and she always gave a brief assessment of the writer's literary skill. From the beginning of her career at Angus and Robertson, she had the almost forensic ability to pinpoint a manuscript's faults in non-judgemental, logical prose. However, one thing she lacked and never developed was a nose for the popular market, a strong sense of what would sell. Her blind spots included books about sport – in 1930s Australia this invariably meant Test cricket – a subject she found boring. She had not been long at A&R when she wrote a 'not recommended' report for a book about Donald Bradman on the grounds that it had little literary merit. Walter Cousins overrode her, naturally, and the book sold thousands of copies.

It must have annoyed the other women in the office to see the flirtatious, elegant and cultured Miss Davis promoted above them all. Partly because of her university degree, but mostly because Beatrice did not gossip with her female colleagues, she was soon branded as stuck-up. Rebecca Wiley in particular thought 'that woman' needed taking down a peg or two. On the outer with the women in the office and not accepted as an equal by the men – no wonder Beatrice later said her first few years at Angus and Robertson had been tense and difficult.

Her colleagues knew very little about Beatrice's private life, and she told them nothing about Frederick Bridges. This was not just because she was a reserved and private person but because she intended to marry him. Beatrice knew the rules: only single women worked, and she had no intention of leaving her new job. At lunchtime on 6 July 1937, when she had been at A&R for only a few months, she slipped out of 89 Castlereagh Street, walked to the Sydney Registry Office, married Frederick Bridges, took off her wedding ring and came back to work. She did not mention her marriage to anyone at A&R for a long time.

Beatrice and Frederick first lived in his rented apartment at Gordon on the north shore. They both enjoyed entertaining, and their double income enabled them to hold large parties. A regular guest was the painter Percy Lindsay, whom Frederick had known for years. Frederick and Beatrice sometimes saw other members of the Lindsay family at Percy's brother Norman's house in Springwood in the Blue Mountains. Norman might even have drawn the beautiful Mrs Bridges; a nymph in one of his etchings is reputed to be Beatrice, wearing nothing but an elaborate headdress.[3]

Not long after they married, Beatrice and Frederick began looking for a house to buy. The north side of the city was rapidly being developed now that the Harbour Bridge had made it accessible, but it was still peaceful and close to harbour and bushland. Professional cellist Tal Craig and his singer/pianist wife Elsie, whom Beatrice had probably met through her musical activities, had bought a steep block of land at Cammeray, overlooking a quiet reach of Middle Harbour. The Craigs were stylish people and they employed an architect to design their dream home: a three-bedroom, two-storey art deco house.

When completed in 1938 and painted white, the house looked as if someone had cut a slice from an ocean liner and set it carefully on a corner of land overlooking a gleaming sheet of water. It was much admired: behind the stairwell was a wall of glass bricks, used for almost the first time in an Australian home. There was space for an outside deck on the first floor, and the living-room floor was specially sprung for parties and dancing. The house even had literary associations, though not very happy ones: out the front was a gum tree from which the bush poet Barcroft Boake had hanged himself with his stockwhip in 1892.

But the Craigs had overcommitted themselves financially and were soon forced to sell. Frederick immediately offered to buy the place, and the owners agreed. Early in 1939 Beatrice and Frederick moved to 102 Cammeray Road, Cammeray, overlooking Folly Point on Middle

Harbour, with Beatrice's piano and two small terriers appropriately named Whisky and Soda. It was a house Beatrice loved from the moment she saw it, and it remained her home for more than fifty years.

Now that Dr and Mrs Bridges were truly At Home, Beatrice was discovering more of Frederick's quirks. She had always known of his disregard for convention. When she decided to join the extremely genteel Queen's Club in the city, she had to state on the application form the clubs to which her husband belonged. Frederick, who ridiculed all clubs as snobbish institutions, took the form and wrote 'Christmas ham club, sixpence a week'. Once, he greeted his party guests in a black cloak that reached from neck to ankle. Not until he turned away to pour the drinks and the cloak swung open did it become obvious that he was naked underneath. Beatrice laughed, but in truth she was ambivalent about this sort of thing. While she always enjoyed people who went their own way regardless of what others thought, and had a large streak of this kind of individualism herself, she also had the Deloitte respect for the rules of 'correct' behaviour.

These conflicting feelings came out in her dealings with Frederick's family. Peter and Robert Bridges had lived with their mother since they were small and Frederick had made little effort to get to know them. Beatrice did not approve of this dereliction of fatherly duty, and she felt that now Frederick's sons were young men, the time had come to mend fences. But Frederick wasn't particularly interested, and Peter was understandably indifferent to a father who had had so little time for him. (Peter's younger brother Robert occasionally spent time with Beatrice and Frederick.) Beatrice commented to Vincentia Anderson that she thought Frederick had been very hard on his children.

In later years, Beatrice was apt to say that she and Frederick had such fun together that the age difference between them did not matter. She might have believed this, but it must have mattered to Frederick, a not particularly good-looking man with a chronic illness whose new wife was not much older than his sons. He loved Beatrice dearly, was kind and generous to her and very proud of her career ambitions, and they were lovers, friends and companions. But like most older husbands, at least since the time of Chaucer, he probably felt insecure, wondering how he could hope to hold on to such a vibrant, clever and attractive young woman. There was also a deep reserve in Beatrice, a sense that she kept some of her own secrets, that he might easily have found frustrating.

Frederick reacted by becoming very possessive. Beatrice was used to this sort of behaviour in men who were interested in her, particularly older ones – Mervyn Archdall being the prime example – and no doubt accepted this calmly. She must have found equanimity difficult, however, on the day Frederick took the album of postcards her father had sent her during the war and burned them all.[4]

It was a shocking thing to do. Frederick knew how much Beatrice had loved her father and what those war postcards meant to her. The most charitable explanation is that Frederick's tuberculosis had made him subject to mood swings and that he became irrational. But burning those postcards does suggest that Frederick considered Charles Herbert Davis to be some kind of rival, that he resented Beatrice's love for her long-dead father. What he did was at best childishly jealous, at worst vindictive. If she hadn't known it before, Beatrice was learning that a much older man is not necessarily an emotionally mature one.

Fighting Words

All through the 1930s the events in Europe – the rise of fascism in Italy and Germany, the Spanish Civil War, Hitler's conquests – had formed a kind of background noise in Australian life, like the constant unsettling murmur of a radio in the next room. When, on the evening of Sunday 3 September 1939, Prime Minister Robert Menzies announced that Australia was at war with Germany, the nation waited to see what would happen next. Like most Australian companies, Angus and Robertson adopted a policy of business as usual. At the end of the 1930s, the book trade was going through a sluggish phase; at Halstead Press there was so little work that over several months in 1938 the proofreader Enid Moon – a very tall woman – had time to knit herself a calf-length woollen dress during working hours.

It seems bizarre to say that the Nazi onslaught on Europe was of great benefit to Angus and Robertson and indirectly to Australian literature. But so it was. U-boat attacks on British shipping soon made the export of British goods, including books, a perilous business. For the first time British publishers allowed their Australian counterparts to print under licence their own editions of English and American books. This was a reversal of current policy: some years before, British publishers, who dominated the Australian market, had formed a cartel to prevent Australian-owned publishing companies from acquiring separate rights in British-originated books. They also agreed not to buy the rights to a

US-originated title unless those rights encompassed all the territories of the British Empire, including Australia. This cosy arrangement also meant, ironically, that Australian writers published overseas received inadequate 'export' royalties in their own country. Not only were Australian readers unable to read an American book except in a British edition (unless they imported it directly from the US), but Australian publishers could not produce their own editions of the money-spinning international bestsellers on which US and UK publishers had always depended for a large part of their revenue. Now the fortunes of war had seen this Traditional Market Agreement temporarily overturned, which meant increased profits for Angus and Robertson.[1]

So, too, did the federal government's early decision to plan and develop their own publishing program of books and pamphlets for civilians as well as soldiers. Not having the capacity to print these in the quantities required, they called on A&R and Halstead Press. For the duration of the war, Angus and Robertson became Australia's de facto Ministry of Information. Always anxious about the company's profitability, Walter Cousins must have been delighted.

Beatrice, however, was able to contain her joy. She now had to edit and check a stream of books, booklets and pamphlets in leaden prose with such titles as *A Manual of Elementary Drill*, *Food Shipment from Australia in War Time* and *Diesel Engine Practice*. She complained to an A&R author, 'I must sweat over execrably written technical works on such subjects as poultry breeding or the wool industry or diseases of the ear, which is apt to make me very cantankerous.'[2]

With the Japanese attack on the US naval base at Pearl Harbor on 7 December 1941 and the fall of Singapore the following February, invasion seemed imminent. By May the enemy were moving towards Port Moresby on Australia's doorstep. Only after the Battle of the Coral Sea in May 1942 were the Japanese forced to retreat. The attack on Sydney Harbour by three Japanese midget submarines at the end of the month was a jolting reminder of what might have been.

Sydney, like other Australian cities, had undergone dramatic changes in the face of war. Never a quiet city, it was now noisier than ever. Beatrice endured the teeth-gritting shriek of the one-o'clock practice air-raid siren, set against the rattle of the trams. The entrances to city buildings were piled high with sand-filled hessian bags in case of bomb blasts; the windows of department stores were either missing or criss-crossed with strips of sticky tan paper to prevent glass shattering. If Beatrice decided to remain at work after hours she emerged from number 89 into a gloomy Castlereagh Street, its streetlights dimmed because of blackout regulations. Her slow bus trip across the Harbour Bridge was followed by a fifteen-minute walk home in the dark.

Angus and Robertson followed the rules laid down by the civil defence authorities. Slit trenches were dug in the grassy strip outside the Halstead Press offices in Nickson Street, Surry Hills, as staff air-raid shelters. But they were too small to take the staff of the printery and it was suggested that a new, bigger shelter be made from the huge rolls of paper in the storeroom: evidently nobody had thought that paper might actually go up in flames. The same combination of bureaucratic solicitude and lack of commonsense was evident at 89 Castlereagh Street, where the official air-raid shelter was the basement. The fact that a bookshop was a prime fire hazard was not considered. And how was Beatrice expected to clamber down three steep flights of wooden stairs without being burned to death?

The often ramshackle preparations for war were marginally less exasperating to Sydneysiders than the government's controls. The amount of regulation because 'there's a war on' confirms the view that during World War II one of the great Australian growth industries was bureaucracy. From about February 1942, in the months when Japanese invasion seemed most probable, the federal government introduced its National Economic Plan. This had far-reaching implications for almost every sphere of daily life, from the rationing of clothes and food to the purchase of capital equipment for business.

It must have seemed to Beatrice and her colleagues that the government was trying to make their jobs as difficult as possible. What was the point of publishing more government pamphlets than Beatrice could handle if the government refused permission to buy more printing machines? There were also massive and continuing problems with paper supplies. As early as June 1940 Walter Cousins wrote to a hopeful author that A&R had too little paper available to indulge in speculative publishing – one of the most convincing reasons ever given by a publisher for rejecting a manuscript. Imported paper was naturally impossible to get; even the poor-quality, yellow-grey paper made in Burnie, Tasmania, was in short supply. It was also expensive, as was bookbinding cloth: according to Walter Cousins, between 1939 and 1947 paper costs increased by 350 per cent and cloth by 300 per cent.[3]

Another constant irritant was 'the Manpower', short for the Federal Directorate of Manpower. This was set up to administer a national register of the working-age population and to provide quotas for jobs, as well as to decide how and where workers could be employed in war-related industries. Even assuming Halstead Press could find and buy the necessary printing and binding machinery at the right price, and assuming they had the paper required, Manpower might not allow them the staff to use any of it.

Despite these problems, A&R was flourishing. By the end of the war, Walter Cousins could boast that 'Nearly every worthwhile book that is published these days goes out of print within a week or two of its publication.'[4] Australian books of general interest – not government-related material or textbooks – occasionally sold out runs of 10 000 copies within three months.

The Commonwealth Literary Fund was also doing its bit for the war effort and for local writers. Set up in 1908 to support creative literature in Australia, this federal government agency had in its early years been almost philanthropic, awarding pensions to distinguished authors and giving occasional financial support to authors and their families. In 1936 Labor leader James Scullin urged Joseph Lyons's conservative government to do more to promote Australian literature among a wider public. This was slow to develop, but four years later – when Australia was at war – the CLF agreed to give fellowships and other direct grants to writers and to subsidise lectures on Australian literature at universities and regional centres.

In April 1944 the CLF established the Australian Pocket Library, a series of cheaply produced paperback editions of Australian books for the armed forces for sale from 1s 3d to 3s a copy. In editions of 25 000 copies each, the Library published such established works as Henry Lawson's stories, as well as *Robbery Under Arms, Man Shy, We of the Never Never, On the Wool Track*, and newer titles such as Gavin Casey's *It's Harder for Girls and Other Stories*, Kylie Tennant's *Tiburon* and Brian Penton's *Landtakers* – twenty-five titles in all.

Australian readers had an unquenchable thirst for true stories about the war. A&R discovered this early in 1941 when George Johnston, then a 29-year-old journalist for the Melbourne *Argus*, wrote *Grey Gladiator*, an account of the cruiser HMAS *Sydney* serving with the British Mediterranean fleet. Its first edition of 1500 sold out within a week; altogether the book sold about 14 000 copies. Johnston, a rapid writer, followed this up two months later with *Battle of the Seaways*, the story of the British naval war. His A&R books *Australia at War* and *New Guinea Diary* also did well. Cousins, who thought Johnston was one of the country's best writers about the war, was irritated when the journalist decided to concentrate on writing fiction. A most successful war book was *Behind Bamboo*, journalist Rohan Rivett's graphic account of his experiences in Japanese prison camps and on the Burma–Thailand railway. Edited by Beatrice and published by A&R in 1946, it went through four impressions by the end of 1947 and by 1950 had sold 43 000 copies.

It is one of publishing's ironies that a best-selling documentary novel about one of Australia's proudest episodes caused Beatrice and A&R more trouble than almost anything else the company published during the war.

In April 1941 the undefeated German army under Rommel was ready to sweep across North Africa. Their only barrier to the Persian Gulf, and Britain's oil supplies, was the fortified town of Tobruk on the Libyan coast, held by the Australian 9th Division. With the 7th Division they built a thirty-mile outer line of defence – about 150 posts protected by barbed wire, tank ditches and mines – as well as an inner series of defences. If the enemy broke through both lines and the mobile reserve failed to stop them, every man in the garrison was told to fight to the death: there would be no surrender. Rommel attacked on 13 April. When the dust settled the following day the Germans had 150 dead and had lost seventeen tanks and twelve supporting aircraft, along with weapons and equipment. The defenders – later called the Rats of Tobruk – with twenty-six dead and sixty-four wounded, had lost two tanks. The garrison held out against the Germans for more than eight months until Rommel withdrew.

Lawson Glassop, a 28-year-old journalist working in Cairo for the *AIF News*, realised that Tobruk was an epic subject for a novel. When the siege was over he interviewed dozens of Rats on leave in Cairo, and worked on his book late at night. He returned to Australia in February 1943 and by the middle of that year had completed *The Rats of Tobruk*, the story of a larrikin furniture salesman named Mick who enlists in the AIF and, with a group of mates, takes part in the siege. Glassop took care to report soldiers' words and feelings accurately, getting away from the literary convention that men at war are steely-chinned heroes. His book was not anti-war in tone – soldiers who refused to do their duty as fighting men were judged harshly both by other characters and the author – but it did break new ground as a graphic and realistic picture of Australian fighting men.

Glassop realised he had a good story and decided to try to publish it in the USA. But first he sent it to Norman Lindsay, a friendly acquaintance of his who, recognising the manuscript's authenticity, showed it to his friend Douglas Stewart. Together they persuaded Glassop to submit it to Angus and Robertson on the grounds that, as the book dealt with Australian soldiers, it should be shown to an Australian publisher, who might later place the book in the US.

A&R accepted *The Rats of Tobruk* almost immediately. 'You've done a great piece of work,' Beatrice wrote to Glassop on 13 September 1943. She added some standard editorial caveats: the narrative was too long in places, elliptical in others, and there were problems with the sequence of material. She also warned of possible libel, but in the light of what followed it is interesting that she never expressed any objection to the characters' use of profanity and blasphemy. Then and always, if Beatrice thought 'language' was appropriate and used effectively in a manuscript, she accepted it. Describing Glassop's novel as an important book, she suggested he rework parts of it and send it back, or better still deliver the manuscript in person so they could work on it together. She said the novel would be published the following February, with a run of 5000 copies – and, she added firmly, its title was now *We Were the Rats*.

All this was heady stuff for Glassop, languishing in a Queensland army press unit. He wanted to work on final revisions with Beatrice as soon as possible, and decided to come down to Sydney. A tanned and cheerful young man presented himself in Beatrice's office in October, but he omitted to mention that he had gone absent without leave. Caught almost immediately, he was docked seven weeks' pay, threatened with court martial and sent to a field punishment centre. The letter he sent to Beatrice shows how severely the army made him suffer for his art.

> I cleaned dixies, made fires, lit fires, tended fires, carried fires, carried water, chopped wood, carried wood, wheeled wood, carried pig food, poured pig food, sanded pig bins, sanded dishes, emptied latrine pans, set out latrine pans, swept the latrine area, swept the shower area, scrubbed benches, scrubbed boards, dug holes, wheeled dirt, filled in holes, hoed weeds, raked weeds, scrubbed tables, scrubbed trestles, shooed cows and above all I marched. I marched in the morning, I marched in the afternoon, I marched in the evening. I would have marched at night but it was too dark . . . [5]

Glassop's glow of martyrdom was extinguished when Beatrice told him his book would be late. By May 1944, with publication apparently no closer and with no word about the fate of his book, the author wrote to Walter Cousins, accusing A&R of letting already successful overseas books take precedence over local ones. (Lawson Glassop seems to have completed the trajectory from gratitude to complaint even faster than the average first-time author.) Cousins apologised in the way he generally did, enumerating his own woes – too many books, too many Manpower restrictions – but it was Beatrice who applied the balm of tact. 'Our chief fault was leading you to believe what we wanted to believe ourselves – that the book would be out in February – when, with government orders to deal with, we were not sufficiently our own masters to promise anything,' she wrote.[6]

Beatrice still thought the book had problems. Glassop was too keen to include factual information about Tobruk, which she said sometimes made the novel read like a newspaper article. Norman Lindsay was less polite: he told Beatrice that while Glassop was a remarkably good reporter of actuality, he had not the dimmest notion of the art of novel writing.[7] But nobody told Glassop; by now he and Beatrice had built up a pleasant, chatty relationship. Four years younger than Beatrice, Glassop apparently treated her as an elder sister, even giving her racing tips: 'Slap the smash on Flight every time she starts,' he wrote to her. 'She's a bobby dazzler.'[8] Beatrice in turn lent a sympathetic ear to Glassop's Byzantine amatory problems, many of which involved a pretty blonde on the A&R staff.

The original manuscript of *We Were the Rats* had weighed in at 200 000 words; Glassop had reluctantly cut about 10 per cent, but Beatrice told him it was still too long. The book simply needed to be condensed, she said, and Glassop could safely leave that to A&R. She did not suggest that he should see either edited manuscript or proofs, and he agreed to review her 'telescoping' when the book was published.

The result was wholly predictable: as soon as Glassop received his copies in September 1944 he hit the roof. His view appeared to be that Beatrice could make whatever changes she liked, provided she didn't actually alter anything. He accused her of tampering with his style and wrongly correcting some of his sentences. Beatrice took a standard editorial fallback position and quoted Fowler's *Modern English Usage*, only to have Glassop retort that if Fowler had been any good he would have written a real book, not a grammar text. Beatrice had imposed her will on the book, and, he wrote, 'If you are going to do that, you might as well put "by so and so as told to Beatrice Davis" on the title page.' Beatrice replied that she thought the published book was fine.[9]

We Were the Rats was a success from the start, selling 10 000 copies in its first year. Reviewers praised its authenticity and energy; only Josephine O'Neill of the Sydney *Daily Telegraph* complained about its 'passages of obscenities', and Vance Palmer on the ABC found it rather crude. Soldiers and their families loved it, none more than the former Rats themselves. Angus and Robertson sold rights in the US, and the novelist John Dos Passos wrote Glassop a letter of congratulation. Now that Lawson Glassop could take the credit for the book's much praised tautness and economy of words, he decided to forgive Beatrice and they were friends again.

Not quite everybody loved the book. In June 1945 the Reverend Gordon Powell wrote to A&R objecting to its 'blasphemy and profanity', singling out a section where a character reads an American girlie magazine aloud to some of his mates. Later the same year a Tasmanian woman read *We Were the Rats* carefully, decided it was obscene and referred it to the secretary of the Tasmanian Women's Non-Party League, who agreed. The woman approached the state minister for customs, who considered the novel indecent and worthy of prosecution. Because the publisher was based in New South Wales, he referred it to that state's chief secretary, who in turn referred the matter to the state crown solicitor. *We Were the Rats* was ruled obscene according to the *Obscene Publications Act 1902* (NSW) – that is, it was found to have a 'tendency to deprave and corrupt' impressionable minds.

The police summonsed A&R, who asked the chief secretary to withdraw the case. He refused, and on 24 April 1946 *We Were the Rats* came before Mr Farringdon, SM. The police case alleging obscenity rested on only five pages: the word 'bloody' appeared on two, one had a quote from 'The Bastard from the Bush'. Two other pages in Chapter 31 comprised the section to which the Reverend Gordon Powell had specifically objected, and some of it is worth quoting to show what the guardians of Australia's morality were up against. In a cave near Tobruk, five Australian soldiers are poring over an American girlie magazine:

'What happened then?' asked Jim.

'Thought you didn't want to listen,' said Gordon. 'She comes across. Turns it on like steam. She pulls her dress off. Listen to this. "He saw her slender fingers unhook her scanty brassière and toss it away from the prominent globes of her breasts. And finally he saw her glorious young body lying irresistibly nude across his lap."'

'Can't stand it,' said Eddie. 'Just can't stand it.' And while the rest of us started to chant 'Stars and Stripes Forever', he got up and went outside.

' "Her soft smooth arms slid about his neck," and she says, "I can see how much fun I missed by remaining a virgin. And I positively do not intend to be one any longer." '

'Had a few virgins in me time,' said Jim slowly, 'but never one like that. It don't seem natural somehow. It was usually pretty tough goin' before they come across.'[10]

Farringdon upheld the case and fined Angus and Robertson £10. A&R quickly mounted an appeal, which was heard two months later before Judge Studdert. The prosecuting barrister said he did not intend to press the matter too strongly as he had read the book himself and enjoyed it. Never, wrote Lawson Glassop to Walter Cousins, had he seen a prosecution so obviously trying to lose a case.[11] He thought the police had been so severely criticised for bringing the case that they were anxious to make amends.

Judge Studdert began by praising *We Were the Rats* as 'a first rate book and a first rate novel', but said that Chapter 31 was the most objectionable part of the book and he could not agree that it was intended to be satirical, as the defence alleged. He concluded: 'I think these pages are just plain filth and I entertain no doubt that they are obscene in fact and in law.'[12]

Angus and Robertson withdrew *We Were the Rats* from the market. Extraordinary as it now seems, the novel stayed out of print until 1961, when it was republished by Horwitz, minus some of the blasphemy and the offending Chapter 31. Lawson Glassop went on to publish other books, but nothing else he ever wrote had the success or the notoriety of *We Were the Rats*.

A&R's willingness to keep out of print a book that had done so well for them is hardly the mark of a brave publisher. The company had already shown similar lack of courage when in 1943 a man with the same name as a character in Kylie Tennant's novel *Ride On Stranger* insisted he had been defamed and demanded financial compensation and the withdrawal of the book from sale. Although Tennant assured A&R that if the matter came to court she would be perfectly happy to settle all costs – the novel was selling well and she was sure that the extra publicity would do it no harm – A&R panicked, withdrew the entire edition from sale and paid the man £250. A furious Kylie Tennant said that it seemed impossible to overestimate a publisher's terror at the prospect of going to court.

For some years after the war, the trouble over *We Were the Rats* became A&R's reason for looking twice at any potentially difficult manuscript. Their timidity cost them one significant Australian war novel: Kenneth Mackenzie's *Dead Men Rising*, about the 1944 breakout of Japanese and Italian POWs from a prison camp at Cowra, western New South Wales. Mackenzie, a well-known poet, had written two previous novels; his first, *The Young Desire It* (1937), about schoolboy sexuality, had caused a fuss. *Dead Men Rising* was also 'difficult', dealing with racism in war. Even though Mackenzie submitted the novel to A&R several years after the war, the publishers turned it down on the rather feeble grounds that it gave an unflattering picture of Australian servicemen and the soldiers who had been in Cowra might object to it. Mackenzie finally published the novel with Jonathan Cape in 1951.[13]

In 1949 a young journalist named Tom (T.A.G.) Hungerford, who had been in Japan with the occupation forces, brought to A&R the massive manuscript of his first novel *Sowers of the Wind*, a large part of which dealt with Australian soldiers in brothels. Beatrice was not at all fazed by the material: she liked the book immediately and accepted the manuscript, though she said A&R could not publish it that year. She suggested that Hungerford enter it in the *Sydney Morning Herald*'s competition for an unpublished novel.[14] He did, and was astonished when it won second prize.

A win in a major literary competition, a good-looking and talented young author and the book's subject should have propelled *Sowers of the Wind* rapidly into print. However, Beatrice now said she thought the book was 'awkward'. This *volte-face* after her initial enthusiasm does suggest that she was following the cautious company line, and also confirms the view that she was sometimes influenced by pressure from Cousins and his colleagues. She couldn't make a decision about publication immediately, she told Hungerford: did he have another novel? As it happened he did: *The Ridge and the River*, the story of an army patrol on Bougainville. Beatrice accepted that too.

Even though she had given him no definite answer about the publication date of *Sowers*, Beatrice was – rather unfairly – proprietorial about it. Clem Christesen, who was scouting for Heinemann in London, wanted to read it and Hungerford referred the request to Beatrice. She said he should do what he thought best, though having accepted *The Ridge and the River* the company certainly considered him an A&R author, despite the delay over *Sowers*. Beatrice's charm and skill in persuading authors to remain with A&R, sometimes against their own best interests, grew more practised with the passing years. She convinced Hungerford to sever any connection with Heinemann.

The Ridge and the River went calmly through the editorial process, though at one point Beatrice asked Hungerford whether he would 'clean it up a bit', as a matter of taste. When Hungerford challenged her, she sent him an alphabetical list, which began: 'A is for arsehole, B is for balls, C is for cunt . . .' and so on down the alphabet. Hungerford, highly amused, agreed to cut out most of these, though on the grounds of authenticity he jibbed at 'P for piss off'.[15]

When it appeared in 1951, *The Ridge and the River* was widely praised for its unsentimentality and frankness – six years after the war it was evidently easier to accept what soldiers were really like – and Tom Hungerford was considered a writer to watch. And still A&R hung on to *Sowers of the Wind*. The next Hungerford novel they published was *Riverslake* (1953), dealing critically with the conditions faced by postwar immigrants. In 1954 A&R decided that Hungerford's reputation was now sufficiently robust to survive the publication of his first book, and *Sowers* sidled on to the market. But by then its time had passed. Several books about the occupation of Japan had now been published, and *Sowers* sank almost without trace. The whole experience made Tom Hungerford disillusioned with Angus and Robertson – he was not even told that his book had appeared until somebody mentioned seeing it in a Perth bookshop – and for some years he stopped writing fiction and returned to journalism. He did not blame Beatrice for his problems with Angus and Robertson and they remained friends – although, according to him, she never apologised for A&R's treatment of *Sowers of the Wind*.

'We Must Remain the Literary Hub of Australia'

Almost as soon as she started at Angus and Robertson in 1937, Beatrice had joined the Society of Women Writers and the Fellowship of Australian Writers, Sydney's only real literary societies. To the monthly seminars or lectures the FAW ran in the Education Department's offices in Bridge Street came most of Sydney's literary luminaries – George Mackaness, Tom Inglis Moore, Miles Franklin, Flora Eldershaw, Marjorie Barnard, Frank Dalby Davison, Norman Lindsay, P.R. Stephensen. Some Beatrice knew through A&R, others she met there, and she became known to a wide cross-section of Sydney writers.

Even though Beatrice's background was as a scientific rather than a literary editor, she had quickly discovered that she loved editing fiction. As she wrote to Lawson Glassop in 1944, 'Producing literature, when I get a chance to deal in it instead of textbooks, is the only thing that makes this job worth while for me.'[1] By now she knew that this was where her future lay.

Beatrice also joined the English Association, encouraged by a new friend, Guy Howarth, who taught literature at the University of Sydney. Founded in 1923 by Professor Sir Mungo MacCallum, the association maintained a lofty intellectual tone, preoccupied with protecting the English language from the corrupting influence of Australian and American slang. (Their quarterly bulletin always had examples of 'the misuse of speech or writing in the English language', and severely mentioned were such usages as 'comics', 'debunking' and 'I will' instead of 'I shall'.) Like the FAW, the English Association met once a month, at the Lyceum Club in the Bank of New South Wales building on the corner of King and George streets, to hear a paper by a guest speaker or a member of the society about an aspect of English literature, and to discuss topics of literary interest over bad sherry and biscuits afterwards.

While Walter Cousins was naturally pleased that the energetic Miss Davis was taking her job seriously enough to network outside office hours, he could not see how her new contacts – those who were not already A&R authors – would benefit the company. Publishing novels, short stories or poetry whose literary merit outweighed their popular appeal was not, Cousins thought, A&R's business. A conservative, quiet and rather owlish man, he was a commercial publisher through and through. George Robertson had published a great deal of fiction and poetry in his time but Cousins, said one of his authors bluntly, had never read a novel in his life. In his view contemporary literature could not compete with the chatty historical non-fiction and adventure yarns by Frank Clune and Ion Idriess, steady sellers for many years. His chief literary advisers were Idriess and E.V. Timms, a writer of historical romances. However, it was not long before Cousins had to modify his views, partly because of a change of staff at the *Bulletin*'s Red Page.

The pink inside cover of the *Bulletin* had provided an outlet for contemporary Australian poets and writers of short fiction since A.G. Stephens founded it in 1896. Under the editorship of Cecil Mann, who became editor in the late 1930s, the Red Page developed a wide-ranging eclecticism: one week it might feature Mallarmé, the next Christopher Brennan. Early in 1939 Mann took on a new assistant, the young New Zealand-born poet Douglas Stewart, recently settled in Sydney. Stewart, who had already published one book of verse, was twenty-six, dark, intense and ambitious. When Mann went into the army in 1940, Stewart – whose flat feet saved him from a military career – took over the Red Page. He remained its editor for more than twenty years.

Stewart started as editor at a time when a whole new generation of Australian poets were either at the peak of their powers or just reaching maturity – they included Ronald McCuaig, Rosemary Dobson, David

Campbell, David Rowbotham, Nancy Keesing, Nan McDonald, Francis Webb and Judith Wright – and he made it his business to encourage and foster their work. He went to a great deal of trouble for *Bulletin* contributors, sometimes helping them revise, though he was careful never to interfere any more than he thought necessary.

Beatrice and Douglas Stewart met shortly after he started at the *Bulletin*. They liked each other immediately, found they had literary tastes in common and knew the same people in Sydney's small literary world. Four years younger than Beatrice, Stewart was a more seasoned judge of poetry. Beatrice expressed great respect for his literary acumen as well as his talent; she always said Douglas Stewart introduced her to the best in current Australian poetry, which became one of her great interests thereafter. Stewart was also an indispensable source of literary gossip at a time when women were not allowed into the public bar of Bateman's, close to the *Bulletin*'s office in lower George Street, or by tradition into Mockbell's coffee shop next door to the *Bulletin*, where many writers and journalists congregated.

It was a happy accident that, when Beatrice advertised for an assistant in 1941, into the office walked another poet.[2] Nan (Nancy) McDonald, a slim and beautiful blonde in her early twenties, had graduated in Arts from the University of Sydney and had recently been doing war work on a pig farm while she wrote her first book of verse. Beatrice probably knew her name already from the Red Page of the *Bulletin*; she hired her immediately and ever afterwards considered it one of her best decisions. Quiet, almost paralysingly self-effacing but with an impish sense of humour, Nan McDonald was, in Beatrice's opinion, 'the most brilliant editor as well as the most enchanting person', who had 'imagination, intelligence, knowledge and feeling', and who was equally proficient in literary fiction, reference works, military manuals and the books of Ion Idriess.[3] She remained Beatrice's lieutenant at Angus and Robertson for more than thirty years.

About a year later Beatrice was introduced to a dark-haired young teacher at Frensham (a private girls' school south of Sydney) by their mutual friend Heather Sherrie. Rosemary Dobson was hoping to leave teaching and go into publishing. Her vocation, however, was poetry.

Beatrice and Douglas Stewart knew and admired her work and Beatrice suggested she start as a proofreader with Grace George before moving over to the editorial department a little later, which she did. Rosemary and Nan shared an office and swiftly became great friends.

Meanwhile, over at the *Bulletin*, Douglas Stewart was becoming increasingly frustrated. While the magazine's management gave him a free hand, Stewart, like every editor before or since, wanted more space, and there was no chance of that. In a magazine that focused on sport, politics and humour he said he felt 'like an outlaw creeping around the outskirts'. Beatrice sympathised. The work of the new generation of poets should be given more of a hearing and Angus and Robertson were the obvious publishers. But how to convince Walter Cousins that A&R should move into literary publishing, especially when this was a synonym for 'books that make no money'?

Help was at hand in the shape of the Commonwealth Literary Fund. A 1940 conference of publishers, booksellers and the CLF presided over by Prime Minister Robert Menzies agreed to consider a scheme for assistance in publishing Australian books recommended by the CLF. This effectively gave a publisher some guarantee against loss in producing non-commercial books. Low-risk literary publishing was now a possibility.

Another factor was the growing wartime demand for Australian books; small print runs of poetry or short fiction could now be produced with a reasonable chance that they would sell. Douglas Stewart argued that A&R should go further. He was sure there was enough literary talent in Australia to support an annual anthology of verse and one of short fiction – perhaps with a run of 500 copies for the poetry, 1000 for the prose. Each could be edited by a different writer every year.

Stewart has always been given the credit for initiating *Australian Poetry* and *Coast to Coast*, but he was not the one who had to persuade Walter Cousins. Beatrice used all her charm to talk her boss into accepting the idea. No doubt she emphasised the low risk and great prestige involved in publishing these anthologies, as well as the editorial and critical expertise A&R now had at its command. Whatever her arguments, Cousins agreed.

The first volume of *Australian Poetry*, edited by Douglas Stewart, appeared in September 1941. Considering its ground-breaking status, it was surprisingly small and unimpressive-looking. Stewart chose a wide range of voices and poetic styles, including work by Mary Gilmore and Furnley Maurice (the pseudonym of Frank Wilmot) in the older, *Bulletin* tradition of bush verse, as well as younger poets such as Stewart himself, Kenneth Slessor, John Shaw Neilson and Robert D. FitzGerald. There was a solid grouping of new voices: Rosemary Dobson, James McAuley, Eve Langley, Elizabeth Riddell. Possibly because of Stewart's own poetic preoccupations – at the time he was writing what he called 'small nature poems' – much of the work is lyrical and pastoral.

Australian Poetry really came into its own with the anthologies of 1943 and 1944. Not even the horrible wartime paper, like shiny beige cardboard flecked with wood shavings, could detract from the quality of the work. Many poems in these editions have become Australian classics. Here are A.D. Hope's 'Return from the Freudian Islands' and 'Australia'; David Campbell's 'The Stockman'; Elizabeth Riddell's 'The Old Sailor'; Judith Wright's 'Bullocky' and 'The Company of Lovers', James McAuley's 'Terra Australis'; Douglas Stewart's 'The Dosser in Springtime', and Kenneth Slessor's 'Beach Burial'.

Giving expression as it did to the work of a new and significant generation of Australian poets, the importance of *Australian Poetry* cannot be overestimated. Certainly, without Beatrice's ability to swing the resources of Angus and Robertson behind it, and her continued support of it, what Douglas Stewart called 'the new movements in Australian literature' would have taken longer to come to public attention. *Australian Poetry* continued to be published, either annually or biennially, until 1973.

Its prose companion *Coast to Coast* also made its first appearance in 1941, compiled and edited by Cecil Mann. Most of the twenty-one stories he selected had already been published in magazines, and some well-known writers were represented: Vance Palmer, Marjorie Barnard, Beatrice's old friend Dal Stivens, Alan Marshall, Frank Dalby Davison, Henrietta Drake-Brockman. Others, such as Douglas Stewart and Hugh McCrae, were better known as poets.

Beatrice herself compiled the 1942 edition of *Coast to Coast*. This was surprising because all her training, as well as an ingrained habit of discretion, had fuelled her belief that an editor's place was in the background, not choosing stories for a collection. She agonised over the job; later in her career, when she had to compile other anthologies, she always took a long time and worried over her choices, often calling on Douglas Stewart for support. Her foreword is reluctant and self-effacing, and she vanishes into the passive voice: 'Contributions were submitted from all parts of Australia . . .' The stories she chose are generally conservative in form, well-defined narratives or character sketches with a twist. The now better-known writers include Henrietta Drake-Brockman, Gavin Casey, Dal Stivens, Marjorie Barnard (represented by 'The Persimmon Tree', later much anthologised). Generally speaking, the stories Beatrice chose do not reflect what became the hallmarks of her literary taste: allusiveness, brilliance of description, dazzling wordplay or evocation of atmosphere. But then, there probably wasn't much of this kind of writing in Australia at the time: the best work of Hal Porter, Eve Langley and Patrick White was still to come.

Short stories were a staple of many magazines and newspapers of the period, including the *Sydney Morning Herald*, the Melbourne *Herald*, *Smith's Weekly*, the *ABC Weekly*, *Home* and *Man*, among others. Having ploughed through more than 500 stories for the 1943 *Coast to Coast*, a rather grumpy Frank Dalby Davison categorised them in his introduction as 'escapist fiction, magazine stories neatly carpentered according to approved commercial blueprints, and meaningless; innocent little pink sugar romances and ten-minute newspaper stories with the verities sacrificed to the indispensable trick ending'. But shining out from the dross that year was well-crafted, mainly realist prose from such writers as D'Arcy Niland, Dal Stivens, John Morrison and Gavin Casey. *Coast to Coast* was published every year until 1948, then biennially from 1949 to 1970. The final volume in the series, edited by Frank Moorhouse, appeared in 1973.

The period during and immediately after World War II was a time of great potential and vitality in Australian writing. Katharine Susannah Prichard, Gavin Casey, Frank Dalby Davison, Eleanor Dark, Kylie

Tennant, Dymphna Cusack, Eve Langley were writing novels; the Jindyworobaks were trying to express mystical union with the spirit of the land in poetry, and the brilliantly mischievous Harold Stewart and James McAuley were bringing forth the poetry of the young genius Ern Malley. This was also the time of the great radio plays. The ABC's Frank Clewlow and Leslie Rees were encouraging Australian dramatists; the ABC held an annual competition for radio plays in verse and Angus and Robertson published the best of them. As Douglas Stewart commented, 'Writers rose and fell or flourished, so it seems, in all directions.'[4]

Three years after helping to set up *Coast to Coast* and *Australian Poetry*, Beatrice used Angus and Robertson to mount a literary rescue operation. In 1939 the English Association had decided to transform their quarterly bulletin into a fully fledged literary magazine named *Southerly*, publishing poetry and stories by Australian writers as well as critical material. From the time it came into being, *Southerly*'s life had hung by a thread. Though contributors were unpaid and the magazine was put together by members of the University of Sydney's English department, headed by Guy Howarth who did the work for nothing, the combination of high printing costs and small circulation was slowly killing the publication. (The only other literary periodicals of note during the war years were the quarterly *Meanjin Papers*, founded in Brisbane by Clem Christesen in 1940 and *Poetry*, started by Flexmore Hudson the following year; both, mostly funded by their creators, were in a similarly parlous state.)

By 1944 *Southerly* was threatened with extinction and Beatrice, a stalwart of the English Association, agreed that something had to be done. Late that year, after discussions with Guy Howarth and Douglas Stewart, she confronted Walter Cousins with the suggestion that Angus and Robertson take over publishing the magazine. The current printers – the Australasian Medical Publishing Co., whom Beatrice knew from her days at the *Medical Journal of Australia* – could continue to print the journal; A&R could finance and distribute it. It would not be too expensive: the print run was only 500 copies and A&R's resources would maximise its sales possibilities. And it could all be done without taking up much of A&R's staff time.

Cousins finally agreed, even though he must have known that publishing *Southerly* was unlikely to make A&R any money. Lacklustre advertising that urged potential subscribers to 'play their part in Australian cultural development' not surprisingly failed to persuade enough people to part with their annual £22 and make *Southerly* profitable, though it became, and has continued to be, a significant force in the study of Australian literature. A&R paid the magazine's bills for many years.

Why did the CLF not see fit to step in and subsidise literary journals? The answer lies in the political ideologies of the time. Labor Prime Minister Ben Chifley considered literary magazines to be elitist, not serving the mass of the people; Robert Menzies, leader of the opposition, was also dead against government money being spent on 'elitist' individual enterprises. As critic and academic Tom Inglis Moore accurately observed, literary magazines got it in the neck both ways. (In 1950 Menzies, who had recently become prime minister for the second time, did manage to find some money for small literary magazines.)

Beatrice showed how keen she was for the company she served to develop and promote new Australian writing. In an undated memo to Angus and Robertson's publishing committee arguing for A&R's involvement in *Southerly* she observed that making the magazine the country's premier literary journal would count in the future 'when, in spite of opposition, we must remain the literary hub of Australia'. It was a means of bringing the best local writing to Angus and Robertson and was important because, Beatrice believed, 'good writers . . . bring the best publicity and prestige'.

The importance Beatrice saw in attracting to A&R writers whose potential was literary, not simply commercial, was echoed by other members of the literary community, notably Douglas Stewart and Norman Lindsay. In 1944 Lindsay wrote to Beatrice, 'I have the sincerest respect for your own soundness of judgement in selecting works of quality . . . but no publishing house can exist as great unless it builds up a strong group of [poets and prose] writers', and he urged her to do what she could to 'stimulate the whole literary aesthetic into strong action'.[5] It was advice and encouragement that Beatrice found highly congenial.

Living on the Edge:
Ernestine Hill

One of our enduring literary images has been the Australian writer as traveller, taking to the track with swag and notebook to discover the 'real Australia' that lies beyond the towns and cities and putting it into words. Henry Lawson, Xavier Herbert, D'Arcy Niland, C.E.W. Bean, Ion Idriess all did it, continuing the tradition that writing about the bush was something that writers – male, of course – did. But the Australian writer who most consistently embraced the wandering life, bringing a journalist's shrewdness and a novelist's insight and descriptive powers to the lives and landscapes of the remote corners of the continent, was a woman. It was Ernestine Hill, as Beatrice once wrote, who most fully showed Australians their own country.[1]

Hill's life as a bush writer began in the early 1930s with a series of articles involving travel around Australia for Sun Newspapers. The vividness and immediacy of her writing quickly found their mark and she undertook similar assignments for a variety of periodicals, notably the monthly magazine *Walkabout*. Her first book, *The Great Australian Loneliness* (published in England in 1937, with an Australian edition in 1940), was based on this journalism. She followed with *Water into Gold* (1937), a history of the Murray River irrigation area. She also did a great deal of work – most of the writing, she later claimed – on Daisy Bates's famous book *The Passing of the Aborigines* (1938).

When Ernestine Hill first approached Angus and Robertson in the early war years, she had firmly established her own literary legend, neatly summarised by a contemporary as 'this slim, dark-eyed girl who appeared seemingly out of nowhere with practically nothing except her horse, her saddle, her typewriter and books and the makings of billy tea and some frugal food . . . and a passion for the land'.[2] Like most romantic legends, this version of Ernestine Hill the indomitable battler cheerfully over-coming the hardships of the outback and writing about them was an oversimplification. She usually claimed she had begun her wandering life in 1933 after the death of her husband, and 'Mr Hill' is mentioned in most of the biographical material about her, but there is no detail about him – indeed, he is something of a mystery. Hill had a son, Robert, born in the 1920s, but she never spoke of his father, and it is likely that Mr Hill never existed. Ernestine Hill kept some areas of her personal life as secret as the indecipherable shorthand code in which she wrote many of her private papers.

Beatrice first met Ernestine Hill early in 1941, after Hill had sent Angus and Robertson the manuscript of her new book. It was com-pletely different from anything else she had published, for it dealt not with outback Australia but with the sea. Further, it was a novelised biog-raphy, the story of the explorer Matthew Flinders, a wanderer after Ernestine Hill's own heart. Matthew Flinders, the man who circumnavi-gated Australia, explored the east coast in a tiny boat and gave the con-tinent its name, was to most Australians a remote historical figure, a hero of primary-school history. But Beatrice read the story of a man whose life had encompassed high adventure, danger and tragedy, who was imprisoned for many years on the island of Mauritius at the behest of the French and cruelly estranged from the love of his life.

Beatrice thought it the best Australian novel she had read in years, and Walter Cousins agreed. 'Our people are very keen on this,' he wrote Alec Chisholm, the eminent naturalist and author who had known Ernestine Hill since her youth in Queensland.[3] The first printing was only 3000 copies, but this was wartime and it was a long book and a first novel. Publication was set for early December 1941.

Trusting her author's research and having confidence in Hill's polished writing style, Beatrice seems hardly to have touched the manuscript, but the project had other problems. The first was its title. Ernestine Hill had wanted to call her novel *He Named Australia*, which A&R rightly thought sounded more like a primary-school social studies textbook than a novel. She also wanted her son Robert to design the jacket. Cousins said no to both, and in October 1941 he asked the illustrator Geoffrey Ingleton to submit a jacket design and to come up with a suitable title for the book. Ingleton obliged with three: *The Sea a Jealous Mistress*; *Mistress Flinders Without a Bonnet* and *My Love Must Wait*. Cousins decided on the last one; Ernestine Hill violently disagreed, bombarding A&R with telegrams of protest. But Cousins could be firm when he chose and he dug his heels in, telling her that if she refused to accept *My Love Must Wait* A&R would not publish the book at all. Hill gave in, and when the book became a success she wrote Ingleton a graceful letter of thanks.

My Love Must Wait was published in November 1941 and it sold well almost immediately, the first run disappearing before Christmas. Its combination of evocative descriptive writing, sound storytelling and detailed research made it enduringly popular; here, as thousands of readers recognised, was a romantic hero who belonged to Australia's history and to nowhere else. The book sold strongly right through the war and after, and went on to become a standard work on Matthew Flinders. It was adapted into a children's comic strip in the *Sydney Morning Herald*, extracts were broadcast over the ABC, and it was used as the basis for textbooks. After the war it was published in the US and the UK. The Australian producer Charles Chauvel bought an option, and Laurence Olivier – who had recently paced the quarterdeck as Nelson in *Lady Hamilton* with Vivien Leigh – was mooted to play Matthew Flinders. Unfortunately, after four years Chauvel dropped the project.

Knowing they had a proven international success on their hands, A&R seemed oddly reluctant to keep *My Love Must Wait* before the public. More than once, after a 10 000 reprint had sold out, the novel stayed out of print for months. A&R were bedevilled by Manpower problems and rising costs all through the war, and juggling priorities at Halstead must have been a nightmare, but it is still a mystery why they did not print larger runs. Perhaps paper shortages were to blame.

In 1948 Cousins wrote to Ernestine Hill that her novel had sold almost 100 000 copies, setting a sales record for a novel written by an Australian author and printed in Australia, though because of rising production costs and a shortage of printing machinery, they were not increasing her royalty rate. Though she thought A&R's economic management left something to be desired, Hill remained gracious.

Her next book was a short burst of patriotism and natural history called *Australia, Land of Contrasts*, published in 1943. However, Ernestine Hill had two much bigger works in mind, which had been germinating for many years. The first was a history of the Flying Doctor Service, a project she tackled with enthusiasm, for she wanted to celebrate the achievements of a service that had started 'where railways end [and] miles begin', whose evolution she had observed for more than fifteen years.[4]

Hill delighted in journeying through the outback to research this book, and wrote to Beatrice in exhilaration about her travels. Her long, detailed letters often made Beatrice feel wistful, even though she did not necessarily want to cook johnny-cakes over a griddle in a duststorm, set up and dismantle a tent every day, or load and carry water for daily baths over hundreds of miles. Beatrice enjoyed getting out of the city – usually to visit relatives, including her brother John and his family in rural New South Wales – but she was basically an urban creature. Even so, the round eternal of the manuscript and the galley proof occasionally made her, like the narrator of 'Clancy of the Overflow', want to take a turn at travelling where the seasons came and went. Hill told her she was being silly: 'Oh, my dear, never envy me. I always feel the waif of the world. That 8.30 to five regime is one of the best things . . . we all grieve most, not about the things we do but of those we have not done.' Yes, retorted Beatrice crisply, but 'You give me, and the world, a wonderful impression of achievement and a life lived as you want it.'[5]

Beatrice probably suspected that Hill was not the calm, quietly resourceful pioneering woman her correspondence conveyed. Far from being a female version of Paterson's Clancy, Hill was slight and wary-looking, with wide dark eyes under a thick fringe, a long narrow face and thin lips. She was a constant smoker who, as the saying went, 'lived on her nerves', and she could be very intense. She was also a creature of contradictions. Compelled to be on the move all her life, she was always telling Beatrice how much she longed to settle down. She needed, she said, a quiet place to work, somewhere to stay, so she could stop her constant travel for a while and write up the vast amount of material she had collected. No sooner did she find such a place than she was off again, happy to be settled only when she was not, and vice versa.

Beatrice received the complete manuscript for the Flying Doctor book just before Christmas 1946, and it was given the matter-of-fact title of *Flying Doctor Calling*. Hill and Beatrice had a few jousts over the editing; Hill criticised Beatrice for being too ready to leach colour from her words for the sake of grammatical exactness. 'If we set out with a copy of [Fowler's *Modern*] *English Usage*,' she wrote half jocularly, 'think of the character we could take out of Mark Twain or even Robert Louis, and as for your friend Hemingway and the moderns, and the newspapers of today!'[6] Beatrice gave some ground, though she insisted on grammatical exactitude.

Flying Doctor Calling did not appear until November 1947, A&R still being plagued by rising costs and a shortage of workers. The book had sold out by Christmas, and a reprint was ordered in January 1948. Australian readers were not reacting to any romantic notion of the Flying Doctor Service, for Ernestine Hill described the lives of the people who lived beyond the farthest roads in words as bleak as any Henry Lawson ever wrote.

Meanwhile she had been collecting material for her masterwork, the story of the Northern Territory. This was a combination of descriptive writing, reportage, personal experience, stories – some true, some yarns – and social history. She carried her material with her everywhere – transcripts of interviews with Territory 'identities', newspaper cuttings going back years, drafts and redrafts of chapters, bank ledgers filled with single-spaced typing, copies of letters to and from friends – a huge amount of paper in boxes or large square tin trunks to protect it from marauding white ants. 'The poor old manuscript has gradually grown deeper through all the last years of travail and travel, becoming less a book than a hypnosis,' she wrote to Beatrice in a letter that enclosed some draft chapters. 'I find on this morning's reckoning that I have written 177 160 words! and still some chapters to go.'[7]

Beatrice must have received this letter with some apprehension. She had no idea how long a book Hill was planning, or what sort of book it was going to be. Hill also had a habit of posting chapters to A&R with no indication of where they belonged. But Beatrice managed to be warmly encouraging, even when Hill told her that an account of the 'haywire history' of the Territory should be a combination of Macaulay, Gibbon and Edgar Allan Poe. Hill continued to worry and to ask Beatrice for reassurance about the monolith that was then called *The Book of the Territory*, asking whether she found it heavy going.

But Beatrice was really enjoying the manuscript and did not hesitate to congratulate the author. 'You have achieved the miracle of being a first-rate writer who is popular as well,' she wrote to her in March 1949. 'There is some magnificent writing here, and I feel so thankful that these stories have been told you before they become formalised in the hands of a mere historian. What a macabre, dramatic, heart-breaking narrative this story makes!'[8] But she did cavil at the size of the book, saying that it would have to cost at least a guinea per copy, about twice the average price. Hill was grateful for her enthusiasm and prepared to be conciliatory. 'I'll cut to make it crisp all the way,' she promised. 'I find that a very good test of direct writing – avoid, even at the cost of what they call "good writing", the condition of mind best described by the blacks as "My ear been knock up." '[9] Beatrice invited her to stay at Folly Point to discuss the cuts, and she accepted with delight.

But she didn't make it to Beatrice's house, going to Narrabeen on Sydney's northern beaches and then on to Frankston in Victoria. From here she wrote Beatrice an apologetic letter. It was July 1949 and Sydney was in the grip of a housing shortage and coal strike, meaning blackouts and no gas. Her son Robert, who had come with her, was out all day and she said she had nothing to do at Narrabeen but listen to the roar of the waves and try to keep the sand and soot down. 'To tell you the truth the newspapers screaming their maledictions . . . made Sydney so much a horror that I had to quit.'[10] A house to work in alone was not for her, she wrote.

So often Ernestine Hill's letters were full of frantic and compulsive activity, of restless erratic movement, rather than the eager discipline of exploration. But as well as the alarming anxiety and depression that her letters often revealed, there was the exhilaration of travel, the exultation in describing what she saw.

In mid-1950 Hill sent Beatrice a sensuously evocative verbal snapshot from Broome:

> I've just seen the famous Broome full moon rise over the mudflats – ebb tide in Dampier Creek – brush of silver and runnels of gold, every cape of dusky mangroves, three old luggers lying over on the sand . . . if you hear of my bones being tucked away in the queer little graveyard out in the pindan, to enjoy the birds and the breeze with Japs, Jews, Frenchmen, Filipinos, Chinese, Malayans, Binghis, old sea-captains and nuns you'll know that's me, happy indeed in the quietness by an ever-changing sea.[11]

A few months later she sent Beatrice some delicate, pink-tinged shells that Beatrice placed on the mantelpiece, as well as prawn paste from Singapore which, Hill said, should be fried in coconut oil to make what sound rather like pappadums. Beatrice served them with sherry before dinner.

Beatrice was still worried that *The Book of the Territory* was too long – it was at least 200 000 words – and suggested it be made into two books instead of one enormous one. No, said Hill, the book had been envisaged, and must stand, as one. Beatrice rather sadly agreed. By October two chapters remained to be written, and Elizabeth Durack had agreed to do line drawings, chapter headings, endpapers and jacket. Late in April 1951 Hill, still in Broome, wrote to say the book was nearly finished: 'I've been grinding away for so long I don't know whether I am a woodpecker or a horse in winkers,' she wrote to Beatrice.[12]

A few weeks later, Beatrice received the final manuscript of the book that was now called simply *The Territory*. Published as one volume in a print run of 15 000 in November 1951, it has an elegiac quality – the story of the first hundred years of settlement, a chronicle of a way of pioneering life that was already disappearing. It blends loving and evocative description, history and adventure, and fifty years after first publication the red dust still clings to its pages.

Angus and Robertson solved the problem of its length by shrinking the type size and conflating paragraphs: it looks rather solid, not exactly user-friendly. But this did not prevent the book receiving rave reviews in Australia and overseas. The *Age* called it 'a notable contribution to Australian literature and a book that will live'. The English reviews were equally flattering, with *John O'London's Weekly* proclaiming that 'Ernestine Hill writes with a fire in her bones, using words as Van Gogh used paint'.[13] A pleased and relieved Ernestine Hill sent a grateful note to Angus and Robertson, describing the book's production as 'beautiful' and adding how delighted she was that the reviews had been so good. She even intended to send all the reviewers a personal note of thanks.

By now Ernestine Hill had an assured and growing reputation. Two of her five books – *My Love Must Wait* and *The Territory* – were considered classics; the latter, one critic wrote, should be in the swag of every Australian. Hill was in her early fifties, and Beatrice, despite any misgivings about 'nerviness', had every reason to believe that more great work lay ahead. But as the 1950s progressed, disquieting signs appeared. Hill was still travelling around Australia, turning up in unexpected places, assuring A&R that she was working hard. To Beatrice's tactful suggestions that she should settle somewhere to help her achieve peace of mind Hill agreed – and the next letter Beatrice received might be from deep in Queensland, or Broome or Alice Springs. There was something driven, panic-stricken, neurotic, about Hill's need to be always on the move.

She was constantly short of money, often asking A&R for advances against royalties. Beatrice and her close friend the author and reviewer Henrietta Drake-Brockman suspected that quite a lot of Hill's money went on supporting her son. The relationship between mother and son was often difficult; Drake-Brockman told Beatrice that she spent hours being 'an ear' for both of them. Beatrice was sympathetic: 'The poor girl, with her temperament as well as Bob to contend with, must have many upsets,' she wrote. 'And I can imagine how difficult it would be for anyone to help her.'[14]

But Hill assured Beatrice that, despite all her problems, she was continuing to write. By early in 1955 she was at work on a new novel, *Johnnie Wise-Cap*. Beatrice and George Ferguson (Walter Cousins's successor) hurried to tell her how much they were looking forward to receiving the manuscript. Hill applied for and received a CLF fellowship and continued to move around Australia, taking her huge trunks and tin boxes of notes with her, sending frequent progress reports. So confident were A&R about *Johnnie Wise-Cap* that they announced its publication for September 1955. The novel was 'the story of an aboriginal taken from his tribe to work with the pearlers at Broome, then brought to Melbourne to live among the white men . . . for the lightness of his skin presents a mystery that several people are determined to solve'.[15]

But month after month passed without A&R seeing a manuscript. Beatrice, who guessed that Hill suffered agonies of worry and self-doubt, did what she could to encourage her. But *Johnnie Wise-Cap* did not materialise, and Hill insisted that her need for money continued to be acute. In 1957 she sent A&R a profit and loss account, describing what she had spent on accommodation (she had been staying on Brampton Island and in Sydney that year) and fares, stationery and small necessities. Beatrice might have felt disquiet about the works in progress Ernestine listed in the same letter. They included 'sixteen books, three volumes of short stories. Ballets, Plays. Volume of notes and work . . . covering travel well over a million miles, with research covering 27 years.'[16] Ernestine Hill was beginning to sound ominously out of control.

Beatrice and George Ferguson insisted that the answer to Hill's problems was to complete *Johnnie Wise-Cap* as soon as possible. George Ferguson even suggested that if Hill provided the framework Beatrice could supply the finishing touches and the novel could be published. But Hill's letters continued to be both panic-stricken and depressed, full of worries about the novel, freelance journalism and other writing. Beatrice tried to soothe her, but she must have remembered a comment by Henrietta Drake-Brockman that with Ernestine 'no line of action is followed consistently for long enough'.[17]

In 1960 the Commonwealth Literary Fund awarded Hill a pension of £7 a week for life – and in August her son Robert wrote to Beatrice that his mother had collapsed and was in hospital in Queensland, confused, thin and very ill. Beatrice was most concerned about her friend and also confessed to Robert, in confidence, that while she was sympathetic to his mother's problems she sometimes wondered whether *Johnnie Wise-Cap* would ever be finished.[18]

Hill recovered but continued to fret. Late in 1960, insisting she needed a decent sum of money with which to buy a place of her own, she offered to sell A&R her copyrights, denying herself all future royalties. Beatrice tried to dissuade her in a letter that, considering Hill's prickliness and sensitivities, was surprisingly tactless:

> How well I understand your need for security and a place of your own to work in! At the same time I know how quickly any lump sum of money you had would be spent, and I should hate to see you with no source of income except [the CLF pension]. Though I personally continue to have confidence that you will complete further work, we have to presume that you may not have the strength to do so.[19]

Ernestine was distressed and angry at what she saw as Beatrice's betrayal. Among a fusillade of furious shorthand on the back of Beatrice's letter, she scrawled 'no longer endure it but I cannot recount my sorrows in your office files'. She had calmed down by the time she replied, asking whether, if A&R did not want to buy her copyrights, they would pay for their temporary assignment. George Ferguson declined the offer on the grounds that it would not be in Hill's best interests (or, indeed, those of A&R: his view was that the older books had a limited earning capacity).

The familiar cycle continued – Hill asking for money, A&R sending advances on royalties when they could, Beatrice suggesting that Hill finish a book and so ease the financial strain, no manuscript turning up. It all became too much for Beatrice early in 1961. In a letter enclosing a contract for the Pacific Books edition of *My Love Must Wait* she wrote:

You really must, my dear Ernestine, sort yourself out to the extent of finishing one book. I know what a tremendous amount of rich material you have gathered; and I know how valuable it would be for Australians even if you did not make it into completed books. But you are primarily a writer, and you simply must go on giving us something to publish . . . If you could finish something you would be solving your own problems – as everyone has to solve his own in the end.[20]

She signed it 'yours with sympathy and affection', but to Hill this was a stinging rebuke. She was now at that stage of defensiveness where her lack of productivity was someone else's fault, especially A&R's. She wrote Beatrice a cranky letter accusing them of being obstructive and demanding they revert her current copyrights to her. Beatrice politely refused.

Beatrice gradually concluded that A&R would never see anything more from Ernestine Hill and she stopped inquiring about her work, so she must have been delighted when on 8 December 1968 Hill wrote a businesslike, sensible letter that gave real promise of a good new book. This was the biography of the legendary Daisy Bates, who had lived among Aboriginal tribes on the Nullarbor from 1912 to 1945 and whose friend and literary collaborator Ernestine had been. She told Beatrice that it was she, not Daisy Bates, who had written Bates's famous book *The Passing of the Aborigines* (1938) from a series of interviews. 'Daisy never touched it,' she wrote, 'but all notes and material were hers.' Drawing on previously unpublished material, Hill had now written about 7000 words on Bates's life, which she had offered to the *Australian* newspaper, with pictures. They had accepted but she then withdrew the material, thinking it would work better as a book. She intended to call it *The Real Kabbarli* and wanted to know whether Angus and Robertson would be interested.

Certainly, replied Beatrice swiftly, though there was a snag: A&R had already contracted a biography of Daisy Bates by Elizabeth Salter. Beatrice did not see this as a real obstacle, though it is not clear why – perhaps she thought Hill would never finish hers. But Hill happily settled down and began to write.

A few months later Beatrice received a letter from Robert Hill. His mother was living with him and his family in Elizabeth, north of Adelaide, he wrote, and she was becoming increasingly difficult. There was nowhere for her to store or sort out her notes, she was ill and needed care.[21] To other friends he gave more details: Ernestine was extremely thin, living on tea, biscuits, Codral and Craven A cigarettes. The weather was hot; she was stubborn, argumentative and broke. Robert Hill told Beatrice that though he had a permanent job at the South Australian School of Art his pay was meagre; he could afford only to rent the house they were living in. Would Angus and Robertson be prepared to enter into a financial relationship, giving him $2000 as a deposit on the purchase of a larger house for them all? The house could be bought in the name of Angus and Robertson unless the publishers accepted his guarantee to repay the deposit as quickly as possible. His mother, he added, knew nothing about the plan.

Beatrice replied frostily that while A&R would do what they could, taking care of an author in this way, even one as valued and respected as Ernestine Hill, was scarcely the firm's responsibility.[22] She was more outspoken in a letter to Henrietta Drake-Brockman, describing Robert as 'quite hopeless'.[23] Robert Hill did not press the point, and there matters rested.

By early 1971 Ernestine Hill was in Queensland, still working on Daisy Bates. She seemed almost back to her old busy self, and was excited because Robert Helpmann, who had long wanted an Australian film project for his friend Katharine Hepburn, was interested in buying the rights to the Bates story. But Hill was now in her seventies and her health was giving way; she was frail, in and out of hospital, battling emphysema and heart trouble, fretting about her notes and manuscripts. More concerned than ever, Beatrice advised her not to worry. She arranged for the National Library to contact Hill and look through her manuscripts and papers, possibly to buy them.[24] Early in 1972 Hill delivered to Angus and Robertson *Kabbarli: A Personal Memoir of Daisy Bates*. It was published in 1973.

But Ernestine Hill did not live to see it in print; she died on 22 August 1972 in Brisbane's St Andrew's Hospital. She left a portable

Olivetti typewriter, a camera and about $100 worth of household goods. There were of course her documents and papers, carted over broken outback roads in duststorms, in blinding heat and in the Wet, obsessively collected, maintained and worried over for so many years. Hill's executor and agent Charles Bateson told Beatrice that they included very little real new material. 'She seems to have spent her last few years looking very busy, but in fact doing no more than retyping, almost without alteration, a chapter or short story she had written several years before,' he wrote.[25] As for *Johnnie Wise-Cap*, the novel that Beatrice had awaited for so many years, only six chapters had ever been written.

'Like a Bird Singing,
She Sings for Herself': Eve Langley

In 1941 Beatrice was invited to be one of three judges of the S.H. Prior Memorial Prize for the best unpublished manuscript of the year. Sponsored by the *Bulletin*, the Prior was one of Australia's few national literary prizes, and previous winners had included Kylie Tennant with *Tiburon*, published in 1935, and Miles Franklin's *All That Swagger*, which appeared the following year.[1] Being on the Prior panel was the beginning of a minor second career for Beatrice as a judge of literary competitions and prizes and an arbiter of taste and quality in the literary world outside Angus and Robertson. While she would certainly have agreed with John Cheever's view that 'fiction is not a competitive sport', she was developing a connoisseur's eye and was keen to discover and reward writing of promise.

One of the 1941 Prior entries was a voluminous manuscript called *The Pea Pickers*, sent from New Zealand by 'Gippsland Overlander' (all entries were submitted under pseudonyms). It was an editor's nightmare – typed in single space on flimsy pink paper with a faded ribbon, words drifting off the edge of the page – but Beatrice had not read many pages before she experienced the prickle of excitement all editors feel when they know they are in the presence of an original new voice. This story of two sisters in their late teens who call themselves Steve and Blue, dress as men and wander around Gippsland and the Australian Alps as itinerant workers had a combination of humour, poetry and vitality

Beatrice had never encountered before. Steve, the storyteller, with her fierce need for romantic love and her contradictory loathing of her own gender ('It was tragic to be only a comical woman when I longed above all things to be a serious and handsome man') was an immensely appealing character.[2] Beatrice was captivated by her sheer joy and exuberance as she and Blue tramped around the countryside, eager for life and experience, always with an eye out for homesteaders who might bestow on them a cup of tea and the odd fried scone. The writing style, too, was strongly individual – the wild juxtaposition of down-to-earth Australian speech and heightened romantic and literary language was just right for the mental landscape of a bookish adolescent girl like Steve. The author, Eve Langley, an Australian in her early thirties who was living in New Zealand, also knew how to evoke the physical landscape: the gum trees, rolling hills, yellow paddocks and overgrown huts of Gippsland. Whenever Beatrice was asked about the books she was proudest of having discovered, she always mentioned *The Pea Pickers*.

Her fellow judges Frank Dalby Davison and H.M. Green were not so sure that *The Pea Pickers* was a worthy winner of the Prior prize. They thought it was too romantic and overwritten, preferring Kylie Tennant's *The Brown Van* (renamed and published as *The Battlers*) or Malcolm Henry Ellis's biography of Lachlan Macquarie. Beatrice argued that, admirable though both these were, they were not in the same street as *The Pea Pickers* for verve, originality and vitality. In the end all the judges had their way: each of the three books was awarded £100.

Apart from Beatrice, the person probably most delighted by the success of *The Pea Pickers* was Douglas Stewart. He had known Eve Langley quite well in New Zealand, admired her richly sensuous poetry, had even been half in love with her. She was certainly attractive: a slight young woman with close-cropped dark hair and green eyes, intense-looking in the Katherine Mansfield style. Though lacking a formal education, she had always been a voracious reader who, like Steve, 'clad her consciousness with scraps of art and literature'. Ruth Park, then a seventeen-year-old copyholder for the *Auckland Star*, had also become a friend; Langley would visit the newspaper's reading room simply to talk, quoting Greek mythology, English literature, history, snatches of other languages. 'She casts treasure around me, not caring whether I pick it up or not,' wrote Park in the first volume of her autobiography. 'Like a bird singing, she sings for herself.'[3] D'Arcy Niland later compared Eve Langley's conversation to a waterfall of sequins.

A woman of dazzling talent, Eve Langley clung desperately to literature: words were almost her only refuge from a life of squalor and misery. Married to an improvident schoolteacher/artist named Hilary Clark, she lived with him and their small daughter in a shed behind an Auckland tenement building, constantly ill, without much money for food, and terrified of being abandoned. Douglas Stewart knew something of this and also realised she was rather odd (she had told him she often ate earth, which she found nourishing), but recognised her extraordinary inner radiance. 'It was squalor, but with a dark little flame in the middle of it,' he said.[4] One of the reasons he was so pleased she had won the Prior – his congratulatory cable to her included the words 'HURRAY HURRAY HURRAY' – was that he knew what a difference the money could make to her and her family.

The enthusiasm of Douglas Stewart and Beatrice for *The Pea Pickers* convinced Walter Cousins that Angus and Robertson should publish it, and Beatrice set to work on the manuscript. It was a long and difficult job, partly because the novel was so discursive – Eve Langley often let her love for out-of-the-way quotation and imagery get the better of her, and long passages of glittering words weighed down the narrative. Beatrice had weeks of cutting and shaping to do. Correspondence with the author was apparently minimal and sporadic; Eve Langley retreated into herself and Beatrice seems to have had a free hand. Langley did not, as her admirers had hoped, use her prize money to buy warmth and security for her family and herself: she spent it on presents, including a wheelchair for an old Maori woman.

The Pea Pickers appeared in mid-1942 and was much praised. Several critics commended its freshness and originality – Frank Dalby Davison observed that it 'had the dew on it' – and early sales were encouraging. It was not universally popular: Miles Franklin considered it phony and disliked it on moral grounds because the main characters stole other people's food. Beatrice defended *The Pea Pickers* and she and Miles had a 'stiff difference of opinion' about it.[5]

With the success of *The Pea Pickers,* Beatrice had every reason to feel elated. For the first time she had discovered and nurtured a writer, perhaps a genius, whose career gave promise of great things. Then, a few months after publication, Angus and Robertson received a letter from Auckland's Public Trustee Office. Eve Langley, 'married woman, a mentally defective person', had been committed to Auckland Mental Hospital. A&R was asked to send the public trustee all Eve Langley's future royalty cheques and statements. Beatrice was appalled; nothing had prepared her for this. Apart from her very real distress about what might have happened to Eve, Beatrice had no way of knowing whether her most brilliant author would ever write another word.

Eve had apparently suffered some kind of psychotic episode, and following the advice of two doctors – no other medical consultation was necessary – her husband Hilary had had her committed to a mental institution indefinitely. Eve was now officially insane, and the State could lock her up and forget about her. And that is what happened: for years, Eve Langley simply disappeared.

Ironically, *The Pea Pickers* continued its life independently of its author's. Dutton in New York published it in 1946, under the title of *Not Yet the Moon*, and were eager to option Langley's next three novels. They were prepared to wait, they said, even though, as they tactfully phrased it, there appeared to be bad news about future work.

Nothing was heard from, or about, Eve Langley for almost eight years. Then in June 1950 Beatrice received a letter from Langley's sister June ('Blue') to say that Eve had been released. June gave a heartrending account of her sister's departure:'On the long coastal journey home [Eve was released into her sister's care] she cried out at the glimpses of earth and sky, an occasional gum tree, and wrung my hand at intervals, how happy we both were . . .'[6] A rather shaky Langley found a job in the bindery of the Auckland Public Library, where she remained for six years. She was very much alone, reluctantly and sporadically supported by her husband, who had no intention of resuming the marriage, and her three children had been taken into care.

Beatrice wrote to Eve Langley in October 1950, her letter combining tact, enthusiasm and a certain caution. 'How many years since we have heard from you! But we do think of you and continue to find *The Pea Pickers* an enchanting book. In fact we hope next year – or it may have to be 1952 – to republish it and to give many more people the pleasure of having copies of their own . . .' She further encouraged Eve with news that the critic and academic editor H.M. Green wanted to include Eve's 'The Celtic Guest' in that year's *Australian Poetry*. 'Life and publishing go on,' she added, 'and I should love to hear from you.'[7]

But it was not until June 1951 that Langley replied. The news was good, she said, she had a new manuscript ready. Its title was *White Topee* and she had been working on it for some time, even during another spell, this time a short one, in Auckland Mental Hospital. It was, she said, hilarious and quite good, and she offered to send it over.

Beatrice was delighted, though the feverishly happy tone of Langley's letter must have been a little worrying. Her next letter was also buoyant, though calmer: 'You have no idea how splendid it is to hear from you again,' she wrote. 'Nearly ten years! No matter what has happened in the interim, my country still stands firm . . .'[8] Presumably she meant the country of her imagination. Another heartening sign was that soon afterwards she sent over some poems.

Early in 1952 the promised manuscript arrived. Beatrice, who was about to go on extended leave – it was her first trip overseas – read it before her departure. Her heart must have plummeted: *White Topee* was a stranger version of *The Pea Pickers*. It had many of the same themes and characters, but much of the *joie de vivre* of the earlier book had gone, replaced by long, introspective monologues.

Nan McDonald, who would be editing *White Topee* in Beatrice's absence, had severe doubts not only about the rambling, sometimes incoherent quality of the new manuscript but about the imperialism of its central image, the white topee. She was also worried about the possibility of libel (Langley used the names of real people) and she noticed that some of the quotations and literary allusions were inaccurate. She wrote in her reader's report:

This novel, pruned and condensed, would certainly be worth publishing. It is written with Eve Langley's characteristic brilliance and

originality and no one else could have written it. But I am afraid
that no amount of editing will be able to make it as good as *The Pea
Pickers* . . . With some writers it might be better not to accept a second novel that is very like the first and inferior to it. But in this case
we may never see a third and there are very few writers of Eve
Langley's quality, even her second-best quality.[9]

The second reader echoed Nan's misgivings, yet Beatrice replied
to Eve Langley in warmer terms than either report seemed to warrant,
perhaps because she knew she would not be editing the novel. She had
read *White Topee* with great pleasure, she wrote, and A&R certainly
wanted to publish it. 'It has those characteristically brilliant passages that
I have come to expect from Eve Langley, but I do think it is a little long,'
she wrote shortly before her departure.[10]

Nan set to work. Like *The Pea Pickers*, the manuscript of *White Topee*
needed a great deal of editing, made more difficult by the author's oddness.
Nan's letters of editorial query were short and tactful, Langley's replies long
and rambling, her enthusiasms and obsessions well to the fore. Though
unsettling as answers to editorial questions, her letters remain fascinating
evidence of a leaping and allusive mind out of control: 'When first in 1900
I saw young men, handsome young men of the Waikato tribe [Eve
Langley was born in 1908] I said to myself that they were descended from
the ancient Greeks. And I called the country not Waikato but Vae Cato,
the woe of Cato from the Latin or Vacao, to empty or to empty out.'[11]

Nan laboured on. According to one account she transferred phrases
Eve used in her letters to enrich, amplify and clarify the manuscript. That
she was able to do this shows how incoherent *White Topee* was, and yet
how all of a piece – in obsessions, style, themes – with so much of Eve
Langley's other writing. The amount and quality of the work Nan
McDonald did supports the theory that editors often do their best work
on the most difficult and unpromising manuscripts. It also shows why
Beatrice considered Nan the best and most sensitive editor in Australia.

While *White Topee* was still being edited, Eve Langley sent in her
third manuscript, *Wild Australia*. This really set off alarm bells at Angus
and Robertson: the book could most kindly be described as dazzlingly

irrational. Many pages were devoted to Eve's account, as Oscar Wilde, of a trip she and her lover Lord Alfred Douglas made to Cairo so that Eve/Oscar could be operated on to become female. Rosemary Dobson reported that the manuscript could not be recommended, though skilful editing and heavy revision would certainly improve it.

Nan McDonald readily conceded that not even the most drastic editing could turn *Wild Australia* into a satisfactory book, and she very tactfully wrote to tell Langley so. 'A writer who has lived with an idea and developed it and become thoroughly familiar with it often fails to realise how baffling it can be if it is presented without explanation to a reader . . . who has not shared in these processes,' she said. [12]

Eve Langley's reply some months later came with a document stating that she had changed her name to Oscar Wilde by deed poll.

> Dear Nan McDonald,
>
> I feel very ill. You are sending WILD AUSTRALIA back to me. I can scarcely belive [*sic*] it. I was banking on the book . . . thought I'd be able to leave the library soon and with the money the Govt gave me, come out here and write more books like it. For it clears my brain to write them. Nan McDonald, DEAR Nan McDonald I AM OSCAR WILDE AND YOU'RE KILLING ME . . . And I hate being Oscar Wilde because NO ONE WANTS OSCAR WILDE, EVER . . . Dear Nan, please reconsider your most awful decision and don't send that book. O I know what death is now . . . [13]

The consternation Nan felt on reading this letter can readily be imagined. How was she to answer it? (And indeed, to whom?) She retreated to the editorial high ground, ignoring the Oscar Wilde problem and addressing her reply to Eve Langley, praising *White Topee* and pointing out that many published authors had subsequent manuscripts rejected. Nan must have been relieved to receive Langley's next letter, written under her own name and much more subdued, even businesslike. She did not refer to *Wild Australia*, simply announcing her intention of sending over another new manuscript, *Bancroft House*. This became an established pattern: Eve Langley apparently did not really intend Angus and Robertson to publish her manuscripts, just to store them for her.

White Topee appeared in mid-1954 to lukewarm reviews: after twelve years the excitement over *The Pea Pickers* had well and truly died down. 'Not so much a novel as a marvellous oddity,' wrote Roger Covell of the Brisbane *Courier-Mail*, recommending that readers approach it with caution. And indeed the author photograph was not reassuring. It showed a very large Eve Langley – she had put on a great deal of weight – in a long fur coat, canvas shoes and a white topee, clutching an elephant gun. (In a letter to A&R she rather endearingly described this image as 'the British housewife on the rampage'.[14])

Langley announced that the New Zealand Literary Fund had asked her to write twenty books, which was fine because she had plenty to write about. In May 1955 she sent A&R *Somewhere East of Suez*, another fragmented and unpublishable manuscript. She had left her job at the Auckland Public Library and late in December 1956 she crossed the Tasman, intent on seeing her publishers and revisiting Gippsland. Before long there she was, a very large woman resplendent in fur coat, man's suit and glistening white solar topee, climbing slowly up the wooden stairs to the editorial floor of 89 Castlereagh Street.

Beatrice and Douglas Stewart met her, and according to Stewart they all had an amiable and sensible discussion about manuscripts and possible future novels. Beatrice, who was meeting Eve for the first time, had quite a different impression. She wrote to her friend Hal Porter, who was working as a librarian in Bairnsdale, Gippsland, that Langley had been 'more eccentric than we could have dreamed of'.[15]

Porter, who had greatly enjoyed *The Pea Pickers*, was intrigued. He discovered that Langley was staying at Metung, not far from where he worked, and telephoned her. Her breathy, little-girl voice led him to expect a frail woman in floating chiffon and silver sandals, fresh from haunts of coot and hern. Instead of which, he said, she was:

> dressed in a navy-blue chalk-stripe double-breasted [suit] à la Menzies, and what I call a publican's cardigan, one of those maroon and fawn things, and a tie with stripes across it. She had quite small

feet in boots, they must have been schoolboy's shoes she had bought
. . . Over this she had flung a very long fur coat, ankle-sweeping,
quite an opulent one, made of black cat or some strange material.
And topping all this, a white topee . . .[16]

Porter went with her as she revisited some of the scenes of *The Pea
Pickers*, and described it as a fascinating experience. She had wonderful
green eyes, like those of *Vanity Fair*'s Becky Sharp, he said, and when
something took her interest she was transformed and became beautiful.
'Drawing from within herself whatever is in a writer of her quality and
a woman of her strange sort, she would come out vivacious, amusing,
intelligent.' But then Eve Langley would retreat into her own mind and
this woman would vanish, to be unnervingly replaced by her alter ego,
Oscar Wilde. She occasionally referred to herself as Oscar, and once
addressed a passing child by that name.

When Porter described the day to Beatrice, she replied that Langley
sounded almost as alarming in Gippsland as she had been at 89
Castlereagh Street. 'I feel drawn and repelled,' she added, 'seeing the richness of her qualities and feeling the pathos of her alienation. There is
really nothing one can do . . .'[17] Beatrice also worried about how Langley
was managing financially. She was probably living on an invalid pension
and meagre royalties. *The Pea Pickers* was still in print – a new reprint was
ordered in 1958 – though *White Topee* had sunk without trace.

And still Eve was writing, writing, pouring out endless manuscripts.
On 19 October 1959 she wrote to Beatrice:

I am just going to pack up the latest book *Last, Loneliest, Loveliest*,
and send it over to you. It's all about my life over on the North
Shore in Auckland and full of rich warm glowing material from a
journal kept in those days of marriage to an artist husband and a
batch of children as well . . . you will get *The Land of the Long White
Cloud* soon. Then comes *Demeter of Dublin Street*, followed by *The
Colossus of Rhodes Street*, then *The Old Mill* . . . Then after this
one comes *Remote, Apart* to be followed by *Portrait of the Artist at
Chelsea* and then *The Saunterers* and *Beautiful Isles of the Sea* and lastly

Apollyon Regius . . . Two books come in between, introducing to
you *The Land of the Long White Cloud* and these are *The Nimrod Type*
and *The Australian* . . . so that's eight to come, no nine with *Golden
Wattle Warriors*, no eleven with *The Nimrod Type* and *The Australian*.

Beatrice staunchly replied that she was delighted Eve was writing so
happily and so prolifically.

It was A&R's usual practice to have two readers' reports done for all
manuscripts submitted. Nan McDonald was given the job of summaris-
ing the latest batch of Langley novels: 'All these novels are shapeless and
lacking in story interest; all have characteristic flashes of brilliance and
originality, and all are distinctly inferior to *The Pea Pickers*,' she wrote.[18] She
concluded that she had probably not done justice to the later manuscripts;
somebody had to read them all, of course, 'but seven full-length works are
too much Eve Langley for anyone to take in a few months without in-
digestion . . . I don't think I could face [any more] for some time to come.'

There was clearly no hope that Eve Langley would ever write
another publishable book. Yet both Beatrice and Nan continued to send
her kind and encouraging letters. 'Heaven knows when we shall be able
to publish all these so attractively titled novels,' wrote Beatrice. 'The point
is that you, with your genius for poetry and fantasy, are a writer for the
few who are capable of appreciating your gifts.'[19] She and Nan knew
that Eve could find refuge in her own mind only by writing endlessly,
that she needed to rework *The Pea Pickers* obsessively in order to try to
make whole her fragmented self. It must have been sad for Beatrice to
see that flashes of the poetic talent she admired so much were still there,
but unreachable, like opal in rock.

Then Langley announced that she thought of settling in Australia,
and asked Beatrice to help her find a very cheap house to buy, costing
between £500 and £1000. Perhaps she had saved this from her royalties over many years, perhaps from a pension; Beatrice never knew, but
she helped Langley apply for an Australian invalid pension, writing on
her behalf to the Department of Social Services, and arranged for information about houses in New South Wales to be sent to her.

Early in 1960 Langley wrote to say she had found a house in

Katoomba, in the Blue Mountains west of Sydney, for the tiny sum of £75. In May she arrived in Australia and went straight up to her new home, which she called 'Iona Lympus'. 'I am settled well among the blue tongued lizards and the tiger snakes and Sydney wattle and waratah at above address,' she wrote to Beatrice in a letter that carried jaunty echoes of *The Pea Pickers*. 'Please forward all mail of a New Zealand or hostile character to same. The house is great . . . Australia Felix or Australia Beatrix it's home to the wanderer and exile and I wish I'd never left it. Love to you and Nan and everyone from Steve.'[20]

From her hut in the Blue Mountains Langley continued to write to Beatrice and to make occasional visits to Sydney. But she had developed a new obsession – to travel to Greece, the home of ancient culture, where she would commune with the ancients and earn her living as an itinerant grape picker. Beatrice and Douglas Stewart considered this ambition another fantasy, but in September 1965 A&R received a letter from H.B. Gullett, Australian ambassador to Greece, telling them that Langley had arrived in Athens, alone and penniless.

Beatrice and Douglas Stewart swung into action. Beatrice prevailed on the A&R accounts department to send Eve a cheque for £50 against royalties for a forthcoming reprint of *The Pea Pickers*, care of the ambassador. She also persuaded Langley's bank to advance her another £300. Douglas Stewart managed to get a grant of £100 from the Commonwealth Literary Fund. In a letter to H.B. Gullett he explained why he and Beatrice had taken such trouble.

> Eve has had a thing about Greece all her life; it is – or Ancient Greece is – her Promised Land and for that reason, if she hasn't gone right off the deep end, we'd love to have her see something of the country before she comes home . . . Would it be possible to let her wander off into Greece for a while, with a small grant, on the understanding that she would keep in touch with the Embassy? Or is she too bad for that?[21]

The trip was not a success. Langley found Athens bleak, hot and hostile. She struggled with luggage, couldn't handle Greek money, and spent a long time tramping the streets, living on scavenged apple peel and biscuits and becoming steadily more bewildered and depressed. The Australian embassy found her somewhere to stay but she felt trapped and once more retreated into her own world. She finally returned to Australia without her luggage, and was back in 'Iona Lympus' by the middle of December.

Early in 1966 Douglas Stewart wrote to her about her financial position, saying he might be able to get further help from the CLF. A month later she replied, mentioning only that she had been ill in Greece. At this point the correspondence faltered. From time to time A&R wrote to her about royalties and other small matters, but there was only silence from her end. Gradually, inexorably, Eve Langley faded into her memories and the landscape of her fantasy.

In 1974 Douglas Stewart's daughter Meg, a writer and filmmaker, decided to make a film about Eve Langley for International Women's Year (1975).[22] She had grown up loving *The Pea Pickers*: her father often spoke of it, her mother, the artist Margaret Coen, would quote a line from it about old boots being the flowers of the Australian bush. Meg, asked to compare two picaresque novels for the New South Wales Leaving Certificate, had chosen *The Pea Pickers* and Fielding's *Tom Jones*. (The examiners had marked her down on the grounds that *The Pea Pickers* was not sufficiently 'literary'.)

In July Meg and her father drove up to Katoomba, intending to talk to Langley about the film. They went out from the town along a winding, uphill bush road and finally came to an old gate with a NO TRESPASSERS sign. Eve Langley's mountain retreat was a decrepit caravan and a dilapidated and rotten wooden shack in scrub overgrown with blackberries. On the ground in front of the shack's open door were three golf clubs, perhaps intended as weapons.

Inside the shack were a rickety bed, a desk and a chair. Bundles of newspaper littered the floor, miscellaneous rubbish was everywhere – an old record player, toys, scraps of clothing, magazines. There was a coal stove and a fireplace but no sign of a radiator or electricity; Tilley lamps evidently provided light. The place must have been freezing in winter, they thought. Eve Langley was not there.

Meg and Douglas Stewart went to the Katoomba police station. They learned that, after a neighbour had noticed uncollected mail in Langley's letterbox, a social worker had called on the afternoon of 1 July. She had found Eve's body in front of the fireplace. Langley had died, probably of arteriosclerosis, at some time during the first two weeks of June. The police statement said that she 'was or had been an author of some note'. One detail in the statement that particularly distressed Douglas Stewart was that her face had been partly eaten by rats.

'Marriage unknown; children unknown; profession nil; time of death 1–13 June 1974,' read the death certificate. Eve Langley had vanished for a third time, this time into the bureaucracy, just another vagrant.

Profession nil: Eve Langley produced one book that Beatrice always considered a novel of rare talent, the first imaginative prose to appear in Australia since Christina Stead began writing.[23] With great regret, Beatrice came to agree with Douglas Stewart, who said, 'What I always felt about Eve, really, you know, was that there was no continuity after *The Pea Pickers*. It was her misfortune and her good luck to do one great work of genius, I think . . . and you can't go on.'[24]

Mrs Frederick Bridges and
Miss Beatrice Davis

At the end of World War II Beatrice was thirty-six. Already she had a touch of the crisp, authoritative manner that came with being efficient and busy, having an assured position and staff of her own. Though she threw herself into her job, it was not her whole life. There was Frederick, of course, and her family. Aunt Enid was now living alone with Granny Deloitte in Neutral Bay, working at clerical or secretarial jobs and settling into the busy, useful life of favourite aunt and keeper of Deloitte family lore. She was still the relative to whom Beatrice felt closest. Her mother Emily, who continued to live alone in Neutral Bay once John and Del were married, was never Beatrice's favourite person, though Beatrice was always the dutiful daughter.

Emily could be difficult, with definite ideas about how things should be done. On the second day of what had been intended as a long visit to her son John and his young family near Narrabri, she announced that she couldn't possibly stay there as she *had* to be near the sea, and insisted on being taken home immediately. Though only in her early sixties, she was developing the imperious manner of an older woman, coupled with a certain vagueness. In fact, she was showing signs of premature dementia. This was a potential worry for Beatrice, as the only one of Emily's children who lived in Sydney.

Though Beatrice was fond of her brothers and made a point of seeing them whenever they were in town, she didn't much like her

sisters-in-law – a lack of warmth, it must be said, that was fully recipro-
cated. They disapproved of Beatrice partly because they suspected she
and Frederick had lived together before marriage. Her city sophistication made the wives of John and Del consider her supercilious and somewhat pretentious, particularly about her job. They also found Frederick's
sense of humour difficult; he had a habit of deliberately putting people
off balance. Once, as Del and his wife arrived at Folly Point for a party,
Frederick greeted them at the door with 'I don't know whether you can
come in. Show us your teeth!'

'Very special and very dear' was how Beatrice described Frederick.
Perhaps she loved him all the more because of the cloud that hung over
their marriage; Frederick's tuberculosis was incurable and they knew their
time together was likely to be short. There was, though, little risk of
Beatrice's contracting the disease: the infection rate among carers was not
very high.[1] Beatrice might also have been influenced by the lingering
Victorian view that TB was a rather romantic disease, associated with
creative, dynamic people. As a doctor, Frederick Bridges knew how limited the treatment was: bed rest at home, ineffective and painful operations involving collapsing the infected lungs, perhaps time in a
sanitorium. Sanitoria of the time were brutal places where, because fresh
air was considered the best treatment for TB sufferers, beds were placed
in front of open windows or on verandahs exposed to freezing winter
nights. Frederick led as normal a life as possible for as long as he could,
but finally had to give up and retire to bed.

Worried though she was about her husband, Beatrice managed to
maintain her calm and businesslike exterior at A&R. By now the staff
knew that she was Mrs Bridges; she probably came clean about her marriage once the shortage of men during wartime allowed married women
to be employed. She did not dwell on her own problems, though occasionally she hinted at them: in 1944 she apologised to Lawson Glassop for
her tardiness in editing *We Were the Rats* because she had been 'off her head
with domestic worries of a fairly sinister sort'.[2] She did not elaborate.

Possessive, even childish though Frederick might have been, as a
doctor he knew precisely what was happening to him and what the
prognosis was. Beatrice could do little in caring for him; she certainly

intended to continue her career after his death, and it would be foolish to allow Frederick's illness to dominate her life entirely. Whatever anguish this realisation caused Beatrice, she accepted it, and maintained her social and professional contacts. Though considerate and practical, she was not the ministering angel type – and Frederick was evidently not the kind of man who expected to be fussed over. Beatrice and Frederick began to lead increasingly separate lives. Del, observing his sister going out one evening with little more than a 'Bye bye, darling' and a kiss on the forehead for her very ill husband, thought she was being hard and selfish, abandoning him for the sake of her own pleasure.

Beatrice did not like to go to social functions alone, and women of her generation were expected to be accompanied. She soon found a very practical solution in the form of Edmund Jeune, known to everyone as Dick, and by 1944 he had become Beatrice's escort. A tall, solid man, bald as an egg – at parties Percy Lindsay used to greet both him and Frederick by bestowing a kiss on each glistening pate – Dick Jeune was a ship's provedore by profession who lived by himself in a hotel room near Circular Quay. Then in his fifties and divorced without children, he had known Beatrice almost as long as she had known Frederick. Children found him very glamorous. Beatrice's nephews firmly believed that in his youth he had been not only a gun-runner but the strong man in a circus, able to lift a horse from the ground by grabbing its mane in his teeth.

Dick Jeune was very particular about such things as dress, speech, correct grammar and the treatment of ladies, although there were times when he forgot to be a gentleman. Once, driving through the city with Beatrice's nephew Charles and attired in his usual town ensemble of tailored suit, snowy shirt and tie, Homburg hat and monocle, he stopped at the traffic lights on the corner of George Street and Martin Place. A rough-looking character took exception to Jeune's resplendent appearance and, as he crossed in front of the car, diverted slightly and rammed the meat pie he was eating through the driver's window onto Jeune's shirt. Dripping meat and gravy, Jeune parked in George Street and got out. Charles watched him stride up the street after his assailant, then saw a well-tailored arm flash forward and a flurry in the crowd as Jeune's victim hit the footpath. Jeune strolled back to his car. 'Bastard!' he growled as he drove off.

Dick Jeune seems to have made it his mission to look after Beatrice, whom he adored, on Frederick's behalf. He was a kind-hearted, dependable man, always willing to escort her to dinners, meetings and the theatre, even though he made no secret of the fact that he found many of these functions excruciating. Some of Beatrice's literary acquaintances – those who did not share her appreciation of human foibles and eccentricity – were bemused by him: why was the dainty, elegant and beautiful Beatrice being seen in public with such a rough diamond? Jeune was rather deaf, and at meetings of the Fellowship of Australian Writers or the English Association was apt to nod off in the front row. A young academic giving a talk at such a meeting was disconcerted at the sight of him, very obviously asleep, and afterwards apologised pointedly for being so boring. 'No, no,' said Jeune briskly. 'That's quite all right. Nobody else has ever apologised.'[3]

Beatrice enjoyed Dick Jeune's company and was grateful for his support, for life was becoming increasingly grim. By June 1945 it was evident that Frederick would not live much longer and he was moved to Prince Alfred Hospital, where he had once been medical superintendent. He died there on 30 July 1945, just before the war ended – and, as Beatrice often bitterly pointed out, not long before the invention of the streptomycin that could have saved him.

In his will, which named Beatrice and his elder son Peter joint trustees and executors, Frederick provided for his young wife generously. After leaving her his personal effects and £500 for each of his sons, he directed that Beatrice should have the net income from his investments during her lifetime. After her death the income would revert to Frederick's sons or their families. As the house at Folly Point was part of the estate, Beatrice had the right to live there for the rest of her life. Despite what she said in later years, she was in a position not to have to work again.

Beatrice was now a widow, living in the house she loved, but alone. Did she wish, even for a moment, that she had had Frederick's child? If so, she never told anyone. However, when her friend Miles Franklin wrote a characteristically sympathetic and generous note the day after she heard of Frederick's death, Beatrice opened her heart just a little.

My dear Miles

It was a wonderful letter you wrote me & it warmed my sad heart. I didn't tell much about Frederick, but I'll tell you about him someday. Have just come home from staying with my brother John on his selection by the Namoi near Narrabri, where I immediately fled. The loveliness of the countryside helped, and hard work, cooking on wood stoves and doing jobs with sheep and cattle.

May I really come to stay with you for a night or two? Perhaps you'd have me one weekend, because weekends will be difficult in this house that was, and is still, Frederick. But I'm going to tear into my job in earnest and, I hope, learn to play the piano again . . . [4]

And so she did.

To the great satisfaction of A&R's management, the Australian publishing boom did not end with the war. 'The future never looked so bright to me and that is saying something,' wrote Walter Cousins in 1948 with giddy optimism, though typically he added his doubts that A&R could keep up the pace.[5] Not that the new poets and prose writers who had come to prominence during the war in *Australian Poetry*, *Coast to Coast* and the *Bulletin* were selling in huge numbers; for A&R the big sellers at the end of the war were still the old stalwarts Ion Idriess and E.V. Timms, as well as Frank Dalby Davison. But newer books were doing well: Rohan Rivett's *Behind Bamboo* had sold almost 30 000 copies, *My Love Must Wait* about 50 000, and two 10 000-copy reprints of *Flying Doctor Calling* had also walked out of the bookshop. George Robertson would have been proud to see how well his company was doing, wrote Cousins: 'We have at this date hardly started publishing.'

But though readers were buying Australian books in greater numbers, the problems of publishing remained. At the end of the war, the

federal government had decided to continue allowing overseas publishers to reprint their books in Australia on generous terms; the Australian
Journalists' Association and the Fellowship of Australian Writers claimed
that cheap paper editions of English-originated work were flooding the
Australian market and putting local writers at a disadvantage.[6] The AJA
and FAW asked for a parliamentary committee to look into the book
publishing industry in Australia, for legislative protection against the
dumping of US-produced books, for a quota system to ensure that bookshops bought at least 20 per cent of new books by Australian authors, and
for tariff protection for the writing and publishing industries. Time after
time since World War II these problems, and solutions, have surfaced.
They can be summed up as a small market in a big country, and they
bedevil Australian book publishers to this day.

The arguments in favour of autonomy for Australian publishers
became even more strident with the reintroduction of the Traditional
Market Agreement, drawn up and enforced by the (UK) Publishers
Association.[7] By 1953 Australia was the world's biggest market for British
books outside the UK, and it might be argued that with such influence
Australian publishers, led by Angus and Robertson, could have tried
harder to negotiate separate rights deals for overseas books.[8] But they did
not, and for many years the Traditional Market Agreement was a
reminder that Australia, certainly in this respect, was still a British colony.

At the beginning of the 1950s Beatrice felt that she, if not Australia,
had quite enough autonomy to be going on with. 'Tearing into her job
in earnest', originally a solace after Frederick's death, gradually became
an end in itself. She told correspondents she was busier than she had ever
been, and in that statement there was a certain pride. Watching Frederick
die had been dreadful and Beatrice still had moments of desolation, but
she had survived. She was continuing to do her job, and to do it as well
as she could.

From the late 1940s Beatrice's department (PBE or 'poor bloody
editorial', as it was sardonically called) had been acquiring the shape it
would maintain throughout the next decade. Beatrice, who at the start
of the war had signed her letters 'Beatrice Davis, Editorial Department'
(never had so few tried to be so many), was, by the end of it, 'Beatrice

Davis, General Editor'. She used this title to differentiate herself and her staff from the very new education department, set up in 1945 and headed by a young, bullet-headed Queenslander named Colin Roderick. Roderick speedily acquired his own staff, as well as an interest in everyone else's job besides his own, and a tendency to inform others that it was educational books that made money, not the literary stuff.

During the war Beatrice had taken on Elisabeth Hughes, whose job was to handle non-fiction, particularly cookery and gardening books. In 1949 John Swindells, one of Guy Howarth's most promising students, was employed as an editorial assistant. He left to travel after a year and was replaced by a dark-haired, judicious young man named Alec Bolton, who remained at Angus and Robertson for fifteen years. He was immediately smitten with Rosemary Dobson; they married in 1951 and a year later she left Angus and Robertson to have their first child.

Though the editorial staff was expanding, their offices in the attic were small and cramped, with no concessions to ventilation or changes in temperature: one winter day Ruth Park saw two of Beatrice's editors actually shivering with cold. At the very top of the stairs was Beatrice's room, with the only door that was ever shut; her secretary Judy Fisher, whose family had known Frederick Bridges, had a small office nearby. The four staff editors shared two further offices. The first held the reference library, which was replenished from the downstairs bookshop whenever necessary, as well as a huge wooden cupboard containing unsolicited manuscripts and those waiting to be edited. Beatrice, as editorial traffic controller, allocated texts according to each staff member's area of expertise. Every manuscript submitted, however hopeless, was read and reported on by two readers, usually from within A&R, though outside experts were sometimes called upon. Unless the books were government publications or works of strong topical interest, there was no urgency in the editing process; editors worked on particular books until they felt they had finished. Indexes were prepared by another editor or a freelancer, often Guy Howarth's wife Lillian.

Opposite Judy Fisher's office was the proofreaders' room. Most of the proofreaders, of course, worked at Halstead Press, but Grace George always had her office in the editorial section and shared it with a copyholder. Beatrice and her editors, who generally worked quietly, were used to the sounds of murmuring from Georgie's room as the copyholder read aloud the original manuscript and the reader marked errors on the proofs. On one notable occasion someone called up the stairs, 'How do you spell "warring"?' The copyholder called back, 'W-h-o-r-i-n-g.'[9]

After Beatrice the senior editor was Nan McDonald, now in her early thirties. Nan's family came from south of Sydney, but she lived with her sister Margaret, who worked in the Mitchell Library. Nan dreaded Beatrice's absences from the office because she then had to write letters and talk to authors, and she was extraordinarily shy. Her other dread was E.V. Timms, a demanding and difficult author who wrote long, bossy letters that she sometimes could not bring herself to read for several days.

Beatrice and her editors spent little time together outside the office, nor did they go to lunch as a group; their main social occasion was the tea break, which Nan in particular insisted upon. At mid-morning and mid-afternoon Judy Fisher or the most junior editor brought the tea tray, with teapot, milk, sugar, cups and spoons, up the narrow staircase from the floor below. Everybody gathered in one of the editorial offices, drank tea, swapped opinions about the manuscripts they were working on, and discussed books and the arts in general. Authors and manuscript readers who were on the premises joined in; a frequent guest was the children's writer Ella McFadyen. Other members of A&R's staff thought the editorial department spent too long over tea, but this was the only time they got together during the day, unless one editor consulted another about a problematic manuscript.

With a staff of editors, Beatrice found that she needed to spend less time doing hands-on editing, though she always worked on the manuscripts of her favourite authors. The newer members of her staff marvelled at the surgical precision and care with which she worked on manuscripts, making marks in tiny handwriting, usually with a foun-tain pen or a fine-nibbed mapping pen and red ink.[10] Beatrice used red, as schoolteachers traditionally did when marking essays, but her manu-scripts looked far more intricate and decorative. 'Your handscript always looks as if it could be played on the piano,' Miles Franklin once told her. The short-story writer Margaret Trist said she didn't mind being corrected by Beatrice because her manuscripts always looked so beautiful.

Although Beatrice's editing might have looked delicate, often it was anything but. Her approach to a now almost forgotten novel, Henrietta Drake-Brockman's *The Wicked and the Fair*, is typical. In August 1956 Beatrice wrote to the author:

> At last *The Wicked and the Fair* is ready for the printer, having been carefully checked and its problems, typographical and other, discussed by me and by Nan McDonald – the two most experienced publishers' editors in the country. I say this to remind you that no suggestion or typographical alteration has been made without due thought, for we do consider this a most important manuscript on which no pains should be spared.

So far so good. But Beatrice continued:

> Since all the points raised are comparatively minor ones, we did not think it necessary to return the ms to you . . . First there are the cuts – all minor but necessary, we think, to avoid blocks in the narrative. A list of these is appended, giving page and line . . . A list of queries is [also] attached. Thirdly, there is the typography, use of caps, hyphens, etc., on which we of course are the experts . . .[11]

Beatrice seldom sent edited manuscripts back, so authors often saw the changes to their manuscript only on proofs. Especially messy manuscripts were often retyped, whereupon Beatrice might show a difficult author a new-looking manuscript with a few red-ink marks added to make the editing look less extensive than it had been.[12]

The cuts Beatrice made to *The Wicked and the Fair* might well have given an author cause for concern – she simply lists them without explaining why they were made. Her changes do seem excessive, even high-handed, but it's possible that she and Henrietta Drake-Brockman, who were good friends, discussed the manuscript in detail face to face during one of Drake-Brockman's visits to Sydney (she lived in Perth).

And Beatrice's questions to the author are always sensible: 'There are no lions in India. Shall we let this pass as a traveller's tale, or change to tiger?'

It was Beatrice's practice to discuss the major problems in a manuscript with its author, in person or by letter, persuade them to rewrite as much as possible, then have the line-by-line editing done, either by herself or a member of her staff. The manuscript was then typeset and the galleys sent to the author. If Beatrice cut too deeply or made changes the author felt were unacceptable, Beatrice either reinstated the disputed text or tried to cajole the author into agreement. It is interesting to see what an interventionist editor Beatrice often was, particularly when in later years she made a point of emphasising that the author's voice and style were sacrosanct.

By 1949 Walter Cousins, having worried his way through the war and its aftermath, needed a rest; he was in his late sixties and his health was uncertain. He had worked for A&R for almost fifty years and, considering his retirement, had already picked out a successor. 'George [Ferguson] has my vision 100% and will carry the torch in the future years,' he wrote to Rebecca Wiley, who had gone to live in the US.[13] 'He has splendid organizing ability and is loved by all.'

It was a logical choice, and an expected one. George Adie Ferguson, son of Sir John Ferguson and grandson of George Robertson, was a loose-limbed, amiable man who had lived and breathed A&R since his youth. He had joined the company in 1931 after leaving university and, in the traditional manner of the heir apparent, he learned the publishing trade from many angles. He sold technical books, handed out the pay envelopes at Halstead Press, even read proofs (his copyholder complained that he constantly sucked hard sweets and never offered her any). During the war he served as a brigade major in the 2nd Division artillery and he returned to Angus and Robertson in 1945, becoming Walter Cousins's deputy. In August 1949, after some months of illness, Walter Cousins died and George Ferguson became publishing director of Angus and Robertson.

Ferguson and Beatrice were almost exact contemporaries: he was a year younger and they had been at the University of Sydney at the same time. They got on well, though temperamentally they could hardly have been more different. Beatrice had undoubtedly sized up her new boss as an easy-going, pleasant young man. George was ostensibly in charge but there was nothing subservient about Beatrice's relationship to him, quite the reverse. Her staff knew that, if Beatrice wished, she could wrap George Ferguson around her little finger.

PART 3
1945–1960

89 Castlereagh Street

'I May Not be a Great Genius . . . but Nevertheless My Tonnage Cannot be Ignored': Miles Franklin

Miles Franklin cast a long shadow. In her fifties when Beatrice met her, she had been one of Australia's best-known literary figures for more than thirty years, *My Brilliant Career* having appeared in June 1901 when she was only twenty-one. Attractive, wilful and opinionated, with a distinct writing voice of her own, Miles Franklin had apparently been destined for a brilliant literary career, and if she never quite repeated the success of her first novel, she nevertheless produced at least a dozen others and collaborated on a well-researched biography of the writer Joseph Furphy. Despite her many years abroad, her subject was almost invariably Australia, particularly the Brindabella country in southern New South Wales where she grew up: with the passing of time, this became an ever more insistent presence in her mind. Her first book displayed the insouciant freshness and high spirits of young womanhood, and as she grew older her writing scarcely changed – though what had been refreshingly casual writing in her youth became perhaps a little forced later in life.

When Beatrice met her, Miles had returned to Australia to live and was an important member of the Sydney literary scene. She had joined the city's major writers' groups and, having forgiven George Robertson for turning down *My Brilliant Career*, she kept a proprietorial eye on Angus and Robertson. She could be sharply critical: A&R, she said, had too many authors and concentrated too much on 'trash'. She and the forthright feminist writer Jean Devanny were once outraged to see that A&R's display for Sydney's Royal Easter Show featured the books of only two novelists: Timms and Idriess.[1]

In some circles Miles was considered cranky. Journalist and short-story writer Thelma Forshaw, who met her at FAW meetings in the early 1940s, described her as having 'a long truculent upper lip, scorn for makeup and dress, the earnest dominating voice propounding – such an aggressively unfurnished personality I found forbidding'.[2] However, to Dal Stivens she was a sweet lady, shy, gentle and generous. 'True, she was feminist' – note the qualification – 'but she was never a battle-axe.' The poet Jill Hellyer saw her as a small, gentle person who wore rose-trimmed hats, was kind to her friends and was retiring and unobtrusive.

None of these spinster characters from Central Casting rings quite true. Certainly Miles Franklin, who was small, straight-backed and snub-nosed, who wore neat collars and brooches, long skirts with polished shoes, and whose twinkling brown eyes were hidden by round glasses, looked like a sweet little old lady. But sweet, retiring spinsters are not gen-erally noted for their robust wit or their idiosyncratic way of looking at the world, as Miles Franklin was. Her voice was slightly deeper than aver-age and she knew how to use it for dramatic effect. She spoke as she wrote, using vivid and pungent imagery from her rural background: to Miles a dishevelled person looked as if he had just burst through a paling fence; Xavier Herbert, struggling over a book for many years, was 'egg-bound'. Her best work is probably the hundreds of letters she wrote to the friends she called her 'congenials', displaying the acuity, tartness and vitality that were so much a part of her personality.

Miles was usually one of the moving spirits at literary meetings, but Beatrice quickly discovered that the assertive opinions which could make Miles appear so formidable were only part of her. 'It was when we were alone, her mask of aggression put aside,' wrote Beatrice in *Overland* magazine years later, 'that I came to know and love her.'[3]

Their relationship became more comfortable, perhaps more equi-table, when they met at A&R as author and editor. Though Miles had a joking, sparring friendship with her near contemporary Walter Cousins, it was Beatrice, young enough to be Miles's daughter, who did the literary spadework on her books. The first Franklin book Beatrice worked on was *Pioneers on Parade* (1939), a novel that Miles co-wrote with Dymphna Cusack lampooning Sydney's sesquicentennial celebrations; Beatrice did very little to their manuscript.

She was more directly involved with Miles's next book, a biography of Joseph Furphy, author of *Such is Life*. A collaboration with Kate Baker, a former teacher who had encouraged and helped Furphy during the writing of his novel and who devoted herself to promoting his work after his death, *Joseph Furphy: The Legend of a Man and His Book* was plagued with problems, not the least being the personality clash of its authors. A&R had planned to publish in 1943, to coincide with the centenary of Furphy's birth and the fortieth anniversary of his novel's first publication, but wartime lack of paper and staff held it up for another year. By the end of 1943 Beatrice had not finished editing the manuscript and the two authors were squabbling about whose name should go first on the title page. Beatrice pushed ahead and Miles thanked her: 'I so much appreciate your toe tracks on the sands of my saga,' she wrote to Beatrice in December 1943.[4] (Since she called the book 'my saga', it's easy to see why she and Baker did not get on.) The book appeared midway through 1944 and, with a reissue of *Such is Life*, set off a revival of interest in Furphy's work.

As well as being literary colleagues, Miles and Beatrice were gradually becoming friends. Miles treated Beatrice like a favourite niece or daughter, scolding her for working too hard. 'Attacking the weeds, running a beautiful house . . . the weight of a great institution on your rare and special gift and all the lame ducks and other calls and connections of life. Where is your love time, your play time, your special outlet music time?' she asked.[5] She also lectured Beatrice about employing her gifts for the betterment of Australian literature, writing, perhaps wistfully, that the younger woman was prettier, better educated and had had greater opportunities than she herself had been offered. Like most people who had anything to do with Angus and Robertson, Miles was shrewdly aware that Beatrice was probably the brightest person in the company, writing to Dymphna Cusack that A&R's general editor was 'the one spark of leaven in directors of sheer stodge', and she noted how writers courted Beatrice.[6]

Miles's friendship was important to Beatrice, who, inclined to be overconscientious, appreciated Miles's bracing approach to life, once telling her that 'I always feel a bit dull compared with you'.[7] (Beatrice's letters could be too eager, even gushy.) And when she travelled overseas for the first time in mid-1952 it was Miles to whom she confided her impressions of London:

> Everything in London was exactly as I had expected it to be, from the smell and the feel of it to the policemen and the lions in Trafalgar Square. I had to force myself to go sightseeing, and settled into a nice little rut in my attic in Bloomsbury Street, going to the-atres, wandering around on buses, and meeting lots of people, and being roused from my lethargy only when somebody had the impertinence to congratulate me on not seeming like an Australian. There's something about the condescension of that remark that always makes me mad with rage. It's difficult to define the differ-ence I feel between the English and us – we are the same people, yet – the class distinctions perhaps strike you most, and the badly fed, runtish look of so many of the lower orders, but you can't gen-eralize. I have still really to talk to English people who have ideas and say what they think, instead of taking refuge in that aloof poise that is sometimes the essence of all rudeness . . . Travelling doesn't make me feel very intelligent, only rather dazed and blotting-paperish. Perhaps I'll feel later on that I've profited from it.[8]

From the late 1940s Beatrice occasionally stayed overnight with Miles at 'Wambrook', Miles's small turn-of-the-century brick cottage about ten minutes' walk from Carlton station on Sydney's southern train line. For Beatrice, who lived on the north side of the harbour and worked in the city, the working-class suburb of Carlton was foreign territory indeed. The house, which had belonged to Miles's mother, had what Vance Palmer called a 'hearty rural atmosphere'. One felt, he said, that there might be a horse hitched to the fence in front and an army of fowls in the backyard.[9] Photographs show a small suburban cottage rather too hemmed-in for a country look, though Miles did keep a few bantams in the backyard, one of which laid her eggs in an ancient felt hat on top of the copper in the outside laundry.

Beatrice was well aware that a visit to 'Wambrook' involved a certain amount of ceremony and preparation: like many older people who spend a lot of time alone, Miles took visitors very seriously. She always gave Beatrice careful and strict instructions about using the outside lavatory, and told her to bring nothing but a comb and toothbrush. 'I have a clean washed hair brush and a tin of salmon,' she told Beatrice. 'If you can eat a salmon mayonnaise, that's one dish without trouble.'[10]

'Wambrook' was very small, though not necessarily cosy. The main room was the parlour, with a mantelpiece on which stood jars of variously coloured earth from different parts of Australia, some collected by Miles, others given her by friends. In the centre, in pride of place, was Miles's Waratah Cup, a Royal Doulton cup and saucer decorated with waratahs. It was a mark of high approval to be invited to take tea from this, and the privileged visitor was also asked to sign and write a note in the visitors' book, known as the Waratah Book, which featured the signatures of Australia's foremost writers. In the parlour, too, was a piano, which Miles often insisted Beatrice play, though she apologised for its poor quality. The rest of the house – two bedrooms, tiny dining room and kitchen – held the solid family furniture that Miles's mother had brought from the country. The house was always tidy, if a little musty.

Though Miles spent very little money, living on the rent from a couple of local shops inherited from her mother as well as her meagre royalties, she was a great stickler for appearances. Beatrice was never a big eater and she must have been dismayed to see fruit, chocolates and cake spread before her while Miles, urging her to eat up, put on a starched white apron and grilled chops and cooked vegetables at the small gas stove. Dinner, in the dining room at the back of the house, was served on a white linen tablecloth with heavy family glassware, crockery and cutlery.

Sitting at the kitchen table, sipping a dry sherry from a specially bought bottle, Beatrice would chat to her hostess. They talked of mutual friends and acquaintances: Dymphna Cusack and Henrietta Drake-Brockman, Douglas Stewart (grudgingly approved of by Miles even though he was a New Zealander), younger writers such as Margaret Trist and Nancy Keesing. They discussed literary politics, particularly the fortunes of the Fellowship of Australian Writers. Miles insisted that the society was going to the dogs, failing to attract real 'writers of tonnage' as members, deploring that significant writers such as Eleanor Dark hardly ever came to meetings. What the country needed, she thought, was a literary organisation prepared to tackle the real issues confronting contemporary writers – more than a tea-and-sandwiches society. It was ridiculous nonsense for leftist writers' groups such as the FAW to send approving cables to their colleagues in Russia, or to order the USA to stop persecuting communist writers: they should be working closer to home. The problem was that all Australia's 'writing guns' were in Melbourne, not Sydney – Vance and Nettie Palmer, Flora Eldershaw, Frank Dalby Davison, Alan Marshall, David Martin, Arthur Upfield – but the country's premier city should be making more of an effort. What was being done to promote Australian writing, to make life easier for local writers, to honour their work? Miles Franklin fretted constantly about the lack of practical support available to Australian writers, and was determined to do something about it.

She and Beatrice, with differing tastes, also argued about what constituted good writing. Beatrice liked vividly descriptive, poetic and inventive prose: then and always she was a great admirer of Eve Langley's work and the short stories of Hal Porter. Miles pooh-poohed the work of both writers, labelling them phony, one of her favourite disparaging adjectives. Beatrice also respected the work of Patrick White: Miles thought his writing was 'by Joyce out of D.H. Lawrence' (not a compliment) and that his first novel, *Happy Valley*, had got the Snowy Mountains – which she considered her own special territory – all wrong. But they both liked the novels of Christina Stead. Beatrice always regretted that Stead was committed to another publisher, while Miles identified with her living abroad for many years while she wrote about Australia.

Miles generally preferred clear, realistic writers whose work echoed her own vision of 'the real Australia', which generally meant life outside the cities. She enjoyed the rough-hewn camaraderie expressed in Sumner Locke Elliott's wartime play *Rusty Bugles* (1948), while Beatrice thought it was too episodic and sparsely plotted to be a successful play. Miles also applauded the courage of Frank Hardy in writing *Power Without Glory* (1950) – not one of Beatrice's favourite books – which brought out her moralistic streak. 'We are just as low in public morality as the USA,' she wrote to Florence James.[11]

But for Miles there was realism and realism. She heartily disliked Ruth Park's *The Harp in the South*, set in the slums of Sydney's Surry Hills, when she read it serialised in the *Sydney Morning Herald* at the end of 1946. 'Ruth Park's great achievement was to fit all those bedbugs into the *Sydney Morning Herald*,' she sniffed to a correspondent. 'She will never surpass that.' Miles seldom missed an opportunity to stick a knife into the young author, criticising everything from her work to her appearance; it was a dislike that was almost obsessive. Ruth Park later speculated that Miles's bitchiness was due to jealousy, which seems a reasonable conclusion.[12] Like Park, Miles had once been a promising and admired young writer, and, not having fully developed that promise, perhaps she found unbearable the thought that another might succeed where she had failed. Miles was also cruelly dismissive of Catherine Gaskin, whose first novel was published when she was sixteen and whose historical novel *Sara Dane*, published in 1954, was a worldwide bestseller.

Miles was always very interested in Beatrice's personal life, though Beatrice did not discuss it with her in any detail, knowing that Miles had her quirks where sex and men were concerned. Energetic and scornful general discussion of male foibles was permissible, but Beatrice's intuition would have told her that discussions of love and loss were touchy. Though Miles had always enjoyed flirting with men, she rejected any closer relationship. She wore a wedding ring for a very typical double reason: to tease people into wondering about her past and to serve as protection against unwanted male attention. Miles herself confided nothing about her private life, telling Beatrice that she would find out everything in her diaries, to be published posthumously. Like Miles's other friends, Beatrice was sceptical about this – why would the obsessively secretive Miles reveal herself on paper, even after her death? (Miles Franklin's diaries, still in the Mitchell Library, have never been published and

Beatrice's instincts were right: they are much less revealing and personal than Miles's letters.)

Some of Miles's friends thought she was afraid of intimacy. Henrietta Drake-Brockman wrote to Beatrice after Miles's death:

> Really a strange, untrusting nature. Perhaps that's why she could never bring herself to marry, or sleep with anybody . . . She only seemed to remember passion in terms of being "adored" by [a man]: What about her own desires? I am certain, really, that Miles never got further than, at best, preliminary skirmishes![13]

Miles had definite views about sexual morality, some of which amused Beatrice. For instance, she disapproved of single women sleeping in double beds, and once Beatrice had gently to persuade her that a woman character in an English novel who quickly yielded to the attentions of a male was not a nymphomaniac.[14]

Miles seems to have been far too fond of Beatrice, however, to judge her according to her own strict rules. She knew that, since Frederick Bridges's death, Dick Jeune was no longer a husband-approved escort but had become firmly ensconced as the man in her life. Like Beatrice's other friends, Miles had met Jeune at literary gatherings; after FAW meetings in the city, he would obligingly go out of his way to run some of Beatrice's friends to Central station in his car. 'He is like the old squatto-cracy, gives his opinions unbridledly,' Miles wrote to Dymphna Cusack.[15] 'B had warned me it was useless to either pinch or hush [him] as it only stimulates him to reiteration.' But she approved of Beatrice's comment that Dick was to be 'bullied and cherished', saying she thought Beatrice well able to do both.

Early in 1950, with money from the Bridges estate, Beatrice bought a property in Tizzana Road, Sackville, about fifty kilometres north-west of Sydney and ninety minutes away by car. She wrote to Henrietta Drake-Brockman about it in July:

> I have acquired about 20 acres of a broken-down orchard with an old ramshackle house on it as a country retreat. It is on the

Hawkesbury River and the scenery is the sort that makes me feel tranquil and happy. She-oak trees and willows on a river bend, orange trees and a lagoon with black swans on it, but fruit has to be picked, and fences put up, and the house tidied up, so it may be some time before it is as peaceful as it should be.[16]

Just down the hill from a picturesque stone church and not far from the local winery, the house, with a verandah on two sides, was intended to be a haven, a place to invite friends for weekends.

It also became the home of Dick Jeune, now retired, who rapidly assumed the mantle of local character. (The house was not far from the local post office which controlled the telephone exchange. Whenever there was a call for Dick, who was deaf as a post, one of the Morley family who ran the post office had to rush down the hill to tell him his phone was ringing. One wonders how he managed to hear the caller.) Dick looked after the orchard and tried his hand at raising poultry: on the electoral roll, no doubt with tongue firmly in cheek, he described himself as a farmer. The place at Sackville gave Beatrice something unique in her life: a place to indulge in tranquil domesticity. 'A weekend at Sackville, packing Valencia oranges, stuffing cushions with kapok, admonishing broody hens and admiring Dick's 200 new chickens,' she wrote to Miles.[17] 'The river looked heavenly with its willow curtains and mountain backdrop, and yesterday we had tea on a boat chuffing down its widest reaches. To retire and live here would be bliss – for a while at least.'

Miles Franklin was one of Beatrice's first visitors at Sackville. The two women continued to see a lot of each other, mainly because Miles's literary career had revived during the 1940s. Not only was there the biography of Joseph Furphy, but Colin Roderick included her work in two anthologies. One of these, *The Australian Novel* (1945), included some of Miles's fiction written under the pseudonym Brent of Bin Bin. Encouraged by this, Miles asked A&R to republish the six novels she had written under that name, though she presented herself not as the author but as Brent's agent. As Beatrice dryly noted years later, it says something for Miles's personality and persuasiveness that A&R agreed.[18] She was also being disingenuous: clearly in Miles's case Beatrice allowed friendship to overrule literary judgement.

Miles Franklin played the Brent of Bin Bin game for years. (She had a tin ear for names; an unpublished novel carried the pseudonym of Mr and Mrs Ogniblat l'Artsau, or Talbingo, Austral[ia], her birthplace, spelled backwards, more or less.) Not only did she quote 'the old gentleman' and write many letters under his name (astute observers noted that Brent used the same typewriter as Miles did), but she once wrote an elaborate account of meeting him. And where did the name come from? Perhaps Miles was giving a defiantly Australian twist to an English form of title, which would have been like her. Beatrice thought Miles knew someone called Brent; the name was printed on a man's collar she found in an old suitcase that Miles left behind after one of her visits.[19] When A&R agreed to publish the Brent of Bin Bin series, Miles told them that the true identity of the author would be revealed when the final volume appeared.

The first two novels in the series, *Up the Country* (1928) and *Ten Creeks Run* (1930), had been published in the UK by Blackwood and edited by Miles's friend Mary Fullerton. In 1950 Beatrice decided to start the A&R series with *Prelude to Waking*, the first manuscript written under the Brent pseudonym, originally submitted to Blackwood – and rejected – under the title of *Merlin of the Empiah*. Beatrice thought there was a very good reason why the novel had never seen the light of day, but she kept her misgivings to herself, even managing to write to Miles about it with some enthusiasm.[20] Angus and Robertson published *Up the Country* and *Ten Creeks Run*, the best two in the series, in 1951, followed by *Cockatoos* (formerly rejected as *The Outside Track*) in 1954, with *Gentlemen at Gyang Gyang* (originally and puzzlingly entitled *Piccadilly's Pants on the Hoof*), and *Back to Bool Bool* in 1956.

In all her dealings with Miles about these books, Beatrice followed the convention that Miles Franklin and Brent of Bin Bin were two different people. She sent letters addressed to Brent of Bin Bin (and deciding how to address him must have caused a few unsettled moments: Brent? Mr Bin Bin? Lord Bin? Beatrice sensibly settled for 'Dear Sir'), c/- Miss Miles Franklin, 26 Grey Street, Carlton, and she wrote to

Miles's other friends about Brent with a straight face: 'Brent, by the way . . . says he will reveal his identity when all six of the books are published but will burn the unpublished volumes, if he is revealed before then. So we are not trying to fathom the mystery, though we are madly curious – and wonder what part Miles might have played. She is inscrutable.'[21] Years later she wrote that she never had the nerve to tell Miles she thought her guilty of pointless deception. 'She could have had reasons that were important to her, and I loved her too much to upset her.'[22]

It is interesting that Angus and Robertson so readily published the Brent of Bin Bin books when their general editor thought them undistinguished at best. After Miles's death, Beatrice allowed herself to be much tougher and franker than she had been while the author was alive: 'With her intelligence, I find it almost incredible that in all those years, with all those rejections, Miles learned almost nothing about literary style. She was an innocent who believed that vitality and love of Australia were enough.'[23] Perhaps Beatrice convinced her male colleagues that Miles's books, however ordinary, should be brought back into print as a contribution to Australian literary history. It is just as likely that she was fond enough of Miles to want to make her happy, to assure her friend that her work had not been forgotten.

Beatrice recognised that the casual, 'spoken' quality of Miles's style translated much better to the lecture hall than to the page. In 1950 Miles gave a series of CLF-sponsored lectures in Perth about Australian literature. Beatrice had offered to read her notes with a view to publication, and she was relieved to find that they were good. Angus and Robertson published the material as a series of essays entitled *Laughter, Not for a Cage* in 1956.

Beatrice continued to keep an anxious and loving eye on Miles, as did Miles's other woman friends. She worried when Miles developed an ulcerated throat in Perth, continued to give her books, sent her a new typewriter when Miles's was being mended. Miles had asked Beatrice to be her literary executor, assuring her that very little needed to be done, but never during her lifetime did Miles Franklin drop so much as a hint about the bountiful gift she was preparing for Australian writers.

In the early 1950s, though she was well into her seventies and battling depression and cardiac problems, Miles was still spirited, not to say
acerbic, defensively quick to stamp on any remark she considered patronising, especially if uttered by a man. She wrote to Dymphna Cusack that
at an English Association dinner she had sat next to 'a Prince Alfred
gun-doctor.[24] He said, "You are a graduate of this university?" I said I was
illiterate. He recovered from that sufficiently to remark that one doesn't
have to go to a university to learn to write. I said no, my mother taught
me my alphabet. That really sunk him . . .'[25]

Despite such flashes of self-assertion or crankiness, Miles often
seemed depressed. Beatrice worried that she spent so much time alone,
but she recognised Miles's impregnable independence and knew there
was little she could do. As Miles's health declined, Beatrice grew more
and more concerned. The final corrections to *Laughter, Not for a Cage*
were due early in 1954, and Miles was unable to decide what to change
and what to leave alone. Realising how ill she was, Beatrice decided to
trouble her no further, giving the manuscript to young Nancy Keesing
for final checking. In June Miles had a heart attack and was taken to the
home of her cousin Mrs Perryman in Cheltenham, a northern suburb of
Sydney, to convalesce. Hating her inability to look after herself, Miles
fretted about her book, alternately demanding to know why it could not
be published immediately and saying she wanted it destroyed.

In August 1954 she wrote to Beatrice saying she was short of breath
with a savage pain under her left collarbone. 'I don't seem to have
enough zip to pull out of this illness if the fact will be that I'm an
invalid,' she wrote in jagged, tiny handwriting. 'I have struggled so long
already. Still not able to read paper or to talk . . . memory gone and I
blame phenobarb.' Beatrice wrote to Miles's former doctor, Douglas
Anderson, the husband of her dear friend Vincentia, describing Miles's
symptoms in detail and asking whether her heart disease was getting
worse. Dr Anderson recommended that she move around as much as
she could, and Miles recovered enough to get out of bed.

In early September she had to go into hospital to have fluid on her
lung removed. The operation went well and she was about to come
home again when she had another heart attack. Miles Franklin died on

19 September 1954 at the age of seventy-five. She had asked for a simple funeral, with no death notice in the *Sydney Morning Herald* and no flowers. In her will she said she wanted her ashes scattered 'on Jounama Creek just opposite the Old Talbingo Homestead where there used to be a crossing'. After all her years away, Miles wanted to return to her birthplace.

'I feel completely bereft when I realise, which is difficult, that she is no longer with us,' wrote Beatrice to the poet Rex Ingamells, who had inquired on behalf of Georgian House whether A&R still intended to publish *Laughter, Not for a Cage*.[26] 'She was trying to go through the ms I had edited, but was not able to complete the job.' The final work on *Laughter* must have been sad and difficult for Beatrice, with Miles's wit and aggressive Australianism permeating every line. When the book appeared in June 1956 Katharine Susannah Prichard wrote to Beatrice to congratulate her:

> As a last word from Miles I felt so moved as I read. Although I read the lectures in manuscript, they seem better and have benefited from careful editing. But the best of Miles is in them – her unique and enigmatic personality. Miles, who seemingly was such a simple lovable person and yet more than that. Someone we never knew . . . [W]ith all her quirks and witty intransigence, she was incomparable . . . [27]

Henrietta Drake-Brockman commented perceptively, 'Dear Miles, what a wit she was, and far from confident, too, in those later days. After all, it was a shield.'[28]

The newspaper tributes and obituaries were respectful – many mentioned the 'unsolved mystery' of Brent of Bin Bin's identity. (Sometimes it seems that nobody fell for Brent of Bin Bin except journalists.) On receiving a copy of *Cockatoos* in October 1954 Dymphna Cusack wrote to Beatrice, 'It is unbearably poignant to open *Cockatoos* and feel again that pulsing vitality, that sparkling commentary on life.'[29]

In 1963 Angus and Robertson published Miles's last book, *Childhood at Brindabella*. An account of her first ten years on her parents' station, it was written in 1952–53, but Miles had been too tired and ill to revise it. She wrote it at the urging of a friend, the children's writer Pixie O'Harris, who wanted her to publish a children's story based on her own early life. At first Miles refused – she loathed stories for children, she said – but the idea of a memoir stuck. Perhaps because it is an autobiography, a deliberate looking back, an attempt to recapture in memory the part of the world that Miles Franklin drew most from, *Childhood at Brindabella* lacks the jauntiness of her other work. But even in a memoir she couldn't be straightforward, changing all the place names and identifying most of the people by their initials. Miles Franklin's need for secrecy pervades even something as charming and unpretentious as *Childhood at Brindabella*.

A few months after Miles's death the Permanent Trustee Company, which administered her estate, wrote to Beatrice that Miles had bequeathed her 'a silver brooch of a fish on a South Sea paddle and a silver necklet in the shape of grape leaves'. Beatrice knew that Miles's important papers had been left to the Mitchell Library and that her accountant and Colin Roderick from A&R had been appointed to burn those marked to be destroyed.[30] Friends and family received small bequests; portraits and manuscripts were to go the Mitchell Library. Miles also decreed that *My Brilliant Career* was not to be reprinted until ten years after her death. But when her will was made public in January 1955, its major clause caused astonishment in Australian literary circles.

Miles Franklin, who, as everybody knew, had led a quiet and frugal life for years, had left almost £8000 for the benefit of Australian writers. Her will stipulated that the Franklin Awards – so named for her family, not for herself – were to be given annually to 'Authors for the advancement improvement and betterment of Australian literature to improve the educational style of such authors to help and give incentive to authors and to provide them with additional monetary amounts and thus enable them to improve their literary efforts'. The will did not specify how many awards there should be, but Miles Franklin seems to have been thinking of only one major prize. This was to be 'awarded for the Novel for the year which is of the highest literary merit and which must present Australian life in any of its phases'. If no novel was deemed worthy of the prize, it should go to a play for stage, radio or television or 'such medium as may develop', though not for farce or musical comedy. The judges of the award, to be chosen by the Permanent Trustee Company, were to be any three among a group comprising Beatrice, the librarian of the Mitchell Library, the poet Ian Mudie (one of Miles's 'congenials'), Colin Roderick, and Miles's accountant George Williams. The trustees could appoint replacement judges and any others they might think fit, and they also had the power to suspend the award of the prize for as long as they wished.

The prize, first given in 1957 and always known as the Miles Franklin Award, was almost unique at the time because it was funded from the income of a person of modest means and was not an endowment made by a corporation or a wealthy individual. The money came from the sale of the Carlton house and the shops Miles had owned, and her royalties, which had been invested by the Permanent Trustee Company. The prize money in the first year of the award was £500, equivalent to more than $10 000 today, and the capital was greatly increased two decades later with the sale of the film rights to *My Brilliant Career*.

Beatrice was not alone in being appalled at the deprivations Miles must have endured for the sake of the award (her unpublished diary entries describe her eating crusts of bread for dinner). She realised, too, that Miles had insisted on the publication of some of her own books partly to increase the amount of money available for writers of greater talent. It was Miles Franklin's last and best-kept secret, and her friends deduced that she must have gained a great deal of satisfaction from it. Beatrice, who described herself as 'bereft' after Miles's death, always recognised her friend's special qualities. As she wrote to Rex Ingamells, 'There was no one like her, nor is there very likely to be again.'[31]

Sydney or the Bush:
Ruth Park and D'Arcy Niland

Sometime in 1943 a young woman made her way through A&R's bookshop and up the steep stairs to the editorial department. Though Ruth Park had been a regular visitor to the bookshop at 89 Castlereagh Street since her arrival in Sydney from New Zealand some months before, this was the first time she had ventured further than the ground floor. Angus and Robertson were considering a collection of her stories for children, and Beatrice had written suggesting they meet to discuss them. Park longed to have a book of her own published under the Angus and Robertson imprint and this was an important meeting. Beatrice she knew by reputation as a witty, stylish and elegant woman – intimidating qualities for a nervous young author. As a freelance writer and journalist Ruth Park had visited newspaper editors such as Eric Baume and Kenneth Slessor, and she assumed that Beatrice also worked in an office reflecting her status: a spacious, well-appointed room gleaming with polished wood, guarded by a dragon-like secretary.[1]

What she saw at the top of the final flight of stairs was an unventilated room with a woman sitting behind a desk that almost filled the entire space. When Beatrice stood up to greet her, Ruth Park noticed how small and pretty she was, with blue eyes, delicate regular features, and dark brown hair pulled back into a graceful knot. Beatrice had started to go grey in her mid-twenties – now, in her thirties, she had bleached a lock of hair above her right eyebrow, a style she maintained for many years. For an established editor greeting a new and unknown author she was surprisingly jittery, lighting a cigarette almost immediately and smoking rapidly throughout the conversation, which did little to put Park at her ease.[2]

For her part, Beatrice saw a tall and slender, neatly dressed young woman with long, red-blonde hair. She knew Ruth Park's work less well than that of her husband D'Arcy Niland, whose story 'The Surrealist' Frank Dalby Davison was about to include in that year's *Coast to Coast*. Park, too, had published short stories, and she and Niland also wrote magazine articles and radio plays. They were barely managing to survive by their writing and they had to be versatile. Beatrice, who viewed literature as a higher calling and knew little about the limitations and imperatives of the marketplace, would not have understood their willingness to write anything and everything. Nor did she have any idea of their domestic circumstances. The wartime housing shortage had forced them to live with their baby daughter in the ramshackle, rat-infested inner-city slum of Surry Hills, a part of the city that for Beatrice, as for most other middle-class Sydney residents, might have been on another planet.

Beatrice and Ruth Park warmed to each other, however, and the young author came away feeling hopeful about her book. She liked Beatrice very much and wanted to know her better. Beatrice liked Park, too, and was disappointed when wartime paper shortages prevented the publication of the children's stories. She had little more contact with Ruth Park until she opened the *Sydney Morning Herald* on the morning of 28 December 1946 and saw the front-page headline 'Woman wins £2000 novel prize'.

The *Herald* had run their first competition for an unpublished novel, war novel, short story and poem, with cash prizes and, for the first three prizewinners in the novel section, the guarantee of publication by Angus and Robertson. Now the judges – Dr A.G. Mitchell, senior lecturer in English at the University of Sydney; critic and academic Tom Inglis Moore; and Leon Gellert, literary editor of the *Herald* – had declared the best novel to be Ruth Park's *The Harp in the South*.

This novel about the Irish–Australian Darcy family in Surry

Hills – the title refers to the symbol of Ireland transferred to the Southern Hemisphere – was praised by the judges for its setting and its 'uncompromising realism'; it was rare, they said, to find a novel with an urban setting. (Other commended novels were set in small country towns, bush settlements or the outback. Even when Australia had been urbanised for at least two generations, the bush was still widely considered the most appropriate subject for fiction.) They made similar comments about the second prizewinner, Jon Cleary's *You Can't See Round Corners*, the story of a rake's progress in another Sydney slum area, Paddington.[3]

The *Herald* delivered a warning about *Harp* in the form of a synopsis: young Roie Darcy becomes pregnant to a Jewish boy, loses the baby after being kicked by Dutch sailors, and eventually falls in love and marries Charlie Rothe (described by the *Herald* as 'part-Aboriginal, but his heart and his soul were completely white'). This was followed by the unsettling statement that the novel was 'not for the squeamish', with the rider that it was nevertheless 'a moral book'. 'If the book is super-realistic it is never deliberately bawdy,' concluded the *Herald*. 'Its quickened sympathy with the lower strata of the proletariat should have a softening effect on the hard rind of social unconcern within Australia.' All this added up to one thing: the *Herald* suspected there would be Trouble.

How right they were. No sooner had *Harp* begun serialisation in twelve close-packed daily *Herald* instalments than readers rushed for pen and paper. Most praised *Harp*'s freshness, vividness and true-to-life characters; if the novel made Sydneysiders aware of the dreadful living conditions endured by some of their fellow citizens, said some, it had earned its place in Australian literature. But others loathed it and accused Ruth Park of bringing disgrace to Sydney and of writing 'filth'. After several days of letters heaping praise or abuse on the novel Warwick Fairfax, managing director of the *Herald*, took the unprecedented step of writing an article to explain the paper's reasons for publishing it. The novel's outspokenness, he said, would be unremarkable in a book from overseas.[4] As Beatrice wrote to Ruth Park a few years later, 'It is odd that we remain wowserish about our own local writing yet accept strong meat from England and America.'[5] Many readers of the stately, sedate

Herald obviously found it much less challenging to read about harsh reality taking place a long way from home.

From a distance of half a century, as Ruth Park has pointed out herself, the furore caused by *The Harp in the South* is bewildering. It is one of Australia's best-loved and most enduringly popular novels, has been translated into thirty-eight languages and made into a television mini-series. The grandchildren of its critics probably studied it at school. So why did it cause such a fuss? In her autobiography, Ruth Park states that the reaction came from her status as a newcomer to Australia and as a woman. There is some evidence for this, particularly as regards gender: a hullabaloo greeted Katharine Susannah Prichard's *Coonardoo,* Kylie Tennant's *The Battlers* and, a few years later, Dymphna Cusack and Florence James's *Come In Spinner.* And while *You Can't See Round Corners* by the Sydney-born Jon Cleary was a tougher and more violent book, it received nothing like the hostile public response of *Harp.*

Beatrice, it must be said, did not care for *The Harp in the South,* which she found too commercial and journalistic and not sufficiently literary for her taste. Douglas Stewart was no supporter of *Harp* either – he had been backing another novel to win the *Herald* competition.[6] Beatrice also disapproved of Angus and Robertson's commitment to publish prizewinners in a literary competition, even the august *Sydney Morning Herald*'s: her view was always that Angus and Robertson must choose the books they wanted. She made no bones about this, telling Ruth Park that *The Harp in the South* was not the sort of book A&R cared to publish, but that they had a gentleman's agreement with the *Herald.*[7] Naturally Ruth Park was dismayed by this and she also felt a sense of foreboding. She knew that a reluctant publisher is little better than none at all, and if someone as influential in A&R as Beatrice did not care for her book, what were its chances of being properly presented to the public? She already had reason for doubt. A&R had not used *Harp*'s serialisation in the *Herald* to generate any publicity for the book; indeed, they never publicised or advertised it at all.[8]

Considering that the book was so controversial and its author so personable (Ruth Park was a young mother), it is extraordinary how little A&R did to promote *The Harp in the South.* They did not publish it until

1948, almost eighteen months after the competition, and then they printed fewer than 5000 copies. Walter Cousins flatly denied that, far from dampening the demand for a book, serialisation generally makes readers want to read it in full. When it finally appeared it sold, as D'Arcy Niland remarked to his wife, like salted peanuts.[9] And still A&R hesitated to reprint; Hedley Jeffries told Ruth Park he had to talk hard to convince them.[10] When Angus and Robertson heard via London that Robert Lusty, publishing director of Michael Joseph, had doubled the first printing order on reading the manuscript, they were pleased for Park but unimpressed.

Despite A&R's efforts, Ruth Park became a successful author and she and Beatrice became friends. Whatever her feelings about The Harp in the South, Beatrice was honestly delighted by Park's success. She took her under her wing and often invited Park to Folly Point. 'We are all such old fuddy-duddies, my pet, you must come along and be young and beautiful,' she told Park (at the time Beatrice was in her late thirties, Park in her mid-twenties). They also occasionally lunched at David Jones in Elizabeth Street, usually after Beatrice's weekly hair appointment in the St James Arcade. A great bond was their shared enthusiasm for The Pea Pickers and Eve Langley – whenever Park visited her family in New Zealand she made a point of writing to Beatrice with news of her.

Beatrice's relationship with Ruth Park shows how easily and well she could distance herself from her role at Angus and Robertson and be simply a friend. She and Park never discussed Park's work, for instance. Park knew that her writing was 'not Beatrice's thing at all' (though Beatrice must have recognised how good it was), and like most writers she was secretive about projects in their early stages.[11] She and Beatrice undoubtedly preserved a tactful silence on the subject of Park's contractual struggles with A&R; Walter Cousins had initially been reluctant to give Park a contract for The Harp in the South, telling her that A&R operated on a handshake.

After the novel became a bestseller in England and the US, it finally dawned on A&R that Ruth Park was a highly profitable author. They published Poor Man's Orange, the sequel to Harp, in 1949 with a print run of 10 000, selling all but 1300 copies in the first four months.[12] The Witch's

Thorn, published in October 1951, had an initial run of 15 000 copies in Australia and New Zealand and became a Book Society choice in the US (the American publishers, Houghton Mifflin, had some trouble with the idiom, wanting to know whether a lamington was a Maori cake). For Ruth Park – to borrow the title of a memoir she and D'Arcy Niland wrote a few years later – the drums had truly gone bang. She was now embarked on a long and distinguished writing career, and described winning the *Herald* competition as 'the biggest break we ever had'.[13]

Meanwhile D'Arcy Niland was beginning to think that, despite the time needed to produce them, there might be something in writing novels. He took time out from short stories and magazine articles and wrote *Gold in the Streets*, a story about the seamy, occasionally violent Sydney he knew. The novel won third prize in the *Herald* competition in 1948, and early in 1950 he submitted it to Angus and Robertson.

The first reader, Alec Bolton, recommended it, though he warned that it contained a number of passages that were 'unswervingly physical'. Beatrice thought it was 'realistic and sordid in the extreme' but could see beyond its subject matter, and her judgement was a considered one:

> The author avoids melodrama – and he is not sentimental. In this respect he outstrips Ruth Park as a writer, but it is extremely doubtful whether his work would have the same popular appeal. Jon Cleary's was a better piece of work in some ways than Ruth Park's, but his novel didn't sell and hers did. To publish a third novel in so short a time with the same Sydney background would perhaps not be wise, though a talent like D'Arcy Niland's cannot be ignored.[14]

A&R turned down *Gold in the Streets*. Beatrice wrote to Ruth Park that the novel was both powerful and beautifully written, and reiterated her view that in some ways Niland surpassed both Park and Jon Cleary as a writer. This seems a tactless statement for an editor to make, though Beatrice was well aware that the Park–Niland literary relationship was not a jealous or competitive one. Beatrice suggested that Niland might consider doing another draft, toning down the violence: 'with his grasp of character, excellent technique and sure sense of drama, he could well become a very fine novelist,' she added, and A&R would certainly be happy to see his next novel.[15]

As rejections with encouragement often do, this had the effect of galvanising Niland to further enthusiasm. He assured Beatrice that he was keen to write another novel, but work would have to wait, 'owing to certain delaying factors, which I hope to tell you about soon. You'll be surprised,' he added. 'I was.'[16]

The delaying factors were born in September. 'How very nice of you to let me know so soon about the twins,' wrote Beatrice soon afterwards. 'Very many congratulations! . . . What an amazing girl Ruth must be to have demanded her writing pad on the twins' birthday!' D'Arcy Niland declared his intention of calling them Angus and Robertson. Pity you can't because they're girls, responded Beatrice, suggesting Angostura and Roberta instead. (They were named Kilmeny Mary and Deborah Mary.)

Park and Niland wrote to Beatrice as if she were an angel and kindly elder sister combined. 'I can't tell you what [your encouragement] means to us,' Park wrote from New Zealand. 'A bit of encouragement and advice from the right person does so much to smooth out the rough places, of which we've had quite a few lately.'[17]

D'Arcy Niland's second novel was *The Big Smoke*, which won second prize in the Commonwealth Jubilee Novel Competition. A&R's first reader thought it was 'an extraordinary mixture of soft-heartedness with extremely gory and repellent toughness', and Beatrice turned it down. She tried to break the news gently to its author:

> You have so much competence and emotional capacity . . . as a writer that I think you must soon produce a real novel that will last, but I do not think this is it. You are still the short-story writer here, and a very good one . . . but your preoccupation with brutality seems almost morbid – as though you thought that only through drawing tough people could you write forcefully. Surely you don't . . . [18]

A disappointed Niland vowed to produce a novel that A&R would accept, but realised that this would have to wait: the bills needed to be

paid: 'I could write a dozen short stories in the time I'd spend labour-
ing over another clunker,' he told his wife disconsolately.[19] Though an
idea for a novel was germinating – the story of an itinerant bush worker
who, to spite his estranged wife, takes his small daughter wandering with
him through the outback – he turned his attention to more promising
short-term prospects. These included more stories and a book on short-
story writing, the latter drawing on the expertise that had enabled him
to support himself as a freelance writer for more than a decade. This was
probably Australia's first 'how to' book on creative writing for the local
market, and Beatrice was dubious about it. She could not believe, she
said, that enough people wanted to write short stories for the book to be
successful. (Perhaps she hadn't looked at A&R's pile of unsolicited
manuscripts for a while.) Niland promptly fired back list upon list of
clubs, groups and other assorted organisations dedicated to the written
word – one newsletter named 'Writers' World' had a circulation of 4000 –
proof that in 1954, as now, Australia was bristling with would-be writers. He finally convinced A&R, and his brisk and practical book, with
its grab-you-by-the-collar title of *Make Your Own Stories Sell*, did well.

But it was his new novel that Niland really cared about. This was the
story of the seasonal worker Macauley who tramps through the towns of
western New South Wales encumbered by his four-year-old daughter
Buster. He sent it to Beatrice early in 1954. The first reports were
cautious, not to say sniffy: 'In his endeavours to be tough, Mr Niland
positively bellows in one's ear,' was the reaction of the first, unnamed,
reader, who thought that the end, where Buster almost dies, was a bit
much – 'I may be wrong but I thought "crises" went out with the advent
of penicillin'. But the reader did think the novel had dignity and the
characters were well drawn. The second reader thought it was written
with colour and vigour but had too many long, gory fights.

Beatrice approached the Commonwealth Literary Fund, and their
reader – possibly Vance Palmer – was much more enthusiastic, com-
menting that the novel had 'vigour which at times rises to genuine
power'. However, the reader thought that the book's violent descriptions
and crudity of language prevented it from being a first-class novel. Like
A&R, the CLF could sometimes be rather prissy.

D'Arcy Niland was becoming nervous. 'Every time the postman whistles I rattle like a loose window,' he wrote to Beatrice.[20] But finally, in June 1954, she wrote with the news that, yes, A&R were interested in publishing the novel, with some revision and perhaps a new title. D'Arcy Niland's cabled reply had all the relief and exhilaration of an author who, after a long struggle, might finally have hit the jackpot: 'WONDERFUL NEWS THANKS A MILLION GOT ANY DRAGONS YOU WANT KILLED'.[21]

Beatrice reported that the publishing committee didn't much like the book's title: *The Shiralee*, they said, was a difficult word that would mean nothing to the reader. D'Arcy Niland defended it strongly, saying that this authentically Australian word, meaning 'swag' or 'burden', summed up the novel's dual theme – that all men need to learn to carry burdens, and that the main character's burden was his daughter.[22] He also pointed out that the public had not hesitated to buy a popular travel book named *Kon-Tiki*. A&R capitulated, though reluctantly: on balance they rightly thought *The Shiralee* a better title than the author's alternative, *A Man Like a Wheel*.

But in the end, Beatrice turned the novel down, on the grounds that the hero was 'such a rough young man'.[23] Ruth Park sent it to a friend in London, who took it to Michael Joseph. They were immediately enthusiastic and offered to publish. When Niland told Beatrice she was annoyed. Why, she asked, would Niland look for a British publisher when Angus and Robertson had recently begun publishing overseas?[24] 'If every author who thinks he has a chance of being accepted by a British publisher leaves us, we have little chance of succeeding with Australian authors in the United Kingdom,' she told him.[25] Her persuasiveness and charm convinced Niland, who agreed to give Angus and Robertson the British Empire rights to his new book. Having a better head for business than her husband, Ruth Park argued that an English publisher would be more likely to sell the book in the UK than A&R, but the deal had been done.

Beatrice's editing of *The Shiralee* was cautious. She thought Macauley's swearing diluted the reader's sympathy for the character, and Niland agreed. But apart from excising the odd 'Christ' or 'Jesus', she made few changes to the manuscript. She remained doubtful about the title, though was reconciled to it when she learned that the London office had no objection. Niland suggested that the novel's flyleaf include a short ballad explaining the meaning of the word 'shiralee', which Ruth Park would write. 'As far as I'm concerned, her name and the fact that we're a team would add something to the book, if only from a publicity angle,' he wrote to Beatrice.[26]

And indeed, by the mid-1950s Ruth Park and D'Arcy Niland were probably Australia's best-known literary couple. Their combination of talent, industry and good looks made them attractive to magazine editors. Not only did they write novels, radio plays, short stories and magazine articles, but they looked after five children; D'Arcy Niland was particularly admired for knowing on which end of a child a nappy went. Their sheer energy and dedication as writers and parents greatly impressed Beatrice, too: more than once she told them she didn't know how they managed everything either. She was particularly struck by the way in which they were able to avoid a clash between their family and professional lives.

In 1956 Park and Niland collaborated on a memoir, *The Drums Go Bang*. With joky line illustrations, and written in the light, breezy style of *The Egg and I*, the book described their early years together, making their struggles to survive as writers in Surry Hills sound difficult but fun.[27] (Many years later, in *Fishing in the Styx*, the second volume of her autobiography, Ruth Park gave a less cheery picture of that time in their lives.)

As a team Park and Niland threw themselves into promoting *The Shiralee*. Some of their less serious ideas amused Beatrice, especially Park's joke that half a dozen swagmen should march into the A&R bookshop and beat up Hedley Jeffries with their billy cans. But they had some good marketing ideas, such as flashing a photograph of the dust jacket on the screens of picture theatres before the main feature started: everything from Holden cars to McNivens icecream was advertised in this way, they said, so why not books? Niland suggested the title be the answer to a quiz question on one of the shows run by the very popular Jack Davey. (This did happen, with no prompting from A&R.)

The Shiralee was published early in 1955 and was an immediate success. It sold more than 20 000 copies in its first six months on the Australian market, and despite A&R's misgivings that the English might find it too slangy and 'essentially Australian', it had sold more than 30 000 copies in the UK by the end of 1956. (The Australian novels that have done best in the UK market have usually dealt with life outside the cities.) *The Shiralee* was a UK Book Society choice and a *Daily Mail* Book of the Month. William Morrow bought it for the US, and German, Dutch, Spanish, Norwegian, Danish and Swedish rights were sold.

Even more exciting was the prospect of *The Shiralee* being made into a film. Niland gave permission for A&R, in the person of Hector MacQuarrie, the New Zealander who ran A&R's London office, to be his agent for the film rights at a commission of 20 per cent. MacQuarrie, a long-time A&R employee whose sojourn in London had made him more British than the British, was very proud of his connections with the UK publishing and film worlds.[28] In April 1955 he cabled A&R that Ealing Studios would film *The Shiralee*, with Peter Finch as Macauley. Finch's versatility and talent as an actor had taken him from being a star of 1940s Australian radio and theatre to success in London. There was a much publicised hunt for someone to play Buster, the part eventually going to a young Australian girl named Dana Wilson. To coincide with the release of the film in 1957, two songs were written to be sold as sheet music – 'The Shiralee' and 'She's Buster, The Swagman's Daughter'.

With the release of the film, sales of the novel rolled on and on: so did *The Shiralee* industry. Little girls were named Shiralee, and so was an Australian racehorse; London's Chelsea Flower Show even launched a rose with that name. (Niland signed a letter to Beatrice's secretary Judy Fisher as 'Petals'.[29]) Niland was now famous: 'Three out of four Australians selected at random could probably tell you who D'Arcy Niland was,' boasted A&R's blurb on the cover of his next novel, *Call Me When the Cross Turns Over* (1957). His two early novels, *Gold in the Streets* and *The Big Smoke*, were published in 1959, though by Horwitz, not Angus and Robertson (Niland had decided not to offer them to A&R again). But not everything was running smoothly. Through inexperience, Hector MacQuarrie had done a disastrous deal on the film rights to *The Shiralee*. Even after the film's success, Park and Niland were closer than they should have been to having, in the words of Australian author Arthur Upfield, 'all the fame and no bloody money'.

Their disappointment over *The Shiralee* film deal might have slightly soured Park and Niland's relationship with Beatrice. Certainly it became less close, though perhaps they were all too busy to see much of each other. Beatrice was put out that Niland had not told her he was writing *Call Me When the Cross Turns Over* – she heard about the new novel from A&R in London. She told him, perhaps a little acidly, that she hoped he would confide in her sometime.

In 1961 Niland started research on the book he had always wanted to write: a biography of his namesake the Australian boxer Les Darcy.[30] By 1963 he had finished his research but he told A&R that he was not ready to show a manuscript. Instead he sent them a novel, *The Apprentices*. Their reaction was so-so. The first reader wrote that, though the novel was 'excruciatingly sentimental', he thought A&R could get away with it. In almost all the A&R correspondence about the work of Ruth Park and D'Arcy Niland enthusiasm is less than total, in spite of the fact that their books were extremely popular. It was left to their American and English publishers to praise the books with a whole heart.

Beatrice's letter to D'Arcy Niland reflected this lukewarm feeling about *The Apprentices*: 'In spite of some readers' doubts about the senti-mentality of the treatment, we believe we can make a go of it; and it has heartwarming qualities that should give great pleasure to many people,' she wrote.[31] Dismayed and, like Ruth Park fifteen years earlier, realising that a publisher without enthusiasm is almost worse than none at all, D'Arcy Niland replied sharply. If A&R didn't want the book, he would send it elsewhere. The novel was quickly accepted by Michael Joseph.

By now Ruth Park and D'Arcy Niland had drifted away from Angus and Robertson. The demands of five growing children and their own international careers – and also disappointment with their treatment by A&R – meant that their contact with Beatrice dwindled. When they did see each other the old affection remained, but the Nilands knew that their attitude to their work, and to publishing generally, was very dif-ferent from Beatrice's. They had learned hard lessons about marketing their work. As they said in *The Drums Go Bang*, they had a product and they lived by selling it; Beatrice had always had a steady job. From the beginning, Park had known that Beatrice lacked marketing intuition, judging a book on literary terms alone; Park never heard her mention readers, only reviewers.

For some years D'Arcy Niland had been seriously ill with heart disease, and in 1967 he suddenly died, aged forty-eight. His last novel, *Dead Men Running*, was published by Hodder and Stoughton in 1969. Beatrice saw little of Ruth Park during the following few years – Park was overseas – but when she went to work for Thomas Nelson in 1973, Park followed her. Beatrice edited her novel *Swords and Crowns and Rings* (1977) – it won the Miles Franklin Award and Miles Franklin would have been appalled – and *Missus*, about the early lives of characters from *The Harp in the South*. Beatrice also edited *Playing Beatie Bow*, which was published in 1980. After thirty-six years, then, her editorial relationship with Ruth Park returned to its beginnings, with a novel for children.

Mixing Their Drinks:
Women Friends, Women Writers

By her early forties, most of Beatrice's time was devoted to her job. Though her brothers and their families, the network of Deloitte relatives, her non-literary friends and her life at Sackville were important to her, her work was the focus of her life. Her role in the literary community depended on more than just her status. Miles Franklin once told Dymphna Cusack that 'everybody' courted Beatrice, for her self, her brain, and because of her position at A&R. Everyone in Australian literary circles either knew Beatrice or had heard of her by now. She had developed many friendships with authors, and as she believed, like Dr Samuel Johnson, that friendships should be kept in constant repair, her literary relationships lasted for many years, some for the whole of her life.

Beatrice was certainly a 'man's woman', as the phrase went – she placed a high premium on male attention – but her most enduring and deepest friendships were with women. Though scarcely the confiding type, she knew how to elicit confidences from other people, and was something of a mother confessor to her staff and some of her authors. Still, being fundamentally interested in her fellow beings, she enjoyed a good gossip as much as anyone, and often met friends to catch up and to swap information. One of her favourite places for lunch was the Queen's Club, which she had joined during the war, nominated by her Deloitte aunts. Situated in a gracious old three-storey building on the corner of King and Macquarie streets, since 1912 the Queen's Club had been a

quiet and genteel city retreat for middle-class women, particularly country visitors. As late as 1958 it was the only women's club in the city that
maintained 24-hour service seven days a week. The second and third
floors were given over to accommodation, and the ground floor had a
lounge where members could relax and peruse copies of *Punch* and the
Tatler direct from Home. But the club's major attraction for Beatrice was
its dining room, where members could entertain their guests in sur-
roundings of tasteful comfort.[1]

In the dining room of the Queen's Club Beatrice regularly lunched
with Connie Robertson, editor of the *Sydney Morning Herald* women's
pages. Ten years older than Beatrice, witty and sharply intelligent and
with a great sense of style, Robertson was very conscious of her literary
connections. She had introduced herself to Ruth Park by saying, 'I am
the daughter of Stephens.'[2] (Her father was A.G. Stephens, founding editor of the *Bulletin's* Red Page.) Many writers whom Robertson had
known during her father's days at the *Bulletin* – Mary Gilmore, Hugh
McCrae, Norman Lindsay, Miles Franklin – were also friends and professional acquaintances of Beatrice's. Meeting as equals, literary-minded
women with responsible jobs, must have been refreshing for both
Beatrice and Connie – and for Gladys Owen, an artist who worked for
the ABC and who usually joined them.

Beatrice's other literary friendships were generally with her women
authors. The relationship between author and editor can be intense and
difficult to parlay into the give-and-take of ordinary friendship, but
Beatrice soon became expert at it. Henrietta Drake-Brockman used to
make a joking distinction between Beatrice her friend and Mrs Bridges
her editor; with the former she enjoyed long gossip sessions by letter,
with the latter she discussed her manuscripts. Beatrice distanced herself
from aspects of A&R's administrative practice: contracts and financial
problems were handled by Walter Cousins or George Ferguson, and it
was not unusual for authors who were arguing over their royalties with
A&R to continue friendly correspondence with Beatrice.

The Perth-based Henrietta Drake-Brockman was one of Beatrice's
closest literary friends. A beaming, large-featured woman with a fond-
ness for wide-brimmed hats, she had a commanding presence; the much

smaller Miles Franklin once described herself as 'under her lee'. Drake-Brockman was the quintessential woman of letters: not only did she write novels and plays, but she edited anthologies and wrote short fiction, biography, radio scripts and children's books. She reviewed books for the ABC and for West Australian newspapers and magazines, and was a founder of the Fellowship of Australian Writers and a member of every literary committee in that state. Her long letters to Beatrice, written in loopy, stylish handwriting, her thoughts linked by dashes, spilled over with opinions on books and people, discussions of literary topics and gossip.

She and Beatrice agreed on many things. They strongly disliked any writing they considered sentimental (which included *The Harp in the South*) and both admired the work of Patrick White, though not unreservedly. Both disliked the way that, even in the 1950s, writers were becoming 'personalities', with their lives being given more attention than their work. Literary politics interested them both, though they were irritated by members of literary societies who were not writers but people merely interested in writing. They agreed with Douglas Stewart's comment that 'people who write poetry are the salt of the earth. But those who *love* it . . . !'[3]

Drake-Brockman and Beatrice knew when to be friends settling down for a good gossip and when, as Drake-Brockman put it, to do some 'straight business talking'. Drake-Brockman had strong reservations about A&R, once telling Miles Franklin that she continued to publish with them only because of her friendship with Beatrice. Perhaps Beatrice knew this; she certainly made concessions to Drake-Brockman, showing her her manuscripts after they had been edited, as well as her proofs. They did not always see eye to eye on editorial style, and Beatrice could be huffy. 'As you say [punctuation] is largely a matter of personal style,' she wrote, 'and if you don't care for our expert advice that's your affair. (Not meaning to be snaky at all.) I myself like punctuation to be fairly logical and as unobtrusive as possible; you like it also as the vehicle of feeling which, I think, the writing itself should convey.'[4]

Drake-Brockman sometimes acted as a literary scout. While researching an historical novel she came across *Australian Legendary Tales* and *More Australian Legendary Tales*, a European retelling of Aboriginal legends by K. Langloh Parker, first published in 1896 and 1898. Langloh Parker had died in 1940 and Drake-Brockman suggested that a selection of the stories be published in one volume, edited by herself. Beatrice agreed to a book of about 70 000 words, which Drake-Brockman painstakingly prepared over many months. Published in 1953, *Australian Legendary Tales* won the Children's Book of the Year Award the following year.

Drake-Brockman's favourite subject was history, particularly that of Western Australia. She sometimes used Beatrice as a sounding board for her ideas on writing history, candidly admitting what she considered to be her own shortcomings. 'I know I am supposed to have the novelist's approach, but . . . I do like facts for their own sake,' she wrote.[5] Once, after criticising E.V. Timms for his clichéd characters, improbable characterisation and habit of including extraneous information for no particular reason, she gave a succinct and thoughtful summary of the problems involved in getting the 'feel' of an historical period:

> It is so hard for us to remember that God and the Devil, Heaven above and hell beneath, existed . . . And that men as adult in every way as ourselves, good business men, shrewd observers, clear thinkers, could travel only as fast as a horse or sail could carry them, and were governed by humours, possessed by demons, knew nothing about their anatomy and physiology or the power of steam or electricity, or even the shape of the world . . . Perhaps it is not possible to write an historical novel at all . . . .It is the *everyday atmosphere* that presents hurdles. Candles, for instance. Our whole world, the night itself, is different, lit only by candles. One must remember never to see a night scene except by candle or flambeau . . . to feel the hand on the sword hilt and the eyes looking for witches and robbers, the moment the sun goes down . . . to FEEL it, not just write about it . . . and at the same time to take it as a matter of course, of everyday existence.[6]

The warm friendship between Drake-Brockman and Beatrice cooled only once, when Beatrice neglected to include any work of Drake-Brockman's in *Short Stories of Australia: The Moderns*, an anthology she compiled and A&R published in 1967. Drake-Brockman was hurt: if Beatrice hadn't had room for a story of hers, she wrote, couldn't she at least have said so, or mentioned Drake-Brockman in the introduction? Beatrice hated feeling she had failed in tact and she wrote back in a fret of remorse, assuring Drake-Brockman that she greatly admired her work and valued her friendship, but that Drake-Brockman's work did not belong in the anthology, and that was that. Drake-Brockman accepted the decision and the friendship remained.

Another of Beatrice's authors with a touch of *grande dame* about her was Ethel Anderson. Born in England of Australian parents in 1883, she married a British Army officer who became private secretary to three successive governors of New South Wales, as well as to the governor-general Lord Gowrie. When Ethel Anderson died in 1958 the London *Times* described her as 'one of the most beloved of those persons who, by virtue of their position, their breadth of sympathy and their charm of character are vital links between the mother-country and the great southern land in which British virtues are finding new and vigorous embodiment'.[7]

Anderson was also a working writer, with three books of short stories to her credit, as well as essays and poetry. A&R brought out one volume of short stories, the posthumous *The Little Ghosts* (1959), her poetry collection *Sunday at Yarralumla* (1947) and *Adventures in Appleshire* (1944), a collection of essays set in England. Beatrice greatly admired the elegance and grace of her writing and often said she wished A&R had published *At Parramatta* (1956), now Anderson's best-known book. Anderson took her work seriously, though rarely herself. As a straight-faced blurb for *Adventures in Appleshire* she suggested: 'Ethel Anderson's *Adventures in Appleshire* is a Van Tromp of a story, sweeping with a broom all other craft out of the way. I have never ever EVER laughed so much in my life . . .', to be signed by her friend, the poet Hugh McCrae. He was a great admirer of hers, and frequently related Andersonian *bons mots* to Beatrice.

Ethel Anderson was a regular visitor to Angus and Robertson. She approved of Beatrice's editors, particularly Rosemary Dobson, who was the granddaughter of the English poet Austin Dobson. Though everybody in the editorial department was fond of Ethel too, they found her visits on the strenuous side. She was almost completely deaf and refused to wear a hearing aid, so that conversation with her involved bellowing into her old-fashioned ear trumpet, which she usually embellished with a scarf to match whatever dress she was wearing.

Some of Beatrice's literary friendships seem rather surprising – that with Kylie Tennant, for instance. How could the comfortably employed Beatrice relate to an outspoken left-wing author of novels about the underprivileged and dispossessed, an author whose world view had been shaped by the Depression, and who once said she was less interested in emotions than in how people made a living 'because I belong to the generation who couldn't get jobs'?[8] Yet Beatrice often forged friendships with women who were very different from herself, particularly if they were talented writers.

Kylie Tennant had a chequered relationship with Angus and Robertson. Her novel *Tiburon*, which won the Prior Memorial Prize in 1935, was turned down by Walter Cousins on the grounds that it was a first novel and therefore too risky to publish. Tennant then wrote *Foveaux* (1939) about early Sydney, followed by *The Brown Van*, which shared the Prior prize with *The Pea Pickers* in 1941 and was published by A&R under the title *The Battlers* (Beatrice preferred its original title). *The Battlers* was also published in the UK and the US, where its novelty was a selling point (the *Cincinnati Enquirer* called it 'a convincing story of migrant workers on the other side of the earth'). Tennant fell foul of A&R over *Ride on Stranger* (1943), which the publishers withdrew from sale because a local Communist Party official had complained about her careless use of his alias; Tennant was particularly disgusted because A&R paid the man more than £200, and she never really forgave them.

The friendship between Kylie Tennant and Beatrice transcended disputes about defamation and differing attitudes to political issues. Beatrice's upbringing, social position, and literary and musical interests placed her firmly in the conservative camp: it is difficult to believe she was ever a Labor voter. The Depression apparently did not politicise her – it is tempting to believe she never came closer to the proletariat than studying it in Zola's *Germinal* at university – and her interest in Australian politics appears to have been purely professional. For instance, she edited H.V. Evatt's *Rum Rebellion* and *Australian Labour Leader*, and she and 'the Doc' became friends, even lunching during the war at Rainaud's, the restaurant in the basement of the Queen's Club. Beatrice did not judge people according to their political affiliations; she and Kylie Tennant were poles apart politically, but both had a wry appreciation of human foibles and similar taste in literature. They also shared a stoic attitude to life. Tennant had to endure family traumas and, like Beatrice, she was not a person who paraded her troubles before the world. She called Beatrice 'a long-distance woman . . . with a heart that nothing can break' and Beatrice once described her as 'a gem of generosity among women'.[9]

In 1952 Henrietta Drake-Brockman wrote wistfully that she wished Beatrice didn't live so far away; she felt rather friendless now that her friend and fellow West Australian writer Katharine Susannah Prichard had become so 'commo in outlook'.[10] Prichard's fiercely idealistic and total commitment to communism, her tireless work for the Australian Communist Party, was understood by few of her writer friends in Western Australia. She had converted to communism as a result of World War I on the grounds that the capitalist system held the seeds of war, and it informed her work from the beginning. A&R had never been her primary publishers, doing only reprints. In 1943 they put *Coonardoo* (1929), *Working Bullocks* (1926) and *Haxby's Circus* (1930) into their wartime paperback Australian Pocket Library series. Uniquely among Angus and Robertson authors, Prichard preferred her books to appear in cheap editions, even the tacky A&R examples, because she felt they made her work more accessible to the people. But Angus and Robertson was tardy in keeping Prichard's books before the public. She wrote to George Ferguson in 1954 pointing out that *Coonardoo* and *Working Bullocks* were in print in French, German, Czech, Slovak, Hungarian, Rumanian, Polish and Russian editions, as well as selling in Austria, Switzerland and Sweden: everywhere, it seemed, except her own country.

Prichard's principles informed other areas of her life. For many years after World War II she would not have labour-saving devices in her house, refusing to use any luxuries denied to the workers. She was incredulous when told in the 1950s that modern Australian workers had washing machines and vacuum cleaners.[11]

Beatrice was a great admirer of Prichard's work, agreeing with Nettie Palmer's 1930 comment that 'we have in Australia a few real writers and Katharine Prichard is one of them'.[12] When *Coonardoo* and *Working Bullocks* were reprinting as A&R paperbacks, Beatrice, who knew Prichard was often short of money, undertook to try to sell serial and broadcasting rights for them. Prichard was grateful. 'It's good to have encounters and find an *esprit de corps* between us,' she wrote to Beatrice in June 1955. 'I like to think of you as one of my friends now, dear Beatrice.'[13] She regretted that their friendship needed to have elements of the businesslike: 'Our brief encounters have always made me feel that I wished you were just a friend and I didn't have to talk about publishing to you.'[14] And: 'Not mixing my drinks – otherwise business and personal relationships – but love to you,' she wrote on another occasion.[15]

Another author who shared Prichard's and Tennant's concern for social justice was Dymphna Cusack, whom Beatrice probably met while working on *Pioneers on Parade* (1939), the satirical novel Cusack wrote with Miles Franklin. Cusack, who suffered from wretched health for most of her life, had caused something of a stir with her first novel *Jungfrau* (1936), which was published by the *Bulletin* and dealt with women's sexual being and needs. After *Pioneers*, she submitted several novels to A&R without success, though Beatrice admired her talent. 'I feel that writing as easily and naturally as you do, you are apt not to take enough care about the details of writing – the art of,' Beatrice told her gently while sending back *Pillar of Fire*.[16] 'But you have such warmth and spontaneity and feeling for the dramatic that your work is tremendously alive.'

During the war, Dymphna Cusack and the journalist and critic Florence James had moved to Hazelbrook in the Blue Mountains (with Dymphna's niece, Florence's two children, three bantams presented by Miles Franklin, two cats and a goat), where they jointly wrote *Four Winds and a Family* (1947), an illustrated children's book about their life in the mountains. They were already researching a more ambitious project: a 'big' novel set in Sydney during 1944, following the fortunes of a group of women involved in various ways with a beauty salon in the Hotel South-Pacific, a thinly disguised Australia Hotel.

Until then women in war novels had generally been wives, mothers, girlfriends or prostitutes who waited in the shadows while the men got on with the fighting. Nobody, in Australia at least, had yet written about women at home in a city at war; women with jobs, boyfriends, problems to solve and ambitions of their own. The novel took Cusack and James two years to write. Both plotted the story, Cusack dictated it into a tape recorder, James transcribed and edited. They kept Beatrice up to date and Beatrice and Walter Cousins responded with eager encouragement.

In 1947 the manuscript of *Come in Spinner* won the Sydney *Daily Telegraph* competition for the best novel of the year, with a prize of £1000 and the promise of publication in Sydney and London. The authors were jubilant until the *Telegraph* asked them to delete large chunks of their manuscript, excising material about the liquor trade and the hotel industry. Cusack and James reduced their work by about half, to 120 000 words, but the *Telegraph* insisted on further cuts, which the authors refused to make. After a great deal of unpleasant toing and froing, the *Telegraph* handed over the prize money and then offered publication not as a book but as an edited supplement to the *Sunday Telegraph*. Cusack and James said no and the London office pulled out of the deal. Three years after the competition, without ever publicly announcing that *Come in Spinner* had won, the *Telegraph* gave up the novel, which was then left without a publisher.

A sympathetic Beatrice had been following this tortuous saga and she liked the novel very much. 'It is a splendid piece of work, thoroughly convincing and alive,' she wrote to Dymphna Cusack. 'What an amazing eye you have for women's appearances and clothes and how skilfully the bawdy touches just stop at the right spot!'[17] With its vivid detail and feeling for Sydney at war – clothes, slang, interior decoration, songs, uniforms, gambling, horse racing – *Come in Spinner* was as much a slice of social history as it was a novel. Cusack and James no doubt expected Angus and Robertson to move swiftly and make an offer for it. Yet, inexplicably, Beatrice remained silent. Perhaps she was waiting for the novel to be offered to A&R. Finally, and probably because there had already been some publicity about the novel in London, Cusack and James accepted an offer from a British publisher.

Heinemann in the UK and William Morrow in the USA snapped up *Come in Spinner* almost immediately. In January 1951 Heinemann printed a first edition of 24 000 copies – about six times the number A&R would have done – and reprinted four times in its first year. The novel sold more than 100 000 copies in its original hardback edition, was translated into eight languages, went into various paperback editions and is still in print. Under the terms of the (British) Traditional Market Agreement, Cusack and James got a 'colonial' or lesser royalty on copies of the UK edition sold outside Britain, including those sold in Australia. Copies sold in Sydney – a city to which the novel owed its very existence – netted its authors relatively little.

Come in Spinner was eventually published by Angus and Robertson; in 1965 A&R bought the paperback rights for their Pacific Books imprint. Beatrice asked for a further 40 000 words to be taken out because of excessive length; the authors refused, pointing out that Heinemann had seen no need for cuts, and Beatrice capitulated. The novel as originally written – all 250 000 words of it, including material about the hotel industry, the liquor trade and horse racing – was not published until 1988, under the supervision of Florence James (Dymphna Cusack had died in 1981). Ironically, the publisher was Richard Walsh of Angus and Robertson.

At the same time as *Come in Spinner*, Dymphna Cusack was working on another kind of book entirely: she was editing the autobiography of a barmaid she had met in Sydney. She was also acting as the book's agent and she sent an early draft to Beatrice early in 1949. While Beatrice found the material fascinating, she thought the book needed filling out and pulling together, and said A&R would not be interested in publishing it until further work had been done. Dymphna Cusack continued working on it and the book became *Caddie, a Sydney Barmaid: An Autobiography Written by Herself*, with an introduction by Cusack. She did not offer it to A&R again but to Constable in London, who published it in 1953.[18]

It is nothing short of mystifying why Beatrice, as a discerning reader and critic, did not move heaven and earth to publish *Come in Spinner* and *Caddie*. She appears to have felt that it was not A&R's place to solicit manuscripts. 'We could, of course, never approach you because this is just not done,' she told Cusack.[19] Beatrice's preference for literary fiction once more blinded her to market realities: when Cusack offered A&R *Say No to Death* in 1949, Beatrice turned it down on the grounds that it was too slight and commercial. Heinemann did a first print run of 25 000 in 1951 and sold the lot. Beatrice also turned down Cusack's *Pacific Paradise*, a play about nuclear weapons – written just before Nevil Shute's *On the Beach* (1957), which became an international hit – on the grounds that plays didn't sell and that A&R were unwilling to take a risk because Cusack was not one of their authors! The play was published and performed in many countries, including China. 'My national pride nags me that I am not published by an Australian publisher,' wrote Cusack ruefully to Beatrice on 23 December 1956.

Dymphna Cusack must have found Beatrice's commercial obtuseness thoroughly frustrating, but the two women maintained a cordial friendship for many years, mostly by letter. Cusack and her husband Norman Freehill lived abroad from 1949 until 1972, writing and travelling, with occasional visits to Australia. In her flowing, dashing writing – so different from Beatrice's neat, minute hand – Dymphna kept Beatrice up to date with her travels and made sure that A&R were well aware of her successes with other publishers.

Early in 1950 she told Beatrice that she had spent the previous Christmas with Christina Stead and her husband William Blake.[20] Beatrice was envious. 'I would love to know Christina,' she wrote, 'since her work has always fascinated me with its extremely imaginative verve and insight.' Stead's 'wild genius', she said, reminded her of Eve Langley. She confessed to Cusack that A&R had already lost one chance of publishing Stead. In November 1949 Beatrice had heard that Stead, looking for an Australian publisher, had sent a manuscript to A&R. Beatrice had been away at the time, and in her absence the manuscript had been rejected by Colin Roderick. He had sent Stead a rather brusque letter which she considered impudent and which understandably annoyed

her.[21] As soon as she found out what had happened, Beatrice hastily
sent a letter to the New York address Christina Stead gave in *Who's Who*,
apologising and asking to see the manuscript again. The letter was
returned unopened.

Beatrice now asked Cusack whether she would be kind enough to
approach Stead on A&R's behalf, explaining that because of Beatrice's
absence and the problems associated with Walter Cousins's illness and
death, the manuscript had not been properly read, and Angus and
Robertson would be delighted if she would reconsider. Cusack did as she
was asked and in March wrote to Beatrice enclosing Stead's address.
She added that she was sure Stead would be interested in being published
by A&R, but that she was justifiably so angry over the treatment she had
received that the first move would have to come from Beatrice.

It was obviously up to Beatrice to try and mend fences. Yet, surprisingly, she delayed writing to Stead. In September – six months
later – she told Dymphna Cusack that she felt 'absurdly diffident' about
doing so. 'I scarcely know what to say, but I suppose people don't mind
even club-footed letters from their admirers. And I should love to be the
means of bringing Christina Stead to A&R's. I will write.'[22] It wasn't like
Beatrice to behave in this way: perhaps her admiration for Stead's talent
had paralysed her, or perhaps she feared another rejection. But then
again, Beatrice had already shown her reluctance to solicit a manuscript
from any author, however desirable. If she did write to Christina Stead
at this time, nothing came of it. Stead was not published by Angus and
Robertson until 1965, when a hardback edition of *Seven Poor Men of
Sydney* was published.

By the mid-1950s Dymphna Cusack's novels and plays had appeared
in twenty-six countries. The *New Zealand Herald* described her as 'a
trailblazer on the Australian literary scene through her emergence as a
best-selling writer around the world'. In 1957 she offered Beatrice the
Australian rights to *Chinese Women Speak*, her study of women in 'the
new' Communist China based on interviews she had conducted with
women from many strata of Chinese society. This time Beatrice agreed,
after an enthusiastic reader's report, but she said that 30 000 words would
have to be cut. (Beatrice's major criticism of most manuscripts was their

length, though she almost never said anything was too short.) Done, said Dymphna Cusack, and the manuscript was accepted in January 1958.

The editing seems to have progressed smoothly, though there was some confusion about spellings. China was in the process of abandoning the old Wade-Giles system of transcribing Chinese characters and Cusack was struggling with the new phonetic system. *Chinese Women Speak* was published in Sydney and London early in 1958 (it was a British Book Society recommendation for May 1959), and appeared in several European countries and in the US. However, the book was remaindered in Australia after only two years. Either it was before its time or – just as likely – A&R had not publicised it sufficiently.

In October 1959 Dymphna Cusack offered A&R her novel *Picnic Races*, set in rural Australia during the 1954–55 wool boom and described by its author as '*Come in Spinner* set in the country', a line that sounds like a publicist's dream. But A&R's readers did not like it. As Beatrice wrote to the author c/- the Writer's Association in Prague, 'We could have accepted in order to have your name on our list, but how could we, in fairness, do an edition of a mere 3500 to 4000 copies, which is all our sales people think they could sell?'[23] She added that almost everybody felt the flavour of the novel was 'somehow dated' and the structure was too amorphous. Dymphna Cusack took exception to this rather tactlessly worded judgement, but did not argue. She sent the novel to Heinemann, who accepted it. Once again, Dymphna Cusack had found a good deal with a publisher other than Angus and Robertson, and she continued to publish her work overseas.

At the end of 1956 Beatrice met a young writer to whom she became not simply an editor, but a friend and mentor. Thea Astley was a quiet, dark-haired Queenslander in her early twenties when she approached A&R with the manuscript of her first novel, *Girl With a Monkey*. She was fifteen years younger than Beatrice but they found they had much in common: both had studied English and French at university, both played the piano and tried to maintain this skill; Astley, however, had become a teacher (a fate Beatrice was always thankful she escaped).

When Beatrice read Astley's first novel she discovered a mind that chimed with her own. Set in Queensland – as have been most of Astley's novels since – *Girl With a Monkey* shows glimmerings of the sardonic and unsentimental observation of human beings, the gift for describing landscape, the wit and saturnine humour that have become such strong features of Astley's novels and short stories. But Beatrice was particularly thrilled to discover a young writer who, like Hal Porter, was beginning to cast off the old realism, the stock-in-trade of the Australian novel, making allusiveness, rhythm and richness of language at least as important as plot and character. It may not be too much to say that, had Beatrice become a novelist, she would have liked to have Thea Astley's voice.

Beatrice was not alone in recognising Astley's individuality. When *Girl With a Monkey* was published in 1958, she gave a copy to the young American editor Frank Thompson, who had come to Australia with his wife and five-year-old daughter to try his luck in publishing and who worked at A&R for a time (eventually heading north to Brisbane, where under his leadership the University of Queensland Press became a significant literary publisher). He later wrote that *Girl With a Monkey* 'blew my mind', as did Hal Porter's *A Handful of Pennies*, which A&R published in the same year. Other Australian writers whose work Thompson had read were:

> okay and even quite amusing but I had felt (perhaps too smugly) that there were similar American writers who were much better. These two new writers, however, were as exciting as I had read anywhere. These Australians were inferior to no one. They could really write. I read both books twice and even today I can remember the thrill of discovery.[24]

Astley and her husband Jack Gregson lived in Epping, a northern Sydney suburb, so she and Beatrice did the detailed editing face to face.[25] Beatrice never interfered – Astley's devotion to correct grammar and usage was often as fierce as Beatrice's own – but occasionally she had to prune. If Astley presented Beatrice with too many overripe adjectives, the editor would draw a line down the page with a dry 'I don't think so, darling.'[26] Disconcerted though she sometimes was, Astley always considered Beatrice an exemplary editor. She credited Beatrice with teaching her how to develop her own natural strengths as a writer – irony, precise use of descriptive language, spareness and accuracy of observation. A series of novels – *A Descant for Gossips* (1960), *The Well Dressed Explorer* (1962), *The Slow Natives* (1965), *A Boat Load of Home Folk* (1968) and *The Acolyte* (1972) – was published by Angus and Robertson and edited by Beatrice. A&R's general editor promoted Astley's career in other ways: as a forceful member of the Miles Franklin Award committee, she influenced the vote in favour of Astley's work more than once.

Astley saw a lot of Beatrice over the years. The women appreciated each other's sometimes sardonic approach to life, and Beatrice enjoyed Astley's slow, droll way of speaking, which gave an extra edge to her wit. They exchanged news, opinions, literary gossip, and Astley occasionally visited Folly Point.

When Beatrice retired from A&R in 1973 Thea Astley wrote:

From my first meeting with her in 1956 until the present day, Beatrice has been a friend, and better than that – a helpful friend who has the capacity to advise without hurt, to correct without making the author feel ashamed or inadequate. This is a truly rare gift. Beatrice had a way of turning corrections into a joke ('I think we'll have a teeny piece of comma here!') that entirely negated any feelings of inadequacy on the writer's part. Beatrice Davis has taught me more about writing than anyone else. But she has, indirectly, and simply by being Beatrice, taught me as much about living. She is a truly great woman.[27]

The League of Gentlemen

'When I think of Beatrice in the 1950s,' said the poet and journalist Elizabeth Riddell, 'I always visualise her on the arm of a well-preserved older gentleman.'[1] Certainly by the time she was in her forties Beatrice had assembled an impressive coterie of male admirers, some of whom were old enough to be her father. When women friends teased her about this, she shrugged and said she found their attentions a bit of a bore, but judging by the flirtatious deference she showed them and the other ways in which she encouraged them, it is impossible to believe she was completely sincere.

Many were Angus and Robertson authors, some from the time of George Robertson. Ion Idriess called her Beatrice Mia and My Favourite Editor-in-Chief; to her he was Dear Favourite Author, and she sent him small notes for his birthday, kept his publishing record up to date for his admirers, made sure he was given copies of new books on anthropology or history. Former prime minister Billy Hughes, whose two volumes of memoirs Beatrice had edited just after the war, was besotted with her. A gnome of a man – 'a bag of bones in gent's natty suiting' Donald Horne called him – Hughes wore a hearing aid that shrieked and crackled, heralding his appearance. 'Where is she?' he would cry as he lurched up the stairs to the editorial attic. 'Where's the woman I'd leave home for?' Beatrice's staff had been instructed to knock at her door if she had been in her office with a male author for more than a few minutes, and one day they realised that Billy Hughes had been closeted with Beatrice for some time and that some very strange noises were coming from inside. An editor knocked and opened the door, to discover Hughes serenading Beatrice with a plaintive ballad from his Welsh homeland.[2]

An admirer of even longer standing was Frank Clune. A cheerful, round-headed and pugnacious man who wore his silvery hair in a spiky crew cut, Clune was an astute businessman and a very hard worker. One of A&R's most successful writers, he produced about sixty books in thirty-five years, on popular Australian history, travel, autobiography, exploration, biography. All were racy and colloquial, and introduced hundreds of thousands of readers to legendary figures and stories of Australia's past. Not only did Clune produce an impressive number of books, he also wrote articles, radio talks and screenplays. Clune did a great deal to popularise Australian history – and writing was not his primary job, for he also ran his own Sydney accountancy business. His letter-heads ('Clune Accounting Systems Limited, Accountants and Auditors, Managing Director: Frank Clune') featured the words 'Author of' with an ever-lengthening list of books. Though he said he treated his work as merchandise, produced at an economical figure to provide a comfort-able profit margin, he was always complaining – as have some Australian popular writers since – that the literati failed to respect his work.

It seems impossible that all Clune's books could have been written by one man, and in fact they weren't. From the time of his early suc-cesses in the 1930s Clune employed P.R. ('Inky') Stephensen, first as his editor, then as his ghost writer: Clune supplied research material and anecdotes and Stephensen structured the books and put them together. Neither Clune nor Stephensen ever claimed that the result was literature, and Beatrice and her staff agreed with them. For years the editorial department's shorthand description of a dreadful travel manuscript was the (apocryphal) first sentence of Clune's *High-ho to London*, describing his parting with his wife Thelma at Sydney airport: 'Well, it's chocks away, and farewell to Brown Eyes!'

Clune's research often left something to be desired. He involved Angus and Robertson in litigation, once because he libelled a bank and then because he adopted the name of a living person for a character in one of his books. He could also be careless about names and dates. These things never worried him unduly: he assumed that a footnote on the appropriate page in the next edition would solve the problem. Beatrice was always asking him to fix things, requests he usually ignored. But he was very fond of 'Beetruss', often declaring that he was in love with her. She was also fond of him, despite his carelessness, which irritated her considerably; she respected his knowledge and efficiency and was amused by his heavy-footed gallantry. She was also shrewd enough to know that his blokey casualness was partly an act. 'I think Frank is really a nice person,' she wrote to Rohan Rivett, 'at heart kind and generous I believe. I should not be surprised if he were really a sensitive, shy type (don't laugh) who hides under that caricature of the Australian that has become his role.'[3] For a long time Frank Clune looked after Beatrice's financial affairs, and almost every year she hosted a birthday lunch for him at the office, or organised a drinks party when he had yet another book published.

Another authorial friend of long standing was Norman Lindsay. Though not really part of the Lindsay inner circle, Beatrice occasionally visited him and his wife Rose at Springwood, usually with Douglas Stewart and his wife Margaret. Beatrice was closer to Norman's elder brother Percy, whom she had known during her marriage and who occasionally came up to Sackville. Her relationship with Norman had its prickles; he could be very prescriptive about what he saw as her role at A&R and she wrote at least one blunt and damning report about a novel of his, which seriously offended him. Because she knew Douglas Stewart admired Lindsay – and also because Lindsay was important to Angus and Robertson, able to transform a book of poetry from a doubtful proposition to a sure seller by adding a drawing or two – Beatrice was usually circumspect. She admired Lindsay's energy and ability to inspire and vitalise other people, and believed that his talent was in making people realise the possibilities they had within themselves.

Beatrice also had a Lindsay connection through the lyric poet Hugh McCrae, who had known Norman and his brothers from the time they were all young writers and artists in Melbourne. A talented illustrator, McCrae had also been a film actor, poetry editor, writer for radio, journalist and public lecturer. He was, however, best known as a poet, having published his first collection, *Satyrs and Sunlight*, in 1909, and four other volumes by 1939. By the time Beatrice met him, probably during the war, the kind of lyricism he and Lindsay celebrated in their art and poetry – nymphs, satyrs and mythic wood-women grafted onto the Australian landscape – was waning in scope and influence, though McCrae's lyric gift was still admired by some younger poets, including Kenneth Slessor and Douglas Stewart.

Even in his early seventies, when Beatrice knew him – he was born in 1876 – Hugh McCrae looked like Hollywood's idea of an older poet: tall, strikingly handsome with a firm profile, white hair and very blue eyes, rather flamboyant in manner. In an admiring piece published by the Sydney *Daily Telegraph* in May 1949, Ronald McKie called him 'the last of the Bohemians' who, he said, could 'easily be a character from the *Odyssey*, or King of the Fairies or a drinking cobber of Villon' (readers of the *Telegraph* in those days presumably knew who Villon was). McCrae, he wrote, talked and laughed constantly in 'volcanic chuckles', discussed everything from pigtails to poetry and claimed he couldn't count or keep money.[4]

In the interview McCrae said he considered himself a living link between Australia's current literary life and that of the 1860s and 1870s. 'I'm the Lazarus of our dead literature,' he added, 'dug up and restored, then varnished, by R.G. Howarth, George Ferguson and Beatrice Davis.' And indeed, during the 1940s and 1950s, A&R published and promoted his work. His collections *Forests of Pan* and *Voice of the Forest Poems*, edited or arranged and introduced by Guy Howarth, were originally published in 1944 and 1945. Beatrice oversaw their passage through the press and Howarth introduced her to McCrae during this period. But it was over his prose collection *Story-book Only* (1948) that he and Beatrice became friends.

Even though they saw each other often, they established a lengthy correspondence. Letter writing was an art McCrae enjoyed and practised constantly: he was well known for his elaborate epistles, full of jokes and anecdotes, often exquisitely decorated with pen and ink or pencil drawings in the margin. Beatrice's letters tended towards the incisive rather than the whimsical, but she was often tempted to write longer letters than usual, if only for the pleasure of receiving his detailed replies. But she never let her guard down: McCrae, she knew, corresponded with many people, and he could be malicious (Douglas Stewart once observed that 'McCrae would write anything in a letter'.[5]) He busily spread the rumour that she was madly in love with the mystical poet Peter Hopegood, another member of what he called her 'seraglio' of older admirers.

Their relationship settled into a pattern that Beatrice often followed with older men: she played the flirtatious, pretty and practical young woman, McCrae the roguish, adoring and romantic swain. Their letters could be teeth-achingly twee: 'You're a darling thing,' he wrote to her on 24 January 1946, 'and when you say your brain (sometimes) resembles suet pudding, I imagine a beatific feast. Truly, I could gobble you up, every bit . . .' He wrote a great deal of this sort of thing, to which Beatrice replied in an amused and businesslike tone while expressing appreciation for his 'delicious nonsense'. In 1949 she wrote to Henrietta Drake-Brockman that 'Hugh has just been in, laughing gaily and telling completely untrue anecdotes with great zest . . . He is a precious person and I hate to think of a landscape without him flitting on and off it.'[6]

Hugh McCrae's nonsense concealed a darker side; his general *bonhomie* and over-heartiness hid shyness, insecurity and a surprising dread of having to talk to people. Several writers commented on his habit of fleeing to avoid conversation. Ethel Anderson once arranged to meet him at home, but as soon as he saw her he leaped from his rocking chair in the living room and bolted to his bedroom; Anderson said that the sight of the chair, still rocking, was the nearest she came to meeting Hugh McCrae for years. He also suffered from depression, which worsened as he aged. Though he had a loving family of three daughters and eight granddaughters (his marriage had been unsuccessful), he often said he felt very much alone.

Beatrice became aware of McCrae's other side while editing his play *The Ship of Heaven* (1951), and he grew increasingly frank about it. 'I'm lucky to have you and George Ferguson to look after me,' he wrote to her in July 1950, 'especially now that I begin to lose my hold on things. This vile melancholia, like a nightmare-octopus, plays with me . . . One doctor attributes it to high blood pressure, plus old age, plus malnutrition, but I myself from inside knowledge am certain that its origin is emotional.'[7] He was sure, he added, that his seventy-fifth birthday would be his last.

He might have been drawing a long bow for the sake of effect –
McCrae could be a hypochondriac – but there was real anxiety in his
words and Beatrice recognised it. Their relationship gradually shifted.
The 'volcanic chuckles' of his laughter became more subdued and he
ceased to play the part of the gallant, amorous poet, becoming warmer
and more reflective. Beatrice responded with kindness, looked after his
literary interests and cheered him up as much as she could.

Early in 1957 she wrote to Guy Howarth, then professor of English
at the University of Cape Town, asking him to edit a selection of Hugh
McCrae's poetry with a biographical introduction. Having worked on
two previous collections, Howarth was a natural choice, and Beatrice
asked whether he could do it soon, while McCrae was still alive:
'Certainly he is a mere eighty years old,' she added, 'but the dear creature
behaves as if he thinks he ought to be dead and will achieve this goal as
soon as possible . . .'[8] McCrae, she wrote, had become rather pathetic,
refusing to see even her, insisting that he couldn't talk or think, or do
anything much. Howarth agreed immediately, and by March Beatrice
was able to tell McCrae that a proper collection of his poetry was under
way. He replied to his 'dearest and only Beatrice' that he was very grateful to be remembered. The thought of the collection cheered him so
much that when Tom Inglis Moore offered to compile and edit a selection of his letters, McCrae accepted. This annoyed Beatrice, who wished
Guy Howarth were editing the letters as well.

Hugh McCrae died on 17 February 1958, before his collected poems
were published. 'No doubt you have already been told of the sadness of
Hugh McCrae's death,' wrote Beatrice to Guy Howarth.[9] 'Our world will
never be quite the same without him: yet he had so withdrawn from
life and so much wanted to die for at least the last three years that his
death did not come too soon.'

As often happens after the death of a writer, McCrae's reputation
dwindled, not helped by the fact that A&R did not publish Howarth's
edition of *The Best Poems of Hugh McCrae* until 1961. Possibly in
memory of old friendship as much as from her admiration for McCrae's
talent, Beatrice undertook to write to Australia's major universities suggesting the book as a set text for literature courses. The response was

lukewarm, even discouraging. Almost all heads of English departments said that there was not a great deal of interest in Australian literature (this was, after all, 1961), and if they were inclined to set another book of Australian poetry they would choose Slessor or Brennan; in any case a guinea a copy was too much for impoverished university students to pay.

The Letters of Hugh McCrae also had a bumpy publishing history. Despite McCrae's agreement, Beatrice had never wanted Tom Inglis Moore as editor, and she sent her own letters from Hugh McCrae to Guy Howarth, hoping to persuade him to take on the job. Douglas Stewart suggested Robert D. FitzGerald. Inglis Moore was understandably annoyed but Beatrice was adamant: her first preference was Guy Howarth, her second FitzGerald.

Howarth pulled out and FitzGerald edited the letters. While he was sorting and compiling McCrae's correspondence – Beatrice complained to Howarth that 'Fitz' had omitted some of the funniest letters because he had no sense of humour – he joked to Beatrice that her letters (which Howarth had sent back from South Africa) began as love letters and ended as diatribes against 'Anguish and Robbery'. Beatrice thought it might be diplomatic not to publish those that were less than flattering about Angus and Robertson on the grounds that they might offend Lady Cowper, Hugh McCrae's daughter and wife of A&R's then chairman Sir Norman Cowper, and so they were omitted. Angus and Robertson published *The Letters of Hugh McCrae* in 1970. By then the world had moved on, and the book did not sell.

In July 1960 Guy Howarth wrote to Beatrice about her relationship with Hugh McCrae:

> What emerges most clearly from the letters is Hughie's passage from an arch or playful affection to genuine love, as well as gratefulness for the personal kindness you showered on him. You knew him for longer – I mean towards the end of his life – than any others of us, and the reward of the relationship, in Hughie's words, is a really precious thing to have . . . You were his nearest friend to the close.[10]

Though Beatrice usually flirted, not always subtly, with any man who crossed her path – one of her women authors once acidly said that flirtation was a reflex with her – she treated her male authors in slightly different ways, depending on their ages. The older ones she 'bullied and cherished' (as she once told Miles Franklin she did to Dick Jeune), thoughtfully organising their manuscripts, looking after them without fuss. Men her own age were comrades or sometimes mildly exasperating younger brothers.

She did not see a great deal of her own brothers during the 1950s. John was still farming at Narrabri and, though his children came down to Folly Point for holidays, he and his wife rarely left the farm. This suited both John's wife and Beatrice very well, given their opinion of each other. Del had been in the navy and left to run a prosperous stock-feed business in Lismore, northern New South Wales, where he lived with his wife and four children. The brothers had different attitudes to their sister and her circle: John was uncomfortable with Beatrice's literary friends, conscious of the fact that he had left school early and gone out to work on the land, but he was very proud of his sister and her accomplishments.[11] Del was extroverted, witty and amusing, a good person at a party. He had become an accomplished jazz pianist, a talent Beatrice rather deplored. '*Must* you play that awful music, darling?' she would ask plaintively. But Beatrice's guests occasionally felt that Del's music enlivened the atmosphere when literary discussion became too inward-looking or intense. Del teased Beatrice, who would smile indulgently: he was always her little brother.

In July 1956 Beatrice learned that Del had been in a horrific, freakish car accident at Tweed Heads, not far from the border of New South Wales and Queensland. He was the passenger in a car that, travelling too fast, had hit the side railing of a wooden bridge. The railing sheered off and a huge splinter went into the side of his head, taking off his ear and going right through his brain. Del was rushed to hospital in Murwillumbah, then to Brisbane. The splinter had seriously infected his brain and he had to undergo eight major operations.

Fortunately the Brisbane hospital had an international brain surgeon on the staff, whom Beatrice happened to know from her days at the

Medical Journal of Australia. She called him and he told her that the splinter had caused an abscess and that Del was not expected to live – news the hospital had kept from Del's wife Joan. Beatrice ensured that Joan was told, and kept in touch with the hospital. Del was in Brisbane Hospital for twelve months, eight on the critical list. Miraculously, he survived.

When he came out of hospital his memory was seriously impaired. He gradually regained some of his skills, learned to read and write again and to play jazz piano. He and his family left Lismore to live in the Sydney suburb of Mosman, and then north of the city at Soldiers Point, near Port Stephens. Del was never quite the same as before the accident, and after the agonising ordeal of his near-death and recovery Beatrice was even more protective towards her little brother.

At work Beatrice could be bossy to men of her own age. While she appeared deferential to George Ferguson, she was often less respectful to him outside the office, occasionally ticking him off for reading less Australian literature than she felt he should have done. Her other male publishing contemporary, Colin Roderick, she found exasperating, particularly his habit of interrupting her at meetings. 'He would say, "Beatrice, let me finish!"' she told Anthony Barker. 'It used to make me furious.' But at some time she must have given him what he construed as encouragement because he asked her to marry him.[12] She turned him down, and when he did marry later he told her, 'Well, Beatrice, you had your chance.'

The poet and novelist Kenneth Mackenzie, four years her junior, Beatrice treated as an honorary younger brother. By the time she met him, during World War II, he was well known as the author of *The Young Desire It* (1937), a semi-autobiographical and, some thought, scandalous novel about the sexual and social awakening of a fifteen-year-old boy at boarding school. He had also published two collections of poetry, *Our Earth* (1937) and *The Moonlit Doorway* (1944). And a few years later he published *Dead Men Rising* (1951), a novel about the 1944 breakout of Japanese and Italian POWs at Cowra, western New South Wales.

If Hugh McCrae looked like the *boulevardier* poet, the last of the bohemians, Kenneth Mackenzie represented the sensitive thoughtful model. Slight and handsome with long, thin hands, clear blue eyes and fair hair, he was a curious mixture of sensuality and anxiety. Although his eager interest in living made him fun to be with, according to his friend Douglas Stewart his nervous tension meant that he was almost unable to handle the rough and tumble of ordinary existence. 'Wild comedy and wild adventures tended to break out wherever he was,' Stewart once wrote – adventures that could be amorous entanglements but that always involved large quantities of alcohol.[13]

Beatrice came to know Mackenzie through Douglas Stewart, who edited his poetry for A&R (he published his fiction in the UK) and who considered Mackenzie to be a poet of fine talent and promise. When she met him, he was living alone on a small property at Kurrajong at the foot of the Blue Mountains while his estranged wife Kate was in Sydney supporting their two children as a teacher. And while Beatrice probably had a more than platonic relationship with him, they were essentially friends. Mackenzie tended to confide in Beatrice as to a sympathetic elder sister.

He also wrote poetry to her. Once, in gratitude because she had found his fountain pen for him – 'now I have him again, with his extra fine golden nib sniffing up the ink and nosing his way along the paper' – he wrote:

> Would I were Dante to your Beatrice
> for it was she who gave that man his pen
> when all (he thought) was lost . . . Never a kiss
> she spared him, and she did not spare him pain
> As you so often me have; she was chaste
> in his undoing and eventual making
> after he went through hell and Paradise
> in her name and – since his heart was breaking
> at least thrice daily – married a sound wife
> and got without complaint a family
> leading a proper ordinary life
> – rather like me, dear B.[14]

Mackenzie was always short of money, and Beatrice gave him journeyman publishing work – basic editing and writing, preparing jacket copy – and tactfully ensured that he had the tools he needed. Knowing that he had no dictionary, she sent him a copy of the *Concise Oxford* with a manuscript she wanted him to rewrite, on the grounds that A&R followed Oxford style. She looked after his literary welfare in other ways: when his novel *The Refuge* was published by Jonathan Cape in London in 1954, she arranged for him to be paid a full royalty on the copies A&R sold in Australia, rather than the more common 'colonial' royalty. 'It will probably mean that we will be paying a bit more for the books, but it will mean more for you,' she wrote to him.[15] She also arranged for him to write the blurb for the Australian edition, which meant another three guineas for him.

In February 1954 Mackenzie went into hospital for a couple of days and suffered a complete nervous and physical breakdown. After he recovered, rather shakily, he went to Perth to look after his sister and her two children, telling Beatrice he could not possibly leave his sister alone, deserted by her husband. He thereby forfeited a job as a book critic for the *Sydney Morning Herald*, as well as further editorial work for A&R. He had also left his own wife and family in dire straits, and Beatrice advanced them £20 to tide them over.

Mackenzie returned in November to be greeted by two pieces of news: he had been awarded a CLF fellowship and Kate intended to divorce him for failing to support his family. He wrote to Beatrice about both events. 'Being quite unable to sleep, I've been working and reading the nights away, hoping for an hour or two's oblivion after dawn or sunrise and usually getting it . . . it all works quite well but dear me, after the years of being a family man . . . I look at myself with astonishment in the mirror and say, So that's the bloke wot spoiled it all?'[16]

Beatrice replied that she was sorry to hear he had been ill and alone, with nobody to look after him, and she could certainly understand what a shock his wife's news had been. But she wasn't about to encourage him in self-pity, either. The CLF grant, she said, was a wise decision on their part and a great blessing, and when he was strong enough he must plunge into work. Her bracing tone and good advice drew from Mackenzie the comment, 'Beatrice, will you marry me? I promise not to support you.'[17]

Kenneth Mackenzie's poem 'Heat' has the following lines:

Well, this is where I go down to the river
the traveller with me said, and turned aside
out of the burnt road, through the black trees
spiking the slope, and went down, and never
came back into the heat from water's ease
in which he swooned, in cool joy, and died . . .[18]

Early in 1955 he drowned in a creek on a friend's property near Goulburn in southern New South Wales – whether deliberately or in a drunken accident is not known. He was forty-one, and left behind an unfinished novel, some short stories, radio plays and poems. But he left no money, not even enough for his funeral. His estrangement from his family was bitter, and it was Angus and Robertson who paid to bury him. Beatrice took charge, even writing to Sydney's Northern Suburbs Crematorium to arrange disposal of Mackenzie's ashes in accordance with the regulations.[19] A few months later she wrote to Harold White, the head librarian of the then Commonwealth National Library in Canberra, asking the library to buy some of Mackenzie's manuscripts for Kate Mackenzie's sake. Even after Kenneth Mackenzie's death, Beatrice was doing what she could to look after him and his family.

Trying Out a Lover's Voice:
Hal Porter

'Fancy you meeting Hal Porter,' wrote Beatrice to Henrietta Drake-Brockman on 19 September 1949. 'He is an amazing creature, the best teller of anecdotes I have ever met and the most entertaining person.' She did not reveal that her own acquaintance with him was closer than these rather breezy comments implied.

Beatrice probably met Hal Porter in 1947, while he was a teacher at the Sydney private boys' school Knox Grammar and writing in his spare time. She certainly knew him through his short stories: 'And from Madame's' had won first prize in a Sydney Sesquicentenary writing competition in 1938.[1] 'At Aunt Sophia's', chosen by Frank Dalby Davison for the 1943 *Coast to Coast*, had been nominated by *Southerly* as the best story in the collection.

It is not difficult to see why Beatrice was attracted to Hal Porter. He had the sort of look that she liked all her life: tall enough, about five foot eleven, with sandy-blond hair, very blue eyes and a clipped, somewhat military moustache (he dyed his hair and moustache blond as he grew older). In his mid-thirties when they met, he looked rather distinguished altogether, in a slightly overripe, tweedy-masculine way. He was also charming, articulate, had a sophisticated, bitchy wit and was frequently very funny. Most importantly, he was a serious writer in the process of developing an individual voice and style, unwilling to compromise what he wanted to say for the sake of popularity. Beatrice always admired his sense of duty to his craft.

Granny Deloitte and her daughters, 1907.
From left: Mary, Brenda, Emily, Phyllis,
Enid

Charles and Emily Davis with John
and Beatrice, 1909

The photograph of John, Del and Beatrice
that Charles Davis carried in his wallet
throughout World War I

The homecoming of Charles and Emily Davis, 1919. Beatrice proudly holds her
father's arm; to her left is John and standing behind her is Aunt Enid. Del holds
the Australian flag, and a smiling Emily in a large hat stands to his right

At 'Lynton', Neutral Bay, circa 1921. Charles Davis stands in the back row on the far left; Beatrice kneels in front of him. On her left sit Granny and Grandfather Deloitte, the latter with Del on his knee. John (in knickerbocker suit) stands on the far right

Year six, Neutral Bay Primary School, 1920. Beatrice is sitting on the far left in the front row

Frederick Bridges at about the time he
and Beatrice met

Enid Deloitte, 1949

The house at Folly Point, not long after it was built. It was Beatrice's home for more than fifty years

Dick Jeune at the wharves, late 1940s

The house at Sackville

Ernestine Hill in the early 1940s, about the time Beatrice met her

Hal Porter, Eve Langley and the original 'Eb' from *The Pea Pickers* at a Gippsland railway station early in 1957

Eve Langley at about the time she visited Angus and Robertson

Tom (T.A.G.) Hungerford, early 1950s

The poet Peter Hopegood, one of
Beatrice's swains, 1950s

Dick Jeune makes a point at dinner, 1950s. Beatrice is on his right; Margaret and
Douglas Stewart sit opposite

Beatrice with Hugh McCrae, Sydney, 1940s

Miles Franklin in a Sydney street, 1949

Ion Idriess, 1950

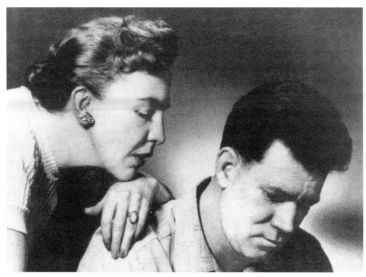

Ruth Park and D'Arcy Niland, early 1950s

Nan McDonald, 1954

Frank Clune, 1940s

Hal Porter, 1959

R.G. Howarth, 1960s

Ivan Southall, circa 1950

Patricia Wrightson, early 1960s

Kylie Tennant and Xavier Herbert, 1960s

Beatrice at Folly Point, 1953

In Beatrice's studio at 221 George Street, early
1960s. From left: George Ferguson, Beatrice,
Alec Bolton, Lyle Blair, Bill Davis

Richard Walsh in the offices of *Oz* magazine, circa 1966

Bookman of the Year, 1977. From left: George Ferguson, Beatrice, National Book
Council president Michael Zifcak

Beatrice in the early 1980s

Some months after their first meeting, Porter joined the Army Education Unit and went to Japan, where for a year or two he taught Australian schoolchildren; thereafter Japan became an important source of inspiration for his novels, plays and stories. He then spent some time in Hobart before returning to Bairnsdale, the Victorian town where he had grown up and where for some years he was the municipal librarian. He was still writing, mainly stories, which were being regularly accepted by the *Bulletin* with the encouragement of the poet and reviewer Ron McCuaig, whom Porter regarded as an early literary mentor. He returned to Beatrice's orbit in 1953 with a sheaf of poems; enough, he said, to make a collection. They were of three main types: 'Australian landscape stuff, fairly outspoken personal stuff (i.e., about persons) and finally some "mental" poetry – you know, ducks, suffering and so on.'[2]

From this point he and Beatrice became much closer; in fact, Porter had decided he was in love with her. From being rather businesslike discussions of future plans, his letters segued into the romantic. Beatrice became 'darling', 'my dearest', 'dear little Beatrice'. On Shire of Bairnsdale writing paper he told her in 1955 that 'You have become the very veins of my bodies – the physical, the mental and, as far as I can judge, the spiritual. All my work from now on is for you . . .'[3] Beatrice was, he said, his muse as well as the woman he loved. 'I think you've turned into an Inspiration.'[4]

Flattered though she no doubt was, there is little evidence that Beatrice took these letters very seriously: her replies, though friendly and warm, were not particularly loverlike. She could see that even Hal Porter's most affectionate, tenderly expressed letters had a studied air. The affection is genuine but they are the work of an actor trying out a lover's voice, placing words carefully for effect, playing Noël Coward to Beatrice's Gertrude Lawrence. Porter's handwriting echoes this self-consciousness. In the early letters his writing is round and loopy, suitable for use on a blackboard, and it steadily evolves into a stylised script that is spikily italic, almost Elizabethan – the writing of someone who intends to have his letters kept for posterity.[5]

Did Beatrice consider Hal Porter more than a friend, more than an occasional flirting companion who shared her sense of wit, perceptive intelligence and liking for good talk and whisky? Were they lovers? It is difficult to say. In 1961 Hal Porter told his biographer Mary Lord that he had never been very interested in a sexual relationship with anyone (he had briefly been married) and that his deepest love had been a young male student in Adelaide. He declared that he needed to live free from strong emotional ties. At the same time he liked people to believe that he and Beatrice enjoyed what he called a 'notable liaison'. After one of Beatrice's parties, when she had gone up to bed, he announced to the remaining guests that he was about to have a bath with his hostess. He sighed and added, 'The things I do for art!'[6] He also spread the rumour that Beatrice was keen to marry him but he had decided against marriage, writing to one friend that 'Ken Slessor thinks it a good idea too but freedom means so much to me that I think not . . . Keeping integrity too may be difficult if one is espoused to the Editor-in-Chief of A&R.'[7] Whether people believed these assertions – Porter was known to be devious – is open to question. He and Beatrice might have had a brief affair, but their relationship was never predominantly physical.

Then and always Beatrice was a staunch champion of Porter's work and did all she could to promote it – as he perceptively commented, she usually had the ability to distinguish between her literary and intellectual judgements and her emotional ones. Early in 1955 he had prepared *The Hexagon*, a collection of forty poems to be published by Lyrebird Writers with CLF support. Angus and Robertson, certainly with some urging from Beatrice, became its publishers. Beatrice, who normally did not consider book design her area of expertise, took a personal interest in the size and shape of the finished book. It was politely received, though Ron McCuaig wrote a negative review in the *Bulletin*. Knowing how grateful Porter had been for his support in the past, Beatrice was furious. Porter was to pay no attention to the article, she wrote angrily: McCuaig was always malicious when he felt someone had a talent greater than his own. He had been just as critical of Douglas Stewart for the same reason, she added.[8]

Beatrice asked Porter to edit the 1957 *Australian Poetry* – not an obvious job for someone who was known as a writer of short stories for the *Bulletin* and who had published only one slim volume of verse.

The resulting book was blisteringly criticised by James McAuley. 'Angus and Robertson really will have to think again about their method of choosing editors for their annual *Australian Poetry*,' he wrote, having a dig at Beatrice or Douglas Stewart.

> This 1957 volume is not the first to have suffered from the appointment of an editor with highly idiosyncratic taste. Mr Hal Porter, to judge from his own work, favours the kind of poetry which is full of bric-a-brac and rococo elaboration, where phrases are quartzed and quincunxed and quizzed into quodlibets of flap-doodle . . . The result is a shocking mess . . .[9]

He further accused Porter of ignoring the work of Judith Wright, Harold Stewart and Vincent Buckley in favour of such lesser lights as Gwen Harwood, Peter Hopegood, Randolph Stow and Bruce Dawe. Porter later described McAuley to Beatrice as nothing but 'a silly little scapular-pinching man'.

More important to Porter than his poetry was his novel *A Handful of Pennies*, based on his experiences as a teacher in Japan. He was enjoying the work, he said, though it was occasionally laborious. 'My eyes are quaite [*sic*] tiny and crimson, but I labour on like one of those dull blokes in *Pilgrim's Progress*,' he wrote to Beatrice.[10] He was not expecting the book to be rapturously received, he said: the main character was homosexual, which would annoy some people, and his comments about the Australian army in Japan could be considered overcritical. But, he said, the novel was highly accessible.

Nan McDonald read the manuscript for A&R. While she agreed with Beatrice, who had also read it, that its brilliance and originality certainly merited publication, she disagreed with Porter's view that the manuscript was easy to read. 'The style is highly polished and finely wrought,' she wrote in an undated reader's report, 'but it is one that is better suited to short stories than to a novel. Over a long course the concentrated richness and the closely packed allusiveness become exhausting. The reader feels he cannot relax for a moment.' In her letter to the author, Beatrice watered this down to a comment that the book was 'brilliant, but a bit too *hard* for the mob', asking Porter to be a little easier on the reader in future.

Nan did the detailed editing on the manuscript, demonstrating the diffidence that occasionally afflicts editors in the presence of highly stylised writers. 'Is "conjole" right?' she asked him. 'I can't find it in our dictionaries. I ask this in humility because your vocabulary gives me an inferiority complex . . . There were three similes I found rather baffling . . . But please don't take the slightest notice of this if you feel they are right, because I'd rather trust your judgment in this matter than my own.'[11]

Because the novel dealt in part with homosexuality, A&R felt they had to handle it with great caution. Porter was asked to delete several tricky passages and to change certain words (substituting 'took' for 'entered', for instance). He graciously agreed to these amendments and the book proceeded towards publication at the usual stately A&R pace, appearing in September 1958. The fuss that Porter had anticipated did not materialise, possibly to his regret. He had recently changed jobs and was living in Shepparton, managing a larger municipal library at an increased salary, and his stories were regularly featured in the *Bulletin* – so often that the Red Page had to run a justification for publishing so many. Porter was riding high; Beatrice was pleased to see him being hailed as a talented new novelist.

Now in his late forties, Porter had a routine. For months he worked hard in provincial Victoria as a librarian, organising branch libraries, producing plays for little theatre groups, being an energetic and efficient member of the local community, while at the same time working equally diligently at whatever writing project engaged him. At such times his life was ascetic and he did not touch alcohol for weeks. But when he had finished his manuscript, or if he felt he needed a break, he took off in search of fun, often coming up to Sydney where he stayed with Beatrice, Kenneth Slessor or other friends.

On these visits he wasted no time in making his presence known. There are many stories of Porter arriving late, drunk and by taxi for dinner at Folly Point, demanding that Beatrice, on her balcony with other guests, throw down her key and let him in. It was not uncommon for someone to visit Beatrice on the morning after a party and find Porter in the living room by himself, drinking whisky, never having gone to bed. Once he telephoned Beatrice's A&R colleague Anthony Barker on Saturday morning at an hour when the sound of the telephone usually brings dread to most people's hearts: 'I'm just about to go to bed,' he said, 'and Beatrice has been nagging me, saying I never get up in time to see you, so I'm making the arrangement now.' Barker went to see him at about midday; Porter looked very spruce after a few hours' sleep, though Beatrice was still in bed. She eventually emerged, immaculately dressed but looking ill and unsteady on her feet (she never admitted to having a hangover). She approached Barker and handed him two small earrings for pierced ears. 'Will you put these in for me?' she asked. [12]

Though Beatrice's staff found Porter amusing and good fun, they also thought he was a bad influence on their boss. Beatrice's liking for a 'teeny piece' of Vat 69 whisky was thoroughly exercised when he was in town. Some resented the way Porter came into her office whenever he felt like it and sat there chatting and smoking as she worked. In exasperation, a junior editor once picked up a snakeskin left in the editorial office by the naturalist Eric Worrall, took it to Beatrice's office and flung it into Porter's lap. He went white with shock and left soon afterwards.

Porter could always rely on Beatrice to forgive him, no matter how badly he behaved. At one celebrated Folly Point party in 1959 her most important guest was Patrick White, who arrived with his partner Manoly Lascaris. White, who had recently won the inaugural Miles Franklin Award for *Voss* and whose *The Aunt's Story* and *The Tree of Man* had made him the most talked about novelist in the country, brought out all Porter's insecurities. Not only had White achieved greater literary success, but he was independently wealthy with an assured social position: Porter came from a modest background and had had to work as an employee all his life. Beatrice was probably unaware of the depth of Porter's jealousy, though she should have realised that anyone who liked being the centre of attention as much as he did was unlikely to welcome the presence of a more successful rival.

Porter and White chatted pleasantly for a while, then White indicated the son of the writer and ABC broadcaster John Thompson, a good-looking young man who was engaged to be married, and asked whether Porter thought this beautiful young man was being married off to prevent him from becoming homosexual. Porter took offence, not at the joke but because White was talking to him as a fellow homosexual – something Porter was not prepared to admit to anybody. He suggested with icy disdain that if White really wanted to know he should ask the young man's mother. It was a definite snub and White was embarrassed and offended; seldom one to give people second chances, he thereafter referred to Porter as 'a detestable man'.[13]

'You should know that my blundering is only that of someone ultimately simple,' wrote Porter to Beatrice – who perhaps chose to believe him – 'and that my love is tediously permanent. I cannot thank you for all you've done for me (I'm not talking about publishing or writers) – I'm fairly safe on the spinning disc of the world, I'm only safe at heart on the pivot – that's you.'[14] On one level he might have meant this, yet he was hardly loyal to her in public. He spread rumours that she had had a long-lasting lesbian relationship with a woman friend who stayed with her at Folly Point for a while; he said that no male author who came to A&R was safe from her. D'Arcy Niland, who once listened to Porter gossiping about Beatrice for some minutes during a dinner party, became so incensed that he stood up, took the much bigger and bulkier Porter firmly by the nose and pulled him out of the room and into a cab outside.

When asked why she spent so much time with Hal Porter when he could be so obnoxious, Beatrice would shrug and say it was because he was fun. In reality, Beatrice had a gift for steadfast friendship and, as she told Xavier Herbert, she never changed her friends. But Porter knew Beatrice well and once told Mary Lord that Beatrice was interested in 'the devil in the basement'. He knew that Beatrice's ladylike exterior hid complex and contradictory elements in herself that she rarely expressed.

As time passed, Beatrice came to regard Porter as a kind of exasperating younger brother, someone to be indulged as well as worried about. 'I feel you may fall among Monsters if you are not careful,' she wrote as he was about to embark on a European trip in 1960. 'I see you rather as a flower girl in Covent Garden than a fastidious passenger driven to grog by the general inanity of shipboard life. Dear old Aunty

Beatrice!'[15] She continued to believe in his talent. Once she wrote to him: 'I can't bear people calling your writing "affected" when I know it is not; I always get furious when they say, "Brilliant, but . . . " '[16]

Porter gave Angus and Robertson his collection of short stories *A Bachelor's Children* which, after minimal editing from Beatrice, was intended for publication in 1960. He went to Europe that year, partly to research a novel, partly to make contacts and to further his career. He left Beatrice with the dedication he intended to add to *A Bachelor's Children*: 'To Beatrice Davis not merely with my personal admiration and deep affection, but also on behalf of those numerous writers – dewy-eyed tyro or hard-bitten professional – to whom she has been a wise guide, a gifted and patient adviser, and a warm-hearted friend.' Before too long, Beatrice would read those words with a fine sense of irony.

Beating the Bibliopolic Babbitts:
Xavier Herbert

When Beatrice joined Angus and Robertson in 1937, one of the up-and-coming writers was a pharmacist-turned-novelist in his late thirties named Francis Xavier Herbert. His novel *Capricornia*, dealing partly with race relations in northern Australia, was creating quite a stir in publishing circles. First published by P.R. Stephensen's Publicist Publishing Co. and winner of a prize in the Sydney sesquicentennial novel competition, it then appeared with A&R in 1938. An immediate success, it was reprinted many times in Australia, published in the UK, where H.G. Wells described it as 'vigorous and distinctive', in the USA and in a clutch of European countries.

Beatrice met Xavier Herbert for the first time early in 1939. He was a bantam rooster of a man with a grating voice, blazing blue eyes and ferociously passionate opinions. Soon after meeting her he announced to Beatrice that he intended to enrich Australian literature, while at the same time declaring that he hated semicolons so much that he had sawed the key off his typewriter. In short, Herbert was a 'character' – not just the 'odd and interesting person' of dictionary definition, but with the added Australian connotation: here was someone who should probably be treated with caution.

Once he had become a successful A&R author, Herbert began to send Walter Cousins long and detailed reports about the progress of his next novel. In January 1940 he wrote:

I can't hurry, I dare not. My present job is not so much to write a novel as to eclipse myself. The fact that I am regarded as an established writer does not mean a thing to me . . . Any fool can fluke a masterpiece and go on turning out imitations of it. I'm no such fool. The great weakness of Australian authors is their lack of sustained power. Who of us has ever turned out more than one masterpiece? None! I am going to do it, or get out![1]

This was not empty boasting. In bombarding poor Walter Cousins with incessant information about his writing techniques, intended wordage, analysis of his own work and occasionally scornful comments about other writers, Herbert was utterly sincere. His commitment to being a writer was wholehearted – he told Cousins he would give up all his bad habits in order to write his book, 'the job of my life'. He stopped smoking and for a while even grew a beard to make himself look more literary.

Cousins, who knew that, apart from his wife Sadie, Herbert had few people with whom he could discuss his work, responded to his remorseless enthusiasm with great kindness. For a while he regularly sent Herbert, who lived in north Queensland, copies of the *Sydney Morning Herald* carefully folded in brown paper, tied with string and labelled. He provided Herbert with white quarto typing paper and once, when the author said the rubber bag holding the ink for his fountain pen had perished, he sent several different types to choose from. But after a while even Cousins wilted under Herbert's barrage. 'You have gone to a great deal of trouble in writing me, which I do appreciate,' Cousins wrote in May 1948, 'but think it quite unnecessary as I always know you are well on the job. However, if you insist on doing these things, I can't stop you.'[2]

But for all Herbert's assurances that he was at the height of his powers, and that no force on earth would stop him producing this great work, etc., A&R had seen nothing. They had been told his novel was called *Soldiers' Women*, but little more than that. 'I sometimes seriously doubt whether any of us will ever see it,' wrote George Ferguson early in 1951 to Archibald Ogden, Herbert's US publisher. 'I am sure that it has

already had too much self-criticism and what it needs now is the critical eye of an experienced editor.'[3]

At this point Beatrice took over the job of extracting Herbert's novel
from him. He was delighted to have a new correspondent, an attractive
woman at that, and immediately began sending her screeds of analysis,
self-criticism and general comments about the art of writing – but no
actual manuscript. Beatrice thanked him politely for giving her so much
information about his methods of working, and regretted that she could
not comment in detail because she had not yet seen a word of his novel.
'Your letter of New Year's Day has indeed convinced me that we must
be patient whether we like it or not,' she wrote. 'But how long, O Lord.'[4]

With her ready appreciation of writers' quirks and respect for
Herbert's dedication, Beatrice warmed to him from the beginning. His
intensity about his work went some way beyond normal writerly ego-
tism, and her reactions display an ironic amusement almost worthy of
Jane Austen. When Herbert announced proudly that he had celebrated
completing a chapter by kicking his landlord, and wrote a little later that
he was having trouble finding a suitable place to live, she told him,
'I hope you will be able to restrain yourself from resorting to tactics
previously used for the landlord.'[5] Her response to his declaration that he
had burned some work without her seeing it was: 'I wish I had been there
to advise you though I don't expect you'd have taken any notice.'

When Herbert finally sent A&R a long chapter later in 1951,
Beatrice was delighted enough to send him a telegram of congratulation.
As far as she could tell, the novel dealt with the lives of a group of women
in the city during World War II, and she said she was impressed by some
of the female characters. She warned him against turning those he disliked into caricatures – a persistent fault in Herbert's writing. 'Bring on
the action and the males!' she invited him. 'Don't overdo the hit and
run style if you can help it; it is vigorous and vivid, but could become
monotonous and tiring to read if you never varied it.'[6]

She warmly supported his application for a Commonwealth Literary
Fund fellowship, assuring the CLF that his novel had reached its final
stages, needing only another year's concentrated work to finish it. She
knew, of course, that she was drawing a long bow, and tried to hurry

Herbert up: 'Some mean minded sceptics even doubt whether you will finish it at all,' she told him. At the same time she astutely described his letter of application to the CLF as 'magnificently temperamental – the man of genius rather than of letters'. He was awarded a fellowship of £200 for a year.

Herbert's lack of curiosity about his fellow human beings was striking. Seldom, if ever, did he ask Beatrice anything about her life or work, or comment on anything she told him that did not deal with his own writing. Beatrice admitted that she was occasionally intimidated by the energy he expended in pursuing his goals. When Herbert announced that, instead of spending his whole time writing, he was chopping wood for a living around Redlynch, near Cairns, she was dismayed: was money so tight? she asked. No, said Herbert, but he liked the balance of manual work and writing.

Just before she left for her first trip overseas in March 1952, Beatrice received part of the third chapter, with Herbert's usual demand for an instant response. Beatrice told him it was difficult to have an overall reaction to a manuscript that arrived in batches: 'I can only . . . ask whether to give more dialogue would be against your religion,' she told him. 'You see these people and scenes so pictorially that they sometimes come across like a silent film.'[7] And with her not around to nag him, she wondered, would he continue to work?

She need not have worried. In July Herbert sent another 70 000 words, which completed the third chapter. 'Mr Herbert says the novel will have thirty-four chapters,' a rather pale-sounding Nan McDonald told George Ferguson. 'They could hardly be on the same scale . . .'[8] Herbert's response was not reassuring. 'I am working as never in my life,' he announced on 29 October in a letter that reached Beatrice on her return to Australia. 'The stuff pours from me . . .' If so, it did not get as far as A&R's office. For the next eighteen months author and editor continued their routine of 'I am working very hard' versus 'Yes, but where *is* it?'

At long last, late in 1955, Xavier Herbert delivered his manuscript. After four years of friendly encouragement and largely humorous nagging, Beatrice must have been relieved to have it all together in one piece. Yet she must also have eyed it with misgiving: it amounted to about a thousand pages and 340 000 words. Then there was the title, not *Soldiers' Women* but the portentous *Of Mars, the Moon and Destiny*.

When Beatrice started to read it, her anxiety hardened into doubt. It wasn't just that the book was far too long to publish profitably: she could see how cutting might be done, though Herbert would almost certainly dislike it. The problem was really the core of the book – Herbert's subject and its treatment. The passionate indignation of his writing, so effective when directed at social and civil wrongs such as the treatment of indigenous Australians, had quite a different flavour when he was dealing with the lives and loves of Sydney women in wartime.

Beatrice acknowledged receipt of the manuscript in a congratulatory telegram and wrote a long letter to Herbert in December 1955, about a month after receiving his manuscript. It was not an easy letter to write: she had to offer praise while at the same time attempting to give a realistic picture of the inherent problems. 'It is a difficult book, Xavier, because it deals almost entirely with sex, yet it is sincere, idealistic and devoid of sensuality,' she wrote.[9] She was also worried about the possibility of prosecution for obscenity. A&R, she said, would do everything possible to make the book successful, but it had to be cut drastically. 'I think you and I shall sort it out without pain on either side,' she assured him.

She should have known better. For an isolated writer like Herbert, who had been worrying at this novel for years and whose exhilaration in putting words on paper had convinced him that the result was a masterpiece, Beatrice's response must have been like a shower of icy water. He was so hurt and depressed that he did not reply immediately, choosing instead to wait for the detailed response Beatrice had promised him.

But she did not reply for three months, procrastinating over a letter she knew would be even more difficult to write than the first. At the same time she had to tell the truth as she saw it, even though her editorial judgement would mean hurting a friend. Honesty won, and she finally wrote:

The spate, the almost frenetic exuberance, the indifference to audience, made me quail at the practical difficulties of publication. Brilliant observation, vivid and vital writing, a passionate hatred of human degradation, an expressed ideal: but too much of everything, the lesson repeated ad nauseam, overwriting and caricature. Frankly, I was appalled by the squalor of your story . . . the sordid drunken scenes, the revolting fornication, made so, of course, by the terrible power of your disgust . . .[10]

She was also unusually frank about the reason for her delay in replying.

Our letters over the years have given me a special attitude to you and your work, an attitude that has made it impossible for me to perform this immediate task with the deliberate judgment and ease I've had to acquire in my normal work. I have enough imagination to be acutely conscious that every manuscript represents a human being, and this makes the job more difficult even when I do not know the authors. With you, it's gone beyond this. I think the emotion, the sense of life and destiny, you have conveyed to me in the writing of your opus has intimidated and embarrassed me – though I am not normally without courage. All I can say now is that I am deeply ashamed at having forsaken you for so long. Certainly I could not let you have Angus & Robertson's verdict (I am not the firm, & could not make a final decision on this myself) until George Ferguson, our publishing director, and other senior people had read the novel too, and until it had been generally discussed, as it has now. But I could have written to you as myself, and shall not forgive myself for not doing so before, even if you can and do.

She wrote him another letter three days later. This time she was Miss Davis, Angus and Robertson's general editor, briskly enumerating the book's problems. She said the manuscript was far too long and could be cut from 340 000 to 120 000 words without difficulty; the brutality of the sexual episodes would shock the average reader; the book could attract prosecution for obscenity. She concluded: 'The power and verve and strength of characterisation are all here, but we feel you have become unaware of audience through absorption in the details of your theme.'

Xavier Herbert reacted as if his muse had suddenly turned on him and bashed him with her lyre. 'How am I to approach you now I find there are two of you, Beatrice my Patroness, who taught me to fear the criticism of none, and Miss Davis the Editress, who presents me with four close-typed pages of tabulated contempt?'[11] He chose to assume that the real Beatrice was the woman who had given him support for so long and that the critical Beatrice was some kind of aberrant being. The real Beatrice had 'plighted her troth' to him over lunch at the Australia Hotel some time before, he said. (Perhaps this was the lunch when, as Beatrice later recalled, he fixed her with an eye glittering like the Ancient Mariner's and talked so long and so intensely about his work that the kitchen had closed before they could order any food.[12]) He hadn't really expected A&R to publish his book, he said; they were nothing but timid traders and money-changers. Above all, he made it very clear that he was not prepared to change a word he had written. 'How my Beatrice would despise me if she . . . heard me agree to deletion of one line of what we have created between us to meet some bibliopolic Babbitt's demands!' he wrote.

After another letter demanding his manuscript back and assuring Beatrice – unnecessarily, one would have thought – that he was 'not commercial in the least', Herbert softened his view slightly. 'I don't think my work is without fault . . .   But with all its faults it is a great piece of work and I think you believe so, Beatrice, though you have been chary of telling me. Can you not tell me now? Can you not come further with me on this great adventure? I would be sad to lose you.'[13]

Herbert's insistence that the real Beatrice was the woman who had showered him with praise and encouragement and that the businesslike adviser was a poisonous changeling left Beatrice with a problem that would give any editor pause. She knew Herbert well enough to under-stand the insecurity behind his hectoring grandiosity. How could she reaffirm her faith in him as a writer – faith he needed and depended upon – while at the same time making him realise that the book he had just spent years writing was almost unpublishable? She tried to steer her way around the problem by emphasising what she saw as her own role, while at the same time playing down her commercial responsibilities. The letter in which she does this is probably the frankest statement Beatrice ever made about the difficulties of carrying out her job while being so closely involved with a manuscript and its author.

> Now Miss D and her associates are banished and I speak as Beatrice, the woman who has that spiritual affinity with the artist, the man of creative purpose; the woman who wants to nurture and cherish selflessly in the truest sense of mothering; the woman I should like to be and perhaps am. Is it enough for me to say that I believe in your sincerity and your talent and your idea, and that if you are satisfied and fulfilled by the work you have achieved, then I am too? . . . I think my official self must have been unconsciously submerged while I knew myself to be involved in your struggle towards the birth. That the finished work should have produced in me such a tormenting conflict was ironic and perhaps inevitable: an awakening to the 'realities' of the commonplace world, a descent into the conventions of a business society. This has made me suffer very much because, unaccustomed to being so divided, I have felt bewildered and uncertain; felt that I was letting you down and myself too – in the cause of 'duty' . . . [W]hile I cannot annihilate the role and the duties and the personality that have resulted from identifying myself with the firm and the job for twenty years, I can still have an inner self that believes with you and collaborates with sincerity and warmth. The situation has no precedent in my experience.[14]

She admitted that the demands he made on her in the role of patroness or partner alarmed her: '[Mine] is often a lonely self that needs sustaining. It does not demand a great deal, and it believes in courage and kindness; it has love and compassion for humanity and admiration for the achievements of the human mind; but it is more apt to accept than to join or lead crusades.' At the same time she thought

A&R should try to find another publisher for the manuscript – though as A&R was by far the biggest trade publisher in the country it's difficult to say which, if any, she had in mind. She even offered to help him explore 'other means of publication', again without giving details.

The unusual intimacy of tone in Beatrice's letters about *Of Mars* – a long way from the lightly ironical, amused manner she had adopted with Herbert earlier in their association – suggests that they became lovers at this point. It is clear that Herbert had amorous feelings towards his editor: according to his biographer Frances de Groen, he included her name in a list of lovers – real or imaginary – he made in a diary of the mid-1950s. Sadie Herbert loathed Beatrice, which implies that she had her suspicions at least. Beatrice told Frances de Groen that she and Herbert went to bed together only once. After they had spent hours at Folly Point drinking and talking, Herbert had followed her into her bedroom, climbed into bed beside her, embraced her and said, 'Gotcha.' He apparently lost interest once he had made his conquest.[15]

Beatrice might have felt able to write so freely to him because she knew that the spectacularly self-absorbed Herbert would be unlikely to judge her or to comment on what she chose to tell him about herself. And he was so wonderfully, bombastically over the top about his emotions in his own letters that perhaps she felt free to respond in kind.

Wanting a second opinion about *Of Mars, the Moon and Destiny*, Herbert showed the manuscript to Kylie Tennant. He told Beatrice that she strongly disliked it, thinking its publication would ruin him. Beatrice was sympathetic, adding she was glad he hadn't taken Tennant's comment too seriously. Meanwhile she worried about Herbert's health. When he told her he was in great pain with rheumatism, she showed his letter to a Macquarie Street specialist she knew who believed, unusually for the 1950s in Sydney, that this kind of pain was often non-physical in origin. He thought the rheumatism was psychosomatic, that Herbert suffered from conflicts based on a sense of guilt, resulting in an unconscious desire for self-punishment. Beatrice relayed this opinion to Herbert, with the qualification that a lot of nonsense was talked about psychiatry, amateur and professional, but that 'self-knowledge must be a good thing if we can ever come by it'. Herbert told her that his rheumatic trouble had been due to an impacted wisdom tooth that had been poisoning him, and that as soon as it had been extracted he put on weight and became so energetic that he bought himself a set of boxing gloves.

Early in January 1957 he wrote an aggressive letter to George Ferguson, saying his health had deteriorated over the period of writing *Of Mars* and because of 'negative dealings' with him and asking for his manuscript back. George Ferguson returned it, no doubt with relief, telling him he was perfectly free to do with it as he liked, but he added that if Herbert decided to divide the work into two novels, or to abridge it in any way, A&R would be happy to discuss it further with him. Herbert then complained to Tom Inglis Moore of the CLF about the treatment he had received from A&R. He accused 'La Davis' of 'silent scheming' to divide the manuscript into two and to publish it as two books (George Ferguson had merely suggested this). He had now decided that as commercial publishers were so mercenary, such 'bibliopolic buzzards', he would try to publish the book himself. Again, nothing came of this, and he seems to have shelved *Of Mars, the Moon and Destiny* for a while.

Herbert had told Beatrice that he had sent several short stories, originally published in the *Australian Journal*, to Walter Cousins some years before; Cousins had put them aside and they were still in A&R's editorial cupboard. The longest was 'Seven Emus' which, at 30 000 words, hardly qualifies as a short story except in Herbert's terms; however, Beatrice said she was sure A&R would be able to publish it. For this story Herbert decided to use unconventional punctuation: a two-dot ellipsis instead of the semicolon (having sawn the key off his typewriter, he presumably needed to find a substitute). Beatrice was very doubtful about this, but agreed to follow his scheme if it really mattered to him. In fact, Beatrice accepted the piece without substantial editing, which encouraged Herbert immensely. Her faith in him, he said, had inspired him to continue. He was already planning an immense novel which he hoped would take in everything he knew about Australia. Early in 1958 he had a title for it: *Poor Fellow My Country*.

A new note was creeping into their correspondence. For the first time

Herbert told Beatrice that he recognised the terrible gap between what he wanted to achieve and his capabilities, and he admitted to a deep sense of failure. 'I've just failed to do what I wanted to do in respect of being a big fellow. I'm only a little fellow . . . I guess I could write only one book, the thing I despise, the old botch of my youth [that is, *Capricornia*].'[16] His life as a human being and a writer, he said, would be worthwhile only if he could produce the work that said everything he wanted to about Australia. Here was the authentic voice of Xavier Herbert the serious and ambitious writer, who had finally gained a measure of self-knowledge in his struggle to write as he wished. In the same letter he acknowledged:

> As you yourself have said, my literary efforts have been voyages of discovery . . . I've only been concerned with the Drama of Life. I see it and feel it very strongly. But I lack the talent to portray it so that my readers will be caught up in it. That's why I have monkied with style. My normal expression is too turgid to be attractive. I've had to fake to attract, it seems. And all fakes fail, of course . . .

If his great work were rejected, he said, he would never write another book, 'nor will I write again to you, except in a tiny business way, because to do so would be too painful. Goodbye, dear Beatrice, and thank you for so much patient endurance of me.' Distressed that he seemed to have lost so much of his confidence, hoping this was only temporary, Beatrice assured him that she would always believe in him and his talent.

When *Seven Emus* was published as a novella in February 1959, it did not find favour. Critics objected to the experimental punctuation (P.R. Stephensen said the book suffered from 'blockage of the colon') and considered Herbert's voice haranguing and ponderous. The book was remaindered within eighteen months of publication. Surprisingly, Herbert was not downhearted. He was very busy, mulling over *Poor Fellow My Country*, working on a novel called *The Little Widow*, which he assured Beatrice she would not like, and revising some short stories. Beatrice, who had been amenable to the style of *Seven Emus*, must have been astonished to be told that he thought its main problem was that he had failed to please his beloved patroness. He had now decided to ditch his 'affected style' and return to a simpler narrative. And the first thing he would do, he said, was to rewrite *Soldiers' Women,* cutting it to about 200 000 words, so that Angus and Robertson could publish it. He concluded with a flourish: 'Surely must I fill the whole frontispiece of that copy of yours' – Beatrice made a practice of asking certain authors, not all, to sign copies of their A&R books – 'with the inscription To Beatrice, my Beloved patroness!'[17]

Beatrice was delighted to hear that he had not only regained his confidence but was determined to revise *Soldiers' Women* (she must also have been relieved that it was no longer to be called *Of Mars, the Moon and Destiny*). She was looking forward, she said, to reading *The Little Widow,* especially if he intended to present it as 'a story and not as a saving-of-the-world pronouncement'.

But when Beatrice did read *The Little Widow* she most emphatically did not like it – Herbert had been right about that – and she wrote to tell him so immediately. Perhaps because Herbert had more or less apologised for ignoring her reservations about the punctuation of *Seven Emus,* Beatrice evidently felt she did not need to mince words; indeed, she was devastatingly blunt. Reading the manuscript, she said, had been hard work. The main character she found an egotistical bore, the account of his motivations unconvincing. Further, Herbert's writing style, with its long sentences and predictable cadences, gave a remoteness, an unreality, to the story. He was also committing his old fault of haranguing the reader. She concluded by asking him to please give the manuscript further thought.[18]

This letter plunged Xavier Herbert right back into despondency. Beatrice's criticism, he said, had convinced him he would have to put the manuscript aside for years. Beatrice then apologised for upsetting him so badly:

I can't bear the thought of this humility and sense of failure in you. You must not be so *absolute.* Surely friends ought to be able to discuss anything at all without such devastating effects. Where has your wonderful confidence gone? . . . You must not make me terrified to talk to you about your work, which means so much to us both . . . Please reassure me by saying that you will start on the revision of *Soldiers' Women* at once. And do me the honour of discussing with me the ways in which you will go about this. You are too much alone in your writing world; and the taking of advice (if you do agree with it) can be a help – it certainly does not mean that you are relying on anyone else or that the book that results will be anything but your own work . . . I know enough of your individuality to know that anything you did would be entirely your own: but no one is infallible and discussion of style and treatment can be stimulating even if it ends in entire disagreement of an amiable kind.[19]

Herbert did remain in contact with her about the progress of *Soldiers' Women*, and by early 1960 the manuscript was ready for editing. Beatrice outlined what she saw as the novel's problems; her main criticisms were overwriting in the descriptive passages, complex sentences that were difficult to read, and intrusion of authorial opinion. Beatrice also attached three pages of editorial comment. Here it is obvious that her professionalism and critical sense overrode her anxiety not to offend Herbert: when it came to the business of detailed editing she was always less concerned with possible bruised feelings – even for someone whose ego was as fragile as Herbert's – than with the business of getting the manuscript as good as possible. Typical comments were: 'You've hypnotised yourself with words here – long-winded and mannered . . . No omelette maker would leave the job even to glance at a newspaper . . . Narrator too much on the stage . . . The anticipation spoils sequence and surprise . . . Don't anticipate.' These pages are among Herbert's papers in the University of Queensland's Fryer Library, and come in a brown manila envelope marked in Herbert's writing 'Beatrice Davis's suggestions for editing S[oldiers']. W[omen] (ignored by F[rancis] X[avier Herbert])'. But he clearly went through them, putting a tick beside almost all Beatrice's comments, which implies that he did at least consider them and more than likely followed most of them.

Herbert was sufficiently grateful for Beatrice's work on the manuscript to propose dedicating *Soldiers' Women* to his 'Beloved Patroness'. Beatrice was embarrassed:

> As a private thing between us [the phrase] has always had for me an affectionate personal, whimsical flavour. But to the general public it would suggest wealth or influence or something inappropriate – particularly when I am in loco publisher. G[eorge] F[erguson] rather raised his eyebrows anyhow pointing out, quite rightly, that publishers or editors should never take credit publicly. Perhaps he would not mind the perfectly plain To BD . . .[20]

In the end Herbert dedicated the book 'To Beatrice Davis', and she told Herbert that her sense of editorial ethics made her feel uncomfortable about even that.

Herbert decided to come to Sydney for the launch. This was symbolically important, he said; he felt he had reached 'the grand climax' of his career. Not having been 'south' for many years, he didn't know what people wore in polite society. He worried whether to bring a dinner jacket. Some of his friends had assured him this wasn't necessary, but, as he told Beatrice, he didn't entirely trust them. He assured her that he did not intend to embarrass her with excessive behaviour. 'I've a feeling you may be a little afraid of that.' And after his trip to Sydney he would return to Redlynch to write what he called 'the last opus', *Poor Fellow My Country*.[21]

But when Herbert came to Sydney he behaved very badly, whether because of shyness, defensiveness or aggression – or perhaps all three. Beatrice found him a room at the Newcastle Hotel in lower George Street, where he slept too little, drank far too much, and picked fights with customers in the bar. He also made a pass at A&R's publicity manager. At the cocktail party Beatrice organised to launch the book, to which she invited a number of other writers, he gave a very long and boring speech. At a Melbourne gathering shortly afterwards he advanced towards the left-wing Jewish writer Judah Waten in a goosestep.[22]

The bad critical reception of *Soldiers' Women*, hard on the heels of Herbert's appalling behaviour, did nothing to diminish his status as a literary celebrity. In 1962 he was invited to the Adelaide Festival of Arts to discuss *Capricornia*, a request that failed to please him. When Rigby's publisher Michael Page made the mistake of saying how much he liked the earlier novel, Herbert snapped, 'Everybody talks to me about that bloody book. Don't they know I've written anything else?'[23] And at a literary gathering at Belair in the Adelaide hills he picked a quarrel with Beatrice, probably on the grounds that he suspected A&R were about to allow *Soldiers' Women* to go out of print. On the same occasion he threw a punch at the Melbourne critic Stephen Murray-Smith. Of course, this sort of behaviour did not bar him from Adelaide or from any other Australian literary festival. Writers' bad behaviour has always been excused – if not actively encouraged – on the grounds that it makes such superb gossip fodder.

Shortly after the Adelaide Festival, Xavier Herbert had yet another fight with A&R. He declared they had taken too long to bring out *Soldiers' Women*, which appeared a year after the final editing had been done, and that he no longer had faith in them as publishers. He there-fore gave his memoir *Disturbing Element* to Cheshire, who brought it out in 1963. If Beatrice felt hurt about his defection, she managed to disguise it. 'I shall not be sorry to relinquish my former editorial role,' she wrote to him, 'though I'd always be glad to help in any way you wish me to.'[24] A&R retrieved Herbert's stories from the days of Walter Cousins, traced some others, and published them all as *Larger Than Life* (1963). Herbert told Beatrice that he did not consider either that book or his memoir to be nearly as important as his 'Maximum Opus': *Poor Fellow My Country*. He worked on it in earnest from about the mid-1960s, while employed part-time as a pharmacist at Atherton District Hospital. 'I've never had such happiness with a book, didn't think it possible,' he wrote.[25]

By now Herbert had struck up a friendship with Hal Porter. Beatrice probably introduced them at the 1962 Adelaide Festival, where all three became drinking companions. In his search for a new audi-ence Herbert quickly and rather naïvely decided that Porter was an ally, a friend, confiding to him in 1963 that 'I still feel very much the bushy-pharmacist who fluked literary eminence'. Herbert admired Porter's writing; Porter's autobiography *The Watcher on the Cast-Iron Balcony* had been published to great acclaim, while *Disturbing Element* had not done nearly as well. The two men shared literary opinions and gossip, including, of course, about Beatrice. Herbert was particularly fascinated by her calm, even under extreme provocation, usually his. 'Have you ever seen her spitting?' he asked Porter. 'I guess not. She has wonderful self-control. I think she smashes things only after one is out of earshot.'[26]

Porter cultivated Herbert, sending him autographed copies of his books and praising his talent. At the same time he was laughing at Herbert behind his back, describing him to Beatrice as 'that poor, sad Xavier' and to other friends as 'quel bloody pathetic bore'. Beatrice took this kind of behaviour from Porter in her stride. She could see similarities between them, as she wrote to Xavier: 'Hal is like you only (as far as I can see) in being dedicated to his writing, and in being completely independent if not isolated from other humans except in detached friendship.'[27] Beatrice understood – none better – how treacherous both men could be.

She and Xavier Herbert continued an occasional friendly correspondence. Late in 1966 he wrote to tell her that he had bought a Land Rover and was thinking of becoming an electrician. Beatrice expressed her admiration; few writers, she said, understood the necessity of having another job for diversion and security. 'You're a very clever boy, really, in your own peculiar way,' she added.[28] He thought he might load up the Land Rover and hawk his wares directly to his public, he said, and perhaps Beatrice could help him. He could dedicate his work to her, calling her the Queen Bee. 'But perhaps what I really meant by it was Queen of the Buzzards. Please don't be offended. If you are a buzzard, you are a very lovely one, a beautiful white buzzard.'[29] Whatever Beatrice's feelings about being compared to a bird of prey – the editor as a vulture feeding off the carcass of literature – she decided to consider it a backhanded compliment. 'I rather like the picture of myself as a white buzzard of kindly mien,' she told him.[30]

Beatrice's friendship, genuine support and enthusiasm for his work were never enough for Xavier Herbert. Late in 1971 he told her that he had made a new friend – Laurie Hergenhan, a reader in English at the University of Queensland (Hergenhan was about forty, Herbert seventy).

Herbert chipped Hergenhan about being 'an akko', or academic, a species of human he declared he detested; Hergenhan did not take offence, which impressed Herbert, as did the fact that Hergenhan had read everything Herbert had written. Herbert quickly nominated Hergenhan as his new patron. 'I'm sure God made him for me, as he did you,' he wrote to Beatrice, saying kindly that he now thought being his patron might be too tough a job for her.[31] Something in him compelled him to reject Beatrice from time to time. As he once confided to Richard Walsh, 'For some reason I have never been able to accept approval or affection of my fellows without a feeling of phoniness.'[32] Before long he was writing to Hergenhan that Beatrice had 'played him for a sucker right from the beginning' and that she was 'a complete cheat'.[33]

Xavier Herbert finished writing *Poor Fellow My Country* at the end of 1973. He had spent nine years on it, though he had mentioned the idea to Beatrice as far back as 1958. Set in northern Australia between 1936 and 1942, the novel explores issues of race, identity and cultural imperialism – all Herbert's obsessions – and he intended it to be the grand summing-up of his life's work. He measured its length as 748 387 words – nearly a quarter of a million words longer than *War and Peace* (in fact, it's more like 900 000 words long) – and it was marketed as the longest novel ever published.

Herbert's new agent, Tim Curnow of Curtis Brown, who was busily sorting out the mess A&R had made of Herbert's royalty payments over the years, advised him to find another publisher. (Beatrice had left the company by then and was working for Thomas Nelson.) Curnow approached William Collins, whose managing director Ken Wilder was energetically steering the company into local publishing. Though Wilder knew of Herbert's reputation as a publisher's nightmare, he was keen to accept *Poor Fellow My Country*. Herbert was pleased too: his contract protected him from any editorial changes or cuts to the manuscript.

Beatrice was not able to tell Herbert how genuinely pleased she was that his novel had finally come to fruition. He quarrelled with her at the beginning of 1974, ostensibly over the fact that she had sent Sadie, who was Jewish, a Christmas card. Her other crime had been to ask, of

Poor Fellow My Country, 'How long is it?' He hated the fact that she typed her letters to him, he told her, and added – more hurtfully – that he had never trusted her as a publisher. Herbert was ill, racked by rheumatism, taking steroids and other drugs that apparently made him more irrational than usual – but Beatrice had helped him as far as she could, and therefore she had to be punished.

A very distressed Beatrice replied on 1 February 1974:

> How could you write me such an unkind, such a spiteful letter? I was truly hurt, and even shocked. I always type letters to my friends; there is no commercial implication; seems sadly to show how little faith you've ever had in me or my long friendship. And surely your bitter stress on the Christmas card impropriety is non-sense. I merely wanted to show Sadie, in the briefest and simplest way, that I'd thought of you both. Really you are a mug, 'Orrible, in spite of your genius, evil or otherwise. I'm naturally panting to see *PFMC* (you must remember I'm an Aust lit addict & devoted to my country's creative writers) but I have no wish to be in any way associated with its publication unless I could help you, which obviously, I can't. So to hell with you, FX, and may even greater fame be yours.

Collins were planning a big launching party for *Poor Fellow My Country*, followed by a black-tie dinner. Herbert told Beatrice he did not want her to attend any of the celebrations: she didn't, which caused a great deal of indignant comment among the literary community.

The publishers stressed the book's size rather than its literary merit (it was known to some of its critics as *Poor Fellow My Reader*) and presented Herbert as a rough-hewn genius. *Poor Fellow My Country* sold out its first run of 14 000 in a fortnight; a month later two-thirds of the second printing – 8000 – had also gone. In 1976, with Beatrice's wholehearted support, it won the Miles Franklin Award. By 1979 the novel had sold almost 70 000 copies in Australia, 30 000 of them in hardback. With Stephen Hawking's *A Brief History of Time*, it may well hold the record for the most unread bestseller in history. *Poor Fellow My Country* desperately needed Beatrice's sympathetic and fearless editorial eye.

Beatrice and Herbert had little to do with each other after that. Now a critically acclaimed author, Herbert became a sort of bush guru, pronouncing from his fastness near Cairns and making occasional visits south, becoming increasingly cantankerous with advancing age. His greatest blow came with the death of Sadie (for whom the adjective 'long-suffering' might have been coined) on 20 September 1979. Beatrice wrote him a sweet and thoughtful note of condolence, to which he did not reply.

Xavier Herbert died in 1984. When Beatrice was first interviewed about him by Frances de Groen, she spoke bitterly about his ingratitude. A little later, and shortly before her own death, she was mellower, recalling Xavier Herbert fondly as a 'dear old boy' who could be both funny and endearing. As Beatrice had once told Herbert, she was more Irish than he was, and she never changed her friends.

No Elves, Dragons or Unicorns: Children's Literature

To most children she knew Beatrice was an exotic creature – smartly dressed, living by herself in a two-storey house; a career woman who worked in an office and who insisted on being called Beatrice, not Auntie Beatrice or Mrs Bridges. She did not encourage children to be spontaneous; when Douglas Stewart's daughter Meg visited Folly Point as a child, she was always on her very best behaviour. She found Beatrice rather cool, not interested in childish concerns, and when Meg showed her an extravagantly praised school project, Beatrice gave it little more than a glance. Yet she was perceptive about presents – once, for her birthday, she gave Meg a tiny gold child's ring set with a turquoise, which Meg loved.

Beatrice was more responsive to children than she sometimes seemed. She enjoyed having her brother John's children, Anne and John, to stay during the Christmas holidays, organising birthday parties for Anne to which she invited the offspring of A&R colleagues. She took Anne and John into the city, to the zoo, and for picnics on the harbour, where Dick Jeune steered into little coves and they would all eat oysters off the rocks. When John was a boarder at a Sydney private school, Beatrice and Dick would take him out (the other boys were impressed by Dick's bald head and tough-guy look). Beatrice was particularly close to her niece. When Anne was small there was talk that Dick and Beatrice might 'adopt' her, at least during the school term. Beatrice, who knew that her brother John was not a great reader, thought Sydney would be more stimulating than Narrabri. Anne's mother refused to consider any such thing.

Though Beatrice occasionally enjoyed the company of children, she was never intuitively connected with them. As far as she was concerned, they could have the so-called magic world of childhood all to themselves. Some children who knew her suspected that she was waiting for them to grow up, to develop a few adult opinions. So it is all the more interesting that in the late 1950s and early 1960s Beatrice played such a key role in the development of Australian children's literature.

The earliest local children's books grafted goblins, elves and small animals from the British Isles onto the Australian landscape. A little later came sunburned copies of English children, until in 1894 Ethel Turner's lively, non-didactic *Seven Little Australians* introduced recognisably Antipodean ones. In 1918 Norman Lindsay's *The Magic Pudding* introduced a very Australian larrikin humour to children's writing, and May Gibbs's *Snugglepot and Cuddlepie* brilliantly transmuted familiar plants and animals of the Australian bush into characters. (Many Australian adults are still unable to look at a mature *Banksia serrata* without thinking of Big Bad Banksia Men.) Before World War II Angus and Robertson published some of the best-known Australian children's books – not just *The Magic Pudding* and May Gibbs's books but Dorothy Wall's *Blinky Bill* (1933), Frank Dalby Davison's *Man-Shy* (1931) and *Children of the Dark People* (1936), and C.J. Dennis's *A Book for Kids* (1921). But despite the quality of much local writing, for many years the children's book section of 89 Castlereagh Street was dominated by books from England and North America. Young readers would move from *Seven Little Australians* to the Canadian *Anne of Green Gables*, from *The Magic Pudding* to Enid Blyton's Famous Five books, or other adventure stories about intrepid British boys and girls. (*Punch* magazine once observed that during World War II English schoolchildren captured more German spies than did British Intelligence.)

From the early 1950s, however, fuelled by increased government spending on education, the growth of libraries in schools and the influence of school librarians, a movement grew in favour of more and better books for Australian children. In 1945 the Children's Book Council was formed in New South Wales and its members, all unpaid volunteers, began holding annual exhibitions of children's books, with the emphasis on Australian titles. They established their own awards in 1946: the first winner of the Children's Book of the Year Award was *The Story of Karrawingi the Emu* by Leslie Rees. Other state children's book councils were formed, amalgamating to form the Australian Children's Book Council in 1959.

As A&R's general editor Beatrice kept an eye on all this, though she was not the company's primary editor of children's fiction. Ella McFadyen, a children's writer who had strong opinions about suitable reading material for young persons, evaluated most of the manuscripts that came into the office. (Describing a murder story in which ants were injected with poison so that their bite would be lethal, she wrote: 'Very fiddly job, injecting ants.') Until the early 1950s, acceptable children's manuscripts were generally prepared for the press by Rosemary Dobson.

In 1951 or early 1952 Joan Phipson, a former schoolmate of Rosemary Dobson's at Frensham, sent A&R a novel for children about a twelve-year-old country girl and a recalcitrant brumby foal. Phipson later said she wrote *Good Luck to the Rider* 'simply to please the child I used to be', and in 1953 it was co-winner of the Children's Book of the Year Award, sharing the prize with a 'boys' book' about aeroplanes. Joan Phipson's writing had an unselfconsciously Australian flavour, her early books reflecting the cheerful rural prosperity of 1950s Australia, though later her work grew darker and more complex. Many of her books have been translated into other languages and several have won prizes, including in 1963 a second Children's Book of the Year Award for *The Family Conspiracy*, also published by Angus and Robertson.

Beatrice was never Joan Phipson's primary editor, and at first Phipson was in awe of her because of her reputation and her patrician manner. But they soon became friends and Beatrice occasionally stayed with Phipson and her husband Colin Fitzhardinge on their property at Mandurama, New South Wales. Once Beatrice was horrified to discover that Phipson did not have *Brewer's Dictionary of Phrase and Fable* and as soon as she returned to Sydney she sent her a copy.

In 1954 A&R received a manuscript from a young writer who lived in the Clarence River region of New South Wales. It was the story of a group of country children who form a secret society and become involved in looking after the local wildlife, and it languished in the unsolicited manuscripts cupboard for more than six months. The author finally wrote a very polite letter to 'The Editor':'With regard to my manuscript *The Crooked Snake* . . . what page are you up to now? Yours faithfully, Patricia Wrightson.'[1]

The letter landed on Beatrice's desk. It made her laugh and she pulled the manuscript out of the cupboard. As soon as she started reading it she could tell that the author knew what she was doing. She liked the story and the characters and before long wrote to Patricia Wrightson that A&R were interested in publishing the book – receiving 'a yell of delight' by return post.[2] Beatrice decided that at 60 000 words *The Crooked Snake* was too long and suggested it be reduced to 40 000. Wrightson argued that cutting it by one-third would destroy whatever life and colour the book possessed. Beatrice responded that it didn't need large slabs cut, just an overall trim. She gave few clues about how this could be done and Wrightson obeyed, though it hurt, taking out one chapter and deleting a word here, a sentence there. She sent the manuscript back to A&R and this time Beatrice accepted it.

The editing process began. Beatrice did the overall editing, handed the manuscript to a member of her staff for the detailed work, and oversaw the result. She took a much more hands-on approach to *The Crooked Snake* than she did with many A&R manuscripts, perhaps because she knew that here she had a young writer of real promise. Wrightson was raw, defensive, full of passionate and unexpressed certainties, intense about her own work; Beatrice reacted with calm and sympathetic logic. As Wrightson later wrote, Beatrice 'recognised a safety valve when it blew, and knew how to release the pressure in a fair and logical way'.[3]

Sometimes author and editor were colleagues at work on a joint project, sometimes they were student and teacher. Beatrice refused to be argued with, bringing the big guns of grammar to bear. 'Fowler says this, and we agree,' she might write, but she also knew how to disarm criticism. 'Yes, we made a mistake.' However, when she saw that Wrightson was adamant about something, she accepted it.

Even so, when Patricia Wrightson saw her galleys she was appalled. A&R's line editor had attacked her text with a brick, she thought, imposing a great many irritating and unnecessary corrections. Very close to the end she saw that a particular passage 'intended to suggest flurry had been tidied up into stodge' and she exploded 'in sheets of burning prose'. Beatrice agreed that the text had been overedited and promised that in future Wrightson would see all edited copy before it was typeset. This concession shows Beatrice's commitment to Patricia Wrightson's development as a writer.

Beatrice professed to know very little about children's literature, but she never believed that a book for children was worth less attention than an adult novel. The important thing was that it be well written. Throughout the editing process she gently encouraged Wrightson to express herself as simply and directly as possible, with no unnecessary adverbs or stylistic tricks, tearing off what Wrightson called 'the crepe-paper frills of schoolroom style'. It was fine, wrote Beatrice, to use 'said' repeatedly, instead of an alternative such as 'smiled', on the grounds that 'you can't smile dialogue'.[4] With illustrations by Margaret Horder, already Australia's best-known children's illustrator, *The Crooked Snake* won the 1956 Children's Book of the Year Award. The judges praised it as 'a really worthwhile story about really normal children . . . characters of children and adults are swiftly and vividly outlined'.

Now Patricia Wrightson began to push the limits of writing for children, to go for more than storytelling, to look below surface realities. Her second novel, *The Bunyip Hole*, was the story of a child who has to come to terms with fear and the possible consequences of cowardice. She felt unsure about the theme: was it too 'heavy' for eleven-year-olds? Was seeing the story through the eyes of one character alone too difficult, even too adult?

Wrightson worried over this for some time and decided to ask Beatrice for her opinion. During a trip to Sydney she called in to

89 Castlereagh Street with her manuscript. Beatrice received her warmly and promised to read *The Bunyip Hole* as soon as possible, but her smile slipped when Wrightson begged her to read it then and there, while she waited. No editor is happy to read a manuscript with the author present (it can of course also be torture for the author) and at first Beatrice refused. But so insistent was Wrightson – she had come so far, she was so anxious to hear what Beatrice thought – that eventually the editor relented.

Beatrice read the manuscript calmly, well aware that on the other side of her desk sat a young author so tense she was almost vibrating. When she had finished, Patricia Wrightson asked her, 'Is a story based on a character study suitable for children?' It was a question Beatrice had never been asked before, and the fact that it needed to be asked shows how undeveloped was Australian children's literature in 1957. Beatrice considered it seriously for a few moments and replied that, yes, this approach was suitable, provided it did not get in the way of the story. Characterisation was important, though secondary.

Wrightson's third novel, *The Rocks of Honey* (1960), dealt with an Aboriginal boy and his problems in coming to terms with white Australia, a provocative theme for a children's book of the time. The core of the story was a chapter entitled 'The Stone Axe', and Wrightson asked Beatrice whether someone who knew and cared about Aboriginal lore and culture would be willing to read it, perhaps a field anthropologist such as Professor A.P. Elkin. Beatrice agreed and in due course returned the manuscript with Elkin's comments. As Wrightson later pointed out, at the end of the 1950s the idea of having an eminent anthropologist check a children's book was unheard of. She 'had only hoped for someone to whom the Koori were real people.'[5]

In such books as *The Nargun and the Stars* (1973), *The Ice is Coming* (1977), *The Dark Bright Water* (1978) and *Behind the Wind* (1981), Patricia Wrightson took elements of Aboriginal folklore and wove them into distinctively Australian fantasies.[6] In a note to *An Older Kind of Magic* (1972) she wrote: 'It is time we stopped trying to see elves and dragons and unicorns in Australia. They have never belonged here, and no ingenuity can make them real. We need to look for another kind of magic, a kind that must have been shaped by the land itself at the edge of Australian vision.' It was this search, this expression of an older kind of magic, that now permeated her work and she has credited Beatrice, her first editor, with being the first to understand what she was trying to do, to give her the freedom to explore what was possible. 'How could a new writer fail to develop, when handled in that way?' she asked.[7]

In late 1953 Beatrice made one of her periodic trips to Melbourne to visit friends and meet Angus and Robertson authors whom she had previously known only on paper. One was a tall, slim and diffident man in his early thirties named Ivan Southall. He had started his writing career at sixteen, selling articles and short stories to Australian newspapers and magazines. 'I don't remember growing up,' he wrote many years later, 'because our little world collapsed when my father died when I was fourteen and I seem to have been working seven days a week from that moment to this.'[8] In August 1948 he had offered Walter Cousins the first in a series of adventure stories about a dashing flying ace named Simon Black, based on Southall's own experiences in the RAAF during World War II (Southall had been awarded the Distinguished Flying Cross at the age of twenty-three). *Meet Simon Black*, its author said, was 'for ages of ten years and up to whatever age the male ceases to be a boy, if ever'.[9] The novel was given an enthusiastic report by George Ferguson's twelve-year-old son John; it was published in 1949 and did well. Southall wrote nine Simon Black books between 1949 and 1961. They were published in London, translated into French (where *Simon Black in Coastal Command* became *Allô Contrôle, Ici Radar*), Swedish, Norwegian and Dutch, and adapted for radio in several countries.

Ivan Southall's first A&R editor was Alec Bolton, with whom he established a warm rapport, but from 1953 Bolton was working mainly on A&R's massive *Australian Encyclopedia* (described in the following chapter) and Beatrice took over. At the time of her visit to Melbourne Southall was living in Monbulk, east of Melbourne across the Dandenongs, with his wife Joy and two small children, making a precarious living as a freelance writer. Beatrice had written asking him to meet her in South Yarra late in the afternoon which, because Southall had no car, meant twelve kilometres by bus, an hour's train journey to Melbourne and a ride in a tram. When he arrived at South Yarra after travelling for most of the day, Southall, who was a shy man and who had thought his meeting with Beatrice would be a private one, was horrified to find her more or less holding court, surrounded by strangers, all of whom seemed cleverer, more articulate and much more sophisticated than he was.[10] Disappointed, he arrived home very early the following morning, having missed the last bus from Ferntree Gully and walked the twelve kilometres home along country roads almost in his sleep.

After this shaky start his association with Beatrice blossomed, and for the next few years she monitored the sales of the Simon Black books. On his behalf she nagged the ABC, who were getting cold feet about broadcasting *Simon Black in Coastal Command* as a radio serial on their *Children's Session* because, they said, it was too violent: later they changed their minds. A heavy smoker herself, Beatrice sympathised with (though never shared) Southall's heroic struggle to give up tobacco. When Southall was approached to write some air force stories for rival publishers Horwitz, he asked Beatrice for permission, saying that the extra money would be useful. Beatrice, unaware that the Southall family were in dire financial straits, with tax problems and a recently born daughter who was seriously retarded, replied coldly that if he needed the money so badly she supposed A&R couldn't stop him. However, when Southall told her he might have to sell the farm, she reacted with sympathy and practical kindness. She immediately asked whether he was being well advised about his tax, suggested he approach John Appleton of the ABC *Children's Session* for possible scriptwriting work, and offered a £300 advance, which Southall accepted. (He solved the most pressing of his financial problems by selling the farm and taking a War Service loan to build a new home.) 'Thanks once again for everything,' he wrote to Beatrice in April 1956. 'You're a pal.'[11] For Beatrice, Ivan Southall seems to have come into the category of younger brother: certainly he felt she considered him a young man in need of care, protection and guidance.[12]

By the early 1960s Southall was doing well with his 'boys' books' about aviation – not just the Simon Black titles, but a history of aviation and another juvenile series of air force stories. He also produced general non-fiction for adults, including a history of his RAAF squadron called *They Shall Not Pass Unseen* (1956); a biography of a World War I ace, *Bluey Truscott* (1958); *Softly Tread the Brave* (1960), about the work of mine disposal officers, and a series called 'War in the Air' (1958–60). But despite his satisfaction in becoming a successful professional writer, Southall was restless. He wanted to extend his range, and the idea of a new kind of book for children kept nagging at him.

In 1961 he began *Hills End*, a short novel about seven children who must deal with a cyclone that destroys half their town, having to survive and keep things going without any adult help. This kind of kids-alone-battling-the-odds story has since become the stock-in-trade of many writers, but in 1961 the idea of children facing a hostile environment by themselves, trying to solve life-threatening problems without a reassuringly happy ending on the horizon, was new in Australian children's fiction. *Hills End* also explored the question Patricia Wrightson had asked Beatrice: 'Is a story based on a character study suitable for children?' The children of *Hills End* were presented as individuals who used their strengths in order to survive.

Hills End took Ivan Southall only about eight weeks to write, and Beatrice edited it lightly. Published early in 1962, it was immediately successful: 'A solid work, strong in action, mood and description', according to the *New York Times Book Review*. It sold in the UK, was nominated a Notable Book by the American Library Association, was published in France, Holland, Norway, Sweden, Belgium and Malaysia. When German translation rights were sold, Southall commented, 'This is something I never imagined while I flogged the Atlantic looking for their beastly U-boats.'[13] *Hills End* put Ivan Southall firmly on the map as a writer of complex, well-crafted books for children, and Simon Black was able to step out of the cockpit.

In 1963 Angus and Robertson employed Joyce Saxby as their children's books editor – making her the first full-time children's books editor in Australia – but because Beatrice had worked with Southall for so long, she continued to edit his books.[14] After the success of *Hills End*, Beatrice told Southall she was looking forward to his next manuscript, and indeed Southall was optimistic about *Crisis at Crowville*, which he thought might even have adult appeal.

Beatrice not only did not like the novel but wrote Southall a letter that shows her at her toughest. She said that she and two other A&R readers had found the adults tedious, the children marginal and the jokes unfunny, and the novel had too little action and too much dialogue. 'This outright rejection does seem terrible and I am so sorry Ivan; but I am sure we are right and that to publish *C at C* would only harm your reputation,' she told him.[15] She judged, correctly, that Southall was enough of a professional to take this devastating criticism. He called it a 'crushing judgment' and insisted that every incident portrayed in the novel was true and that he knew the characters. 'But,' he added, 'you don't know them – so the book means nothing. Therein is its failure . . . There must be lessons I can learn from it, though not yet.'[16] He was depressed: what if *Hills End* had been just a flash in the pan? Maybe he was kidding himself, he wrote; perhaps years of writing non-fiction had corroded his style and he was nothing more than 'the modest hack I once believed myself to be'.

Southall sat down at his desk and tried again. Before long he sent Beatrice five chapters of a new novel for teenagers. Beatrice's response, though gentler, was essentially the same as before: he was looking at things from an adult point of view, not letting the children in the story take leading roles. Further, he was 'chuckling on the sidelines', enjoying his own humour too much.[17] Southall did not waste any time in being offended: Beatrice's comments, he wrote, had been pretty much what he expected and he agreed with many of her criticisms. What disturbed him was his own level of self-delusion. He hadn't seen that he was writing from an adult point of view. He thought he had got out of touch, and wondered whether perhaps he didn't know how to write books for children any more.

He told Beatrice he would give it one more try. He was developing another book for teenagers, which was coming along very slowly. If this failed, he said, he would abandon all thought of writing juvenile fiction and concentrate on turning out tradesmanlike documentary books. For the rest of 1964 he worked on this novel, sending Beatrice worried bulletins from time to time. He thought it was tense and tight; his wife Joy said it was terrific; he was happy with the way it was going; he really didn't know whether it was worth anything. Finally, on 23 January 1965, he sent Beatrice the manuscript 'with prayerful HOPES' and was sufficiently worried about it to write to her four hours later with a minor correction. He called the novel *Ash Road*.

Like *Hills End*, *Ash Road* pits a group of children against ferocious odds, having to survive without adult help, but this time the agent of destruction is not a natural disaster but an accidentally started bushfire. Nan McDonald, A&R's first reader, found it grimmer than its predecessor, which worried her slightly. 'The characters of the children are well drawn, but seem less vivid than those in *Hills End*, probably because the crisis here is of a more active and developing kind, the terror and drama of the fire inevitably take the centre of the stage and overshadow human personalities.' But she thought it must be published: 'I doubt if there is a more memorable bushfire in Australian literature, and this alone should make the book a classic.'[18]

A delighted Beatrice agreed and, knowing what acceptance would mean to Southall, sent him a telegram on 3 February: 'CONGRATULATIONS ASH ROAD SPLENDID WORK WRITING BEATRICE'. She got an immediate response: 'HALLELUJAH IVAN'.

But Beatrice had a niggling doubt about the book's grimness and asked Kath Commins, reviewer of children's books for the *Sydney Morning Herald*, for an opinion. Commins's response is interesting as a 1960s contribution to the continuing debate about proper reading matter for children. 'I know that Southall was criticised by the judges of the Book of the Year for the "agonising pitch" of the suspense engendered in *Hills End*,' wrote Commins. 'I didn't agree.'[19] She liked *Ash Road* for its realism, pointing out that from their earliest years children live on familiar terms with fear and anxiety, and bushfires are part of Australian bush life. 'I think we adults reading children's books need to remember, constantly, that we are very remote from today's children,' she added. 'I think the children of today would take the disaster at *Ash Road* in their stride while reading about it.' Her only criticism was that the novel was 'a bit moralistic' but this could be fixed at the editing stage. Beatrice agreed.

Mainly because of cataclysmic changes to A&R (described in 'Bringing the Pirates on Board'), Beatrice did not edit *Ash Road*, and in succeeding years her editorial relationship with Ivan Southall became more remote. He remained an A&R author for a long time. For *Ash Road*, which was published in twenty countries between 1965 and 1990, he won the first of his four Children's Book of the Year Awards, while with *Josh* (1971) he became the first children's writer outside the UK to be awarded the British Library Association's Carnegie Medal.

But before all that happened, and after the first success of *Ash Road*, Southall wrote to Beatrice: 'I have hopes that rather than having entered my "prime" I may only be just beginning and that everything else has been part of the apprenticeship. Even the two or three horrible failures that A&R has seen fit to turn away have been very valuable – even if costly – experience.'[20] Ivan Southall always credited Beatrice with teaching him lessons about writing that he needed to learn.[21]

Plain Sailing: Angus and Robertson During the 1950s

In 1959 Beatrice reached two milestones: she turned fifty and she celebrated twenty-two years as general editor for Angus and Robertson. There is no reason to believe she made an issue of either of these anniversaries. If she mourned her lost youth she did not say so: hers was not a generation that worshipped youth. The way women dressed – stiff skirts, hair permed into rigid waves, little hats, gloves, elaborate makeup, seamed stockings, high-heeled shoes – made them look older than they do now. Long hair, jeans, sandals, psychedelic fabrics – the clothes of a generation at play – were about to become fashionable, but not quite yet.

Beatrice often referred to her 'advanced age', perhaps because she started to go grey when she was quite young. When in 1950 Rohan Rivett had asked for permission to abandon 'Miss Davis', Beatrice replied, 'Yes, please do call me Beatrice in spite of my advancing years. It makes me feel younger.'[1] She was almost forty-two. As with many elegant women, the look she chose in her youth she maintained all her life. Being small and slim, she favoured neat prints over splashy designs; her hemlines were no shorter than knee length, and she generally wore straight or slightly flared skirts, classic suits with short fitted jackets, collared dresses with narrow belts, discreet earrings and small brooches. Because she was vain about her legs and wanted to look taller, she usually wore very high heels.

By the late 1950s Beatrice's air of authority also made her seem older than she was. She was being called the *grande dame* of Australian publishing – not a title given to a young person. Her position as A&R's literary powerbroker made some writers wary of her, including Geoffrey Dutton, who met her for the first time in the late 1950s.[2] Douglas Stewart had told him that Beatrice could be fierce and abrupt if she wished, but that it was mostly an act. This bluntness became more pronounced as Beatrice got older, particularly after a couple of whiskies.

Like most prominent people who don't much care about popular opinion, Beatrice was a target for gossip, mainly about her sex life. She didn't altogether discourage speculation, once announcing at a party, 'All I need is ten lovers and a good bottle of whisky!' Everybody knew about Dick Jeune; not many were aware that the weekends she didn't go to Sackville she often spent with Geoffrey Burgoyne, a journalist and writer of about Jeune's age who was also a friend of Henrietta Drake-Brockman's. Beatrice was careful to ensure that Jeune and Burgoyne seldom met: they knew about each other and were jealous. There were other lovers. Her attitude was 'It's only sex, darling, just a bit of fun.'

The rumours about Beatrice were predictable. She was supposed to be sexually voracious, a real man-eater. (According to Geoffrey Dutton, when Patrick White heard she had edited *Soldiers' Women*, White sniffed, 'She's probably one of them.') It was said that no male writer would be published by A&R unless he slept with her, and that it was never safe to be alone with her – an interesting thought considering the dimensions of Beatrice's office. She was supposed to have been George Ferguson's mistress for many years. There were stories that she was bisexual: several incidents are claimed, rather tenuously, to support this view. In the ladies' room during the Adelaide Festival in 1960 she fingered a brooch that the wife of a young poet was wearing on her blouse, saying it was similar to one she owned; after a few drinks she flung her arm around a girl's shoulders in the back of a cab; Hal Porter claimed that a woman friend who stayed at Folly Point for some months was Beatrice's lover.

It's almost impossible to sort fact from fiction here. Some people who knew Beatrice well have said that nothing she did would surprise them;

others are horrified, distressed or amused about the stories, particularly the rumours of lesbian relationships. Close to the end of her life Beatrice said to Anthony Barker, 'I feel dreadful . . . I do hope I haven't got AIDS. But then I haven't had homosexual sex for some years now.'[3] This startling statement was probably ironic: it sounds like her kind of tease. Like many women of her class and generation, she expressed a dismissive tolerance for homosexual men; while she was emotionally closer to women than to men, this closeness was not necessarily sexual.

Rumours about Beatrice's sex life, like most gossip, reveal more about those telling the stories than they do about her. A single, highly intelligent and attractive woman whose job gave her power over the literary destinies of men was bound to make a fair proportion of them feel insecure, particularly if they had tried to flirt with her and she had rebuffed them. Beatrice often made no attempt to pander to the male ego, rather the reverse. 'Leslie,' she once told the theatre historian and children's writer Leslie Rees during a party, 'you can't write. You *know* you can't.'[4] Another reason for the hostile rumours is simple: Beatrice kept to her own rules and standards. She made no secret of the fact that she was strongly sensual and enjoyed sex, but she had a code of honour. She kept that part of her life private, didn't gossip or go into details about it. In short, Beatrice was a gentleman.

By today's standards the editorial department Beatrice controlled in the 1950s was uncommercial to the point of perversity. A&R's aim was to publish as many books as possible about Australia and by Australian authors. Ensuring that these books came out at the optimum times for sales – for Christmas or Mother's Day, for example – was not considered important. Books were published only after they had been through the editorial and production processes, and no editor was ever castigated for spending too much time on a manuscript. Print runs were often decided by a combination of caution and race memory, and occasionally the printers at Halstead were asked to give an estimate. This was less lunatic than it sounds; some had been there for more than forty years, and their estimates, based on knowledge of previous publications, were often at least as accurate as the calculations of today's publishing bean counters.

Beatrice never thought popular taste an important indicator of good publishing, a view sometimes shared by A&R's management. In 1952 A&R published *Alien Son* by Judah Waten, a collection of linked, semi-autobiographical stories about a Jewish migrant family in Western Australia during World War I, and one of the first significant pieces of fiction about the Australian migrant experience. A&R published 2000 copies with CLF support; readers recognised the vitality and freshness of the material and the book sold out quickly. But George Ferguson decided not to reprint on the grounds that doing a small quantity – say a thousand – was 'not economically viable', and A&R did not wish to publish any more than that. It was easier to let the book go out of print. Waten's politics might have been a consideration too: he belonged to the Communist Party at a time when echoes of US paranoia were drifting over to Australia and when the Menzies government had already attempted to introduce anti-communist measures.

Beatrice agreed with Ferguson's decision, on slightly different grounds; while she recognised Waten's ability, she said she found his work depressing. But the CLF were appalled. For God's sake, they said, keep *Alien Son* in print, and if more money was needed, the CLF would willingly supply it. Angus and Robertson reprinted. This must be the only time in Australian literary history that a government-sponsored body, and a conservative one at that, has gone against a publisher's decision and insisted on subsidising a book by an author whose political views they opposed.

The book that Beatrice most famously turned down for Angus and Robertson also dealt with the migrant experience, though in different terms. In late 1956 a young boy brought into the office the manuscript of a novel by his father, a former pharmacist named John O'Grady, and gave it to Colin Roderick, who had edited textbooks by O'Grady's brother Frank. The book was *They're a Weird Mob*, which purported to be the autobiography of Nino Culotta, a young Italian who tries to make sense of the Australian language and way of life. Roderick later said he started reading and couldn't stop laughing, and he wrote Beatrice a memo saying that, with Lennie Lower's *Here's Luck*, this was a great example of cultural clowning. It would sell thousands of copies and should be published immediately.

A recommendation from Colin Roderick was hardly a passport to Beatrice's favour. Not having time to read the manuscript herself, she gave it to a reader, who thought that, though the author had a 'marvellous' knowledge of current Australian slang and could write convincing dialogue, the book lacked plot, and the incidents, though sometimes funny, were not sufficiently exciting to maintain interest. The reader added: 'Perhaps as a series in some periodical . . . "Days in the life of a New Australian" or something of the kind, would have a success . . . It's pleasant to read anything so competent but I doubt its success published in its present form as a book.' A second reader complained that, although the manuscript had flashes of humour, there was far too much about damp courses, concrete foundations and other aspects of the building trade. (Given *Weird Mob*'s subsequent history, it's probably fortunate for the A&R readers that they are anonymous.)

Reports and manuscript went to Beatrice, who replied to John O'Grady on 30 January 1957. As she usually did when she had not read a manuscript herself, she paraphrased the readers' comments: 'In spite of some very amusing incidents and a fine command of Australian slang, Nino's story would not, in our readers' opinion, make a successful book. It is felt that the plot is not strong enough and that there is too much detail about various building operations.' And she repeated the suggestion that *They're a Weird Mob* could make a series of magazine articles.

The rest, as they say, is history. John O'Grady took his manuscript to Sam Ure Smith, who grabbed it with both hands and sold 300 000 copies in its first three years. It was made into a feature film starring the Italian actor Walter Chiari, and by 1981 it had been reprinted forty-seven times.

They're a Weird Mob is close to the top of A&R's list of 'books that got away' – although, because it was printed at Halstead and distributed by Angus and Robertson, the company did make money out of it.[5] Turning it down did nothing for Beatrice's reputation as a publisher, and people who thought she was too big for her high-heeled boots – and there were a number – were pleased that she had made such a spectacular error of judgement. However, her rejection of *Weird Mob* is not really surprising. She was not inclined to trust Colin Roderick's opinion and she would have concluded that the manuscript was just another would-be humorous novel, no different from a dozen others the editorial department rejected every year. Had she read the manuscript herself, she would probably have come to the same conclusion. When *They're a Weird Mob* became so successful and Beatrice was reminded that she had turned it down, she was regretful but not devastated. For her, inadvertently rejecting Christina Stead was a much graver matter, though Stead sold less than one-tenth as well.

Nor is it entirely fair to stigmatise Beatrice for her lack of focus on profitability. The department she ran was surprisingly unfettered by commercial imperatives; indeed, the editorial section dwelt in splendid fiscal and intellectual isolation from the rest of Angus and Robertson. Beatrice and her staff were not responsible for preparing the budgets for books, for instance: that was the job of the finance or production department. Beatrice probably knew how well books had sold only if editorial corrections had to be made for a reprint. With its lack of deadlines and its staff occupied with the careful weighing and measuring of words, 'poor bloody editorial' resembled an old-fashioned university liberal arts department more than an arm of a modern publishing company.

Beatrice carried on a tradition that dates at least from the Middle Ages: as a guide, mentor and teacher to her staff, whom she trained on the job, she was in effect the leader of a craft guild. The team of editors Beatrice trained in the 1950s and 1960s – Nan McDonald, Alec Bolton, Elisabeth Hughes, Elizabeth Wood-Ellem, Janet Bennett, Anthony Barker, Eric Russell – were some of the best in Australia. Beatrice parcelled out the manuscripts from the editorial cupboard; she read the most promising ones herself, but all the editors were expected to read and report on some, and to write individual letters of rejection. The rule was to try to say something pleasant, or at least not too discouraging, about the manuscript, although Beatrice did not always follow this herself. Every manuscript received was reported on, and the reports were typed and filed by one of the typists downstairs in case the author submitted the same manuscript under a different title. Editors sometimes read manuscripts while they ate lunch at their desks, and according to legend, someone's ham sandwich once disappeared into a rejected manuscript.

As time went on, A&R's editors developed areas of expertise. Poetry and fiction were usually edited by Nan McDonald or Rosemary Dobson, practical books such as gardening and cookery were given to Elisabeth Hughes, Eric Russell was generally allotted large, intricate books such as H.M. Green's *A History of Australian Literature*. But whether the book was on sheep diseases or partial dentures, was a children's story or a biography, most of A&R's editors could handle anything.

Training was a part of her job that Beatrice took very seriously. 'Darling,' she would say to new editors in impressive tones, 'if you make a mistake in print, it will haunt you for the rest of your life.' Elizabeth Wood-Ellem remembers that when she joined the department in 1953 with a BA from the University of Melbourne, she spent her first year having everything she did scrutinised by Elisabeth Hughes, whom Beatrice had personally trained, while Beatrice – of whom Wood-Ellem was somewhat in awe – kept a strict eye on her progress.[6] Wood-Ellem sometimes found this careful inspection painful, but by the end of her first year she knew the basics of her craft thoroughly.

Beatrice did not confine her training to hands-on editing. She asked Henry Mund – the head of A&R's production department and a German immigrant of immense learning about books, as well as a gifted typographer – to give a series of talks to her staff about typefaces and book design. So, too, did Halstead's head printer Leslie Apthorp, formerly employed by the great printers Jarrolds of Norwich.

Alec Bolton, who joined Beatrice's editorial department shortly after the war, often said its fact-checking expertise was comparable with that of the *New Yorker* magazine.[7] For general inquiries, editors used their own books, consulted those in the bookshop or went to the public library. Wood-Ellem once spent three weeks in the Mitchell Library checking Miles Franklin's quotations in *Laughter, Not for a Cage*. An excellent memory was an indispensable asset; editors were expected to notice, for example, that the American general who fought in the Philippines during World War II might be Douglas Macarthur on page 47 and Doug

McArthur on page 195. Authors who wilfully allowed inaccuracies in their manuscripts drove the editors mad. The worst offenders were Ion Idriess and, especially, Frank Clune. When an editor pointed out that Clune had given the same ship two different names, he solved the problem by tossing a coin.[8]

Copy editing or line editing was an orderly process, though sometimes messy. Manuscripts were supposed to be submitted on double-spaced foolscap or quarto, typed on one side of the paper, with wide margins to allow plenty of room for editing, which was always done in red. As well as a small bottle of red ink and a mapping or fountain pen, standard editorial equipment included a pair of scissors, Sellotape and a pot of glue. There were basically two ways to restructure a manuscript: retype the whole thing again or cut it up, rearrange it and type additional bits. Correction fluid did not exist: an editor who changed her mind about alterations in a manuscript retyped the passage and stuck it into the appropriate place.[9] Everybody knew how to type. Mistakes were erased with a special hard tan-coloured eraser that smudged the carbon paper used for making copies.

Editors worked from nine to five-thirty Monday to Friday, and the staff – not Beatrice – took turns to come in on Saturdays in case an author turned up or telephoned. In 1954 the starting wage was £7 a week: low pay, especially for a university graduate, of whom there were several on the staff. Equal work for equal pay did not exist. Though the women editors were doing the same work as their male counterparts, their small brown pay packets never held as much cash. Elizabeth Wood-Ellem, with a medical student husband to support, was paid less than Eric Russell, who had no dependants. Some were also irritated by the convention that the men on the staff, apart from their immediate colleagues, called the women by their first names, while they were obliged to address the men as 'Mr'.

The editorial department conducted a love–hate relationship with production – the part of A&R responsible for metamorphosing a stack of edited manuscript into finished, bound books. Frank Thompson, who had been trained as an editor, was offered a job in the production department in 1958. George Ferguson assured him that Henry Mund would look after him, as would John Holland and Anne Davis, Beatrice's niece, who had been working there.[10] Before Thompson could take up the job, however, Henry Mund died of a heart attack, John Holland went to New York, and Anne Davis married and left A&R. Horrified and in-experienced, Thompson was the sole member of the department at a time when A&R were doing 150 new books and reprints a year. John Ferguson, George's son, who had been learning the business at Halstead, soon joined and both young men had to learn their jobs very rapidly.

This was often made difficult by the editorial department and the printers at Halstead. Once a pictorial book about South-East Asia was ready to print, except that the editorial department had failed to supply a caption for one of the photographs. The printer, whose name was Thode, told the production department that they had to get the cap-tion by noon. Editorial promised to supply it, which they did at two that afternoon, and Frank Thompson called Halstead with the caption. 'Too late,' said Thode. 'We've printed.' Thompson gulped and said, 'Who wrote the caption?' 'I did,' said Thode. 'It was just an ordinary bloody street scene somewhere, so I called it "A sunny day in Bangkok."'

Like many other long-term A&R employees, Beatrice felt she was part of something great. Angus and Robertson wasn't just a printing, book-selling and publishing company – it was part of the intellectual fabric of Australia, like the University of Sydney or the Australian Broadcasting Commission. George Ferguson believed, as his grandfather had done, that A&R's publishing should express and reflect as far as possible the work of the community's best minds. 'We are dispensers, not prescribers,' he once said.[11] The first question must always be: is this book worth pub-lishing? If so, it should be published, and the question of profit, though important, must be secondary.

It was this attitude, this sense of *noblesse oblige* inherited from George Robertson, that led the company to embark on publishing projects where profit came a long way behind commitment to Australian literary culture. The seven-volume *Bibliography of Australia*, a list of printed materials published between 1784 and 1900 and the life's work of George

Ferguson's father Mr Justice J. A. Ferguson, appeared between 1941 and 1969. Angus and Robertson also published Percival Serle's two-volume *Dictionary of Australian Biography* (1949), F.T. Macartney's revision of Morris Miller's *Australian Literature* (1956) and H.M. Green's two-volume *A History of Australian Literature* (1961) – all indispensable reference books whose worth was far greater than their profitability.

But by far the biggest and most ambitious project Angus and Robertson undertook, and still one of the biggest and most complex enterprises in Australian publishing history, was the second version of the *Australian Encyclopedia*. This ran to ten volumes – nine plus an index – took ten years to complete, featured the work of more than 400 contributors, most of whom were authorities on their particular subjects, and dealt with almost every phase of Australian life. The list of subject headings alone consisted of 220 typed quarto pages, each with twenty-seven entries. The whole project was a problem for Beatrice, mainly because it gobbled up so much in the way of editorial resources. Some of her best and most experienced editors – Janet Bennett, Eric Russell, Alec Bolton – were seconded to the encyclopedia, which often overstretched the production and printing departments as well.

Work on the encyclopedia had begun as early as 1949, when Walter Cousins engaged Alexander (Alec) Chisholm as chief editor. 'Chis' was a noted journalist and newspaper editor with a wide range of interests; as well as a great deal of journalism he wrote many books on natural history and several about Australian literary figures. A man with the air of a scruffy, snappy terrier, Chisholm was jealous of his knowledge and intolerant of any opposition. The rivalry between him and the historian Malcolm Ellis was a standing joke in A&R's editorial department: their correspondence over the encyclopedia, which began 'Dear Alec' and 'Dear Malcolm' ground to a halt many years later under the permafrost of 'Dear Chisholm' and 'Dear Ellis'. Chisholm had a literal sense of humour that depended heavily on puns, and he often regaled Walter Cousins and later George Ferguson with solemn and smutty schoolboy jokes. On an impressive range of letterheads – Royal Australian Ornithologists' Union, Field Naturalists of Victoria and eventually *Australian Encyclopedia* Editor-in-Chief Alec H. Chisholm – Chis solicited contributions in courtly prose, complete with such phrases as 'in a jamb' and 'fie upon you' and signed 'Ffy yours', following the nineteenth-century tendency to delete unnecessary letters when the mning is clr. Chisholm oversaw about 6000 entries which were written, subbed, retyped, read (by himself or his deputy Bruce Pratt), set, proofed, read, corrected, sent to the author, corrected, pasted up, made up, proofed again, read and corrected before being printed and bound.[12]

His zeal for knowledge led him to some bizarre information. Having read somewhere that the Australian Aborigines were the hairiest race in the world, he thought an article on the physical characteristics of the white Australian should include some reference to hair. To Professor Abbie of the University of Adelaide he mused:'Hair seems to grow more quickly in this country than in Britain – the Duke of Gloucester told me in 1945 that he had to get his hair cut here almost twice as often as he did at Home!'[13] Professor Abbie thought the Duke of Gloucester was talking through his hat.

Apart from a large map printed on English paper, the encyclopedia was a proudly Australian enterprise. The paper stock – 100 tonnes of it – was specially made at Burnie, Tasmania, and the stock for the black and white photographs came from Ballarat. Most of the printing blocks were made in Halstead's engraving department, all the printing was done at Halstead and only Australian materials were used in the binding.

The *Australian Encyclopedia*, launched at the Australian Book Fair in Melbourne in March 1958 and published early in June, was universally hailed as a major event in the history of Australian publishing. 'Our greatest work of reference by several million words,' enthused the *Age*, which devoted almost a page to it. In recognition of his role, Alec Chisholm was awarded an OBE in the Queen's Birthday Honours that year.

Angus and Robertson's high-minded sense of duty also extended to its employees, though it did not go as far as paying them high salaries. The house magazine *Fragment*, named for A&R's cable address, was a lavish publication that appeared intermittently between 1954 and 1959, and was more than a transmitter of social news. In the words of A.A. Ritchie, the chairman of directors, its aim was nothing less than 'to give members of the firm a better knowledge of books, of the men and women who write them, and of our fellow members who edit, produce and sell them [and] to preserve the personal atmosphere of the firm . . .'[14] Before Halstead Press moved from Surry Hills in 1957, the home addresses of all Halstead employees were checked and a map prepared. A site south-west of the city near a railway station was convenient for the greatest number of people, and so Halstead moved to such an area, at Kingsgrove.

Those who worked for Angus and Robertson were expected to follow high standards of dress and behaviour, especially when dealing with the public. It was an age when people smoked in the office and drank alcohol during the day; the men frequently went down to the pub at lunchtime. The management of the bookshop warned employees against drinking on the job. An undated memo ran:

> Members of the Board, their friends and relations and customers have lodged complaints about the smell of liquor on assistants' breath during working hours. Actual names have been submitted but will not be mentioned unless there is a repetition. Should this occur the offender's name will be posted on the Notice Boards. Two offences will result in dismissal. With Christmas almost with us and acquaintances extending invitations to "have one" it will be difficult to avoid . . . but YOU HAVE BEEN WARNED.

This kind of headmaster-ticking-off-the-school-assembly prose was not unusual in A&R memos.

In the 1950s Angus and Robertson was doing well. They could afford to pour vast resources into a huge project for ten years without getting a penny back. Halstead Press, which printed books for most of Australia's publishers, expanded and moved to a modern, bigger plant. The bookshop remained one of the best in the country, employing about 300 in selling and allied service departments (general office, advertising, purchasing, mail orders) in Sydney and Melbourne. The retail operation in Australia and in the UK was going strong. Even publishing, the least profitable part of the company, was booming.

Like other employees, Beatrice assumed she had a job for life. And why not? Anyone looking at the company's history over the last forty years – and that included George Ferguson and the board of directors – had good grounds for concluding that Angus and Robertson, the colossus of Australian publishing, was set for further growth and continued prosperity. Which just shows what an unreliable guide history can be.

Bringing the Pirates on Board:
The Battles for Angus and Robertson

To many people inside and outside Angus and Robertson, it seemed extraordinary that Beatrice had so little authority except within her own department. She was obviously one of the most intelligent and experienced people in the company and yet men with less knowledge, talent and force of personality had greater status. While she had a more responsible job than any other woman in the company and had been at A&R for over twenty years, she had never been invited onto the board of directors. George Ferguson adopted his grandfather's practice of recruiting long-serving employees to the board, but this did not apply to women.

Beatrice's staff were angry at this perceived slight, but Beatrice herself apparently passed it off with a shrug. She did not want to be a company director; finance and profit-and-loss statements were of little interest to her and she didn't have a particularly high opinion of the board members. As long as she was allowed to run her own department and to publish books she considered worthy, she was content. But a series of devastating events was about to destroy not only her ability to do her job, but the job itself.

Since 1951 a New Zealand-born businessman named Walter Burns had been quietly buying shares in Angus and Robertson through his Sydney stockbroker Arthur Hordern. Burns's various business ventures had made him wealthy, and for some years he had been a real-estate developer. Had Burns appeared about thirty years later he would have been called an entrepreneur, although he was anything but flashy. On the contrary, he looked like one of the bank managers he dealt with: about five and a half feet tall, neatly dressed, with grey eyes and greying dark hair and an alert, brisk manner. The only unusual thing about him was his voice: a benign growth had been removed from his larynx and he could speak only in a rasping whisper. This disconcerted many people, and Burns, a small man anxious to exercise authority – he was known as the Pocket Battleship – knew how to turn it to his advantage.

By 1958 Walter Burns had become the major shareholder in Angus and Robertson. The board considered him a sensible, intelligent man with a good grasp of business principles. They themselves were hardly a dynamic group. A.A. Ritchie, then in his early seventies and an A&R employee for the greater part of his working life, had been a director since 1923. George Ferguson, appointed in the 1930s, had never worked for another company, nor had his fellow board member Aubrey Cousins. The business of their monthly board meetings consisted largely of listing share transfers and approving such things as Christmas bonuses to the staff. Over the years the seven-member board of directors of Angus and Robertson had acquired the torpid complacency of a nineteenth-century gentleman's club.

There were signs that this pleasant, patrician style of operation was losing its effectiveness. Though the shareholders were happy with their returns, a firmer hand was needed on the financial and marketing tiller. It was a warning sign that the bookshop, one of the biggest in the world, with a credit customer and mail-order list of more than 200 000, was forced every year to run huge bargain sales in order to clear its stocks. The *Australian Encyclopedia*, the jewel in A&R's crown, had not sold as well as it might, mainly because the company had done little to promote it – by giving special deals, for example, to schools or universities. The sales force, hamstrung by the company's lack of energy, were becoming increasingly frustrated. A&R were losing authors to newer, hungrier publishers, and were commissioning few books of their own. The company was beginning to drift.

George Ferguson, who controlled the board, thought that the

culture of A&R had become too inward-looking. The board needed new blood. In August 1959, when one of the longest-serving A&R directors retired, Ferguson invited Burns, whom he liked and respected, to fill the vacancy, and Burns agreed. In welcoming him, Ferguson and his fellow directors did not stop to wonder why a real-estate developer who had no real interest in the publishing business had spent so much time and energy on becoming A&R's major shareholder and joining the board.

To those with greater financial sophistication the answer was clear: Angus and Robertson, which owned very valuable property in the Sydney and Melbourne CBDs, was sitting on a gold mine. The directors knew that their real estate was worth a great deal, but as the company was making a reasonable profit and the shareholders were happy, they could see no reason to realise their assets, or even to determine their value. Already one large company had suggested that 89 Castlereagh Street be torn down, redeveloped and leased back to A&R, an offer greeted by scandalised incomprehension.[1] Angus and Robertson were booksellers and publishers, not dealers in real estate; property was to be used, not speculated with. There was no reason to seek liquidity. The same line of thinking applied to buying other companies: why would Australia's most venerable and esteemed publishing, printing and bookselling company want to become bigger players on the business scene?

But Walter Burns had no time for the views of cautious Scottish–Australian booksellers: he was a businessman who saw a golden opportunity. Once on the board he helped drive out two more directors, including the chairman A.A. Ritchie, then persuaded the rest to appoint his own nominees, making his stockbroker Anthony Hordern chairman. In a surprisingly short time Burns and his nominees had a majority on the board, and by the end of 1959 Walter Burns was managing director of Angus and Robertson, with George Ferguson as his subordinate.

Burns then assumed extraordinary powers to split the company's operations into several wholly owned subsidiaries: A&R (Publishers) Pty Ltd, A&R (Bookshops) Pty Ltd, Halstead Press Pty Ltd, and HEC Robinson Pty Ltd. The last, a retailer and publisher of maps, was a new acquisition. Burns also bought up as subsidiary companies the

Melbourne booksellers and publishers Robertson and Mullens, the Sydney stationers and booksellers Swain and Co., Albert's Bookshop in Perth, and other retail outlets in Australia, New Zealand and London. Having split the retailing, publishing and printing sections of the company into three separate divisions, each with its own director, Burns further diminished George Ferguson's role by putting him in charge of the publishing division only, and forcing Ferguson to dismiss his right-hand man and chief supporter, the production manager Paul Tracy, who had worked for A&R for many years.

To many at A&R, Ferguson acquiesced in all this far too readily. He was like the commander of a brigantine who, having invited another mariner on board and shown him all over the ship, suddenly finds him hoisting the skull and crossbones and can do nothing about it. Ferguson's apparent helplessness must have made Beatrice feel that he could not be relied upon as a strong ally if Burns continued to move against the publishing department.

Burns then invented a new position: director of publishing, whose job was to create books – to think of ideas, to commission and publish new books, as well as to liaise between the sales and editorial departments, keeping a check on books published, their costs and scheduling. 'We only want to publish bestsellers,' Burns declared, causing a great deal of irritated amusement in the editorial department – so he had found someone with a magic formula, had he? Someone whose judgement was so infallible that he could change book publishing from a gamble into a business with hard-and-fast rules? Marketing books was like selling toothpaste, was it?

Beatrice knew she wouldn't get the job. Burns clearly did not consider her and her department sufficiently attuned to commercial realities (and besides, she was a woman). Burns appointed Alec Bolton – a man fifteen years younger than Beatrice, whom she had trained – to be her immediate boss. Beatrice's staff were furious about the decision, and Bolton was distressed and embarrassed, assuring Beatrice that he would always consult her and defer to her greater experience. Beatrice herself said little; perhaps she was relieved that she would not have to work directly to Burns.

Probably to further divide the staff, and also to get rid of George Ferguson, Burns now decreed that the publishing division (including the production and sales departments as well as editorial) should leave 89 Castlereagh Street. The bookshop would remain on the ground floor for the time being, but there were plans to redevelop the rest of the building. So at the end of June 1960 Beatrice and her department moved to the fourth floor of 221 George Street, one of a row of terraces near the Newcastle Hotel and above the premises of the newly acquired Robinson's Maps. Moving from the office she had occupied for twenty-three years was a wrench, and recovering from the chaos took time, but by October Beatrice was able to write to Sadie Herbert that 'The new quarters are really much pleasanter and cleaner, and all should be well when we get under way again properly.'[2]

This resolutely positive response was typical of Beatrice's reactions to Burns and his plans, at least in public. Keeping a calm front was second nature, and she could see no point in alarming or unsettling her authors: in spite of these upheavals, A&R were still A&R. 'It does not matter that our present managing director, Mr Burns, has had no publishing experience; for we have,' she wrote to Xavier Herbert in July 1960 (she was in the throes of editing *Soldiers' Women*).[3] 'He is certainly interested in our making more money out of publishing; but that will be all to the good for our authors; and we still intend to publish the best possible books we can get – and to sell them.' She did, however, permit herself to add that 'life is not easy here'.

It certainly was not, working with someone whose attitude to books and publishing was the antithesis of hers. In the *Observer* of 26 November, Burns spelled out his philosophy in detail – that of economic rationalists the world over:

> The tendency among book men to restrict their contacts to their own trade breeds a smugness and conservatism that makes book publishing and book selling a potential bonanza for those who can break with tradition, broaden their horizons and treat books for what they are – merchandise to be manufactured and sold as quickly as possible . . . The publication of literary masterpieces and

prestige works, with appeal to a limited market, is not the obligation of a public company . . . The main responsibility for what
might be termed prestige publishing rests with the universities
and similar institutions. In a public company the publisher's first
responsibility is to the shareholders, and if he undertakes a
programme with undue emphasis on prestige works he courts
financial disaster . . . [S]uccessful marketing depends on good
marketing research; too many publishers rely on experience and
intuition. This is not good enough. If [market research] is desirable
and necessary to the marketing of other commodities, why not
books?[4]

In October Angus and Robertson held a mammoth book sale,
unloading many of their 'prestige' books at ridiculously low prices. The
sell-off delighted discerning book buyers all over the country. But
Adelaide's Max Harris, while appreciating the opportunity to pick up
most books in A&R's poetry catalogue for a shilling a copy, sounded a
note of disquiet. A&R clearly intended to publish fewer 'serious' books
in future, he wrote, but what did that leave them with? He listed the current program: Christopher Brennan, a comedy about a family running
a bush pub, one or two Ion Idriesses, popular novels . . . not a very
impressive list. A&R's retreat from serious, heavyweight publishing
would leave a gap in the market; the other major local publishers, though
perhaps more dynamic, were unlikely to fill it because such books were
not profitable.[5]

Burns's next innovation was to set up what he called a committee of
review: editors, sales reps and sales assistants were to meet regularly in
order to decide print runs and prices for all upcoming titles. The sales
force approved of this – they felt they had not been consulted enough –
but Beatrice found these meetings, which she usually chaired, intensely
irritating because she felt the decisions ignored questions of quality.
Soldiers' Women had been costed at 32s 6d a copy, which was expensive,
and the committee decided a better price would be 22s 6d a copy, so the
book would have to be shortened. No editor has ever taken kindly to
sales or marketing people deciding on the length of a book to fit a

particular price, especially if they haven't read it. Almost every meeting featured this sort of clash between salespeople and editors, and Beatrice was soon thoroughly sick of arguing.

She may even have considered resigning: with a steady, though small, income from the Bridges estate she could just have afforded not to work. But she felt she was part of Angus and Robertson; it was her life, she didn't want to let her authors down, and where would she go? Apart from A&R the biggest publisher was probably F.W. Cheshire, who brought out about twenty books a year. Other significant publishers were Melbourne University Press, Jacaranda, Shakespeare Head Press, Ure Smith, Horwitz, Oxford University Press and Georgian House. Of these the 'serious' publishers – Cheshire, OUP, MUP and Georgian House – were based in Melbourne and, even assuming any of those was able to offer her an editorial job, Beatrice had no intention of leaving Sydney. There was no alternative: she had to stay.

In August 1960 Burns appointed P.R. Stephensen, writer, editor and sometime literary agent, to develop a paperback list. George Ferguson had always been against paperback publishing; paperbacks weren't 'real' books, he felt, and the success of Allen Lane's Penguins had not changed his mind. A&R were not set up for paperback publishing, and the quality of Australian paperbacks (those printed by Horwitz, for instance) was generally poor. For months Stephensen had been urging Burns to start a paperback list – up to 100 000 copies per title – running off the Angus and Robertson backlist or any other Australian books that looked promising.[6] He said he was confident that with his experience and contacts he could find two hundred titles a year, from either reprints or new manuscripts, to be printed in England for worldwide distribution. The whole idea greatly appealed to Burns. Paperbacks were cheap, the books already existed, and buying books from other publishers was much less risky than publishing A&R's own. Burns was more than ready to boldly go where Allen Lane had gone before.

Beatrice considered this a disaster in the making. Why choose someone as erratic and unbusinesslike as Stephensen to run the program? Where would he find enough material? Who would oversee production of these books, and how would they sell 100 000 copies of books that most potential buyers had probably already read? None of these questions apparently occurred to Burns, who speedily and without consulting George Ferguson or anyone else appointed Stephensen at a salary considerably higher than Beatrice's.

The word spread that Burns intended to stop A&R doing any original publishing at all, relying for profits on buying books from elsewhere and putting existing A&R titles into paperback. Beatrice's worst fears were confirmed when in late September or early October the publishing department was ordered to stop work altogether, ostensibly while a new costing system was fine-tuned and budgets revised. The staff were not laid off, just told to await developments, and in the meantime everybody was supposed to fill in a form indicating their place in the company and how they related to other departments. Halstead's binding machines were shut down in mid-flow, and a run of textbooks for the following year was abandoned, costing the company thousands.[7]

Beatrice swiftly decided that the ruling was absurd, and she and her staff continued to edit, proof and check books as usual. With incoming jobs dwindling, the production department spent much of its time calculating page extents in all typefaces in all sizes for all books. (This turned out to be very useful in years to come, as they could calculate, say, how many pages a 70 000-word manuscript would make in a particular typeface and book size.) The freeze lasted for about six months.

From being a company that took pride in its relationship with its staff, a company where people trusted each other, Angus and Robertson had become a place where the atmosphere was poisonous, thick with suspicion. Staff who favoured Burns's reforms were hardly on speaking terms with those who supported George Ferguson and traditional publishing. Everyone was unhappy. The resignations began. Among the first to leave was Alec Bolton, who found the pressure of his new job intolerable. After only a few months he stormed into George Ferguson's office, deeply upset, declaring, that he could not accept the decisions Burns was making.[8] When Burns sold the *Australian Encyclopedia* to the Grolier Society for a ridiculously low £100 000 – after ten expensive years in preparation the encyclopedia had hardly been on the market long enough to recoup any costs – its associate editor Bruce Pratt went with it. David Moore, who had worked on the *Encyclopedia* and moved to editing non-fiction, also left, as did Quinton Davis (no relation to Beatrice), the art director. When Davis left, Burns abolished the art department. In all, the publishing division was reduced from thirty to eighteen people, which Burns considered quite large enough. Beatrice's secretary Judy Fisher often went home in tears during this spate of resignations and dismissals, wondering whether Beatrice herself would be the next to go.[9]

Burns and his plans for Angus and Robertson were generally treated admiringly in the press; he was called the 'stormy petrel' of publishing and described as 'shrewd, vital, likeable, bold'.[10] Among those impressed was the writer Colin Simpson, a former journalist who combined work in an advertising agency with the writing of successful travel books. Burns's plans agreed with his own views on marketing books – not least his own – and in mid-1960 he left his well-paid job to become Burns's personal assistant. He quickly realised that the managing director knew little about marketing books, became disillusioned and resigned after only a month.

Simpson then became one of Burns's chief critics, a change that did not go unnoticed. As a correspondent in the *Observer* noted:

> An equilibrist who could thus establish a footing in each of the two camps at A&R in rapid and vacillating succession, while at the same time maintaining a foothold in the advertising business, and all the time balancing a chip on his shoulder and pushing his own barrow, deserves all the applause that such an acrobatic feat could earn for him.[11]

Simpson took particular exception to Burns's enthusiasm for paperback publishing and his assertion that the hardback had had its day. In Simpson's opinion, paperbacks would never replace hardbacks, as readers and buyers wanted something good-looking they could keep. He might have been George Ferguson when he declared, 'The culture of this country is bound up with the hardback book; and I do not propose to stand by and see Mr Burns or anyone else "merchandise" the book

culture of this country out of existence.'[12] Having changed sides so com-
prehensively, Simpson now began to mobilise other authors against
Burns and his further plans for Angus and Robertson.

'The situation will not be solved until after the annual general
meeting,' wrote Beatrice to Xavier Herbert in October 1960.[13] 'We have
a reasonable chance of winning the cause of Publishing versus Finance,
and it is of tremendous importance that we should win.' It certainly
was. Burns, who with his supporters just held the balance of power on
the board, was now discussing with Sir Frank Packer the possibility of
Packer's Consolidated Press Holdings buying out Burns's interest. For
Beatrice and the other Ferguson supporters, the thought of A&R being
merged with a newspaper empire was almost as bad as anything Burns
alone could do.

At a board meeting on 18 October the situation seemed to improve.
Anthony Hordern suddenly resigned as the chairman and in his place
was elected Norman Cowper, who had strong links with Angus
and Robertson. Just as importantly Arthur Swain, whose bookselling and
stationery business Burns had bought and who owned a large parcel of
A&R shares, declared himself in support of the Ferguson forces
and deposed Burns as managing director. Though he remained on the
board, Burns lost his dominant position.

So far so good. Like other members of the pro-Ferguson group,
Beatrice believed that the annual general meeting in December – at
which, ironically, almost the whole board except Walter Burns was up
for re-election – would see Publishing defeat Finance. However, a week
before the AGM it became clear that Arthur Swain, with his large block
of shares, had switched sides. He and Burns had nominated a board that
excluded George Ferguson and his supporters altogether.

There was very little time before the meeting and the situation was
desperate. But a large number of shareholders were uncommitted to
either side, and they could be reached. Beatrice swung into action,
contacting every shareholder she knew, urging them to support the
Ferguson forces. Hedley Jeffries spread the word down in the bookshop;
Mary Gilmore and others did what they could. Colin Roderick
collected evidence that state education departments all over Australia

were alarmed at the non-appearance of textbooks for the 1961 school year and had little confidence in the way Burns was running A&R's publishing. Simpson mobilised thirty-four prominent A&R authors, including Ruth Park, D'Arcy Niland, Kenneth Slessor and May Gibbs, to sign a statement to be presented at the AGM that they would never publish with A&R again if Burns and his nominees succeeded.

It all ended very quickly. At the AGM a majority of A&R's share-holders supported the traditional, anti-Burns forces, and the Ferguson team was elected to the board. Burns remained but his supporters were in the minority. Sam Ure Smith, a rival publisher who had helped gar-ner support for the Ferguson faction, had agreed to signal the result of the meeting from his city office window; a white handkerchief meant victory, a piece of paper with a red cross defeat. A jubilant Ure Smith hoisted the handkerchief and before long, with a bottle of champagne and a group of supporters, he rushed down the King Street hill to 221 George Street to join the A&R staff in a victory celebration.

The literary community was almost as relieved and delighted. 'I feel sure George Robertson was sooling on the archangels,' wrote Dame Mary Gilmore to George Ferguson on 26 December 1960. And a fortnight after the meeting a thankful Beatrice wrote to Xavier Herbert:'It was quite amazing how the old shareholders stood by – as well as our many friends in the book world. It has all been very exhaust-ing and worrying, but now we can go ahead with a will. There is a tremendous amount of reconstruction to be done . . . I hope 1961 will be a very good year. At least it could not be worse than 1960.'[14] Her exhilaration withstood even an *Observer* article in which Colin Simpson failed to deny credit for the entire triumph.[15]

This was not quite the end of the story. Almost a year later, in November 1961, A&R learned that Sir Frank Packer had bought Arthur Swain's shares – Packer also held many of his own – and that Australian Consolidated Holdings now owned about 20 per cent of A&R. But Packer wasn't about to come on board the good ship A&R – he wanted to ram it. He demanded two further seats on the board, and when that was rejected he went into full-scale takeover mode. Before the AGM on 15 December a tremendous proxy battle ensued. Colin Roderick, who had been nominated to the board, thought the day could be won if enough shares were mobilised. He organised a clever share-splitting arrangement that denied Packer control of the company.[16]

Early in 1962 Walter Burns resigned from the board, stipulating ill health. But Packer still had a seat on the board as well as his large share-holding. In May 1962 he cabled A&R from New York that he intended to sell his shares to an American company, but gave A&R the chance of acquiring them. George Ferguson immediately asked a number of British publishers for their help in getting rid of Packer. In his letter to Sir Stanley Unwin (of George Allen & Unwin), he added, 'I certainly do not need to tell you the consequence that could flow in the Australian book trade from having A&R in American hands. I realise that if the Americans want to enter Australia we can't stop them, but their road will be much harder if they don't have the resources of A&R than if they do.'[17] In order to keep the Americans from invading their patch, a group of British publishers led by William Collins — reluctantly, because Collins itself was just about to start publishing in Australia and was unwilling to tie up funds — agreed to buy Packer's share of A&R. They paid well above market price for them, and Frank Packer sold out of Angus and Robertson at a tidy profit, as he had almost certainly intended.[18] It was understood that, when A&R's share price rose to the price Collins had paid, the British publisher would sell its shares to buyers friendly to the A&R board. In the meantime Collins would not interfere in A&R in any way, and hoped to be free of its investment within three years.[19]

So Angus and Robertson was safe again, free to pick up the pieces and carry on publishing as before. But despite George Ferguson's repeated insistence that 'all this is behind us', the company had been shaken to its core. In only three years it had gone from an old-fashioned, paternalistic organisation, owned and managed by its employees, where, in the words of Colin Roderick, 'the sun was as likely to fall out of the sky as something to go wrong', to one that had come within a whisker of its staff losing control altogether.[20]

The person hardest hit by the events of 1960 was probably George Ferguson. Ever since joining the company as a young man in 1931 he had worked for the cause of Australian books, overseen the expansion in publishing of poetry, literary fiction, educational texts and writing for children, and forged important links between Australian and overseas publishers. He had served the interests of A&R's shareholders and carried on the business honourably and with profit, in the tradition of his grandfather George Robertson. And now, because of his naïvety, trusting benevolence and lack of business acumen, he had almost lost it all. Colin Roderick always believed that 'the advent of Burns . . . totally undermined [Ferguson's] moral universe' and destroyed his faith in human beings.[21]

There was other fallout. P.R. Stephensen was left with a half-formed paperback publishing scheme and no home for it. At first he thought of selling his list to Consolidated Press but they were not interested, then he considered floating his own company, again unsuccessfully. He took legal steps to get his promised salary back; eventually some accommodation was reached but from then on he bitterly referred to the company as 'Anguish and Robberson'.[22]

And what of Beatrice? With Angus and Robertson restored she was able to return to work, though perhaps in a less committed spirit than before. The events of 1960 had shaken her badly. For the first time she realised how vulnerable she was, how easily everything she had built up could be destroyed. Never again would her position be as secure.

221 George Street

The Backroom Girl Moves up Front

The new offices at 221 George Street were in a part of Sydney that Beatrice had once known well, and in 1960 it was surprisingly unchanged. Still there, a few doors down from A&R, was the now dilapidated old building where she had rented a room, with divan bed and gas ring, twenty-five years before.[1] The warehouses of Circular Quay remained, as did the seagulls, the green-and-cream ferries held at anchor by creaking ropes, and the sharp smell of tar and salt.

A&R's office was close to two well-known pubs, the Brooklyn and the Newcastle, and the latter, run by Jim Buckley, speedily became the A&R watering hole. Beatrice often dispatched members of her staff to the bottle department to replenish her supplies of red wine or Vat 69 whisky, as well as soda in metal-netted siphons. Though slightly more refined than the Brooklyn, the Newcastle nevertheless had a certain roughness. Frank Thompson, sent to buy a bottle of red wine for an office party and having already had a glass or two, once had difficulty with the word 'Cawarra' (a cheap local brand). The barmaid thought he meant Corio, a vile Australian whisky, but Thompson loudly insisted on red wine. The man next to him at the bar looked him up and down contemptuously. "E wants a bottle a plonk, the bloody poofter!' he announced to the dusty bar, and turned his back.[2]

The area was showing signs of gentrification. Near the Newcastle was the Andronicus coffee shop, where A&R staff on their way to the office from Wynyard station could enjoy a cup of real coffee, still a novelty in the Sydney of the early 1960s. And close to the office was John Huie's, one of the first wine bars in town where, unlike the pubs, patrons could have a meal as well as drink their red wine or hock, lime and soda. Huie's served French bread rolls with ham and salad and became a favoured place for A&R staff lunches – during the 1960s it was also one of Sydney's best jazz venues.

At number 221 the educational and technical publishing division shared the ground floor with Robinson's Maps – once it became known that A&R had moved, staff in the map shop as well as the education department had to cope with would-be authors – while the production department was on the third floor and editorial on the fourth. It was ironic that the publishing staff of A&R had Walter Burns to thank for new offices that, for comfort and safety, far surpassed those at 89 Castlereagh Street. Not that they were particularly lavish – one newspaper article described them as being 'austerely finished old Edwardian chambers perfumed with that delightful ink and paper smell given off by the books stacked on tables, desks, chairs and portions of the floor', and noted that Beatrice's room had no pictures on the wall and a view of a brick wall and a square of corrugated-iron roof, painted red.[3]

The fourth floor, with the editors at one end and Georgie and her proofreaders at the other, was bisected by a lift-well housing an ancient birdcage lift with doors on two sides protected by a metal concertina arrangement that pinched the fingers of the unwary. Hal Porter, who once described Beatrice as 'a celestial friend and a comforting goddess', said it was 'proper to ascend' to visit her, but a lurch upwards in a clanging, grating lift had very little in common with a glide to the summit of Mount Olympus. Most people found it faster and more comfortable to take the stairs that circled the lift-well. It was an office joke that if the two elderly cleaners happened to be mopping the stairs, whoever used the lift knew all about their family and medical problems by the fourth floor. Once when Beatrice was holding a celebration to launch a new travel book by Colin Simpson, the party was well under way when the author arrived. The lift became stuck between the third and fourth floors and, as getting him out was impossible, guests passed him food and drink for a couple of hours until help came. (It would be nice to say that the book being launched was *The Country Upstairs*, Simpson's book about Japan, but it wasn't.)

Beatrice had not been at 221 George Street very long before she decided that her office wasn't really suitable for entertaining. Though she continued to invite people to lunch at the Queen's Club, she really wanted a place in the city where she could host large parties. She found it in the building next door, which was almost identical to 221 except that it was a honeycomb of little rooms, some the offices of small businesses, others rented out as studios. Such places were disappearing fast as city rents increased. On the first floor of 219 George Street was a large room that, years before, had been a studio for Thea Proctor and Roland Wakelin. Beatrice arranged to rent it from its current tenant, the artist and children's writer Elisabeth MacIntyre. 'Beatrice's studio', as this was immediately called, was an austere place, with board floors and an open balcony facing the street, furnished with a *chaise longue*, a rickety table, and butter boxes painted in different colours, originally seats for models and students. The most startling item was an old pale grey dentist's cabinet with narrow pull-out trays for instruments. Its reason for being there was a mystery, but the shelves made excellent glass holders during parties. Off the studio was a tiny kitchen with a sink, a draining board and a brass tap, and Beatrice added a refrigerator to provide ice for drinks.

The studio was used a great deal, usually for drinks parties after work and occasionally for larger functions, such as book launches. Beatrice also allowed the PEN (Poets, Essayists, Novelists) club and the Australian Society of Authors, founded in 1961, to use it for their evening meetings. She paid for the drink and food herself – George Ferguson was never very keen on entertaining – and her staff would go to David Jones further up George Street to buy bread, cheese and pâté. Almost anyone in Sydney who was a writer of any kind came to Beatrice's studio; the parties tended to be large and raucous, with some guests (notably Colin Simpson and Hal Porter) having to be poured into taxis afterwards.

Beatrice had Sir Frank Packer to thank for another development in her working life. In 1960 Packer had bought the *Bulletin* and merged it with the *Observer*, planning to turn the result into a news magazine.

Douglas Stewart recognised that this spelled doom for the *Bulletin*'s literary section, including the Red Page. 'On the day we were taken over by Packer,' he said later, 'we were all assembled in the *Bulletin* corridors and old Sir Frank got up on the landing there and made a genial speech saying we were not to worry:"There may be a few staff changes I suppose, but don't worry about your jobs." . . . I applied that very afternoon to Angus and Robertson.'[4] He was not the only one. The *Bulletin*'s literary editor Ronald McCuaig also approached A&R, as did Douglas Stewart's assistant John Abernethy. McCuaig went to Canberra, but Stewart and Abernethy both joined Angus and Robertson.

Stewart came in three days a week to oversee and give some direction to A&R's poetry list. His brief was also to develop Sirius Books, a paperback series of Australian classics heavily dependent on A&R's backlist. (At last George Ferguson had got the message about paperbacks.) Stewart was a quick and efficient worker who came in at about ten, worked for two or three hours before lunch, came back to the office afterwards and went home at about four-thirty. Beatrice was delighted to have her old friend and colleague in the office, readily available for consultation.

She was less pleased to see John Abernethy. Then in his early thirties, Abernethy had been a proofreader for the *Sydney Morning Herald* before moving to the reading room of the *Bulletin*. A man of wide-ranging intelligence and literary knowledge, as Douglas Stewart quickly recognised, Abernethy was tall and broad, with dark hair and eyes, large features and a hearty voice. Though Beatrice recognised that he was highly intelligent and well informed, she found him a little too insistent for her taste.

Before long Abernethy was in charge of Angus and Robertson's local publishing. Beatrice must have had a weary sense of déjà vu – this was the second time in two years that a man almost young enough to be her son had been promoted over her. But George Ferguson had learned from the Burns and Packer episodes: if A&R were to continue to be competitive, especially with new publishers in the field, they had to get out and find and promote new authors. Abernethy never shared Beatrice's view that if people did not choose to be published by Angus and Robertson it was undignified to try to persuade them. In 1966 one of his friends, a young writer named Thomas Keneally, was about to have his second novel published by Cassell. Abernethy, who very much wanted him for A&R, brought the new manuscript into the office for everyone to read and make editorial suggestions. Keneally's novel was called *Larks and Heroes*; Anthony Barker, a relatively new member of the editorial staff, suggested the addition of '*Bring*'.[5] *Bring Larks and Heroes* won the 1967 Miles Franklin Award and Keneally published several novels with Angus and Robertson thereafter, edited by John Abernethy. Abernethy was also keen to persuade Patrick White to publish with A&R in Australia, and White toyed with the idea but his London agent advised him against it. A significant writer who appeared at this time was David Ireland, whom Douglas Stewart found and supported.

Beatrice's job had not dwindled in importance: she was still in charge of the editorial department and she and her editors continued to work as they had always done. She was also getting some publicity: a 1964 article in the Sydney *Sun* described her as one of Australia's few women in a top-rank executive job.[6] (Less flatteringly, journalist John Yeomans called her 'a handsome, middle-aged veteran of the struggle to establish a viable book-publishing industry in this country' as well as 'intensely shy'.) But it was true that Beatrice had less influence on publishing decisions than before, as Abernethy was taking over her territory of local fiction, and it was from about this point that Beatrice quietly began to turn away from the new order and concentrate on the authors with whom she felt most comfortable.

Foremost among these was Hal Porter. In June 1960 he began to drop coy, leaden hints that he was becoming friendly with 'a Mr Eliot (Thomas Stearns) and Mr Osborne (Charles)', two of the movers and shakers at Faber and Faber. He had already assured Beatrice that he was busily at work on his new novel *The Tilted Cross*. Porter always worked fast and in concentrated bursts, and he said he was writing about 4000 words a day – especially impressive because he wrote every word in his elaborate longhand. 'I'd love to be one of those clever people who take a year or more to write a novel,' he wrote to Beatrice. 'Much more gracious I feel than an immoderate few months' stint which leaves one with pinpoint ruby eyes and looking generally as though one has been slept in.'[7]

The Tilted Cross, a convict novel set in Tasmania and based on the career of the convicted forger Thomas Griffiths Wainewright, was, thought Nan McDonald, a much more powerful and developed work than *A Handful of Pennies*, though the oddities of the dialogue made the manuscript rather heavy going. She was also unsure about some of the elaborate language and the melodramatic nature of the action, but considered that grotesquerie was part of Porter's makeup as a writer and recommended publication.

Beatrice conveyed the news to Porter. Perhaps she was less enthusiastic about *The Tilted Cross* than he thought she should have been, for in January 1961 he casually dropped the bombshell that he had offered it to Faber, who, he said, were extremely impressed. They were only sorry that they would be unable to publish it in spring, but had to wait until the early autumn. Wasn't Beatrice pleased for him?

Accustomed though she was to Porter's unswerving self-interest, Beatrice must have been angry and disappointed at this betrayal. Porter knew that, even though the contract for the novel had not been signed, it was on A&R's schedule for the coming year, along with his short-story collection *A Bachelor's Children,* which he had dedicated to Beatrice. Showing considerable restraint, she wrote to Porter that it was 'rather a shock' to learn that he wanted to go with Faber. What about his moral obligation to A&R, not to mention his view that Australians should be published in their native country first?

Her view was echoed in literary circles, where Porter's 'sellout' caused a great deal of heated discussion.[8] Thea Astley took the view that Porter had betrayed his Australianness; Frank Thompson thought Beatrice was being 'too bloody kind to an author who had ratted on her, no matter how good he was'. Beatrice naturally did not show her real feelings in public, merely saying that if Porter was to make a living as a writer, he needed to go elsewhere.

Porter's reply to Beatrice's letter was disingenuous. Under normal circumstances he would not have sent his novel to another publisher, he wrote. But he had not realised the danger Walter Burns posed to

A&R, and he was afraid of being left out on a limb, with no publisher and two books. 'I am shocked and mortally sorry about A&R's present unhappy attitude,' he added. 'It didn't dawn on me that they'd be anything but pleased by my success.'⁹ He said he was wholly committed to Faber, who would be much better for him in every possible way. He was sad, really, rather than angry and unduly critical of A&R, and he hoped Beatrice would understand.

Beatrice might have retorted that Porter could have discussed his worries with her, and that it might also have helped to know how far his discussions with Faber had gone. However, her reply was generous:'Your uncertainties as to our future make your attitude and actions perfectly understandable,' she wrote to him. 'With our best wishes for the success of the novel and the growth of your name and fame.'¹⁰ When *The Tilted Cross* was glowingly reviewed in the *Times Literary Supplement* she wrote to congratulate him; when Beatrice was editing *A Bachelor's Children* for publication the following year, she wrote to ask whether he would agree to have *The Tilted Cross* added to the list of books by the same author opposite the title page, even though it was not an Angus and Robertson title. But she did not let him off entirely. While she was pleased that *A Bachelor's Children* would be dedicated to her, she added tartly, 'I should of course be most flattered, but I have a nasty memory of your saying that you paid off debts and closed accounts by this curious means, so perhaps I would rather not be mentioned after all?'

Porter was working as the librarian in Shepparton while he wrote his next book. This, he told Beatrice, was a childhood autobiography covering his life until his mother's death when he was eighteen, and he already had a title for it:*The Watcher on the Cast-Iron Balcony*. It was developing slowly, he said, partly because he needed to sift his memories carefully, but largely because he was struggling with problems of technique in portraying himself, particularly as a precocious child. He kept Beatrice posted on his progress and she encouraged him, though she must have realised he was unlikely to offer the manuscript to Angus and Robertson.

Indeed, it was Faber who published *The Watcher on the Cast-Iron Balcony*, in August 1963. Porter said it was 'as true as I could get', and its imaginative (though not necessarily factual) truth, even through the artificial, allusive writing, makes it one of the best things he ever wrote. The English reviews were generally admiring, but there was some alarm that because Porter had discussed his early homosexual feelings the book might be banned in Australia. It wasn't, but Porter took advantage of the possibility, with fellow writers protesting on his behalf against possible censorship. He boasted to Beatrice that he had perversely written an anonymous letter to the *Age* in support of censorship, which was not published, convincing him that the Australian literary scene was riddled with communists and fellow travellers. Hal Porter's political views seldom veered towards the centre, let alone left of it.

Porter was now riding high. *Watcher* and *A Bachelor's Children* had consolidated his literary reputation and both were selling steadily, and Hal Porter the urbane writer, the suave *boulevardier*, gave a number of radio and newspaper interviews. But as enjoyable as all this attention was, he didn't let it slow down his working pace. Already he was preparing a second volume of memoirs, a play and another book of short stories. He wanted to call the stories *Say to Me Ronald* but agreed to Beatrice's suggested title *The Cats of Venice*. The collection was published by Angus and Robertson in 1965 to good reviews.

Porter offered *The Paper Chase*, his second volume of autobiography, to Faber in 1966. They turned it down on the grounds that it was more likely to sell in Australia than in Britain, and Porter unhesitatingly offered it to Angus and Robertson. Beatrice knew, of course, that A&R were second choice, but did not say so. She professed to admire it greatly and said A&R were 'mad keen' to publish it as soon as possible. This enthusiasm, verging on gush, concealed some of Beatrice's disappointment about the manuscript itself. She told Porter that it wasn't quite as good as *Watcher*, mainly because the focal points of home and family were missing and the narrative was more episodic.

The Paper Chase was published by Angus and Robertson, in Australia and the UK, at the end of 1966. Only one review, in the *New Statesman* in January 1967, was less than wholly favourable. It was written by a young Australian who had lived in Britain for some years, and Alec Bolton (who had by then joined A&R's London office) sent the clipping to John Abernethy with the query: 'Should I know who Clive James is?' James's review went beyond the usual criticism that Porter's writing was affected: 'His prose . . . is so relentlessly too-much that a momentary descent to mere sufficiency would probably look like a lapse,' he wrote, before making some pungent comments about what he saw as the parochialism of Australian writing. '[Porter's]hyped-up writing is thought to be all right because it is Australian writing, the neanderthal opinions are thought to be all right because they are Australian opinions, the echoes from Proust . . . are thought to be all right because, even if Patrick White has established himself in Tolstoy's boots, the cork-lined room for an Australian Proust is to be let furnished.'[11] He did allow that *The Paper Chase* had virtues 'which have little to do with Australian writing and everything to do with Mr Porter. He has ambition and the means to meet it, an uncanny memory for detail and the patience to set it down, and a sure sense that this is an adventure of the mind.'

Porter did not take the adverse criticism very seriously, perhaps because it appeared in a leftish periodical. By now he was turning to John Abernethy for literary guidance and advice as much as to Beatrice; Porter liked having a man-to-man beer in the Newcastle, discussing literary projects. Abernethy had suggested one that Porter liked: a non-fiction study of modern Japan. He agreed to do it, and in 1967 set off for a year's travel and research there.

While he was in Japan Porter wrote to Beatrice assuring her and A&R that he was working hard, though he said the book was at present little more than a series of travel impressions. He was honour bound to submit his next manuscript to Faber, who had published the text of his play *The Professor* (1966) and had first option on his next book. This wasn't a problem, he said – he would offer them a book of verse which they would be bound to reject. When Faber duly did, Porter told Beatrice he was clear of his obligation to them and free to offer A&R not only the book of poems, but also his book on Japan. Beatrice was pleased and offered an advance on the Japan book, which he accepted.

Porter sent this manuscript, *The Actors*, to John Abernethy in December 1967, but most uncharacteristically added that he wasn't sure of its worth and that Abernethy or 'dear little Beatrice' could cut it as much as they liked. Abernethy said he liked the work, which he thought had some of Porter's best writing, though Porter disagreed. Beatrice was also doubtful, and after reading it again Abernethy changed his mind. The problem, he now thought, was the tone, what he called 'the bitter, almost nagging note that keeps creeping in', as well as a strong dash of anti-Japanese prejudice. Beatrice, who agreed that Porter laid himself open to charges of racism, asked him to go through the manuscript again. Porter agreed with unusual docility to do whatever A&R thought was necessary. 'As you know,' he wrote, 'I'm not (in a book of this sort anyway) the sort of author who cherishes what he has written,' he wrote, which must have been news to Beatrice. 'Relax!'[12]

But before A&R had finished preparing *The Actors* for publication, John Abernethy received a disturbing letter from Charles Monteith of Faber and Faber. In 1965, he said, Faber had suggested that Porter write a book on Japan for them, and for three years Porter had been working on it with his Faber editor Frank Pike. Faber had even written a letter of support for the book to help Porter in his application for a Churchill Fellowship. (It was unsuccessful.) The company had made a formal offer for the book in January 1967 and clearly understood that it was theirs. Then Porter's London agent Robin Dalton told them she had heard that A&R had 'commissioned' the Japan book and were going to publish it. Monteith wrote that, though Faber had no legal claim against Porter, they naturally felt very annoyed about the episode.[13]

Beatrice and John Abernethy agreed that, though Porter's behaviour was, as Beatrice said, 'ghastly', Angus and Robertson should certainly keep *The Actors*. So Abernethy wrote a letter of rueful courtesy to Charles Monteith, who replied graciously: no hard feelings on either side. 'Hal is an unsatisfactory customer, isn't he?' added Monteith, British publisherspeak underlining the fact that, if Hal Porter had ever doubted it, his career as a Faber author was now at an end.[14]

The Actors did not sell. Haruko Morika, who reviewed it in *Nation* in November 1968, described it as 'stifling in its lack of common humanity'. Porter did much better with his book of Japanese stories, *Mr Butterfry and Other Tales of New Japan*, which A&R published in 1970. Beatrice told the author that she did admire the stories and found them horrifying and fascinating, and they appeared with very little editorial change.

A *Bulletin* interview in April 1969 leaned heavily on Porter's dear-boy, gin-and-tonic style, fully displayed for the occasion. Beatrice wondered why journalists always tried to make Porter even more like himself than he was. As he aged, Porter was increasingly trapped in his own persona. Ken Wilder, who came out from London to run the Australian office of William Collins (and who was Collins's representative on the A&R board after the events of 1962), considered him 'a sort of colonial Bertie Wooster'.[15]

Beatrice was always after Porter to write another novel, and was gratified when the manuscript of *The Right Thing* turned up at the end of 1968. She even had A&R type it so it could be entered in the 1969 Adelaide *Advertiser* competition for an unpublished novel. Unfortunately, nobody at A&R liked it much: Douglas Stewart described it, in an undated reader's report, as 'naïve, amateurish, melodramatic and indeed ludicrous'. A&R turned it down, a slightly embarrassing decision because it then won a prize.

With A&R's blessing Porter approached Rigby, who accepted the novel – which then promptly won another prize, this time in the 1970 Captain Cook Bicentenary literary competition. There were raised eyebrows at A&R, and Beatrice valiantly wrote a letter of congratulation. 'I suppose you're committed now to Rigby for *The Right Thing*,' she said, 'which we did not turn down but wanted you to revise. (I knew you wouldn't.)'[16]

It was probably because she knew Porter so well that Beatrice always forgave his treacheries: there was no point in suddenly being upset over behaviour she had accepted for almost twenty years. Beatrice was aware she was one of three women whom Porter called his 'old girlfriends' – the others were his divorced wife and a friend, Margaret Ward.[17] He used to say that they would all sit in bathchairs with golden wheels, looking at the sunset in the old folks' home. This prospect was still a safe distance away, and in the meantime Beatrice could still write to Porter:'I wish you could come to Sydney. You could stay with me if you promised not to keep me up grogging on all night and not to bring lonely taxi-drivers in for a drink at 3 am.'[18]

During all the A&R upheavals of the late 1950s and early 1960s Beatrice continued with the other, unpaid, part of her job: supporting Australian literature. At various times she was on the committees of Sydney's three major literary societies: the English Association, the Fellowship of Australian Writers and PEN. All had regular evening meetings, all existed to celebrate literature, and because Sydney was a small place, they all had practically the same membership.[19] For a long time the English Association and the Fellowship of Australian Writers met at the Feminist Club room at 77 King Street in the city.

PEN was more political than the others, the local branch of an international organisation that had been genuinely influential during the Cold War. It was a vigorous group, with committed members who had some literary prescience, nominating Patrick White for the Nobel Prize some years before his award in 1973. During the 1960s they held some outstanding functions, including a dinner for English novelist Angus Wilson, a reception at the University of Sydney for Yevgeny Yevtushenko and, in conjunction with the English Association and undoubtedly of great significance to Beatrice, a reception in July 1969 for Christina Stead on her first visit to Australia for forty years.

This last occasion cannot have been entirely comfortable for Beatrice, nor was it for Stead herself. Stead's shyness about meeting strangers had hardened into a defensiveness that at the age of sixty-seven could make her intimidating. Beatrice was well aware that though she might express her sincere admiration for Stead's work, A&R had shown itself to be generally indifferent to it, which Stead of course knew too. Indeed, fifteen years after A&R had turned Stead down, only three of her novels were in print in Australian editions: A&R hardbacks of *For Love Alone* and *Seven Poor Men of Sydney* and a Sun Books paperback of *The Salzburg Tales*.[20] Beatrice and Christina Stead met at the PEN meeting and probably encountered each other at the FAW a little later, but not surprisingly their acquaintance failed to ripen.

Though Beatrice's position at A&R was gradually changing, in the wider literary community she was just as influential as ever, largely because of her work as a judge of the Miles Franklin Award. Early in 1957 Beatrice, with the other judges named in Miles's will – Colin Roderick, the Mitchell Librarian Jean F. Arnot, poet Ian Mudie, and Miles's accountant George Williams – met to decide upon the first winner. There were nineteen entries, including the text of Ray Lawler's play *Summer of the Seventeenth Doll*, and Beatrice had probably read most of them already. She had even edited several, including Henrietta Drake-Brockman's *The Wicked and the Fair* and the light novel *Green Leaves* by Helen Fowler. One she hadn't read – *They're a Weird Mob* – but she had the opportunity to do so now. (Given that, over the years, the Miles Franklin has become *the* prize for an Australian literary novel, it is interesting to see how many 'popular' novels were submitted in its first few years.)

On 2 April 1958, more than a year after the winner was chosen, Beatrice, the other judges and distinguished guests assembled in the Rural Bank in Martin Place, a building whose banking chamber featured a bas-relief of art deco sheep, horses and horny-handed sons of toil that Miles Franklin would certainly have approved of. Beatrice listened while the chairman of the panel, Colin Roderick, announced that the unanimous choice for the first Miles Franklin Award was *Voss* by Patrick White. Prime Minister Robert Menzies, no less, presented a cheque for £500 to the author, describing his fifth novel as a 'quite remarkable work' that, like much other Australian writing, was growing away from excessive attention to earthy humour and beginning to explore the psychological aspects of character. Either Menzies had actually read *Voss* or he or one of his staff had taken a good look at the judges' report.

Though Beatrice admired White's work, she did not love it wholeheartedly, thinking some of his writing overelaborate. Generally she regarded him as she did Christina Stead: a gifted writer of whom she was slightly in awe because of personality as well as talent. Her relationship with White had never been wholly comfortable; perhaps she thought he blamed her for the unpleasant little contretemps with Hal Porter at Folly Point. She knew how cruel and witty White could be; she might not have known that he consistently referred to her as 'Beatrice Davis, BA', with a downward inflection that consigned her firmly to the ranks of the literal-minded, schoolteacherly and pretentious who, he considered, ruled Australia's intellectual roost.[21]

White won the Miles Franklin Award again in 1961 for *Riders in the Chariot*, and *The Solid Mandala* was chosen in 1966. However, learning that his publishers Eyre & Spottiswoode had entered *The Solid Mandala* without his knowledge or consent, he withdrew it just before the announcement was made in April, suggesting the award should be divided between Elizabeth Harrower for *The Watch Tower* and Peter Mathers for *Trap*.[22] The judges decided on the latter.

Judges' decisions were not always unanimous, as the judges' report made a point of mentioning. When Randolph Stow won with *To the Islands* in 1958, two of the five judges preferred *Into the Morning* by Elizabeth Webb. (There were some interesting contenders that year, including Elizabeth Harrower's *The Long Prospect*, Christopher Koch's *The Boys in the Island* and Thea Astley's first novel, *Girl With a Monkey*.) In 1962 the judges were so far from unanimity that the prize was shared between Thea Astley for *The Well Dressed Explorer* and George Turner for *The Cupboard Under the Stairs*. The judges' meetings must have been lively: two voted for Astley, two for Turner and one for *Amid the Plenty* by Gavin Casey. There is little doubt which novel Beatrice favoured. In her judges' report – judges took it in turns to chair the committee – she gave *Explorer* high praise, saying that the main character George Brewster 'may become as memorable in Australian writing as Sinclair Lewis' Mr Babbitt', while her comments on George Turner's novel have the lacklustre blandness of mediocre jacket copy: 'an absorbing, compassionate story of a man's struggle for normality in a country town after treatment in a mental hospital'.[23]

Beatrice maintained that she hated making public speeches, but she always spoke clearly and calmly, often without notes. Although she gave the impression that she was good at speaking off the cuff, she took her responsibility seriously and thoroughly rehearsed her speeches. The judges' reports she prepared and delivered for the Miles Franklin Award were always direct and succinct, seldom leaving listeners in any doubt about her opinion of the prize-winning book. Beatrice seldom bothered with the usual anodyne remarks that all entrants were equally worthy and the judges had difficulty making up their minds. When Stow's *To the Islands* won in 1958, Beatrice said that of the seventeen novels

submitted, six showed genuine literary quality and twelve mature narrative competence, the message being that only Stow had demonstrated
both. Her comments on Peter Mathers's *Trap* began, rather predictably, by
calling it a literary tour de force showing great comic and satiric talent,
but she then said it was 'a very unpleasant book indeed'. (She wasn't alone
there: Sir Roy McKerihan, who presented the prize to Mathers's brother
in the author's absence, said, 'There are parts I wouldn't like my wife to
read.') Beatrice's straightforward approach was very much in the spirit of
Miles Franklin herself.

One novel very much in the Franklin spirit was *Careful, He Might
Hear You* by Sumner Locke Elliott, the winner in 1963. In a year that
saw a record twenty-nine entries, with novels by Barbara Jefferis,
Randolph Stow, Jessica Anderson and Gavin Casey, the judges chose the
novel that was probably most closely linked with Miles herself in its evocation of a vanished Australia. But Miles Franklin's personal taste was
never a consistently strong factor, a question that came up for debate in
1959 when the prize was posthumously awarded to Vance Palmer for *The
Big Fellow*. Palmer had died the same year and it was argued that the prize
should have gone to a living novelist, as Miles had surely intended. (The
question of 'what Miles would have liked' had disappeared entirely
by 1977, the year Ruth Park won the Award for *Swords and Crowns
and Rings*.[24])

People who serve on the same committees year after year grow to
understand each other's literary tastes, prejudices and blind spots, and this
was certainly true of the Miles Franklin committee. Beatrice always
looked for writing that transmuted everyday life in an imaginative way,
reserving special scorn for 'roast and boil prose' and for flatly written studies of domestic life. At the same time she demanded clarity and precision
in writing, echoing her own cast of mind and tendency to succinctness.
She disliked writing that was too 'experimental' (as demonstrated by
her reaction to *Trap*) and she liked a strong narrative line with memorable
characters. Beatrice also had a sharp eye for personal relationships
described in a way that she thought did not ring true: 'Well, you just can't
believe that,' she would say dismissively.[25] Her opinions, however, were
not always fully formed. Several writers remember that if dinner

conversation at Folly Point turned to the Miles Franklin Award, Beatrice would canvass her guests' opinions of various writers' talent without quite admitting those writers were candidates, probably to reinforce her own instincts and judgements.

The Miles Franklin judging process was mostly harmonious. Beatrice got on well with Jean Arnot and subsequent Mitchell librarians, and she and Ian Mudie were on cordial terms. Colin Roderick she found more difficult, partly because he persisted in interrupting and talking over his fellow judges: she considered him a cross they all had to bear. She also deplored his habit, after he had resigned from A&R in 1966 and gone to live in north Queensland, of reviewing some of the entries in the *Townsville Bulletin*, signalling those he preferred before any decision had been made.

Quite often Beatrice and Leonie Kramer, professor of English at Sydney University who joined the Miles Franklin committee in the mid-1960s, sided against Roderick. The two women formed a friendship that transcended work on the Miles Franklin committee and it is not difficult to see why. Though Kramer was younger than Beatrice, they were both highly intelligent women who had carved out positions for themselves in traditionally male environments; they were quick at sizing people up, knew how to be charming to men, were articulate and impatient with waffle or prevarication. Above all, perhaps, neither particularly cared what people thought. (Another possible bond between them was that Patrick White disliked them both.) As a combination on the committee, they could be formidable – though always with great politeness.

As time passed, the Miles Franklin Award became only one of several major Australian literary prizes, and as Beatrice gradually withdrew from prominence in literary circles she began to find reading for the prize a bit of a chore. It was a way of keeping up with what Australian novelists were writing, but she found herself less and less in sympathy with that, too. However, she never missed a committee meeting unless she was really ill. Being on the Miles Franklin Award committee was a duty Beatrice had assumed, and she had a strong sense of duty. Besides, she felt she owed it to Miles.

In March 1960 Beatrice flew to Adelaide for the third Miles Franklin Award presentation, the only time in its history that this event has taken place outside Sydney. The chair that year was the South Australian-based poet Ian Mudie, and the presentation was the centrepiece of the very first Writers' Week, now a celebrated segment of the Adelaide Festival of Arts.

The first Writers' Week was a sedate affair. Shoehorned into the festival almost as an afterthought, it was intended to be a chance for Australian writers to get together. One of the early organisers constantly referred to Writers' Week as a 'safety valve': the assumption being, presumably, that if Australian writers were left in their solitary garrets their frustration, despair and loneliness would cause them to explode. Invitations to overseas visitors came later, as did the emphasis on readers casually 'meeting the author'. During those early Writers' Weeks, small numbers of earnest and dedicated readers would turn up to the forbidding lecture theatre at the State Library of South Australia to hear authors talking about the place of Australian literature in education or the existence of specifically Australian poetry. The whole university/tutorial atmosphere suggested that Australian literature was a worthy pursuit: indeed, good for you.

Those first Writers' Weeks give a depressing insight into the status of Australian literature in the early 1960s. Though Australian novels were increasingly appearing on university curricula, though Australian literature qualified for a university chair (in 1962, at the University of Sydney, with G.A. Wilkes its first professor), those who wrote it were not highly valued. In the words of Geoffrey Dutton, an Australian writer was still considered 'a pretty crook sort of minor tradesman'.[26] Being a writer in Australia was considered character-building, too; in 1962 Frank Dalby Davison suggested that writers should be content with a fairly low standard of living. 'Domestic women', he said, had it easier than the men, as they were supported by their husbands and could set aside part of the day for writing.

Writers' Week gradually widened in scope and diminished in earnestness, and from the start Beatrice was an important participant. Her eminence, knowledge of writers and social skills made her an obvious choice as a chair of panel sessions. But with her elegant, immaculate style of dressing, her quick intelligence and rather patrician manner, she could be headmistressy. When she chaired a tribute to Kenneth Slessor in 1974, David Malouf wrote:

> Like a good hostess she put us at ease, she invited us in, she offered to share with us some of the secrets of that close circle of friends and colleagues who had known Slessor and shared his work. But in doing so she remained, for all her graciousness, just a little proprietorial. One was given the clear sense that however well we might have known Slessor from our reading, we hadn't known him as the platform did. We were outsiders.[27]

Beatrice never enjoyed being on Writers' Week panels: she went to Adelaide every second year only as part of what she called her 'duty to literature'. Once her task was over she had a much better time, catching up with writers she hadn't seen for years and meeting new ones. Hal Porter and Xavier Herbert, fixtures at the early festivals, always sought her out. 'Let's go and annoy Beatrice,' Porter would say to Herbert, as if they were a couple of naughty children, and they would all go drinking together. At the 1968 Writers' Week the Adelaide-based A&R children's editor Barbara Ker Wilson hosted a party to launch several books. It was hot, and Beatrice wanted to wear a strapless dress but did not have a suitable bra. Not wanting her nipples to show through the light fabric, she appealed to Ker Wilson for help. 'Oh,' said Ker Wilson, 'that's easy. You put a bandaid across them, it's the same colour as your skin and nobody will know the difference.' Beatrice followed her advice. At the end of the evening, unable to bring herself to rip the bandaids off her breasts, she had to ask Ker Wilson to do it for her.

Not all Beatrice's encounters in Adelaide were literary, even peripherally. At the very first Writers' Week in 1960 she met a man who became very important to her. One afternoon she was holding court at the bar in the South Australian Hotel when the husband of an Adelaide-based relative introduced her to his companion John Broadbent, a solicitor. Beatrice shook hands with Broadbent and both of them liked what they saw. Broadbent, a few years younger than Beatrice, was a powerfully built man, not particularly tall, well dressed, with blue eyes and a moustache. Based in Sydney, he was a former Rat of Tobruk who had won the DSO and usually led his battalion at the Anzac Day march. Intelligent, well read, interested in writing, good-looking with a military bearing and a pleasant speaking voice, he was everything that Beatrice admired. Not only did he have the same medals as her adored father, he even looked a little like Charles Herbert Davis. They very soon became lovers, spending time together on weekends at Folly Point (Broadbent was married) or attending literary gatherings. 'We had no responsibilities except to our congeniality,' Broadbent said many years later.[28] Their relationship lasted more than thirty years.

Bartonry and Walshism

In the 1960s many people thought Beatrice's life ran on oiled wheels. She seemed to have organised everything as she wanted it; she loved the house at Folly Point, her job was satisfying, her social life pleasant. In John Broadbent she had a regular, undemanding male companion to squire her to literary gatherings in town, while there was Sackville and Dick Jeune if she felt she needed to escape to a country retreat.

Dick was now in his late seventies and quite happy to live up on the Hawkesbury, growing oranges and avocados and guarding his chickens against marauding foxes. In twenty years the house at Tizzana Road had hardly changed. Beatrice had had the phone put on, and electricity had replaced its original kerosene lamps, but it was still basically an old wooden farmhouse. Inside the layout was simple – a central living room furnished with books and pictures, including some prized watercolours and etchings, and a double-brick fireplace at the farthest end. Dick's desk was on the side overlooking the verandah and the river, while two small bedrooms led off it, along with a tiny kitchen, scullery and bathroom. Occasionally a horse would wander over to the house and poke its nose through the kitchen window.

Beatrice loved Folly Point, but the house at Sackville was her special place. Getting there was a chore: when she left the office on Fridays she had about an hour's train journey to Windsor, laden with food for the weekend, then she had to take a taxi at the station for a twenty-minute drive over dirt roads to the house. But once she arrived, for two days she could stop being Beatrice Davis, editor, and forget about work and books. She rarely brought manuscripts to the house, and if she had invited friends for the weekend, as she often did, they rarely talked about literature.

The locals were used to seeing her occasionally, and she was on friendly terms with them all, but they knew Dick better. Now a bull-necked, tanned old man in ancient baggy shorts and a shirt or safari jacket – he never dressed up in the country – Dick was often to be seen riding along the dusty road on his tractor. He was as tough as old boots. Beatrice's nephew Charles, staying for the weekend, saw him stride into the living room one morning looking a bit shaken, and help himself to a large whisky. This seemed odd behaviour on a Saturday morning, and Charles asked whether anything was wrong. Dick shook his head. 'Fell off the bloody roof,' he growled.

Beatrice continued to see a great deal of her family. Her mother Emily had died, after a long illness and with dementia, in October 1952. True to her usual practice, Beatrice had said little about this at the time, or later, and any comments she made generally demonstrated that she and Emily had never become close. But her mother's death affected Beatrice. Knowing that dementia often runs in families, as she aged she was increasingly haunted by the fear that such a fate might be in store for her.

Granny Deloitte had also died, leaving Beatrice's Aunt Enid free to be an independent single woman. With very little money of her own, she moved into a small rented apartment on the north side of Sydney Harbour, supporting herself by doing clerical jobs. Her only indulgence was travel; unlike her niece Beatrice she enjoyed seeing new places by herself. Under a veneer of gentlewomanly grandeur, Enid was also very friendly, and her address books were crammed with the names and phone numbers of friends she had made in Sydney and abroad. On her first trips to England after World War II she capitalised on her not particularly close family connection with the international accountancy firm Deloittes, made friends with the chairman in London, and kept in touch with him and the company executives. When the firm's Sydney office held special events, Enid Deloitte was always invited.

Beatrice was very fond of Enid – the only person in the world, possibly apart from Dick Jeune, who still thought of her as 'dear little Beatrice'. Every year Beatrice organised a birthday party for her aunt at Folly Point. Aunt and niece had many things in common: they lived alone, were unmarried and earned their own living, though Enid was more interested in Deloitte family matters and family history. Beatrice's worldliness in sexual matters was unknown to her aunt, who, belonging to a generation that recalled the scandalous Oscar Wilde, confided in her eighties to her great-niece Anne, 'There's a lot of talk around the place about homosexuals. But, you know, I've never been really sure what they *do*.'

Another crucial difference between them was their attitude to money. Enid lived frugally – Beatrice used to joke that her aunt could hold a party for thirty people on one bottle of sherry – and she was a good manager, for she had never had much money of her own. She saved enough to take two extensive overseas trips and used a small inheritance from a friend to buy her own apartment in Cremorne, north of the harbour. Beatrice, on the other hand, had always had the cushion of the Bridges estate, and with her Angus and Robertson salary she was quite well off. But she spent money as fast as she earned it – on clothes, entertaining, books, the house. Enid was far more fiscally sophisticated, in fact more of a modern working woman, making her own financial decisions independently, whereas Beatrice considered such matters irksome, preferring to let others handle them for her.

Through the 1960s and into the 1970s Beatrice's Sydney was being torn down, reshaped, beginning to turn from a shabby Victorian seaport to a more modern-looking city. Change was literally in the air as the westerlies blew around the raw, gritty dust of demolished buildings. It seemed an appropriate time for Angus and Robertson, that grand old edifice that had stood unchallenged for the best part of a century, to be challenged by sleeker, more functional publishing companies, all of them of British or American design.

The first of these was Penguin Books, which had opened a sales office in Melbourne just after the war. In 1961 they started a local publishing operation, intending to produce quality paperbacks by finding good local books to reprint as well as commissioning originals. Brian Stonier was managing director, with Geoffrey Dutton and Max Harris as literary advisers. Penguin were challenging A&R in a field that George Ferguson had entered with some reluctance, and indeed the Pacific Books imprint (initially edited by Douglas Stewart) was not proving particularly successful, partly because the titles brought back into print ranged right across A&R's list without much focus. Judith Wright was disconcerted to find *The Generations of Men* being publicised at the same time as a book about spiders.[1] Pacific Books also looked cheaper than the Australian Penguins, which generally had better quality paper and binding. With the added advantage of the Penguin name and prestige, Penguins sold better than their A&R competitors from the first.

Penguin and Sun Books – a new paperback publishing company set up in 1965 by former Penguin staff members Geoffrey Dutton, Max Harris and Brian Stonier, with George Smith – found Angus and Robertson exasperating to deal with. Whenever Beatrice or Douglas Stewart was asked to release the paperback rights to various A&R titles, they often refused on the grounds, usually spurious, that they intended to issue those books in paperback themselves. Geoffrey Dutton said he grew tired of having Sun Books act as talent scouts for A&R, particularly when a title had been out of print for many years.[2] When A&R did agree to relinquish a title, their judgement let them down: they gave Sun Books the rights to Judah Waten's *Alien Son*, which turned out to be one of the new company's bestsellers.

A new generation of 'larrikin publishers' was taking on A&R at their own game, showing entrepreneurial skill and creative flair.[3] Andrew Fabinyi, who had come to Australia as a postwar refugee, was building up F.W. Cheshire in Melbourne; Frank Eyre was running Oxford University Press in Melbourne. During the 1950s and 1960s it was these companies, not Angus and Robertson, who published Australia's most significant non-fiction, including A.A. Phillips's *The Australian Tradition* (1958), Russel Ward's *The Australian Legend* (1958), Robin Boyd's *The Australian Ugliness* (1960), Donald Horne's *The Lucky Country* (1964) and

Geoffrey Blainey's *The Tyranny of Distance* (1966). Oxford University Press were developing a list of children's books to rival A&R's. The Angus and Robertson speciality, books that should be published regardless of profit, was no longer their monopoly; Manning Clark's *History of Australia* and the *Australian Dictionary of Biography* came from Melbourne University Press. Brian Clouston and Lloyd O'Neil (who had started his publishing career as a bookshop assistant at 89 Castlereagh Street) co-founded Jacaranda Press in the 1950s, publishing educational books, natural history, fiction and poetry – again, A&R's traditional areas. In 1960 O'Neil left Jacaranda to establish Lansdowne Press, which made a killing with books about sport. And the Americans could not be kept out of the Australian market forever: a number of US-based companies were publishing books for the tertiary educational market.[4]

At a time when almost all worthwhile Australian books had been stamped with A&R's logo of the thistle and waratah, it had made sense for A&R to publish right across the range, from novels to poetry to children's books, natural history, biography and educational texts. But now, with increased competition from other publishers, A&R was casting around for a niche to call their own. In October 1969 John Abernethy expressed his concerns to George Ferguson:

> Time and again in New York I got the impression that the A&R general list, as expressed in the current Sydney and London catalogues, was at best puzzling and at worst off-putting, for New York editors . . . it was clear that many editors wondered how anyone with a list as relatively small as ours could make a good job of being so many different kinds of publisher at once . . . We came away, in fact, with the feeling that except in educational and children's books (the only parts of our list that appear to have unity of character and direction) A&R presents a disturbingly diffuse and unkempt image to the world.[5]

A&R were also slow to respond to new trends in publishing. Though the company spent time and money establishing a presence in Asia, they continued to use Halstead Press to print their full-colour books, while their competitors had turned to the Hong Kong and Singapore companies that produced better-looking books more cheaply. A telling anecdote in this context is the story of Neville Cayley's *What Bird is That?*, which had been a good seller for A&R since its first appearance in 1931. In the early 1960s it came up for yet another reprint, but the original blocks with their small coloured drawings were too worn to be printed from. Books on natural history with large and detailed photographs were doing well in the USA and in Britain, and A&R had the opportunity of revamping the book's format. But management decided to leave it just as it was: Cayley, they said, was a classic and readers would expect no changes. The original drawings were scaled down so the tiny pictures looked just as they had always done. Lansdowne soon began publishing natural history books intended for use in the field and sales of Cayley – and other old-fashioned-looking A&R natural history books – dropped dramatically.

As Frank Thompson has pointed out, to stay in business publishers need to be attuned to what people want, have a feel for new trends, work out which books will catch the public eye. They need to be able to catch the next wave – and there were times when A&R didn't seem to realise the surf was up.[6] George Ferguson's 'we are dispensers not prescribers' – his precept that A&R's job was not to decide what people should read but to give them what they wanted – was altogether too passive, too reactive for the new publishing scene.

Watching Angus and Robertson with frustration and foreboding was Ken Wilder, managing director of Collins Australia and the Collins representative on the A&R board.[7] His position was a difficult one. When Collins bought Packer's A&R shares in 1962, they had agreed to keep them only until they could be sold to a friendly buyer without loss, which everyone anticipated would happen within three years. But eight years later Collins still had almost £1 million tied up in A&R – money that could have been financing their own Australian publishing operation. Collins had also agreed not to interfere in the running of A&R in any way, but Wilder found George Ferguson's less-than-dynamic management style increasingly frustrating (and Ferguson, of course, was uncomfortable about having a rival publisher present at board meetings).

The situation pleased nobody, though apparently Angus and Robertson had come to accept Collins as a permanent feature of their managerial landscape.

Then, early in 1969, Ken Wilder dropped a bombshell. Collins had decided to cut their losses and withdraw their shareholding from Angus and Robertson. Their own local publishing program had been successful, they wished to expand, and they needed the money to finance this and to set up a new distribution plant near Moss Vale, south of Sydney. They would not pull out immediately, but would give Angus and Robertson a year to find a friendly shareholder. To George Ferguson, Collins's decision was not merely a blow but an affront, almost a betrayal. He and the board had clearly forgotten that Collins had bought into A&R simply to prevent an American publisher from controlling the company, and that the arrangement had never been intended to last forever.

One way out of A&R's dilemma – and an argument for the view that what happened next could have been prevented – was to raise money on the value of the shares, rebuild 89 Castlereagh Street and develop the property, or sell it to a developer and lease it back. Here was another opportunity for A&R to realise their assets, capitalise on their real estate and, by becoming liquid, get themselves out of trouble. But despite their narrow escape from Burns a decade before, the board maintained their traditional view: Angus and Robertson were publishers, not dealers in real estate. For them, selling or borrowing against their property was like trying to run a shipping company by selling the ships. The board did nothing, and early in 1970 Collins pulled out of Angus and Robertson. And, just as there had been ten years before, someone was waiting in the wings.

Gordon Barton was a young businessman whose company, the International Parcel Express Company (IPEC), had made large profits in the transport business and who was looking to expand. He already had an interest in publishing, though not through books: his newspaper *Nation Review* was essential reading for anyone under thirty-five who wanted a quizzical and irreverent slant on Australian life and politics. He ran a think tank called Tjuringa Securities, cheekily named after the sacred Aboriginal objects but with the even cheekier twist that Tjuringa Securities removed objects from other companies. They were in fact asset strippers, corporate raiders, among the first in Australia.

Barton not only had his eye on Angus and Robertson, but he could see exactly how to go about acquiring it. It wasn't difficult. IPEC had a share in the Anthony Hordern office building on the southern side of the CBD, which was coveted by the AMP Society. AMP also wanted the Angus and Robertson bookshop at 89 Castlereagh Street to complete their Centrepoint development. IPEC and AMP did what amounted to a straight swap. AMP put up the money, IPEC did a deal with Collins, who got cash for their shares, and Angus and Robertson's shareholders got cash and IPEC shares. AMP got the site at 89 Castlereagh Street, Collins the value of its shareholding, IPEC the company. By the end of 1970, after more than eighty years as a family concern, and without a struggle, Angus and Robertson belonged to Gordon Barton.[8]

Many people could not understand (some still can't) why George Ferguson and the board failed to act sooner to keep the company in their hands. There is an argument that the Barton takeover need never have happened. At the time George Ferguson apparently considered it as something of an act of God. He wrote to Rohan Rivett in mid-1970:

> We withstood the battle and the breeze for nearly ninety years on our own and could have gone on doing it. But we have to take life as it comes and make the best of it and this we here are prepared to do, providing that Barton is fair dinkum. He says that he intends to carry the place on as it is, etc., etc., but one knows that these things are usually said on occasions like this and only too often they are not meant. Whether he means it or not I don't know yet . . . The big question is whether in fact we are really going to have a say in things or not. If not, then there's no point in staying and I should probably say goodbye to the old firm after forty years' service. But we'll see.[9]

The swiftness and efficiency of the Barton takeover left A&R employees confused, almost shell-shocked. 'It feels strange to know we are the property of someone else,' wrote Beatrice to Hal Porter at the end of 1970.[10] At least Gordon Barton didn't want to close down A&R's publishing: Beatrice and her colleagues had to take what comfort they could from that.

Shortly after he took over Angus and Robertson in 1970 Gordon Barton hosted a staff party at the Phillip's Foote steakhouse in the Rocks area. With its bare flagstone floors, rough wooden benches and tables, and nineteenth-century-style handbills on the walls, the restaurant might have been deliberately chosen as the backdrop for the speech Barton made. He was well aware, he said, that Angus and Robertson was part of Australia's history, a great Australian institution whose character he would always recognise and respect. He would never relinquish A&R, he did not want to change things: the message was 'steady as she goes'. As Beatrice listened to these reassuring words, she must have wondered whether Barton's assurances of continuity were as ersatz as the restaurant's gas-fed log fires.

Rumours were flying. Paul Hamlyn, who had made a fortune publishing big commercial picture books, was alleged to have told Barton to turn the bookshop into a supermarket and to publish only non-literary works. It was also said that Barton intended to abandon publishing altogether and sell off A&R's list to the highest bidder. No one knew what to think, everybody was jumpy. 'The situation made us all slightly eccentric,' said Barbara Ker Wilson. 'People went slightly mad for a while. It was like a divorce, I think.'[11]

The first round of changes in management came quickly. Gordon McCarthy, the young accountant who had helped broker the AMP deal for Barton, was put in charge of A&R's publishing and bookselling, a huge job. Under him were John Abernethy, who continued to be the publisher of fiction and general books – McCarthy never had any great interest in publishing – and Bruce Semler, director of the education division. Barbara Ker Wilson went to run children's book publishing from A&R's London office. One person Barton had to handle carefully was John Ferguson, not only a friend but the assumed heir apparent. Barton sent him off to manage the London office with broad hints to the effect that it was not unknown for a general who was sent to the provinces to return later and lead Rome.

Everybody had been wondering when George Ferguson would go. He had been almost completely marginalised, and early in 1971 he resigned after forty years with A&R. His decision was not unexpected: the last few years had been difficult for him. He had always been interested in publishing politics and over the years had cultivated friendships with Hamish Hamilton, Sir Stanley Unwin, Sir William Collins, and other leading British publishers; now those contacts would prove useful in his new position as the first staff director of the Australian Book Publishers' Association. Ferguson was sixty, two years younger than Beatrice. His departure was another nail in the coffin of the old A&R, and it must have underlined Beatrice's sense of insecurity and apprehension about the future.

An even more decisive break with A&R's past came later in 1971 when Angus and Robertson left 89 Castlereagh Street. Ever since David Angus and George Robertson set up their bookselling business, number 89 had been a Sydney institution. Now the stock was moved to a more modern store in Pitt Street, part of the Centrepoint complex. To Australia's book buyers, the demise of the bookshop was the most obvious and the saddest symbol of the changes in Angus and Robertson. Number 89 Castlereagh Street stood empty, a dismal cavern, until the building was finally demolished in 1975. A branch of the ANZ bank now stands on the site.

With the bookshop went many employees who had spent their working lives there, including the head fiction-and-general buyer, Hedley Jeffries. His domain was vanishing and he had little interest in the new premises in Pitt Street. For years his ambition had been to work in Hatchard's bookshop, Piccadilly, and he decided to retire and go to London to fulfil his dream. Alas, Hatchard's management considered him too old to be on their staff and he returned sadly to Australia.

Other changes struck further blows to A&R's heart. First under George Robertson, then under George Ferguson, the company had taken pride in the number of men who had worked for the company all their lives, literally 'man and boy'. Perhaps a dozen were left, mostly in their eighties, and they were working not out of love for the company but because they could not afford to retire. With all its paternalistic attitudes, Angus and Robertson (like other companies of its vintage, admittedly) had never had a proper superannuation plan. Halstead Press, for whom most of these men worked, had also become a liability, unable to compete with cheaper offshore printing prices. Gordon Barton sold Halstead Press to John Sands in 1972 and the old printers and type-setters were dismissed with *ex gratia* payments. The following year the education division was sold to McGraw-Hill.

In March 1972 the publishing department moved from 221 George Street across the harbour to a boxlike new two-storey office at Glover Street, Cremorne. Beatrice thoroughly disliked the change, not least because she would have to give up her studio at 219 George Street. She conceded that the new offices were within easy reach of Folly Point and close to Aunt Enid's apartment, but this was just one more upheaval she could do without. She thought the new quarters 'hideous' and hated the colour scheme. 'The new office . . . is painted bright yellow, inside and out, to cheer us all up,' she commented acidly to Hal Porter.[12]

The move to Cremorne heralded a change in management that would affect her more than she ever suspected at the time. Gordon Barton announced that he was appointing a new publisher so that Gordon McCarthy could concentrate on the retail side of the business. This development immediately caused an outbreak of turf wars. John Abernethy, Bruce Semler and John Ferguson all felt entitled to the job. While Beatrice had never had managerial aspirations outside her own department, with another level of management above her she was now just one of the working editors, which she did not like. The other editors who worked with her were resentful on her behalf as well as their own.

With all these clashing ambitions and disappointments, the atmos-phere at A&R was thoroughly unpleasant, so Gordon Barton decided to appoint a publisher from outside the company. When he made his choice, the staff, and others in the industry, were stunned. Richard Walsh? The gadfly publisher and editor of Barton's cheeky, scrappy *Nation Review*? Why would Barton choose an abrasive thirty-year-old iconoclast, the former editor of the satirical magazine *Oz* whose natural habitat was apparently hot water, to find and publish books for a traditional company like Angus and Robertson? Shaking their heads, A&R's competitors considered Barton's choice downright eccentric. 'Richard's bright, but he doesn't know anything about book publishing,' was the general view.

But Barton wasn't looking for an experienced publisher. He liked what Walsh was doing on *Nation Review* and could see that this young medical graduate turned magazine editor, ten years younger than he, represented the assertive, well-educated, progressive generation that would shortly sweep Gough Whitlam's Labor Party into office. There was a youthful impatience about Walsh, a willingness to chop away dead wood, to bring in fresh ideas, and Barton thought that was just what Angus and Robertson required.

From the beginning Walsh was keen to take on the job: he loved books, could see that A&R was creaking, and he was bristling with ideas. He and John Abernethy were friends, on the same wavelength, with similar tastes; Walsh approved of Abernethy's attempts to make A&R's fiction publishing less conservative. The change in career direction – dodging defamation writs on the *Review* one minute, running A&R's publishing the next – didn't faze him at all, but he wanted to hang on to *Nation Review*. He and Barton reached a compromise – reluctantly on Barton's part – whereby Walsh would spend half his working week in Sydney, half at the *Review* in Melbourne. Walsh handed over the *Review*'s editing to George Munster and John Hepworth, though in effect he continued to run it. He was soon doing two full-time jobs simultaneously, running from one to the other, devoting only two days a week to the more difficult and demanding, which he would have to learn from scratch. He was frequently seen hurrying out of the office on the way to the airport with a colleague running beside him, into the street or the car park, needing a decision.

Walsh began overhauling the editorial department. For many years the royalty records system had been in the hands of Bert Iliffe, who had devised a Byzantine system for recording and paying royalties that was the bane of A&R's authors' lives and that nobody understood. A member of the clerical staff was seconded to help streamline the system and shortly afterwards Iliffe, then in his eighties, left the company.

Beatrice soon discovered that Richard Walsh needed to be involved in every aspect of A&R, including the running of the editorial department. He decided to change A&R's system of reporting on manuscripts. Instead of having two readers report on every one that came in, he set up a 'poison-tasting' system, with one person responsible for looking through all the unsolicited manuscripts, culling those considered unsuitable and sending them straight back with rejection letters. He told Abernethy, Beatrice, Douglas Stewart and the other editors that they would no longer evaluate all the fiction that came in, that a junior editor or clerical assistant would do the initial sorting: 'I want my senior editors editing manuscripts, not reading crap,' he said bluntly. Beatrice took this as a slap in the face. Reading bad manuscripts and writing reports about them was not her favourite occupation, but she did not like losing part of the job she had always done.

More infuriating still she found the types of books and authors being encouraged by 'the boy publisher', as she disdainfully called her new boss. Walsh's view was essentially the same as that of his contemporary, the writer and publisher Michael Wilding, who wrote:

> We knew there was good prose around that wasn't surfacing in the quarterlies or the overground publishing houses . . . no more formula bush tales, no more restrictions to the beginning-middle-end story, no more preconceptions about a well-rounded tale . . . we wanted to provide space for the varieties of stories that weren't being catered for.[13]

It was these new writers – Wilding, Frank Moorhouse, Kate Jennings, Bob Adamson, Pamela Brown – Richard Walsh was after. They were not the authors Beatrice understood or wanted. She considered Frank Moorhouse's short-story collection *The Americans, Baby* (1972) banal, the treatment of sex clinical and vulgar. She was much more comfortable with Dal Stivens's *A Horse of Air* than with David Ireland's *The Unknown Industrial Prisoner*; had more common ground with Hal Porter's artfully crafted novel *The Right Thing* than the harsh, confronting collection of antiwar poetry *We Took Their Orders and Are Dead*.

Walsh was also making wide-ranging changes in the presentation of A&R's books. The Pacific Books imprint was abandoned; paperbacks were put into either A&R Classics (often backlist titles whose paperback rights had been reclaimed from other publishers) or the much more commercial Arkon. Tie-ins – books published on the back of a film or TV series – were introduced, often profitably. The paperback of *My Brilliant Career* with the film's stars, Sam Neill and Judy Davis, on the cover might have helped generate money for the Franklin estate and the Miles Franklin Award, but Beatrice considered that Richard Walsh took the tie-in to new depths. Nothing could have been further from the Angus and Robertson she had known than the novelisation of the raunchy TV soap opera *Number 96*, or a re-release of Norman Lindsay's novel *The Cousin from Fiji* with a voluptuous actress from the ABC-TV adaptation on the cover.

The days when Colin Simpson, Frank Clune and Ion Idriess had been the mainstays of the non-fiction list had long gone. Clune's books slipped out of print; one or two Idriess titles were kept for the sake of the Australiana boom in the wake of the Captain Cook bicentenary, but the market was disappearing. 'It was a new audience out there,' said Richard Walsh years later. 'Australian readers were younger, becoming more sophisticated. They wanted Frank Moorhouse, not Frank Clune.'[14] Drawing on his *Nation Review* and magazine background, Walsh began to commission books from journalists and columnists – 'newspaper' not 'book' people – and to produce their work for the mass market. These cheap paperbacks were not meant to last but to supplement what people were reading in the newspapers, and they were instantly popular.

Beatrice never troubled to hide her feelings about her new boss. 'Despite Bartonry and Walshism we remain A&R,' was her comment to Hal Porter, striking her usual note of fortitude under extreme difficulty.[15] Very quietly and politely, with a flick of ridicule or a disdainfully raised eyebrow, she resisted almost everything Walsh was doing. He found this infuriating: he would much rather have had a head-on argument than be forced to contend with these ladylike tactics. Beatrice's 'extraordinarily genteel' persona irritated him; her squeamish approach to graphic sex in print he found hypocritical considering her own history. 'Her belief was that you could do what you liked, but you didn't talk about it, and you didn't write about it either, and that was fine,' he said.[16]

Of course the conflict between Walsh and Beatrice involved more than generationally opposed attitudes to sex in print, differences in political consciousness or tastes in literature. Scathing about certain authors and their work Beatrice often was, but her whole professional life had expressed her sense of stewardship about good writing, her belief that her responsibility as an editor involved maintaining standards of writing and of authorship. Her sense of authority in Angus and Robertson and within the wider literary community had derived from this role of gate-keeper, being the person who knew what was 'good'. Now she had to contend with someone who, as she saw it, encouraged crudity above craft, dismissing her notions of quality in writing or publishing as old-fashioned or irrelevant. It was partly the difference between a woman who took the primacy of the written word for granted, who had been a teenager before radio came to Australia and a mature adult before television began and who therefore considered mass media little more than interesting and occasionally useful diversions, and a young man for whom books, though vitally important, were part of a larger media mix, with television, newspapers, the movies, even cartoons helping to influence opinion.

In that era of impatient change that was the early 1970s the antagonism between Beatrice Davis and Richard Walsh was a microcosm of the conflict being played out in boardrooms, workplaces, educational institutions – even families – throughout Australia. Beatrice looked at Walsh and saw a shaggy-haired young man who thought he knew it all; Walsh looked at Beatrice and saw the purse-lipped, conservative representative of a bygone generation.

It must be said that on a day-to-day level Beatrice was not the only member of the staff who found Walsh difficult to deal with. As another editor remarked, even when you agreed with what he was doing, there was something about him that really annoyed you. Often making decisions on the run, doing too much at once, Walsh appeared to have no time for people's feelings or sensitivities. There is no way he could have changed A&R as much as he did without arousing antagonism, of course, but his decisiveness could look like cockiness; his anxiety, interventionist style and inability to delegate seemed presumptuous interference, and his brusque energy came across as a lack of respect for the experience and expertise of others.

The staff's hostility became so obvious and upsetting that Walsh considered resigning: when he was offered a job in television he almost took it. But partly from pure stubbornness, he decided to stick with A&R. The staff were often as depressed as he was, though for different reasons; many people felt that with the advent of Barton the heart had gone out of the place. Beatrice and her editors sometimes sat in her office and talked about the good old days, always ending with the same question: How had this been allowed to happen?' 'I suppose A&R was an idyllic kind of publishing ethos that couldn't go on forever,' said Beatrice's editorial colleague Marilyn Stacy years later. 'We were in a time warp, really.'[17]

Then, late in 1972, when morale was at its lowest, the company suffered another heavy blow. For months John Abernethy had been under severe stress, working too hard, drinking too much, trying to deal not only with a huge workload but with a difficult personal life. Shortly before Christmas he went on leave, checking himself into the Langton Clinic, a Sydney drug and alcohol rehabilitation facility, to dry himself out. A few days later, he suffered a heart attack and died there.

Everybody was appalled: Abernethy was only in his forties. His death was particularly shattering for Richard Walsh, who had lost his only ally. Walsh was so upset that one or two of the editors wondered whether he felt partially responsible for Abernethy's death by working him so hard. It was a very bad time.

After Abernethy's death Walsh became head of the general books division as well as managing director, and the conflict between him and Beatrice intensified. She drew her own editorial staff around her, including those now working from home such as Elisabeth Hughes and Nan McDonald, both of whom had developed health problems (Nan had cancer). To Walsh, as to Abernethy before him, Beatrice's editorial department was an implacably ladylike women's club. Her editors were always polite enough but their animosity was constant. As well as his other responsibilities Walsh liked editing books, especially the racier titles he was then commissioning. The editorial staff never cared for these, and Beatrice in particular found Walsh's assumption of the editorial role intensely annoying. She let her friends in the literary community know that in her opinion A&R had gone to the dogs, that despite all her efforts standards of editing and publishing had slipped. This was not like Beatrice. During the Burns business she had been tight-lipped about internal company matters, but now she probably felt that this was no longer the company to which she had owed such loyalty. The word spread that Walsh was an immature young man on a learning curve who was doing a great deal of damage to little purpose.

Walsh was furious. With her formidable contacts and her ability to patronise him, Beatrice was white-anting him at every turn, publicly as well as privately. 'It was like working with a prim headmistress who permanently disapproved,' he said years later. 'I'd been through that – had a fairly tough time at school as a matter of fact – and I no longer needed to go off to a place of work each day where there was a senior employee who disapproved of me.'[18] In his view Beatrice had never come to terms with A&R's need to make money and she wasn't trying to attract new authors; in effect, she was fighting a rearguard action during a taste revolution. Walsh wanted to employ editors more in tune with his ambitions for the company and he felt that Beatrice was blocking him.

Late in February 1973 Richard Walsh called Beatrice into his office. He suggested she become a consultant rather than a full-time staff member, being paid a certain amount per annum to work from home editing the books of 'her' A&R authors. An affronted Beatrice refused point blank. Walsh then told her he had no alternative: Angus and Robertson would have to let her go.

Beatrice was never one to display emotion, not even about being fired. 'I'm not surprised,' she said calmly – and given the situation between her and Walsh, this was probably true. 'I don't want you to go tomorrow,' he said. 'Just come back and tell me when you've made other arrangements and we'll talk about it.' Walsh knew Beatrice had no superannuation, and believing she was not in a good financial position he offered her an *ex gratia* payment. Though not ungenerous, it was certainly not commensurate with her thirty-six years at A&R.[19]

When the word spread that Beatrice had been dismissed, and callously, according to popular opinion, most people were shocked. They had heard of similar ruthless sackings in the US, but this was the first time such a thing had happened in Australian publishing. The Australian Society of Authors wrote that Beatrice was 'irreplaceable'; some of her longtime authors, including Thea Astley and Hal Porter, announced that they were leaving Angus and Robertson out of loyalty to her. 'The mythology about Beatrice was among the authors, certainly not in house by that time,' said Richard Walsh. 'She did have a lot of charisma, and while she was there she was very much an icon. But the new authors we were bringing on couldn't relate to her.'[20]

Nan McDonald, Elisabeth Hughes and John Tranter (who had been at A&R only a matter of months as their Singapore-based education editor) were dismissed at the same time as Beatrice.[21] Douglas Stewart put in his resignation soon afterwards, and others left as well. 'Even the tea-lady was retrenched,' wrote Anthony Barker, who resigned at the end of 1973. 'She had left in fine style, demanding a bunch of long-stemmed roses from Richard Walsh – and getting them – and then refusing to come out of her kitchen when the party in her honour was being held.'[22]

Beatrice left Angus and Robertson at the end of April 1973. She was sixty-four. 'A bit of a shock (though I hope I muffled this up) to find you're not wanted,' she told Xavier Herbert months later.[23] She didn't complain about what had happened but instead took a positive attitude, speaking to friends and family of her future plans: she could catch up on reading, it was a good time for an overseas trip, she could take Dick Jeune, now in his eighties, on a European holiday. She was not destitute. But some of those who knew her well believe that she never really recovered from being sacked from the company she had served so loyally for thirty-six years.

Folly Point and Hunters Hill

'I Thought You Needed Me Most'

In March 1973 the senior publishing staff of Thomas Nelson (Australia) Ltd – managing director Al Knight, publisher Anne Godden, senior editor Sue Ebury – heard that Beatrice had been fired from Angus and Robertson and was soon to leave. Like almost everybody in the literary community, they were appalled. They also saw Beatrice's dismissal as an opportunity.

Nelson, whose Australian office was in Melbourne, were at a crucial stage of development. Like several other English-based publishers, they had established a small sales presence in Australia many years before, chiefly to sell educational books. They had begun publishing for the local educational market in the mid-1960s and were now ready to expand into general publishing. They needed a Sydney-based editor with good contacts, someone who knew how to build a list, whose reputation would bring prestigious authors to Nelson. Al Knight lost no time in offering Beatrice the job.

Nelson's was not the only offer Beatrice received, but it was the one that suited her best. She would be given a regular salary, not a contract, so her finances – always a concern for a woman who tended to let money slip through her fingers – would remain secure. Al Knight had proposed she work at home, so Folly Point would effectively become Nelson's Sydney headquarters. Beatrice could work at a desk in her study, a pleasant room with a porthole window that faced the harbour. After the past few years at Angus and Robertson, she must have been relieved at the prospect of simply doing her job, maintaining her literary contacts, without having to bother about office politics. She must also have been pleased that Al Knight, a Canadian publisher whom she did not know, had sought her out, that he and Anne Godden admired and respected her work enough to want her. Characteristically, she expressed none of these feelings to her new employers. 'I came to Nelson because I thought you needed me most,' she told Anne Godden. Shaken by events at A&R she might have been, but she was a woman who knew her own worth.

Beatrice did not start at Nelson immediately but took almost a year off. Now was the time for the visit to Europe she felt she owed herself. She had not been out of Australia since her anxious trip in the early 1950s, when she had been on unpaid leave, spending as little as possible, trying to make contacts for Angus and Robertson and seething at British condescension. Now she could splurge some of her severance pay, knowing she had a regular salary to look forward to, so this trip would be very different. This time she wanted to go 'with Dick (just 87) under my right arm while I organise travel and things with my left', she told Xavier Herbert.[1]

While she was away, several of her friends and former authors got together to decide how best to commemorate her years at Angus and Robertson and her contribution to Australian literature. They decided on a testimonial volume, and Colin Simpson set about collecting contributions from eighty Australian authors – writers of fiction, non-fiction, poetry, children's books, as far as possible covering the range of her work at Angus and Robertson. Bound in dark blue cloth with 'A Tribute to Beatrice Davis' lettered in gold on the cover, the book, now in the State Library of New South Wales, is a fascinating record of Beatrice's editorial career. It bears out the fact that, like most editors, she probably spent more time editing non-fiction of various kinds than fiction. Among the contributors were anthropologist A.P. Elkin, Ion Idriess ('Our Favourite Editor, We of the Pen and Brush, salute thee!'); Douglas M. Barrie, author of *The Australian Blood Horse*, the 1956 Australian Book of the Year known to Beatrice's staff as The Australian Bloody Horse; H.G. Belschner, who wrote one of A&R's most successful books, *Sheep*

Management and Diseases (it sold for a guinea and, this being the price of one sheep at the time, was a bargain). Also a successful author was Helen M. Cox, author of *The Hostess Cookbook*, edited by Beatrice in 1949 and still in print twenty-three years later; her book probably stood second only to A&R's *Commonsense Cookery Book* on whose back, as George Ferguson once pointed out, much of A&R's fiction and poetry was published. Beatrice enjoyed editing cookery books – the order and precision of ingredients and methods appealed to her – though she often had arguments with the reps, usually male, who could never see why anybody would need more than one.

The book of tributes also gives a range of reactions to Beatrice's job as editor. Some of her authors thought of her as a strict but fair English teacher. Joan Phipson frankly admitted to being terrified of Beatrice when she first met her, hoping to meet the editor's exacting standards. Like several other contributors, Tom Hungerford provided a variation on the idea of the iron fist in a velvet glove: 'So quiet was she, so self-deprecating and humorous that even after 20 years I can't believe she was ever an editor,' he wrote. Cyril Pearl, whose *Morrison of Peking* A&R had published in 1967, added a witty comment:

> *To Beatrice Davis*
> *Rara avis*
> *Whose counsel, tempered with a smile*
> *Helped many a lame writer over his style.*

Some of the most thoughtful assessments of Beatrice's career came, predictably, from her A&R colleagues. Douglas Stewart wrote:

> I think it would be true to say that Beatrice initiated or revived the publishing policy which George Ferguson, always with her active participation, kept in operation so long and so successfully, which means that, as much as anyone else, and more than most, she has kept Australian literature alive for more than a quarter of a century.

George Ferguson added:

No other editor can possibly claim to have had so much influence during almost four vital decades of development in Australian publishing. When Beatrice came into A&R Australian publishing differed little from what it had been in the nineties. When she left it had been transformed into the third force in publishing in the English language; and no one had played a more important part than she had.

It was a cheerful Beatrice who wrote to Xavier Herbert in January 1974, about a month before she started her new job. The trip, she said, had been a good move. She had been able:

to see that Dick lived before he died (he enjoyed every minute); to confirm my divorce from the old firm; and to make me more than thankful that I had Australia to come home to. Anyhow I've now joined the ancient firm of Thomas Nelson (estab 1872) . . . I find them wonderful people – vital, enthusiastic and competent – and it will be fun to work for them as an editor in Sydney, with my office here at home. I'm sorry to say so, since you categorically hate all publishers; but publishing is my game, my way of life, if I have to earn a living.[2]

Nelson's Australian office was true to its UK origins, it was even something of an outpost of Empire. Al Knight was Canadian; English-born Anne Godden had worked as an editor in colonial Africa; Sue Ebury, originally from New Zealand, was married to a member of the English aristocracy; another editor, English-born Liz Macdonald, had studied at university in London and worked for Oxford University Press in the UK. Beatrice was the only Australian on the senior editorial staff. The editorial offices were on the upper floor of an ancient building in Little Collins Street, an English-looking part of Melbourne that, with its deciduous tree-lined wide streets and solid grey Victorian buildings, kept the less refined aspects of Australia at bay.

While Beatrice rejoiced to find herself working for a company where her expertise was respected and valued, she was not entirely confident. At sixty-five she was the oldest editor and she would be working directly on manuscripts for the first time in some years: could she still do it? A month or two after she started at Nelson, Anthony Barker dropped in to see her and over a glass or two of whisky – usually when Beatrice's anxieties came out – she worried about the amount of work she had taken on.[3]

However, she was encouraged to find that she resumed the rhythms and skills of close, detailed editing very quickly. She revived other habits of years: quick and decisive evaluation of manuscripts, efficient use of words and time. Some of her younger Nelson colleagues found her insistence on high standards of editorial practice and behaviour rather formidable. She even reminded Sue Ebury of her children's nanny. Ebury felt that Beatrice would have been very much at home in a certain stratum of literary London – the cultivated, well-read world of Muriel Spark and Iris Murdoch, of Michael Joseph, George Weidenfeld and Sir William Collins.[4]

When they came to know Beatrice better, her colleagues picked up occasional hints that this woman of the world, this lucid, clever judge of manuscripts, was less secure than she seemed. Just occasionally, when she was caught off balance – perhaps by an allusion to a book she hadn't read, or a production procedure that was unfamiliar – her response had a touch of defensiveness. Was this, Sue Ebury wondered, because she still felt vulnerable after what had happened at Angus and Robertson?

In December 1976 the National Book Council named Beatrice Bookman of the Year. This was the first time a woman, and an editor, had won the award, but Beatrice – no lover of inclusive language – was content to be a bookman, not a bookperson. There were tributes from several of her friends and former colleagues, including Nancy Keesing, George Ferguson and Douglas Stewart. At a dinner in her honour she nailed her traditional editorial colours to the mast, mourning what she saw as the decline in standards of language use. Another thing she deplored was the growing commercialisation of publishing generally. When Suzanne Lunney interviewed her for the oral history archives of the National Library of Australia in 1977, Beatrice cut off her reverent questions about literature with:'The sad thing about publishing is . . . you talk about publishing as though it were literature, well it's not! That's the merest fraction of it. It's usually books of information.'

Beatrice was gradually, though reluctantly, coming to terms with the way publishing had changed. Events at Angus and Robertson had more or less forced her into becoming the standard-bearer for Fowler and the *Oxford English Dictionary*, and with a staff of editors she had been able to choose the manuscripts she wished to work on – usually those of authors whose writing she knew. Now she found herself editing a wide range of manuscripts by authors whose only common denominator was that they lived in Sydney and were being published by Thomas Nelson, and her mapping pen and red ink were working overtime. Sue Ebury, the editorial liaison between Beatrice and Nelson's Melbourne-based production department, admired her meticulous work but was given the distinct impression that the authors with whom Beatrice had worked at A&R had been better writers, whose manuscripts needed less editorial attention than Nelson's. If she was trying to make Nelson believe that she had done little rewriting in the past and was not used to performing radical surgery on manuscripts, Beatrice was being disingenuous.

One of her chief delights was working with some of her favourite authors. Thea Astley had decided that Beatrice was her editor, rather than A&R being her publishers, and moved across to Nelson while Beatrice was there. Over *A Kindness Cup* and *Hunting the Wild Pineapple*, they renewed their friendly editorial relationship. Hal Porter went to Nelson for *The Extra*, the third part of his autobiography, and a book of stories, *The Clairvoyant Goat*. Nelson's staff became participants in the Hal Porter show, having dinner with him or accompanying him on pub crawls while they tried not to drink as much as he did. Robert Sessions – the young Englishman who became Nelson's publishing director when Anne Godden and Al Knight left to set up their own company Hyland House – took over the role of chief minder. Porter often spoke of Beatrice, who Sessions suspected was the only woman the writer had ever really loved, though his behaviour was hardly loverlike.

When Porter was with Beatrice at Folly Point he drank too much, said outrageous things and generally behaved like a naughty schoolboy, while Beatrice played the stern but indulgent parent or teacher. It was not particularly pleasant to watch, but both Beatrice and Porter appeared to derive great enjoyment from carrying out what was by now a well-established double act.[5]

Not all Beatrice's relationships with authors who followed her to Nelson proceeded on such predictable lines. In 1976 Nelson accepted Ruth Park's *Swords and Crowns and Rings*. Bob Sessions, who had come to Nelson from Penguin, had wanted to publish it as the first hardback under the Viking imprint, but had let it go; Penguin were nervous about hardback fiction and he knew it needed to be cut substantially. Beatrice had misgivings about the novel, which she thought sentimental and too long, but Nelson were keen to do it and Sessions was happy for Beatrice to handle it because of her experience and her friendship with the author. Park cut 30 000 words out of the manuscript and the novel was edited and published. *Swords and Crowns and Rings* won the 1977 Miles Franklin Award, went into paperback and sold well. Beatrice later edited other books of Ruth Park's, including *Playing Beatie Bow* (1980), the Children's Book of the Year in 1981.

Beatrice had been working for Nelson for some months when Les Murray showed her the draft of a novel dealing with Indonesia during the events of 1965, when President Sukarno took his country on a collision course with the West, causing a bloodbath and his own downfall. The manuscript was currently on offer in London and had the intriguing title of *The Year of Living Dangerously*. Its author was Murray's friend Christopher Koch. Beatrice knew Koch as a promising young writer: they had met in the late 1950s after Hamish Hamilton published his first novel *The Boys in the Island* (1958), and they had a mutual friend in Hal Porter. As soon as she read the new manuscript Beatrice was enthusiastic: here was the first significant Australian novel about Indonesia. Koch wished to publish his new novel in the UK and Australia simultaneously, and so it was jointly published by Nelson and Michael Joseph.

In late 1977 the editing process began, Beatrice and Koch working by letter. Koch was living in Launceston, having recently left his job in the ABC Radio education department to write full-time. At first he was a little suspicious of Beatrice: he thought her literary tastes were 'a bit arty', she had worked for a company that took advantage of being Australia's only significant publisher to treat local writers badly, and she had a reputation for being high-handed, ruling her little empire 'like the czarina'. On *The Year of Living Dangerously* editor and author worked together amicably enough – when Beatrice said the manuscript was too long Koch cut it by one-third, and he agreed to most of her other suggested changes – though prickles were never far below the surface. At one point in the novel two of the main characters realised they were in love and Beatrice snapped, 'For God's sake, Christopher, can't you get them to show more feeling than this?' Koch argued back heatedly, eventually agreed to look at the passage again, decided Beatrice was right and reworked it. They had touchy discussions about grammar (the use of 'that' as distinct from 'which') and Koch felt that Beatrice's insistence on correct usage sometimes chopped into the rhythm of his sentences, but each emerged with respect for the other's professionalism, and Koch had no doubt that Beatrice's work had improved his book. *The Year of Living Dangerously* became a bestseller and a newspaper headline catchphrase; it won the *Age* Book of the Year Award in 1978 and a National Book Council award the following year. It was made into a successful movie starring Mel Gibson, Linda Hunt and Sigourney Weaver.

But the cordiality between Beatrice and Christopher Koch soured at a private dinner to celebrate the NBC award. After a whisky or two, Beatrice compared him unfavourably with another contemporary writer she admired; her tendency to be excessively forthright, to put it mildly, was increasing with age and was exacerbated by alcohol. It was as if all those years of editorial good manners and gentlewomanly behaviour had to find an outlet, as if for every ladylike action there had to be an equal and opposite waspish, even spiteful, reaction. Koch wrote her a hurt and angry letter, and he and Beatrice were not on speaking terms for some time. But when in 1985 Koch's novel *The Doubleman* won the Miles Franklin Award, Beatrice went up to congratulate him at the prize-giving event. They chatted amicably for a while, and Beatrice suddenly said, 'Christopher, this is ridiculous. Let's make up, shall we?' So they did.[6]

In the Australia Day honours of 1981 Beatrice was made an AM for her services to Australian literature (she had been made an MBE in 1965). She was naturally pleased and wrote to Hal Porter, one of her nominators: 'Thank you for putting in the word that helped the Powers to give me an AM. It was gratifying to the old girl.'[7] At about the same time she was awarded an Emeritus Fellowship by the Literature Board of the Australia Council. This scheme, set up by the old Commonwealth Literary Fund, allowed for a small annuity to a group of no more than twenty writers. Beatrice's was worth $5000 per annum to begin with, increasing in November 1987 to $8750, and her fellowship remains the only one ever given to a book editor. But ironically, in the midst of these honours, when the often thankless role of the book editor was being acknowledged and Beatrice was finally achieving public recognition as the doyenne of her profession, she was about to lose her job for the second time.

By 1980 the UK owners of Thomas Nelson were taking a long, hard look at their Australian program. Publishing in Australia was growing more competitive, profit margins steadily tighter, and while the Australian company had published some profitable books, they had also lost money on novels and poetry. The parent company decided to cut back on general publishing and concentrate on educational and special-ist works with a guaranteed market. There would be staff cutbacks: there was no further need for a separate Sydney office with an editor being paid a salary.

This decision, which he could do nothing to influence, deeply upset Bob Sessions. He had very much enjoyed his visits to Folly Point, talk-ing to Beatrice over whisky and soda about the Nelson list, about other authors and their books, discussing Australian writing in general. His conversations with Beatrice, he felt, had given him a real 'feel' for Australian literature and he was grateful to her. Twenty-five years Beatrice's junior, he was also a little in love with her: her vitality, sensu-ality, wit and elegance had scarcely diminished with the years. She always called him Robert, never Bob, and his staff at Nelson watched with amusement as he gradually grew more urbane, taking to whisky instead of beer, and smoking cigars. Sessions also protected Beatrice. In her

seventies, she was starting to slow down, to miss small points on manuscripts. Once Sessions suggested as tactfully as possible that she might like
to concentrate on structural editing, leaving the very detailed work to
others. Beatrice was affronted by this, pointing out that she had been
employed to do a complete editorial job. Sessions said no more but
quietly made sure that her manuscripts were checked by a Nelson in-
house editor without Beatrice's knowledge. Now, after seven years, he
was being forced to tell her that her services were no longer required.

Feeling dreadful, he broke the news as gently as possible on his next visit
to Sydney. He said she could become a consultant, perhaps do some freelance work. Beatrice took the blow calmly, as she did all setbacks, saying she
had been expecting it for some time (which Sessions did not believe). Her
stoicism and tact made him feel even worse. The next day he received a curt
phone call from John Broadbent, whom Sessions had met in Beatrice's
company once or twice, with a request for a meeting at Broadbent's club.
As soon as Sessions appeared, Broadbent went on the attack. Was Nelson
aware that Beatrice didn't own the house she lived in, that it belonged to
her late husband's estate? Did Sessions realise that this forced retirement
would 'probably kill' Beatrice? What was he going to do about it?

Broadbent's knight-errantry sent Sessions back to Folly Point the
next day, telling Beatrice he would do anything he could to reverse
Nelson's decision. Whatever Beatrice might have felt about her lover discussing her financial situation with her employer, she was firm: she
wouldn't hear of any change, she would accept Nelson's decision and
things must stay as they were. (Of course her financial position was not
as dire as Broadbent had painted it.) They arranged that she would be
paid a small retainer to oversee the last of Nelson's general list.[8]

Beatrice stopped being a full-time employee of Thomas Nelson in
April 1981, a few months after her seventy-second birthday. Most
women of her age and background would have retired gracefully but at
no time, then or ever, did Beatrice intend to disappear entirely. As she
had once told Xavier Herbert, publishing was her way of life, and she saw
no reason why that should change.

After a three-month trip to Europe she returned to Sydney invigor-
ated, telling Hal Porter she was 'glad indeed to sink back into my rut of

domesticity, friends and relations, work offered and accepted'.[9] She had work to finish off for Nelson and she was now editing manuscripts for other publishers, including the new Sydney firm of Mead and Beckett, run by Rod Mead and Barbara Beckett.

Late in 1980, while Beatrice was still at Nelson, Patrick Gallagher, managing director of Allen & Unwin Australia, asked her to edit the manuscript that had won a new award for an unpublished novel by a writer under the age of thirty.[10] Though the English-born Gallagher had been in Australia for several years he knew little about Beatrice; Allen & Unwin were publishers of non-fiction and academic books and this was their first foray into fiction. Sponsored by the Vogel bread company and the *Australian* newspaper, the prize, then worth $10 000, was Australia's richest for a young writer. The winner, Paul Radley from Newcastle, New South Wales, was only eighteen; his winning novel *Jack Rivers and Me* was the story of five-year-old Peanut, his imaginary friend Jack Rivers, and life in the country town of Boomeroo.

Radley was the latest beneficiary of the perennial Australian eagerness to find brilliant new young writers.[11] In the press and on television he was portrayed as a rustic genius, a young man who, after an indifferent education, had somehow found the assurance, style and craft to write a prize-winning novel. He also seemed to need his family around him a great deal, especially his great-uncle Jack.

Beatrice worked with Paul Radley by letter. The manuscript was too long, she wrote in November 1980, mostly because he 'went on', spoiling effects by adding sometimes tedious dialogue. She worried about the fact that the main character could not possibly have reproduced grown-up conversations – 'Remarkable child though he is, P. is only five' – and sent three and a half pages of her usual crisp, occasionally elliptical notes. But Beatrice also gave Radley a great deal of latitude: 'please rewrite these four lines retaining their lyrical quality', or 'see if you can make him sound more natural', for instance. She wasn't going to hold his hand or be his mentor, but simply give guidance. 'Remember I'm a helper, as all editors should be,' she told him.

At least once she had to reprove him. 'You really do owe it to your-self (money apart) to take your writing more seriously than you appear to do,' she wrote to him in February 1981. 'It is a demanding art or craft, and you have the essential qualities of humanity and imagination. Your appearing (in spite of your modesty) so cavalier, even arrogant, about it disturbs me because I believe good writing is so important – and so rare. But if you just don't want to be a writer, that's that.'[12] Her words take on a new resonance in view of what was to happen fifteen years later.

Beatrice became firm friends with Patrick Gallagher, then in his early thirties. The Allen & Unwin offices were not far from Beatrice's house and Gallagher occasionally called in to see her on the way home from work. Their only disagreement came when *Jack Rivers and Me* was ready for publication and Gallagher assumed that Beatrice wanted her name as editor on the imprint page. Beatrice let him know in no uncer-tain terms what she thought of editors who thrust themselves forward in this way.

Jack Rivers and Me was published in mid-1981 to generally admiring reviews. It was called 'a type of Australian *Under Milk Wood*' and praised for its 'great vitality and assurance' as well as Radley's 'highly individual talent'. Beatrice edited its sequel, *My Blue-Checker Corker and Me*, which she considered much better written, though she declined to work on the third in the series, *Good Mates!*, saying she was too old.

Paul Radley looked set to stay in the pantheon of young Australian writers for some time. He was named Young Australian of the Year in 1982 and won a writers' fellowship to St Andrews University in Scotland. However, *Good Mates!* did not sell well and he published no more; it was assumed that he had exhausted this seam of working-class Australian life and his success had been a flash in the pan.

In March 1996, four years after Beatrice's death, Paul Radley, then thirty-three, caused a sensation by announcing that he had not written one word of *Jack Rivers and Me* or the other two novels published under his name. They had all been the work of his great-uncle Jack Radley. Why he confessed at this particular time has never been clear, but he said that living with the deception had been eating away at him for years. Two months later, Jack Radley explained that he had compiled the manuscripts from material used in his own unpublished short stories; his great-nephew's contribution had been to tape conversations in pubs and elsewhere.[13] When Beatrice's pages of corrections, suggestions and changes arrived, Jack Radley had read them out while Paul amended the manuscript. Anything more difficult than a simple change of word, any rewriting or changing of tone Jack Radley did himself.

A frustrated writer for much of his life, Jack Radley said he had entered *Jack Rivers and Me* for the Vogel Award as a protest against age discrimination, with the $10 000 prize an added inducement. He said that he and his great-nephew had signed a legal agreement giving Jack the right to write and publish books using Paul's name. The scheme fell apart when the two men quarrelled: when the story broke, Jack Radley said he and his great-nephew had not spoken for six years.

Could Beatrice have guessed that Paul Radley was a fraud? According to Jack Radley she had met Paul only twice, when he came down from Newcastle to visit her at Folly Point. On both occasions he was very much accompanied by Jack and said hardly a word for himself. When Beatrice asked him what books he had read, he mentioned Steinbeck's *The Pearl* and Hemingway's *The Old Man and the Sea*, but that was all, whereas Jack Radley spoke with enthusiasm of his own reading – Joyce, Dickens, Shakespeare, Jane Austen – and he and Beatrice had a long and pleasant discussion about books while Paul remained silent. As Beatrice saw the Radleys to the door, she looked sharply from one to the other and said, 'So writing runs in the family, does it?'[14]

Beatrice was no fool. She had known and worked with writers for more than forty years. Presented with a totally inarticulate author who didn't appear to have any pride of ownership in his words and a much older, better read and watchful minder on whom the author seemed dependent even for literary opinions, she must have thought something strange was going on. Her comment that 'writing runs in the family' – if she was quoted accurately – seems to confirm that she had her suspicions.

But if Beatrice did suspect that Paul Radley had not written those books, she did not say so to Patrick Gallagher or to anyone else, which again is what one would expect from her. She was an editor, employed to straighten out a manuscript for publication: it was not her place to make any comments about putative authorship. Weighing up the evidence – Beatrice's shrewdness, her knowledge of authors and writing, her professional discretion, her view of her role – it is quite likely that about Paul Radley, as about so much else in her life, Beatrice knew what the story was but wasn't saying.

The Final Chapter

'I'm trudging along, with more jobs to do than I can comfortably manage,' wrote Beatrice happily to Hal Porter on 12 June 1983. She had recently joined the judging panel of the New South Wales Premier's Literary Awards – 'Quite fun, really, if time permitted,' she told Porter – and was preparing an anthology of Australian verse, commissioned by Mead and Beckett in association with Nelson. The collection was to cover Australian poetry from the earliest days of European settlement to the present, with suitable illustrations. Beatrice chose the poems and wrote the introduction. She enjoyed the job, although as usual she agonised over her choices and the order of poems, asking Douglas Stewart for his advice. *The Illustrated Treasury of Australian Verse* was published in 1984 and was generally well received, though Beatrice was criticised for failing to include any Aboriginal works.[1]

In July 1982 she received an unexpected offer: Richard Walsh invited her to write her memoirs for Angus and Robertson. She must have been struck by the irony of being invited back to A&R by the man who had dismissed her, and not as an editor but as an author. She toyed with the idea but finally said no, though the gracious tone of her reply suggests that she was flattered to be asked. 'The project would need qualities I don't believe I have,' she wrote. 'Perhaps my critical sense has squashed any creative ability I have; but I don't think I'm a good enough writer – not good enough, anyway, to satisfy myself.'[2]

Keeping busy was something of a solace; it stopped Beatrice thinking about the past. A significant piece had fallen out of her world with
the death of Dick Jeune in 1976. As much in thrall to Beatrice at the
age of eighty-nine as when he had first met her forty years before, Dick
had seemed as indestructible as the farmhouse in Tizzana Road, though
he grew deafer and more irritable with every passing year. For a long
time he had conducted a guerrilla war with the local church, whose
roadway went across a corner of his property, and the locals believed that
his complaints to the council about the state of the roads had irritated
them so much that they laid down a stretch of tarred road – the only one
in the immediate vicinity – outside his house.

Beatrice often came to see him on weekends, as she had done for so
many years, though visits to Sackville were becoming a mixed blessing.
The area was now a popular weekend retreat, with the quiet of the
Hawkesbury shattered by the whine of speedboats towing waterskiers.
Dick Jeune had declared war on the lot of them, threatening to hurl
empty beer bottles from the verandah as his enemies zipped along the
river.

In the early 1970s Dick began to slow down, and heart trouble and
chronic nephritis forced him into hospital with increasing frequency. On
7 July 1976 he died of pneumonia in Mosman District Hospital. Beatrice
made the final arrangements for him. Considering how long he had been
part of her life, she seems to have known surprisingly little about him.
Giving his full name as Edmund Lawson Jeune on his death certificate,
Beatrice nevertheless wrote 'unknown' against questions about his
marriage and whether he had children. Like many gentlemen of his
era, Edmund Lawson Jeune had evidently kept many things about his life
to himself.

After Dick Jeune died the house at Sackville remained empty, for
Beatrice no longer had the heart to go up there often. Then one afternoon about two months after Dick's death, local residents noticed thick
black smoke coming from that part of Tizzana Road. By the time anyone got there, fire had completely destroyed Beatrice's house. Gone were
valuable books and paintings, including works by Percy and Norman
Lindsay, with, it is said, the drawing that showed a young Beatrice in

nothing but an elaborate headdress. Nobody ever knew exactly how the fire started. Beatrice was convinced it was the work of waterskiers, revenge for Dick's vendetta; some local residents thought it was arson to cover robbery, others heard that behind the house some young boys had lit a campfire that burned out of control.

Beatrice was devastated. The house and its contents had not been insured: even if they had been, some things were irreplaceable. She had lost not just books and paintings she had loved, but with Dick Jeune and the house had gone almost her last remaining link to Frederick Bridges and her marriage. She was forced to sell the property for land value alone. Beatrice could hardly be described as sentimental, but this double blow left her depressed for a long time.[3]

The ranks of her friends and colleagues were beginning to thin. In June 1983 she wrote to Hal Porter about 'several sadnesses', including the death of her nephew John in a drowning accident and Colin Simpson's death from liver cancer in February. 'You spoke of your once pretty play-girls falling off the twig; and no doubt anyone is liable at any moment . . .' she told him.[4]

Friends were worth so much, and after years of friendship there was no point in changing them. Beatrice's friendship with Hal Porter had survived even a 1977 trip they made to Tasmania during which Porter deserted her to look up old haunts and friends, leaving her alone in a Hobart motel room to smoke, read Thomas Hardy and seethe. In the 1982 Queen's Birthday honours Porter was awarded an AM, the same honour Beatrice had been given nearly eighteen months earlier, and she sympathised – without too much irony – that it hadn't been the knight-hood he wanted. But she was greatly worried and concerned when in July that year Porter, who now lived in Ballarat, was arrested and tried for shoplifting and was released on a $140 bond. Beatrice heard of this not from him but from a Sydney newspaper and immediately sent a telegram of love and support, offering to put him up for a few days in Sydney if he needed it.

On 24 July 1983 Hal Porter was crossing a street in Ballarat on his way to visit a friend when a car driven by a drunken driver knocked him down. He suffered massive brain damage and for more than a year remained in a coma in Ballarat hospitals. After fourteen months without regaining consciousness, he died on 29 September 1984 at the age of seventy-three. A couple of years before, Beatrice had written to him: 'There's no one like you, my dear, and you'll always be precious to me.'[5] For more than forty years Beatrice had been his loyal and loving friend; to her he was irreplaceable.

Xavier Herbert also died that year. Though he and Beatrice had not been in regular contact for some years, Beatrice had always been fond of him, in spite of constant temptation to the contrary. A more personal – and more devastating – loss came in mid-1985 with the death of Douglas Stewart. After he and Beatrice had left Angus and Robertson in the early 1970s they remained close, and she had been grateful for his help with *The Illustrated Treasury of Australian Verse* the year before. She had always greatly valued his advice. 'It was so marvellous to be able to ring him up and say, "Doug, what do you think about this?" ' she said in a radio interview after his death, 'and he could always give you a completely sane, unprejudiced judgement based on taste and knowledge.'[6] At least once she had returned the compliment, writing a short profile of him for an Independent Theatre performance of *Ned Kelly*: 'His interests are fishing and poetry, both noble sports.'

After Stewart's death, Beatrice became friendlier with his wife Margaret and daughter Meg. 'Mum and I used to joke because we didn't think she was very keen on us,' said Meg Stewart. 'She was always very nice to us, of course, but Dad was the one. I remember after he died she had us over for lunch and seemed to be quite happy because she could have a conversation about current books with me . . . she would ring up and say how much she missed him.'[7] Beatrice never stopped missing Douglas Stewart.

As she gradually worked less during the 1980s, Beatrice turned her attention to her house and garden. For her, however, gardening largely meant doing a little light weeding in a large and becoming hat; after a while she tired of this and employed a gardener. She decided to have a spiral stairway added to the outside of the house, leading to the flat roof, so guests could enjoy the wonderful view over Middle Harbour. It was an attractive idea but Peter Bridges, who thought Beatrice could be cavalier about the estate, pointed out that having people stand on a flat roof would cause problems. Beatrice went ahead and sure enough the roof, punctured by the stiletto-heeled shoes of her guests, leaked during rain and had to be fixed. The incident did not increase warmth of feeling between Peter and Beatrice.

Though Beatrice could be thoughtless about such matters, in other ways she was anything but casual. As she aged, keeping up appearances was more important than ever. When Anthony Barker visited her unexpectedly one day, she was distressed. 'I haven't even got my lipstick on,' she told him. 'You don't realise how important these things are to women of my generation.' She was still swift to correct bad grammar or usage – one of her pet hates was 'hopefully' used to mean 'with any luck' – and she stuck to her gentlewoman's manners, never wearing scent (which she refused to call 'perfume') in the mornings, or white in the evenings. She cooked a proper meal – meat and vegetables – every evening and set the table for dinner with fresh napkins and candles, even when she was eating by herself. None of her friends could ever imagine Beatrice having fish and chips in front of the television set. To a younger generation her insistence on good form was sometimes quaint, like something out of a novel by Ivy Compton-Burnett, one of Beatrice's favourite writers.

She and John Broadbent continued to see each other, though their relationship gradually changed. When he became involved with another woman she was upset – she wasn't used to rivals – though one or two of her friends were less than sympathetic. As she had more or less taken him for granted, they thought she had only herself to blame. Beatrice steeled herself to behave beautifully, making a point of inviting the other woman to lunch and speaking to her in her native French (she came from Belgium). But once Beatrice forgot herself and snapped at the woman, who told John. He accused Beatrice of being indiscreet, and the fact that she had let her guard down, had compromised her own standards of behaviour, upset Beatrice as much as did Broadbent's criticism.

Beatrice had learned to drive in her forties and used to take Aunt Enid for drives, chatting as they bowled merrily along Military Road. It can safely be said that the attention to detail that was so much a part of

Beatrice's profession never extended to driving. Once she stopped outside her house to collect something, got out and forgot to put the handbrake on. The car rolled down the steep hill towards the harbour, hit another car and came to a halt, a side panel severely dented. Before the police came Beatrice had the presence of mind to say to the car's owner, her neighbour, 'You, I am sure, will be a gentleman about this.' It says something for Beatrice's charm that he was. On another occasion she started her car, bent down to retrieve a torch from the back seat and panicked when the car moved. She failed to stop it and it travelled out of the garage. Before it came to a halt on the other side of the road, Beatrice had fractured her sternum, probably against the steering wheel. Her niece Anne pleaded with the police to take away Beatrice's licence, but they only laughed. To the huge relief of her family, Beatrice eventually got rid of her car.

Until she turned eighty Beatrice had been fairly healthy, despite emphysema due to heavy smoking, but on 17 April 1989, after attending a party at the University of Sydney to celebrate *Southerly*'s fiftieth anniversary, her leg gave way when she was getting ready for bed and she fell heavily to the floor. As she lay on the upstairs bedroom carpet she realised her left femur was broken. It was about ten o'clock, the house was dark and quiet and she was alone. The telephone was downstairs and on the other side of the house.

Nobody who cared about Beatrice likes to think of what happened next. Exerting every bit of her courage and self-control, in excruciating pain, she dragged herself slowly across the bedroom floor and down the semicircular carpeted staircase, stopping to rest after every effort. The night must have seemed like an eternity. Seven hours later, at five in the morning, she managed to get to the hall phone and telephoned a neighbour, who let himself into the house and called an ambulance.

That fall was a *coup de vieux* for Beatrice: she was suddenly an old woman. She endured a series of operations and stays in hospital, becoming weaker and shakier. She never spoke of the pain she was in, only regretting that she was left with one leg two or three inches shorter than the other and had to wear a built-up shoe. 'I think I'll start wearing clothes like Edith Sitwell,' she told Anthony Barker crisply. 'Long, flowing dresses down to the ground and interesting hats.'

But she had iron determination and every intention of continuing to do exactly as she wished for as long as possible. She smuggled cigarettes into hospital and continued to smoke even when she had to use an oxygen mask for her emphysema; a horrified doctor took away her cigarettes before she caused an explosion. She kept whisky in the hospital locker, telling her visitors that what the hospital staff didn't know wouldn't hurt them. They weren't always so blind: a Scottish nurses' aide told her severely that he could smell the water of Scotland in her room. Her supplies were confiscated and she was lectured like a naughty little girl, but she managed to con people into bringing her more.

Beatrice never liked visitors when she was at her lowest in hospital; only old friends and family were allowed to see her. She didn't always welcome them, either. Once her brother John, who was also very ill, came to see her and found her propped up in bed with books all over the blankets, a table set up beside her and nurses fussing around. She was reading for the Miles Franklin Award. 'Wait a while, will you, darling?' she said to her brother. 'I'm busy.' Having been familiar with Beatrice's imperious manner since she was about two years old John refused to accept this, and they quarrelled.

Between spells in hospital Beatrice returned to Folly Point, determined to look after herself at home. But it was a struggle and she grew increasingly depressed. 'What do you think I should do?' she asked Anthony Barker in January 1990. 'Give up and die or battle on?' It was said half jokingly, but she worried about being able to continue living alone. What she needed, she decided, was a larger house with a garden, one without stairs but with high ceilings and some grandeur. 'It doesn't matter if it isn't in a fashionable suburb,' she said. 'Neutral Bay or Mosman will do.' Nobody had the heart to tell her that those suburbs hadn't been unfashionable or cheap for nearly forty years.

Physical discomfort was bad enough, but Beatrice could set her teeth and endure that. Her greatest fear was not pain but losing her mind; she could not forget her mother's dementia. She could hardly bear to finish

David Malouf's novel *The Great World*, which she was judging for the Miles Franklin Award, after reading its opening description of a dotty old woman 'likely to say things, and do things too, that you weren't expecting and could make neither head nor tail of'.[8] She constantly tested her memory on the titles and authors of books, abruptly asking friends and former colleagues such questions as 'John Tierney wrote *The Advancement of Spencer Button*, didn't he?' She was reassured to find that she had a much better memory for books and writers than most people she knew.

But her body was failing her. However determined she was to manage on her own, this was becoming impossible. Not that Beatrice admitted any such thing: when her family arranged for domestic help in the house she would exhaust herself by getting up early, doing the housework and sweetly sending the cleaner away. But for her to continue living at Folly Point the house would have to be modified extensively, with a bedroom and bathroom put in downstairs – this, with other necessary changes, would be expensive. Everyone was afraid she would fall again, and she clearly needed to move to a facility where she could be looked after.

Naturally Beatrice hated the idea of leaving her home of almost fifty years, but she realised that her physical condition was deteriorating. At about this time she began to give away her possessions, particularly her library. Some books she sold, but mostly she said, 'Darling, if you want this, you can have it,' as she handed to friends and relatives modern first editions, books that had belonged to Frederick, Angus and Robertson titles signed by their authors. Soon relatively little was left.[9]

Peter Bridges arranged for the sale of Folly Point in November 1990 and for the purchase of a unit in Hunters Hill Lodge, a retirement village in an elegant north-west suburb. Beatrice moved the following January. The idea of communal living had appalled her – eating in the dining room with 'all those common people' – but once she was settled she found there were compensations. Remaining aloof from her neighbours meant spending a lot of time alone, which was boring, and she began to enter into the life of the place. Hunters Hill Lodge was close to a shopping centre with a good restaurant, so she could still invite people to dinner, even though she did not cook it.

Not long after Beatrice moved to Hunters Hill Aunt Enid, who was well into her nineties, died. She continued to look after 'dear little Beatrice' even after death, leaving her niece the money from the sale of her home unit. A delighted Beatrice spent some of it on morale-boosting small luxuries: facials, nail treatments, having her hair done.

She was still a judge of the Miles Franklin Award and her authors, former colleagues and friends were always happy to see her at literary dinners. It was reassuring to find that she continued to be important to the people she valued. And though she sometimes called herself 'the old girl' or 'the old fossil', she was rather enjoying a new role as a literary resource. Her memories and knowledge of Australian writers and writing were much sought after; 'Davis, Beatrice' appeared more and more often in the indexes of Australian literary biographies. However, while she was willing to set the record straight about other writers, she was still uncomfortable with direct questioning about herself. When Anthony Barker interviewed her for *One of the First and One of the Finest* she complained that he was taking her 'too seriously', was impatient with some of his questions – she didn't always remember events accurately – and when the work was completed in July 1990 she wouldn't read it.[10] The only editorial suggestion she made, true to form, was that the book should be shorter, even though it was only forty-seven pages long.

In February 1992 Beatrice was awarded an honorary doctorate of letters (*honoris causa*) from her alma mater, the University of Sydney. The degree was presented by the vice-chancellor, Professor D. McNicoll, with Beatrice's friend Professor Dame Leonie Kramer, the chancellor, presiding. Beatrice sat in a wheelchair, a small, spidery figure, her hair carefully done for the occasion, pearl earrings and makeup perfectly applied, wearing a blue and red long-sleeved dress, her black bag in her lap. She said she could have walked onto the stage to accept her degree, but because she was so tiny the gown would have swamped her. It was an occasion she greatly enjoyed.

'Sometimes I feel I'd like to go to sleep one night and not wake up,' Beatrice told Anthony Barker early in 1990. Her wish was granted: she died peacefully during the night of Sunday 24 May 1992.[11]

The funeral service, conducted at Beatrice's request by her former colleague Marilyn Stacy, who had changed an editorial career for an ecclesiastic one, was delayed until the following Friday so that John Broadbent, who had been in Belgium when Beatrice died, could return. Friends, authors and former colleagues packed the chapel at Sydney's Northern Suburbs Crematorium. It was an informal service: Beatrice had instructed Marilyn Stacy, 'Don't put too much God into it, darling,' and Stacy complied.

A few weeks later there was a memorial gathering at the State Library of New South Wales, where Beatrice had so often presented the judges' report of the Miles Franklin Award. With enormous affection writers, journalists, family and friends spoke of her calm thoughtfulness, her kindness, warmth, wit, her occasional sharpness – and above all her duty to her craft. Beatrice, who shrugged off such things and once said, 'I've been given far more attention than I deserve,' would have been embarrassed but pleased. She might also have appreciated that a travelling fellowship for editors, jointly funded by the Literature Board and Australian publishers and established in 1991, has been named after her.

Beatrice was unique in Australian letters in being able to create her own niche, to invent her job. Before she joined Angus and Robertson, editing had been a schoolteacher's skill, done on a book-by-book basis without much attempt at consistency. By her own practice and the training of her staff, she brought it to the status of a craft, with its own exacting standards. Part of her legacy is the question asked by a generation of editors, 'What would Beatrice have done?'

She was a commanding presence in Australia's literary community. Did she long to work in a wider world, did she feel her gifts would have been better appreciated in New York or London? Perhaps. She was a proud Australian, though she doubtless felt Australia needed a fair amount of brushing-up.

Did Beatrice have a vision for Australian literature? Finding the documentary narrative style of much local fiction flat and uninteresting, she was always attentive to writers who went beyond storytelling to explore ways of writing that dominated and transformed their subject matter, who found new ways to describe the experience of being Australian. She gave Thea Astley, Patricia Wrightson and dozens of other writers the astute sympathy and acceptance they needed in developing their own voices, and she did it calmly, self-effacingly and with tact. As a judge of the Miles Franklin Award, she had a great influence on the public view of what constituted good Australian writing – recognising and celebrating the work of novelists who are now considered some of our best.

Had Beatrice possessed good marketing sense she could have been a distinguished publisher, but control of this sort was never what she wanted. According to Geoffrey Dutton, Patrick White nastily referred to her as 'the bottleneck of Australian literature': in fact, she was the exact opposite. She was a conduit, a facilitator, making contacts, bringing people together. 'I had such good conversations in her house,' said Ruth Park, and her words have been echoed by other writers. Beatrice was a true reader, a lover of words and books and good writing, a sometimes ironic appreciator of the quirks of human nature. She once described herself as 'addicted to Australian literature'. At a time when Australia was a small country that took almost perverse pride in its anti-intellectualism, she affirmed the importance of our writers in every aspect of her working life. Australian literature will always be in her debt.

She had, in the end, a rather ambivalent attitude to her position as an editor. While she insisted that her job was to remain invisible, if she hid her light under a bushel she rather liked people to know where that bushel was. 'Someday,' she said to Anthony Barker, 'someone will write a full-length book about me.'

ACKNOWLEDGEMENTS

I owe a special debt of gratitude to Beatrice's niece Anne Dowey, who very generously gave me access to a wealth of Davis and Deloitte family material, as well as answering innumerable questions about her aunt. I am grateful to the Literature Fund of the Australia Council for grants that enabled me to research and draft this manuscript. Thanks also to the Council of the State Library of New South Wales for the award of the C.H. Currey Memorial Fellowship in 1996, which enabled me to begin research, and to members of the State Library staff, particularly curator of manuscripts Paul Brunton, and Louise Anemaat, Rosemary Block, Jennifer Broomhead and Judy Nelson; chief librarian Roslyn Follett and the staff of the Fryer Library, University of Queensland; manuscripts librarian Graeme Powell and the staff of the National Library of Australia, Canberra; staff at the La Trobe Library, Melbourne; Michelle Nichols of the Hawkesbury City Library; staff at the Bendigo Library and members of the Bendigo Historical Society. Seminars sponsored by the Research Institute for History and the Social Sciences, University of Sydney, provided stimulating insights into the problems and practice of biography.

Thanks to the following for their invaluable help in research: Anthony Barker, the late John Curtain, Frances de Groen, Richard Gill, Kerryn Goldsworthy, Dr Bridget Griffen-Foley, Professor Harry Heseltine, Neil James, Professor Charles Kerr, Susan Lever, Valerie Lawson, Drusilla Modjeska, Meaghan Morris, Craig Munro, Robyn Sinclair, Tom Shapcott.

Many friends and colleagues of Beatrice kindly gave up their time to answer questions for this book. Grateful thanks to Vincentia Anderson, Thea Astley, Anthony Barker, Lyle Blair, the late Alec Bolton, June

Bonser, Peter and Doreen Bridges, John Broadbent, Charles Davis, Rosemary Dobson, the late Geoffrey Dutton, Sue Ebury, John Ferguson, the late Dorothy Fillingham, Elizabeth Fulton, Patrick Gallagher, Anne Godden, Elva Hoy, Elisabeth Hughes, Tom Hungerford, Barbara Ker Wilson, Professor Leonie Kramer, Christopher Koch, Margot Ludovici, Mary Lord, Enid Moon, Frank Moorhouse, Geoff Morley, Ruth Park, Nancy Phelan, Joan Phipson, Jack Radley, Leslie Rees, the late Elizabeth Riddell, the late Professor Colin Roderick, Robert Sessions, Ivan Southall, Marilyn Stacy, Marley Stephen, Meg Stewart, Frank Thompson, Judy Wallace, Richard Walsh, Ken Wilder, Elizabeth Wood-Ellem, Patricia Wrightson.

Thanks to my agent Rosemary Creswell, to Robert Sessions and Clare Forster of Penguin Books, and to indexer Garry Cousins. To Meredith Rose particular thanks: I do not think this book could have had a better editor.

Finally, my thanks to friends and family who put up with long and detailed replies to the question 'How's Beatrice going?'; to Suzanne Falkiner for her astute and perceptive reading of an earlier draft of this book; and to my partner John Tuchin, who has lived with Beatrice almost as long as I have and whose thoughtful encouragement and support were invaluable.

Beatrice's family photographs appear courtesy of Anne Dowey. The photograph of Ernestine Hill is reproduced by permission of the Fryer Library, University of Queensland. Photographs of Frank Clune, Miles Franklin, Xavier Herbert, R.G. Howarth, Ion Idriess, Nan McDonald, D'Arcy Niland, Ruth Park, Ivan Southall, Kylie Tennant, Richard Walsh and Patricia Wrightson are reproduced by permission of the National Library of Australia. The photograph of Beatrice at Folly Point is by Bill Davis; that of Beatrice in the early 1980s is by Alec Bolton.

NOTES

Little Sweetheart

1 J.K. Haken, *Australian Dictionary of Biography 1891–1939*, pp. 237–8.

2 'Wyoming' belonged to Quarton Levitt Deloitte for more than fifty years. Though the house still exists and was being restored at the time of writing, the only surviving reminder of the Deloitte name is Deloitte Avenue, a narrow thoroughfare that skirts the park at Birchgrove, running from Louisa Road to Wharf Road.

3 She is called Emily here, of course, to distinguish her from her daughter Beatrice.

The Family Intellectual Becomes an Editor

1 Beatrice's paternal grandparents both died in 1907: in 1928 Charles's two brothers and two sisters were still living.

2 Taking shorthand was a skill that never deserted Beatrice: at Angus and Robertson she kept very clear and accurate Pitman notes of phone messages.

3 213B stood roughly on the site of the present Regent Hotel.

4 Many years later this doctor gratified Beatrice enormously by telling her how bitterly he regretted not having married her himself.

5 Vincentia and her husband had four sons, the second of whom, also named Doug, became a well-known journalist and columnist on the *Sydney Morning Herald*. Beatrice's place as assistant editor of the *Medical Journal of Australia* was taken by Dorothy Tremlett, a colleague of hers at school and university. Mervyn Archdall continued to edit the *MJA* until he retired on 31 August 1957, his seventy-third birthday. He died a week later, on 6 September.

The Story of Angus and Robertson

1 Quoted in A.W. Barker, *George Robertson: A Publishing Life in Letters*, University of Queensland Press, Brisbane, 1993, p. 14.

2 This story comes from Alec Chisholm's tribute to George Robertson after his death (Melbourne *Argus*, 2 September 1933). According to *The Oxford Companion to Australian Literature*, there was no definitive edition of Lawson's verse until Colin Roderick published a three-volume *Collected Verse* in 1967–69.

3 Quoted in Barker, op. cit., p. 72. This view – that good grammar and proper speech were supremely important, regardless of context – persisted in Australia for many years, and not just in literature. According to actor Leonard Teale, who was playing the part

of an uneducated stockman in a 1950s ABC radio production, producer John Thompson would not allow him to drop aitches and final 'g's because, he said, 'people should not talk like that'.

4   George Robertson wanted his son Douglas to succeed him, but though Douglas worked in the shop for more than twenty years, his heart was not in A&R. He was a skilled builder and carpenter, not a bookseller. Father and son quarrelled seriously in the 1920s and Douglas sold his A&R shares. Their estrangement remained bitter to the end. A descendant of Douglas's is the composer Ross Edwards. (Source: Anthony Barker, letter to J.K., 12 February 2002.)

'That Woman'

1   Detailed information about life at A&R in the 1930s comes from J.K. interview with the late Enid Moon, a proofreader with Halstead for many years who died in her nineties in 1999.

2   Interview B.D. with National Library of Australia, 1977.

3   This, a Davis family story, may well be true. Beatrice owned several works by Percy and Norman Lindsay, and apparently showed this picture to at least one member of her family.

4   Beatrice told her brother John about this many years later.

Fighting Words

1   Between 1938 and 1945 A&R's yearly production of Australian books of all kinds, including educational titles, was 73 per cent of their total (quoted by George Ferguson in his submission to the British Publishers' Association UNESCO inquiry in 1954).

2   B.D. to Lawson Glassop, 3 March 1944.

3   Walter Cousins to J.K. Moir, Moir Collection, State Library of Victoria, undated.

4   Walter Cousins to Clive Evatt, 4 February 1945.

5   Lawson Glassop to B.D., 30 November 1943.

6   B.D. to Lawson Glassop, 12 May 1943.

7   This is a bit rich coming from Norman Lindsay, several of whose novels Beatrice turned down on the grounds of poor plotting and inadequate characterisation.

8   Lawson Glassop to B.D., 28 March 1943.

9   Lawson Glassop to B.D., 13 November 1944; B.D. to Lawson Glassop, 27 November 1944; Lawson Glassop to B.D., 1 December 1944.

10   The 'obscene' extract is given in full in *Fighting Words*, edited by Carl Harrison-Ford, published by Lothian in 1986.

11   Lawson Glassop to Walter Cousins, 9 June 1946.

12   'Boyd v Angus & Robertson Ltd Judgement' in Lawson Glassop file, Mitchell Library, Sydney.

13   *Dead Men Rising* was not published in Australia until 1969, when ironically A&R brought it out as part of their paperback Australian Classics series.

14   For more details about this competition, which was an important one in its day, see the chapter on Ruth Park and D'Arcy Niland.

15   Interview Tom Hungerford with J.K., 27 October 1998.

'We Must Remain the Literary Hub of Australia'

1   B.D. to Lawson Glassop, 12 May 1944.

2   Beatrice's first assistant was the young university student Nuri Mas, who stayed less than a year. She later became a journalist and writer for children.

3   Interview B.D. with National Library of Australia, 1977.

4   Douglas Stewart, *Norman Lindsay: A Personal Memoir*, Thomas Nelson, Melbourne, 1975, p. 32.

5   Norman Lindsay to B.D., 1944, undated.

Living on the Edge: Ernestine Hill

1   B.D. draft blurb for *The Territory* in Hill file, Angus and Robertson collection, Mitchell Library.

2   Notes by Rene Foster in the Ernestine Hill papers, Fryer Library, University of Queensland.

3   Walter Cousins to Alec Chisholm, 25 November 1941.

4   Ernestine Hill, *The Territory*, Angus and Robertson, Sydney, 1951, p. 1.

5   Ernestine Hill to B.D., 22 June 1948; B.D. to Ernestine Hill, 13 July 1948.

6   Ernestine Hill to B.D., 20 December 1946.

7   Ernestine Hill to B.D., 14 May 1948.

8   B.D. to Ernestine Hill, 15 March 1949.

9   Ernestine Hill to B.D., 22 March 1949.

10   Ernestine Hill to B.D., 30 July 1949.

11   Ernestine Hill to B.D., 17 June 1950.

12   Ernestine Hill to B.D., 23 April 1951.

13   Quoted in A&R publicity material of September 1952 for a proposed second edition of *The Territory*.

14   B.D. to Henrietta Drake-Brockman, 21 June 1950.

15   *Fragment*, May 1955, p. 6.

16   Ernestine Hill to B.D., undated, 1957.

17   Henrietta Drake-Brockman to B.D., 21 June 1950.

18   B.D. to Robert Hill, 17 August 1960.

19   B.D. to Ernestine Hill, 23 October 1960.

20   B.D. to Ernestine Hill, 20 March 1961.

21   Robert Hill to B.D., 5 March 1969.

22   B.D. to Robert Hill, 14 March 1969.

23   B.D. to Henrietta Drake-Brockman, 22 March 1969.

24   Ernestine Hill's papers are now in the National Library of Australia and the Fryer Library, University of Queensland.

25   Charles Bateson to B.D., 29 January 1973.

'She Sings for Herself': Eve Langley

1   The S.H. Prior Memorial Prize was named after Samuel Henry Prior, editor of the
      Bulletin from 1915 to 1933 and an enthusiast for new Australian writing. It was awarded
      annually between 1935 and 1946.

2   Eve Langley, *The Pea Pickers*, Angus and Robertson, Sydney, 1942, p. 6.

3   Ruth Park, *A Fence Around the Cuckoo*, Viking, Melbourne, 1992, pp. 233–4.

4   Interview Douglas Stewart with Meg Stewart for *The Shadows are Different*, Meg
      Stewart's ABC radio portrait of Eve Langley, in the Stewart papers, Mitchell Library.

5   Miles Franklin to Mary Fullerton, 4 July 1943, quoted in Jill Roe (ed.), *My Congenials*,
      Vol. 2, Angus and Robertson, Sydney, 1993, p. 94.

6   June Langley to B.D., 24 June 1950.

7   B.D. to Eve Langley, 26 October 1950.

8   Eve Langley to B.D., 17 September 1951.

9   Nan McDonald, reader's report, March 1952.

10   B.D. to Eve Langley, 19 March 1952.

11   Eve Langley to Nan McDonald, 13 October 1952.

12   Nan McDonald to Eve Langley, early October 1953.

13   Eve Langley to Nan McDonald, 12 April 1954.

14   Eve Langley to Nan McDonald, 14 April 1954.

15   B.D. to Hal Porter, 5 December 1956.

16   This account of Hal Porter's meeting with Eve Langley is taken from his interview with
      Meg Stewart, broadcast on ABC radio in 1977 as *Hal Porter Remembers Eve Langley*.

17   B.D. to Hal Porter, 30 May 1957.

18   Nan McDonald, reader's report, early 1960.

19   B.D. to Eve Langley, 7 January 1960.

20   Eve Langley to B.D., 9 June 1960.

21   Douglas Stewart to H.B. Gullett, 29 September 1965.

22   Interview Meg Stewart with J.K., 12 February 1997.

23   B.D. said this several times: in an interview with Elizabeth Riddell, the *Australian*, 9
      February 1974; in a taped interview with Suzanne Lunney for the National Library of
      Australia's oral history project, May 1977; in an interview with Meg Stewart for the
      ABC radio program *The Shadows Are Different*, broadcast 18 September 1977.

24   Interview Douglas Stewart with Meg Stewart for *The Shadows are Different*, Stewart
      papers, Mitchell Library.

Mrs Bridges and Miss Davis

1   According to Professor Charles Kerr of the Department of Public Health, University
      of Sydney (communication with J.K., 30 June 2000), TB infection was spread by oral
      means. Being a doctor, Frederick Bridges would have been careful to disinfect such
      things as glasses and toothbrushes. People often took such risks with TB in its man-
      ageable stages, and did not greatly compromise their sex lives.

2   B.D. to Lawson Glassop, 28 July 1944.

3   Interview Harry Heseltine (who was also present at the talk concerned) with J.K., 16 February 2000.

4   B.D. to Miles Franklin, 22 August 1945.

5   Walter Cousins to Rebecca Wiley, 28 April 1948.

6   'The case for Australian Authors and Artists', prepared by the Australian Journalists' Association and the Fellowship of Australian Writers, no date, but internal evidence suggests 1946–47.

7   In 1953, according to the (UK) Publishers Association, the traditional British market was Aden, Australia, Burma, Canada, Ceylon, Cyprus, Egypt, Republic of Ireland, Hong Kong, India, Iraq, Jamaica, Israel, Jordan, Kenya, New Guinea, New Zealand, Northern Ireland, Pacific Islands, Pakistan, Palestine, South Africa, Uganda. Figures from the same source for approximate values of book trade exports for the UK in the calendar year 1953 include Australia £3 500 000; USA £2 300 000; South Africa £2 100 000.

8   At the end of the war other players in the Australian publishing scene included Consolidated Press, Melbourne University Press, Robertson and Mullens, Lothian, Ure Smith, Cheshire, Shakespeare Head Press, Currawong, and Whitcombe and Tombs. Most of these published educational books.

9   Elizabeth Wood-Ellem to J.K., 5 December 1999.

10   Elisabeth Hughes to J.K., 30 May 1999.

11   B.D. to Henrietta Drake-Brockman, 10 August 1956.

12   According to Robert Grundy, a young accountant at A&R during the late 1960s, who handled the typists' invoices.

13   Walter Cousins to Rebecca Wiley, 28 April 1948.

'My Tonnage Cannot be Ignored': Miles Franklin

1   Miles Franklin to Dymphna Cusack, 28 April 1953.

2   Quoted in Nancy Keesing's memoir *Riding the Elephant*, Allen & Unwin, Sydney, 1988, p. 74.

3   Beatrice Davis, 'An enigmatic woman', *Overland* 91, 1983, p. 23.

4   Miles Franklin to B.D., 30 December 1943.

5   Miles Franklin to B.D., 6 May 1953.

6   Miles Franklin to Dymphna Cusack, 1 May 1951.

7   B.D. to Miles Franklin, 26 August 1949.

8   B.D. to Miles Franklin, 10 August 1952.

9   Vance Palmer, *ABC Weekly*, 11 December 1954.

10   Miles Franklin to B.D., 9 January 1953.

11   Miles Franklin to Florence James, 16 September 1950.

12   Ruth Park, *Fishing in the Styx*, Viking, Melbourne, 1993, pp. 150–1.

13 Henrietta Drake-Brockman to B.D., 26 June 1956.

14 B.D., *Overland*, op. cit.

15 Miles Franklin to Dymphna Cusack, 14 November 1950.

16 B.D. to Henrietta Drake-Brockman, 31 July 1950.

17 B.D. to Miles Franklin, 14 November 1953.

18 B.D., *Overland*, op. cit.

19 Ibid.

20 As she makes clear in her *Overland* article, op.cit.

21 B.D. to Henrietta Drake-Brockman, 11 July 1950.

22 B.D., *Overland*, op. cit.

23 Ibid.

24 'Gun', meaning champion, usually applied to a shearer: another example of Miles Franklin's rural vocabulary.

25 Miles Franklin to Dymphna Cusack, 2 November 1950.

26 B.D. to Rex Ingamells, 12 October 1954.

27 Katharine Susannah Prichard to B.D., 24 June 1956.

28 Henrietta Drake-Brockman to B.D., 13 July 1960.

29 Dymphna Cusack to B.D., 12 October 1954.

30 B.D. to Rex Ingamells, 12 October 1954.

31 Ibid.

Ruth Park and D'Arcy Niland

1   Ruth Park to J.K., 25 May 1997.

2   At the time Beatrice was consumed with worry about the health of Frederick Bridges. Like most of Beatrice's authors, Park knew nothing about this.

3   Third prizewinner was Queensland writer Esther Roland for her bush novel *I Camp Here*.

4   Warwick Fairfax, 'Why We Print This Story', *Sydney Morning Herald*, 11 January 1947.

5   B.D. to Ruth Park, 6 March 1950.

6   Ruth Park to J.K., 25 May 1997.

7   Ruth Park, *Fishing in the Styx*, p. 151; Ruth Park to J.K. 25 May 1997.

8   Ruth Park to Bob Sessions, 13 January 2001.

9   Ruth Park, *Fishing in the Styx*, pp. 180–1.

10 Ruth Park to J.K., 25 May 1997.

11 Ibid.

12 B.D. to Ruth Park, 7 March 1950.

13   Ruth Park and D'Arcy Niland, *The Drums Go Bang!*, Angus and Robertson, 1956, p. 192.

14   B.D. editorial report, February 1950.

15   B.D. to Ruth Park, 18 April 1950.

16   D'Arcy Niland to B.D., 30 August 1950.

17   Ruth Park to B.D., 10 October 1950.

18   B.D. to D'Arcy Niland, 14 January 1952.

19   Ruth Park, *Fishing in the Styx*, p. 181.

20   D'Arcy Niland to B.D., 14 January 1952.

21   D'Arcy Niland to B.D., 15 June 1954.

22   According to G.A. Wilkes' *Dictionary of Australian Colloquialisms*, the word 'shiralee', in the sense in which Niland used it, meaning 'swag' and by extension 'burden', was rare until D'Arcy Niland's novel was published.

23   Ruth Park to Bob Sessions, 13 January 2001.

24   A&R opened a distribution office in London in the early 1950s, and by the end of the decade their British publishing had grown from five titles in 1954 to seventeen by 1959, with average edition sizes of 4000.

25   B.D. to D'Arcy Niland, 17 September 1954.

26   D'Arcy Niland to B.D., 6 October 1954.

27   *The Egg and I* is American writer Betty Macdonald's amusing story of a hapless young couple trying to run a chicken farm. It was published in 1945 and became a worldwide bestseller and the basis for a series of films starring two of the characters, Ma and Pa Kettle.

28   MacQuarrie was also a sometime A&R author, having written several travel books, one dealing with a trip around the world in his Baby Austin in the 1930s. When he and the Baby Austin reached Hollywood, the film star Douglas Fairbanks demonstrated his swashbuckling credentials by leaping over the car.

29   D'Arcy Niland to Judy Fisher, 9 February 1965.

30   The biography, entitled *Home Before Dark*, was completed after Niland's death by Ruth Park and Rafe Champion, and published by Viking in 1995.

31   B.D. to D'Arcy Niland, 17 August 1964.

Women Friends, Women Writers

1   Much of this information comes from *The Queen's Club: Some Memories and Records of the First Fifty-Eight Years* by E.M. Tildesley, privately printed by Halstead Press in 1970. The Queen's Club has a footnote in literary history. As recounted by Robin Dalton in her very funny memoir *Aunts Up the Cross*, her father, a doctor, was visiting a patient on one of the club's residential upper floors early one morning. Men were strictly forbidden to go beyond the first floor, and as he came down the stairs he was met by an outraged staff member in dressing gown and curlers who demanded to know what he was doing there. 'Ssh!' whispered the doctor. 'I overslept.' (Robin Dalton, *Aunts Up the Cross*, Viking, Melbourne, 1998 p. 107).

2   Ruth Park to J.K., 25 May 1997.

3   Quoted in Nancy Keesing, *Riding the Elephant*, Allen & Unwin, Sydney, 1989, p. 89.

4   B.D. to Henrietta Drake-Brockman, 17 February 1948.

5   Henrietta Drake-Brockman to B.D., 26 July 1967.

6   Henrietta Drake-Brockman to B.D. c.1955, letter undated.

7   *The Times*, August 1958 (undated, sent to Beatrice by Anderson's daughter Bethia Foote).

8   From an article by John Hetherington in the Vance Palmer papers, quoted by Drusilla Modjeska in *Exiles at Home*, Angus and Robertson, Sydney, 1982, p. 230.

9   Tribute volume on Beatrice's retirement from A&R, 1974; B.D. to Xavier Herbert, 24 November 1966.

10 Henrietta Drake-Brockman to B.D., March 1952 (she often didn't bother with exact dates).

11 Ric Throssell, *Wild Weeds and Wind Flowers*, Angus and Robertson, Sydney, 1975, p. 221.

12 Ibid., p. 77.

13 Katharine Susannah Prichard to B.D., 28 June 1955.

14 Katharine Susannah Prichard to B.D., early in 1960, letter undated.

15 Katharine Susannah Prichard to B.D., 1 November 1955.

16 B.D. to Dymphna Cusack, 4 October 1949.

17 B.D. to Dymphna Cusack, 19 September 1950.

18 *Caddie* was made into a successful Australian film, directed by Donald Crombie and starring Helen Morse, in 1976.

19 B.D. to Dymphna Cusack, 12 March 1957.

20 Dymphna Cusack to B.D., 9 January 1950.

21 Hazel Rowley, *Christina Stead: A Biography*, William Heinemann, Melbourne, 1993, p. 351.

22 B.D. to Dymphna Cusack, 19 September 1950.

23 B.D. to Dymphna Cusack, 4 November 1959.

24 Extract from Frank Thompson's speech for the memorial gathering for B.D. on 5 June 1992, State Library of New South Wales.

25 This is why there is comparatively little fine detail about B.D.'s working methods with Astley. Those details are much easier to trace, of course, when Beatrice was working with an author who lived interstate.

26 Conversation Thea Astley with J.K., 5 August 1998.

27 B.D. tribute volume, 1974.

The League of Gentlemen

1   Interview Elizabeth Riddell with J.K., 14 August 1996.

2   Anthony Barker, *One of the First and One of the Finest: Beatrice Davis, Book Editor*, The Society of Editors, (Vic.), Melbourne, 1991, p. 23.

3   B.D. to Rohan Rivett, 2 April 1952.

4   Ronald McKie, *Daily Telegraph*, 7 May 1949.

5   Douglas Stewart, *Norman Lindsay*, Thomas Nelson, Melbourne, 1975, p. 61.

6   B.D. to Henrietta Drake-Brockman, 15 March 1949.

7   Hugh McCrae to B.D., 27 July 1950.

8   B.D. to Guy Howarth, 19 February 1957.

9   B.D. to Guy Howarth, 24 February 1958.

10   Guy Howarth to B.D., 10 June 1960.

11   He expressed his pride in Beatrice to another farmer, who happened to be a writer: Eric Rolls.

12   So Beatrice told her colleague Anthony Barker years later: interview Anthony Barker with J.K., 12 July 1998.

13   Douglas Stewart, *Norman Lindsay*, Thomas Nelson, Melbourne, 1975, p. 65.

14   Kenneth Mackenzie to BD, 15 March 1953.

15   B.D. to Kenneth Mackenzie, 14 August 1953.

16   Kenneth Mackenzie to B.D., 17 November 1954.

17   Kenneth Mackenzie to B.D., 20 November 1954.

18   Quoted in *Modern Australian Verse*, selected by Douglas Stewart, Angus and Robertson, Sydney, 1964. 'Heat' was first published in the *Bulletin*, 1 February 1939.

19   B.D. to Cremation Society, Northern Suburbs Crematorium, 31 May 1955. She added: 'No plaque or casket is required either by the author's widow or by this firm.'

Trying Out a Lover's Voice: Hal Porter

1   Retitled 'Waterfront', the story was included in Porter's short-story collection *A Bachelor's Children* in 1962.

2   Hal Porter to B.D., 6 October 1953.

3   Hal Porter to B.D., 7 February 1955.

4   Ibid.

5   As indeed they were, in the Mitchell Library, State Library of New South Wales, and many other places, all carefully noted and annotated by the author.

6   Conversation Harry Heseltine with J.K., 16 February 2000.

7   Hal Porter to Ann Jennings, 12 August 1955, quoted in Mary Lord, *Hal Porter*, Random House, Sydney, 1993, p. 111.

8   B.D. to Hal Porter, 8 August 1955.

9   James McAuley, *Observer*, 8 March 1958.

10   Hal Porter to B.D., 28 April 1956.

11   Nan McDonald to Hal Porter, 22 February 1958.

12   J.K. conversation with Anthony Barker, 11 September 1996.

13   Mary Lord, op. cit., p. 129; David Marr, *Patrick White*, Random House, Sydney, 1991, pp. 523–4. Other versions of this story, which has done the literary rounds over the

years, state that it was Porter who made the remark about Thompson's son, not White, who was offended that Porter had implied he, White, was homosexual.

14 Hal Porter to B.D., 15 January 1960.

15 B.D. to Hal Porter, 7 January 1960.

16 B.D. to Hal Porter, 18 March 1959.

Beating the Bibliopolic Babbitts: Xavier Herbert

1   Xavier Herbert to Walter Cousins, 19 January 1940.

2   Walter Cousins to Xavier Herbert, 19 May 1948.

3   George Ferguson to Archibald Ogden, 18 January 1951.

4   B.D. to Xavier Herbert, 22 January 1951.

5   B.D. to Xavier Herbert, 10 July 1951.

6   B.D. to Xavier Herbert, 14 October 1951.

7   B.D. to Xavier Herbert, 22 March 1953.

8   Nan McDonald to George Ferguson, 2 July 1953.

9   B.D. to Xavier Herbert, 21 December 1955.

10 B.D. to Xavier Herbert, 17 March 1956.

11 Xavier Herbert to B.D., 1 May 1956.

12 Interview B.D. with Craig Munro as part of his research for *Inky Stephensen: Wild Man of Letters*.

13 Xavier Herbert to B.D., 31 May 1956.

14 B.D. to Xavier Herbert, 1 July 1956.

15 Communication Frances de Groen with J.K., 2 December 1999.

16 Xavier Herbert to B.D., 11 March 1958.

17 Xavier Herbert to B.D., 14 April 1959.

18 B.D. to Xavier Herbert, 9 March 1959.

19 B.D. to Xavier Herbert, 13 March 1959.

20 B.D. to Xavier Herbert, 15 February 1961.

21 Xavier Herbert to B.D., 20 June 1961.

22 Frances de Groen, *Xavier Herbert*, University of Queensland Press, 1999, p. 188 et seq.

23 Ruth Starke, *Writers, Readers and Rebels*, Wakefield Press, 1998, p. 90.

24 B.D. to Xavier Herbert, 5 August 1962.

25 Xavier Herbert to B.D., 22 November 1964.

26 Xavier Herbert to Hal Porter, 24 June 1974.

27 B.D. to Xavier Herbert, 24 November 1966.

28 Ibid.

29   Xavier Herbert to B.D., 16 November 1966.

30   B.D. to Xavier Herbert, 24 November 1966.

31   Xavier Herbert to B.D., 9 October 1971.

32   Xavier Herbert to Richard Walsh, 16 August 1976.

33   Frances de Groen, op. cit., pp. 226–7.

Children's Literature

1   Patricia Wrightson to J.K., 4 May 1999.

2   Ibid.

3   Patricia Wrightson in 'A Tribute to Beatrice Davis', 1973.

4   Patricia Wrightson, letter to J.K., 4 May 1999.

5   Ibid.

6   While in the 1960s–80s such use of Aboriginal culture was seen as a radical and posi-
     tive move, there is today a greater awareness that many Indigenous people are opposed
     to their culture being used in this way.

7   Patricia Wrightson in 'A Tribute to Beatrice Davis', 1973.

8   Ivan Southall to Alec Bolton, 26 June 1953.

9   Ibid.

10   Ivan Southall to J.K., 18 April 1999.

11   Ivan Southall to B.D., 11 April 1956.

12   Ivan Southall to J.K., 18 April 1999.

13   Ivan Southall to B.D., 22 July 1964.

14   Joyce Saxby died of cancer a few months after she started at A&R. She was replaced for
     a while by John Abernethy, then by Barbara Ker Wilson.

15   B.D. to Ivan Southall, 3 September 1964.

16   Ivan Southall to B.D., 16 September 1964.

17   B.D. to Ivan Southall, 28 September 1964.

18   Nan McDonald, reader's report, 29 January 1965.

19   Kath Commins to B.D., 8 February 1965.

20   Ivan Southall to John Abernethy, 9 February 1965.

21   Ivan Southall's hobby is growing fuchsias, and in 1997 he registered with the American
     Fuchsia Society an elegant blue and white flower known as the Beatrice Davis.

Angus and Robertson During the 1950s

1   B.D. to Rohan Rivett, 15 December 1950.

2   Interview Geoffrey Dutton with J.K., 14 October 1996.

3   Conversation Anthony Barker with J.K., 18 May 1997.

4   Interview Leslie Rees with J.K., 18 August 1998.

5   Colin Roderick later said (conversation with J.K., May 1999) that A.A. Ritchie, chairman of the A&R board, asked him in the early 1960s, 'Why can't we publish a bestseller like *Weird Mob*?' Roderick lost no time in telling him the story, and Ritchie told him to extract his memo to Beatrice from the files, presumably so there would be no record of the mistake. The memo is now in the Colin Roderick papers, National Library of Australia. Beatrice's letter of rejection and the two readers' reports are in the Angus and Robertson collection, State Library of New South Wales.

6   Elizabeth Wood-Ellem to J.K., 5 December 1999.

7   Alec Bolton, 'Publishing in an Age of Innocence: Angus and Robertson in the 1950s', a talk given for the Canberra Book History group on 29 November 1994.

8   Elizabeth Wood-Ellem, op cit.

9   At this time editors trained at Melbourne University Press apparently used a glass rod and a bottle of bleach as correcting agents: bleach was carefully spread over the offending passage with a glass rod, the editor waited for it to dry and fade and then typed over it. But no A&R sources remember anything like that in Beatrice's department.

10   Interview Frank Thompson with J.K., 12 September 1996.

11   Neil James, 'Basically We Thought About Books: An Oral History with George Ferguson', unpublished.

12   Bruce Pratt, 'The *Australian Encyclopedia*: A Summary of its Production and Publication' in *Fragment* (A&R house journal), no. 11, June 1959, p.3.

13   Alec Chisholm to Professor Abbie, 6 February 1950.

14   *Fragment*, no. 1, editorial, 1954.

The Battles for Angus and Robertson

1   Interview Alec Bolton with J.K., 30 September 1996.

2   B.D. to Sadie Herbert, 11 October 1960.

3   B.D. to Xavier Herbert, 15 July 1960.

4   Walter V. Burns, 'Books as merchandise', *Observer*, 26 November 1960.

5   Max Harris, *Observer*, 26 November 1960.

6   See Craig Munro, *Inky Stephensen: Wild Man of Letters*, University of Queensland Press, Brisbane, 1992, p. 262 et seq.

7   According to one figure, Halstead Press's trading profit went down from £37 000 to £580 during the time Burns was managing director.

8   Bolton moved to Ure Smith, where he remained until 1966, when he rejoined A&R to run their London office. He finally resigned from Angus and Robertson in 1970.

9   Interview Judy Wallace, née Fisher, with J.K., 12 February 1996.

10   *Observer*, 11 July 1960.

11   *Observer*, 24 December 1960.

12 Ibid.

13 B.D. to Xavier Herbert, 13 October 1960.

14 B.D. to Xavier Herbert, 30 December 1960.

15 Peter Coleman, 'The Architect of Victory', *Observer*, 7 January 1961.

16 During the meeting at which this was decided, telegrams of support from A&R authors were read out. There were so many of these that Packer lost patience and allegedly exploded, 'Look, is this a shareholders' meeting or a bloody wedding?'

17 George Ferguson to Sir Stanley Unwin, 25 May 1962.

18 Packer's biographer Bridget Griffen-Foley doubts that Packer was seriously holding talks with US publishers; more than likely he was simply trying to push up the price of his shares. See Griffen-Foley, *Sir Frank Packer: The Young Master*, HarperCollins, Sydney, 2000, p. 250.

19 Ken Wilder, *The Company You Keep: A Publisher's Memoir*, State Library of NSW Press, Sydney, 1994, p. 68.

20 Interview Colin Roderick with Neil James, November 1996.

21 Ibid.

22 The usual variant was 'Anguish and Robbery'.

The Backroom Girl Moves up Front

1   The building containing Beatrice's old bedsit was pulled down to make way for the Regent Hotel; the site of A&R's offices is now occupied by a Harry Seidler-designed office building.

2   Recalled by Frank Thompson in his address for B.D. memorial gathering at the State Library of New South Wales, 5 June 1992.

3   John Yeomans, 'An Introduction to the Shy First Lady of Publishing', Sydney *Sun*, 23 October 1964.

4   Douglas Stewart to Suzanne Lunney, oral history program, National Library of Australia, 1977.

5   Conversation Anthony Barker with J.K., February 1996.

6   John Yeomans, op. cit.

7   Hal Porter to B.D., 12 September 1958.

8   Frank Thompson, address to B.D. memorial gathering at the State Library of New South Wales, 5 June 1992.

9   Hal Porter to B.D., 26 January 1961.

10 B.D. to Hal Porter, 31 January 1961.

11 Clive James, *New Statesman,* January 1967.

12 Hal Porter to B.D., 18 December 1967.

13 Charles Monteith to John Abernethy, 10 January 1968.

14 Charles Monteith to John Abernethy, 9 February 1968.

15 Conversation Ken Wilder with J.K., 29 May 1997.

16 B.D. to Hal Porter, 12 May 1970.

17   Mary Lord, *Hal Porter: Man of Many Parts*, Random House, Sydney, 1993, p. 221.

18   B.D. to Hal Porter, 10 August 1972.

19   When Dal Stivens and a group of Australian writers got together to form the Australian Society of Authors in 1961, these configurations changed slightly.

20   Hazel Rowley, *Christina Stead: A Biography*, William Heinemann, Melbourne, 1993, p. 446.

21   According to Geoffrey Dutton, among others.

22   David Marr, *Patrick White: A Life*, Random House, Sydney, 1990, p. 464.

23   Despite A&R's pre-eminent position and the presence of Beatrice and Colin Roderick on the judging panel, Angus and Robertson books did not win the Miles Franklin Award any more often than those of other publishers.

24   One wonders what Miles Franklin – or Beatrice herself, for that matter – would have thought of 1995's winner, Helen Darville's *The Hand That Signed the Paper*.

25   These comments about Beatrice's taste come from Professor Harry Heseltine, who was on the Miles Franklin judging committee with her from 1978 to 1991.

26   Quoted in Ruth Starke, *Writers, Readers and Rebels*, Wakefield Press, Adelaide, 1998, p. ix.

27   Ibid. p. 47. Malouf described Beatrice as 'tall' – she was evidently being a particularly *grande dame* that day.

28   Interview John Broadbent with J.K., 21 January 1999.

Bartonry and Walshism

1   Interview Douglas Stewart with National Library of Australia, 1977.

2   Interview Geoffrey Dutton with J.K., 14 October 1997.

3   The term 'larrikin publishers' was first used by Laurie Muller, then publishing director of Lansdowne Press and later of the University of Queensland Press.

4   See Michael Zifcak, 'The Evolution of Australian Publishing', *Logos* 1/3, Whurr Publishers 1990. At about this time the publishing scene was beginning to metastasise, or at least to sound like the 'begat' bits of the Old Testament. O'Neil sold Lansdowne to Cheshire in 1962; Cheshire was sold to IPC of London and the Melbourne printers Wilkie & Co. in 1964 – they had already bought Jacaranda from Brian Clouston. In 1969 IPC, through their Hamlyn Books division, bought the Wilkie share and made Cheshire, Lansdowne and Jacaranda subsidiary companies.

5   John Abernethy to George Ferguson, 7 October 1969.

6   Interview Frank Thompson with J.K., 23 July 1997.

7   Interview Ken Wilder with J.K., 29 May 1997.

8   Although the deal between IPEC and AMP did not give Gordon Barton a majority shareholding in Angus and Robertson, he had now become the largest shareholder and was therefore in a position to make a takeover bid. Angus and Robertson, in response, could have adopted a share-splitting strategy using preference shares – similar to the one that defeated Frank Packer – but they did not. According to Colin Roderick (who was inteviewed by Neil James in November 1996), among others, the AMP put up the $9 million Barton needed to take over Angus and Robertson on the condition that he would let them have the site. No formal record of the deal apparently survives.

9   George Ferguson to Rohan Rivett, 30 July 1970.

10   B.D. to Hal Porter, 14 December 1970.

11   Interview Barbara Ker Wilson with J.K., 27 January 1998.

12   B.D. to Hal Porter, 12 September 1972.

13   Michael Wilding in *Days of Wine and Rage*, ed. Frank Moorhouse, Penguin, Melbourne, 1980, p. 149.

14   Interview Richard Walsh with J.K., 12 May 1999.

15   B.D. to Hal Porter, 13 September 1972.

16   Interview Richard Walsh with J.K., 12 May 1999.

17   Interview Marilyn Stacy with J.K., 18 April 1997.

18   Interview Richard Walsh with J.K., 12 May 1999.

19   Ibid. The common view that A&R didn't give Beatrice any kind of payout is inaccurate.

20   Ibid.

21   Nan McDonald, who had been very ill for some time, died in 1974.

22   Anthony Barker, *One of the First and One of the Finest: Beatrice Davis, Book Editor*, The Society of Editors (Vic.), Melbourne, 1991, p. 39.

23   B.D. to Xavier Herbert, 22 January 1974.

'I Thought You Needed Me Most'

1   B.D. to Xavier Herbert, 22 January 1974.

2   Ibid.

3   Anthony Barker, diary note, May 1974.

4   Communication Sue Ebury with J.K., August 2000.

5   Communication Bob Sessions with J.K., 10 April 2000.

6   Conversation Christopher Koch with J.K., 12 January 2000.

7   B.D. to Hal Porter, 9 February 1981.

8   According to Beatrice's correspondence with the Literature Board, in 1984 her annual income was $19 641; in 1987 it was $22 817. During the 1980s it hovered around the $20 000 per annum mark, not lavish by any means but enough to live on, considering the Bridges estate paid expenses associated with the house.

9   B.D. to Hal Porter, 13 October 1981.

10   In 1982 the age limit was raised to thirty-five.

11   In 1930 Katharine Susannah Prichard wrote a sardonic letter to a friend saying she wished her current work were her first novel so that people would make a fuss of her as a new young writer.

12   B.D. to Paul Radley, 3 February 1981.

13   Susan Wyndham, 'They Said I Was Too Old: Vogel Hoaxer Explains', *Sydney Morning Herald*, 29 May 1996.

14   Interview Jack Radley with J.K., 12 July 1996.

The Final Chapter

1 It was republished in 1996 by the State Library of NSW Press, with a new introduction by Jamie Grant, who also chose some new work.

2 B.D. to Richard Walsh, 14 July 1982.

3 All that remains of the house in Tizzana Road, Sackville, is the ruined double-brick chimney that used to be at one end of the living room. It is almost completely buried under nettles and morning glory, and difficult to find.

4 B.D. to Hal Porter, 22 June 1983.

5 B.D. to Hal Porter, 14 June 1981.

6 Quoted in Anthony Barker, *One of the First and One of the Finest: Beatrice Davis, Book Editor*, The Society of Editors (Vic.), Melbourne, 1991, pp. 41–2.

7 Interview Meg Stewart with J.K., 14 January 1996.

8 David Malouf, *The Great World*, Pan Macmillan, Sydney, 1990, p. 3.

9 After her death there was some confusion about Beatrice's intentions, and a certain amount of bad feeling about what she had intended to leave to whom.

10 A.W. Barker, diary note, 16 July 1990.

11 Her brother John died exactly a week later and Del, who had cancer, died a few months later.

WRITERS AND THEIR WORKS

The following is a list of the major writers mentioned in the text, and their most important publications.

Anderson, Ethel (1883–1958)

Poetry: *Squatter's Luck and Other Poems* (1942), *Sunday at Yarralumla* (1947), Essays: *Adventures in Appleshire* (1944), *Timeless Garden* (1945). Short fiction: *Indian Tales* (1948), *At Parramatta* (1956), *The Little Ghosts* (1959), *The Best of Ethel Anderson* (edited by J.D. Pringle 1973).

Astley, Thea (1925–)

Novels: *Girl With a Monkey* (1958), *A Descant for Gossips* (1960), *The Well Dressed Explorer* (1962), *The Slow Natives* (1965), *A Boatload of Home Folk* (1968), *The Acolyte* (1972), *A Kindness Cup* (1974), *An Item from the Late News* (1982), *Beachmasters* (1985), *It's Raining in Mango* (1987), *Reaching Tin River* (1990), *Vanishing Points* (1992), *Coda* (1994), *The Multiple Effects of Rainshadow* (1996), *Drylands* (1999). Short fiction: *Hunting the Wild Pineapple* (1979), *Collected Short Stories* (1997).

Bean, Charles Edwin Woodrow (1879–1968)

Non-fiction: *On the Wool Track* (1910), *The Dreadnought of the Darling* (1911), *Flagships Three* (1913), *The Official History of Australia in the War of 1914–1918* in twelve volumes (editor, 1921–1942), *Anzac to Amiens* (1946).

Casey, Gavin (1907–64)

Short fiction: *It's Harder for Girls* (1942), republished as *Short Shift Saturday* and *Other Stories* (1973), *Birds of a Feather* (1943). Novels: *Downhill is Easier* (1945), *The Wits Are Out* (1947), *City of Men* (1950), *Snowball* (1958), *Amid the Plenty* (1962), *The Man Whose Name Was Mud* (1963).

Chisholm, Alexander Hugh (1890–1977)

Editor-in-chief of the *Australian Encyclopedia* (1958).

Cleary, Jon (1917–)

Author of more than fifty novels, including *You Can't See Round Corners* (1947), *The Sundowners* (1952), *The Green Helmet* (1957), *North from Thursday* (1960), *The High Commissioner* (1966), *High Road to China* (1977), *A Very Private War* (1980).

Clune, Frank (1893–1971)

Author of more than sixty popular histories, travel books, autobiographical works, many in collaboration with P.R. Stephensen. Titles include *Try Anything Once* (1933), *Dig* (1937), *Tobruk to Turkey* (1943), *Ben Hall the Bushranger* (1947), *High-ho to London* (1948), *The Kelly Hunters* (1954), *Bound for Botany Bay* (1964), *Journey to Pitcairn* (1966).

Cusack, Dymphna (1902–1981)

Novels: *Jungfrau* (1936), *Pioneers on Parade* (with Miles Franklin 1939), *Come in Spinner* (with Florence James 1951), *Say No to Death* (1951), *Southern Steel* (1953), *The Sun in Exile* (1955), *Heatwave in Berlin* (1961), *Picnic Races* (1962), *Black Lightning* (1964), *The Sun is Not Enough* (1967), *The Half Burnt Tree* (1969), *A Bough in Hell* (1971). Non-fiction: *Caddie, a Sydney Barmaid: An Autobiography Written by Herself* (edited with introduction 1953), *Chinese Women Speak* (1958), *Holiday Among the Russians* (1964), *Illyria Reborn* (1966). Also plays, books for children.

Davison, Frank Dalby (1893–1970)

Fiction: *Man-Shy* (1931), *Forever Morning* (1931), *Children of the Dark People* (1935), *The Woman at the Mill* (1940), *Dusty* (1946), *The White Thorntree* (1968).

Dennis, C.J. (Clarence James) (1876–1936)

Poetry: *Backblock Ballads and Other Verses* (1913), *The Songs of a Sentimental Bloke* (1915), *The Moods of Ginger Mick* (1916), *The Glugs of Gosh* (1917), *A Book for Kids* (1921).

Dobson, Rosemary (1920–)

Poetry: *In a Convex Mirror* (1944), *The Ship of Ice* (1948), *Child with a Cockatoo* (1955), *Selected Poems* (1963), *Cock Crow* (1965), *Selected Poems* (1973), *Greek Coins* (1977), *Over the Frontier* (1978), *The Three Fates and Other Poems* (1984).

Drake-Brockman, Henrietta (1901–1968)

Novels: *Blue North* (1934), *Sheba Lane* (1936), *Younger Sons* (1937), *The Fatal Days* (1947), *The Wicked and the Fair* (1957). Short fiction: *Sydney or the Bush* (1948). Non-fiction: *Voyage to Disaster: The Life of Francis Pelsaert* (1963).

Franklin, Stella Maria Miles (1879–1954)

Novels: *My Brilliant Career* (1901), *Some Everyday Folk and Dawn* (1909), *Old Blastus of Bandicoot* (1931), *Bring the Monkey* (1933), *All That Swagger* (1936), *Pioneers on Parade* (with Dymphna Cusack 1939), *My Career Goes Bung* (1946), *Childhood at Brindabella*

(1963), *On Dearborn Street* (1982). Non-fiction: *Joseph Furphy: The Legend of a Man and His Book* (with Kate Baker 1944). Essays: *Laughter Not for a Cage* (1956). As Brent of Bin Bin: *Up the Country* (1928), *Ten Creeks Run* (1930), *Back to Bool Bool* (1931), *Prelude to Waking* (1950), *Cockatoos* (1954), *Gentlemen at Gyang Gyang* (1956).

Gibbs, May (1876–1969)

For children: *Gumnut Babies* (1916), *Snugglepot and Cuddlepie* (1918), *Little Ragged Blossom* (1920), *Bib and Bub* (1925), *Mr and Mrs Bear and Friends* (1943), *The Complete Adventures of Snugglepot and Cuddlepie* (1940).

Gilmore, Mary (1865–1962)

Poetry: *Marri'd and Other Verses* (1910), *The Passionate Heart* (1918), *The Tilted Cart* (1925), *The Wild Swan* (1930), *Under the Wilgas* (1932), *Battlefields* (1939), *Fourteen Men* (1954). Non-fiction: *Old Days, Old Ways* (1934), *More Recollections* (1935).

Glassop, Lawson (1913–1966)

We Were the Rats (1944), *Susan and the Bogeywomp* (1947), *Lucky Palmer* (1949), *The Rats in New Guinea* (1963).

Herbert, Xavier (1901–1984)

Capricornia (1938), *Seven Emus* (1959), *Soldiers' Women* (1961), *Larger than Life* (1963), *Disturbing Element* (1963), *Poor Fellow My Country* (1975).

Hill, Ernestine (1899–1972)

Non-fiction: *The Great Australian Loneliness* (1937), *Water Into Gold* (1937), *The Passing of the Aborigines* (with Daisy Bates 1938), *Australia, Land of Contrasts* (1943), *Flying Doctor Calling* (1947), *The Territory* (1951), *Kabbarli: A Personal Memoir of Daisy Bates* (1973). Fiction: *My Love Must Wait* (1941).

Hungerford, T.A.G. (Thomas Arthur Guy) (1915–)

Novels: *The Ridge and the River* (1951), *Riverslake* (1953), *Sowers of the Wind* (1954), *Shake the Golden Bough* (1963). Short fiction: *Wong Chu and the Queen's Letterbox* (1977). *Short Fiction* (edited Peter Cowan 1989). Autobiography: *Stories from Suburban Road* (1984), *A Knockabout with a Slouch Hat* (1985), *Red Rover All Over* (1986).

Idriess, Ion L. (1889–1979)

More than forty books, mainly factual adventure stories, including *Madman's Island* (1927), *Prospecting for Gold* (1931), *Lasseter's Last Ride* (1931), *Flynn of the Inland* (1932), *Gold-Dust and Ashes* (1933), *The Cattle King* (1936), *Headhunters of the Coral Sea* (1940), six military handbooks in the *Australian Guerrilla* series (1942), *The Red Chief* (1953).

Ireland, David (1927–)

Novels: *The Chantic Bird* (1968), *The Unknown Industrial Prisoner* (1971), *The Flesheaters* (1972), *Burn* (1974), *The Glass Canoe* (1976), *A Woman of the Future* (1979), *City of Women* (1981), *Archimedes and the Seagle* (1984), *Bloodfather* (1987), *The Chosen* (1997).

James, Florence (1902–1993)

With Dymphna Cusack: *Four Winds and a Family* (1947), *Come in, Spinner* (1951).

Jose, A.W. (Arthur Wilberforce) (1863–1934)

Poetry: *Sun and Cloud on River and Sea* (under pseudonym 'Ishmael Dare' 1888). Non-fiction: *A Short History of Australasia* (1899), *The Romantic Nineties* (1933). Editor-in chief of the first *Australian Encyclopedia* (1925–1926).

Keesing, Nancy (1923–1993)

Non-fiction: *Australian Bush Ballads* (1955), *Old Bush Songs* (1957), *The Pacific Book of Bush Ballads* (1967) (all with Douglas Stewart); *Garden Island People* (1975), *Riding the Elephant* (1988). Children's novels, critical essays.

Keneally, Thomas (1935–)

Novels: *The Place at Whitton* (1964), *The Fear* (1965), republished as *By the Line* (1989) *Bring Larks and Heroes* (1967), *Three Cheers for the Paraclete* (1968), *The Survivor* (1969), *A Dutiful Daughter* (1971), *The Chant of Jimmie Blacksmith* (1972), *Blood Red, Sister Rose* (1974), *Gossip from the Forest* (1975), *A Season in Purgatory* (1976), *A Victim of the Aurora* (1977), *Passenger* (1979), *Confederates* (1979), *The Cut-Rate Kingdom* (1980), *Schindler's Ark* (1982), *A Family Madness* (1985), *The Playmaker* (1987), *Towards Asmara* (1988), *Flying Hero Class* (1991), *Woman of the Inner Sea* (1992), *Jacko* (1993), *A River Town* (1995) *Bettany's Book* (2000). Non-fiction: *Outback* (1983), *Now and in Time to Be* (1991), *Our Republic* (1993), *Homebush Boy* (1995), *The Great Shame: A Story of the Irish in the Old World and the New* (1998).

Koch, Christopher J. (1932–)

Novels: *The Boys in the Island* (1958, revised 1974), *Across the Sea Wall* (1965, revised 1982), *The Year of Living Dangerously* (1978), *The Doubleman* (1985), *Highways to a War* (1995), *Out of Ireland* (1999). Essays: *Crossing the Gap* (1987).

Langley, Eve (1908–1973)

Novels: *The Pea Pickers* (1942), *White Topee* (1954).

Lindsay, Norman (1879–1969)

Novels: *A Curate in Bohemia* (1913), *Redheap* (US 1930, Australia 1959), *Saturdee* (1933), *Age of Consent* (1938), *The Cousin From Fiji* (1945). Non-fiction: *Bohemians of the Bulletin* (1965), *My Mask* (1970). For children: *The Magic Pudding* (1918).

McCrae, Hugh (1876–1958)

Poetry: *Satyrs and Sunlight* (1909), *Colombine* (1920), *Idyllia* (1922), *Poems* (1939), *Forests of Pan* (1944), *Voice of the Forest* (1945), *The Best Poems of Hugh McCrae* (edited R.G. Howarth 1961), *The Ship of Heaven* (1951). Short fiction: *Storybook Only* (1948). Non-fiction: *The Letters of Hugh McCrae* (edited R.D. FitzGerald 1970).

McDonald, Nan (Nancy) (1921–1974)

Poetry: *Pacific Sea* (1947), *The Lonely Fire* (1954), *The Lighthouse and Other Poems* (1959), *Selected Poems* (1969). Edited *Australian Poetry* (1953).

Mackenzie, Kenneth (1913–1955)

Novels: *The Young Desire It* (1937), *Chosen People* (1938), *Dead Men Rising* (1951), *The Refuge* (1954). Poetry: *Our Earth* (1937), *The Moonlit Doorway* (1944), *The Poems of Kenneth Mackenzie* (1972).

Moorhouse, Frank (1938–)

Short fiction: *Futility and Other Animals* (1969), *The Americans, Baby* (1972), *The Electrical Experience* (1974), *Conferenceville* (1976), *Tales of Mystery and Romance* (1977), *The Everlasting Secret Family and Other Secrets* (1980), *Selected Stories* (1982), *Room Service* (1985), *The Coca-Cola Kid* (1985), *Forty-Seventeen* (1988), *Fictions 88* (1988), *Lateshows* (1990), *Loose Living* (1995). Edited *Coast to Coast: Australian Stories* (1973), *The State of the Art: Australian Short Stories* (1983). Novels: *Grand Days* (1993), *Dark Palace* (2000). Non-fiction: *Days of Wine and Rage* (1980).

Niland, D'Arcy (1919–1967)

Novels: *The Shiralee* (1955), *Call Me When the Cross Turns Over* (1957), *Gold in the Streets* (1959), *The Big Smoke* (1969), *The Apprentices* (1965), *Dead Men Running* (1969). Short fiction: *The Ballad of the Fat Bushranger* (1961), *Logan's Girl* (1961), *Dadda Jumped Over Two Elephants* (1961), *Pairs and Loners* (1966), *Penguin Best Stories of D'Arcy Niland* (edited by Ruth Park 1987). Non-fiction: *Make Your Own Stories Sell* (1955).

O'Grady, John (1907–1981)

They're a Weird Mob (1957), *Cop This Lot* (1960), *Gone Fishin'* (1962), *No Kava for Johnny* (1961), *Aussie English* (1965), *Gone Troppo* (1968), *There Was a Kid* (1977).

Park, Ruth (1923–)

Fiction: *The Harp in the South* (1948), *Poor Man's Orange* (1949), *The Witch's Thorn* (1951), *A Power of Roses* (1953), *Pink Flannel* (1955), *One a Pecker, Two a Pecker* (1957), *The Good Looking Women* (1961), *Swords and Crowns and Rings* (1977), *Missus* (1985). For children: *Playing Beatie Bow* (1980), *When the Wind Changed* (1980). Non-fiction: *The Drums Go Bang!* (1956), *Companion Guide to Sydney* (1973), *A Fence Around the Cuckoo* (1992), *Fishing in the Styx* (1993), *Home Before Dark* (with Rafe Champion 1995). Edited *Penguin Best Stories of D'Arcy Niland* (1987).

Phipson, Joan (1912–)

More than thirty novels for young people, including *Christmas in the Sun* (1951), *Good Luck to the Rider* (1953), *Six and Silver* (1954), *The Family Conspiracy* (1962), *The Haunted Night* (1970), *The Way Home* (1973), *Bird Smugglers* (1977), *Keep Calm* (1978), *The Grannie Season* (1985), *Hit and Run* (1986).

Porter, Hal (1911–1984)

Novels: *A Handful of Pennies* (1958), *The Tilted Cross* (1961), *The Right Thing* (1971). Short fiction: *A Bachelor's Children* (1960), *The Cats of Venice* (1965), *Mr Butterfry and Other Tales of New Japan* (1970), *Selected Stories* (1971), *Fredo Fuss Love Life* (1974), *The Clairvoyant Goat* (1981). Autobiography: *The Watcher on the Cast-Iron Balcony* (1963), *The Paper Chase* (1966), *The Extra* (1975). Non-fiction: *Stars of Australian Stage and Screen* (1965), *The Actors* (1968), *Bairnsdale: Portrait of an Australian Country Town* (1977). Edited *Australian Poetry* (1957), *Coast to Coast* (1962). Poetry: *The Hexagon* (1956), *Elijah's Ravens* (1968), *In an Australian Country Graveyard* (1974).

Prichard, Katharine Susannah (1883–1969)

Novels: *The Pioneers* (1915), *Windlestraws* (1916), *Black Opal* (1921), *Working Bullocks* (1926), *Coonardoo* (1929), *Haxby's Circus* (1930), *Intimate Strangers* (1937), *Moon of Desire* (1941), *The Roaring Nineties* (1946), *Golden Miles* (1948), *Winged Seeds* (1950), *Subtle Flame* (1967). Memoir: *Child of the Hurricane* (1963).

Rees, Leslie (1905–2000)

For children: Digit Dick series (1942–82), *Karrawingi the Emu* (1946), many others. Non-fiction: *Towards an Australian Drama* (1953), *A History of Australian Drama* (1973, 1978, 1987), *Hold Fast to Dreams*, 1982. Edited four collections of plays, with Ruth Park adapted *The Harp in the South* for the stage (1949).

Riddell, Elizabeth (1910–2000)

Poetry: *The Untrammelled* (1940), *Poems* (1948), *Forbears* (1961), *Occasions of Birds* (1987), *From the Midnight Courtyard* (1989), *Selected Poems* (1992).

Rivett, Rohan (1917–1977)

Non-fiction: *Behind Bamboo* (1946), *Australian Citizen* (1965), *Australia* (1968), *David Rivett* (1971).

Roderick, Colin (1911–2000)

Non-fiction: Several biographical/critical studies of Henry Lawson including *Henry Lawson: A Life* (1991), biographies including *In Mortal Bondage* (1948, biography of Rosa Praed), *Miles Franklin: Her Brilliant Career* (1982), *Leichhardt: The Dauntless Explorer* (1988), *Banjo Paterson: Poet By Accident* (1993). Edited Henry Lawson's *Collected Verse* (1967–1969), *Collected Prose* (1972).

Simpson, Colin (1908–1983)

As journalist on the Sydney *Sun*, credited with revealing Ern Malley hoax (5 June 1944). Author of *Adam in Ochre* (1951), *Come Away, Pearler* (1952), *Adam with Arrows* (1953), *Adam in Plumes* (1954), *Wake Up in Europe* (1960), *Greece: The Unclouded Eye* (1968), *The New Australia* (1971).

Southall, Ivan (1921–)

Simon Black series 1950–1961, other books for children including: *Hills End* (1962), *Ash Road* (1965), *To the Wild Sky* (1967), *Finn's Folly* (1969), *Sly Old Wardrobe* (1969), *Chinaman's Reef is Ours* (1970), *Bread and Honey* (1970), *Josh* (1971), *Fly West* (1974), *What About Tomorrow* (1977), *Over the Top* (1980), *Blackbird* (1988), *The Mysterious World of Marcus Leadbeater* (1990), *Ziggurat* (1997). Non-fiction: *They Shall Not Pass Unseen* (1956), *Bluey Truscott* (1958), *Softly Tread the Brave* (1960), *War in the Air* series 1958–60.

Stead, Christina (1902–1983)

Novels: *The Salzburg Tales* (1934), *Seven Poor Men of Sydney* (1934), *The Beauties and the Furies* (1936), *House of All Nations* (1938), *The Man Who Loved Children* (1940), *For Love Alone* (1944), *Letty Fox: Her Luck* (1946), *A Little Tea, A Little Chat* (1948), *The People with the Dogs* (1952), *Cotter's England* (1967), *The Little Hotel* (1973), *Miss Herbert, The Suburban Housewife* (1976), *Ocean of Story* (1985), *I'm Dying Laughing* (1987). Novellas: *The Puzzleheaded Girl* (1967).

Stewart, Douglas (1913–1985)

Poetry: *Green Lions* (1936), *The White Cry* (1939), *Elegy for an Airman* (1940), *Sonnets to the Unknown Soldier* (1941), *The Dosser in Springtime* (1946), *Glencoe* (1947), *Sun Orchids* (1952), *The Birdsville Track* (1955), *Rutherford* (1962), *Selected Poems* (1962, 1973), *Collected Poems* (1967). Verse dramas: *The Fire on the Snow* (1941), *Ned Kelly* (1942), *The Golden Lover* (1944), *Shipwreck* (1947), *Fisher's Ghost* (1960). Short fiction: *The Girl With Red Hair* (1944). Essays: *The Flesh and the Spirit* (1948), *The Broad Stream* (1975). Editor/anthologist: (with Nancy Keesing) *Australian Bush Ballads* (1955), *Old Bush Songs* (1957), *Pacific Book of Bush Ballads* (1967), *Kenneth Mackenzie: Selected Poems* (1961), *Modern Australian Verse* (1964), *Hugh McCrae: Selected Poems* (1966), *Short Stories of Australia: The Lawson Tradition* (1967), *The Wide Brown Land* (1971). Non-fiction: *Norman Lindsay: A Personal Memoir* (1975), *A Man of Sydney* (Kenneth Slessor) (1977), *Writers of the Bulletin* (1977), *Springtime in Taranaki* (1983).

Stivens, Dal (1911–1997)

Short stories: *The Tramp and Other Stories* (1936), *The Courtship of Uncle Henry* (1946), *The Gambling Ghost and Other Tales* (1953), *Ironbark Bill* (1955), *The Scholarly Mouse and Other Tales* (1957), *Selected Stories* (1969), *The Unicorn and Other Tales* (1976), *The Demon Bowler and Other Cricket Stories* (1979), edited *Coast to Coast* (1958). Novels: *Jimmy Brockett* (1951), *The Wide Arch* (1958), *Three Persons Make a Tiger* (1968), *A Horse of Air* (1970).

Tennant, Kylie (1912–1988)

Novels: *Tiburon* (1935), *The Battlers* (1941), *Foveaux* (1939), *Ride On, Stranger* (1943), *Time Enough Later* (1945), *Lost Haven* (1946), *The Joyful Condemned* (1953), republished as *Tell Morning This* (1967), *The Honey Flow* (1956), *Tantavallon* (1983). Non-fiction: *Australia: Her Story* (1953), *Speak You So Gently* (1959), *Evatt: Politics and Justice* (1970), *The Missing Heir* (1986). For children: *Tether a Dragon* (1952), *All the Proud Tribesmen* (1959).

Timms, E.V. (Edward Vivian)(1895–1960)

Prolific writer of historical romances, including *Forever to Remain* (1948), *The Pathway of the Sun* (1949), *The Beckoning Shore* (1950), *The Valleys Beyond* (1951).

Waten, Judah (1911–1985)

Short stories: *Alien Son* (1952), *Love and Rebellion* (1978). Novels: *The Unbending* (1954), *Shares in Murder* (1957), *Time of Conflict* (1961), *Distant Land* (1964), *Season of Youth* (1966), *So Far No Further* (1971), *Scenes from Revolutionary Life* (1982).

White, Patrick (1912–1990)

Novels: *Happy Valley* (1939), *The Living and the Dead* (1941), *The Aunt's Story* (1948), *The Tree of Man* (1955), *Voss* (1957), *Riders in the Chariot* (1961), *The Solid Mandala* (1966), *The Vivisector* (1970), *The Eye of the Storm* (1973), *A Fringe of Leaves* (1976), *The Twyborn Affair* (1979), *Memoirs of Many in One* (1987). Short fiction: *The Burnt Ones* (1964), *The Cockatoos* (1974), *The Night the Prowler* (1978), *Three Uneasy Pieces* (1988). Memoir: *Flaws in the Glass* (1982).

Wright, Judith (1915–2000)

Poetry: *The Moving Image* (1946), *Woman to Man* (1949), *The Gateway* (1953), *The Two Fires* (1955), *Birds* (1960), *Five Senses* (1963), *City Sunrise* (1964), *The Other Half* (1966), *Alive: Poems 1971–1972* (1973), *Fourth Quarter and Other Poems* (1976), *Collected Poems 1941–1970* (1971), *The Double Tree: Selected Poems 1942–1976* (1978). Non-fiction: *The Generations of Men* (1959), *The Coral Battleground* (1977), *The Cry for the Dead* (1981) *Half a Lifetime* (1999). Short fiction: *The Nature of Love* (1997). Criticism: *Preoccupations in Australian Poetry* (1965).

Wrightson, Patricia (1921–)

Children's novels: *The Crooked Snake* (1955), *The Bunyip Hole* (1957), *The Rocks of Honey* (1960), *The Feather Star* (1962), *Down to Earth* (1965), *I Own the Racecourse!* (1968), *An Older Kind of Magic* (1972), *The Nargun and the Stars* (1973), *The Ice is Coming* (1977), *The Dark Bright Water* (1978), *Behind the Wind* (1981), *Balyet* (1989), *Song of Wirrun* (1993), *A Little Fear* (1993), *Shadows of Time* (1994), *Rattler's Place* (1997).

BIBLIOGRAPHY

Manuscripts

State Library of New South Wales

When Angus and Robertson was sold to Gordon Barton in 1970, a large number of office files was bought by the State Library of New South Wales and housed in the Mitchell Library. These files (ML MSS 3269) run from the early 1930s to the late 1960s – a separate collection traces A&R's early years – and without them this book could not have been written. They contain Beatrice's letters to authors, theirs to her, readers' reports, office memoranda, scribbled notes, publicity material, newspaper cuttings, and even, very occasionally, statements of accounts. The following is a list of the major files consulted from this collection: Anderson, Ethel T.; Angus & Robertson; Australian Classics; *Australian Poetry*; A&R internal mail; Royalties; Astley, Thea; Australian Department of Manpower; Commonwealth Literary Fund; *Australian Encyclopedia*; Baker, Kate; Baker, Sidney J.; Barnard, Marjorie; Bean, C.E.W.; Bolton, Alec; Drake-Brockman, Henrietta; Bruce, Mary Grant; Casey, Gavin; Cayley, Neville; Chauvel, Charles; Chisholm, Alexander; Cousins, Walter; Cusack, Dymphna; Davison, Frank Dalby; Dennis, C.J.; Dobson, Rosemary; Durack, Mary; Dutton, Geoffrey; Ellis, Malcolm Henry; Evatt, H. V.; Fellowship of Australian Writers;. Ferguson, George Adie; FitzGerald, R.D.; Forshaw, Thelma; Franklin, Miles; Gaskin, Catherine; Gibbs, May; Gilmore, Mary; Halstead Press Pty Ltd; Haylen, Leslie; Herbert, Xavier; Hill, Ernestine; Hungerford, T.A.G.; Ireland, David; Jacaranda Press; James, Florence; Jose, A.W.; Keesing, Nancy; Keneally, Thomas; Langley, Eve; Lawson, Henry; Lindsay, Norman; McCrae, Hugh; McCuaig, Ronald; McDonald, Nan; McFadyen, Ella; Mackenzie, Kenneth; Mann, Cecil; Menzies, Sir Robert Gordon; Moore, Tom Inglis; Niland, D'Arcy; Park, Ruth; Penton, Brian; Phelan, Nancy; Phillips, A.A.; Phipson, Joan; Porter, Hal; Prichard, Katharine Susannah; Publishers' Association of Australia; Rees, Leslie; Riddell, Elizabeth; Rivett, Rohan; Roderick, Colin; Rolls, Eric; Salter, Elizabeth; Saxby, Joyce; Sheppard, Alex; Simpson, Colin; Slessor, Kenneth; Society of Women Writers of NSW; Southall, Ivan; *Southerly* magazine; Stephensen, P.R.; Stewart, Douglas; Stivens, Dal; Stone, Walter; Stow, Randolph; Tennant, Kylie; Timms, E.V.; Tracy, Paul; Trist, Margaret; Waten, Judah; White, Myrtle Rose; White, Patrick; Wiley, Rebecca; Wilson, Barbara Ker; Wrightson, Patricia.

Also consulted were the papers of Miles Franklin and Florence James, and Enid Moon's unpublished manuscript, *Memoirs of a Galley Slave*.

National Library of Australia

The papers of Beatrice Davis, Xavier Herbert, Ernestine Hill, Hal Porter, Colin Roderick, Dal Stivens, Kylie Tennant.

Fryer Library, University of Queensland
The papers of Thea Astley, Thelma Forshaw, Xavier Herbert, Ernestine Hill.

Newspapers and periodicals

Age, Argus, Australian, Australian Women's Weekly, Bendigo Advertiser, Daily Telegraph, Fragment (house magazine of Angus and Robertson), *Meanjin, Observer, Overland, Publishing Studies, Southerly, Sunday Telegraph, Sydney Morning Herald.*

Books

Barker, Anthony, *George Robertson: A Publishing Life in Letters*, University of Queensland Press, St Lucia, 1993.

—— *One of the First and One of the Finest: Beatrice Davis, Book Editor*, The Society of Editors (Vic.), Melbourne, 1991.

—— *Dear Robertson: Letters to an Australian Publisher*, Angus and Robertson, Sydney, 1982.

Coleman, Peter, *Obscenity, Blasphemy, Sedition*, Angus and Robertson, Sydney, 1974.

Davis, Beatrice, ed., *Coast to Coast: Australian Stories 1942*, Angus and Robertson, Sydney, 1943.

——, ed., *The Moderns*, Angus and Robertson, Sydney, 1967.

de Groen, Frances, *Xavier Herbert*, University of Queensland Press, St Lucia, 1999.

Dutton, Geoffrey *A Rare Bird: Penguin Books in Australia 1946–96*, Penguin, Melbourne, 1996.

Eley, Beverley, *Ion Idriess*, Editions Tom Thompson, Potts Point, 1995.

Fairey, Eric, *The 38th Battalion*, Bendigo Advertiser, Bendigo, 1920.

Falkiner, Suzanne, *The Writers' Landscape: Wilderness*, Simon and Schuster, Sydney, 1992.

—— *The Writers' Landscape: Settlement*, Simon and Schuster, Sydney, 1992.

Gill, Lydia, *My Town: Sydney in the 1930s*, State Library of NSW Press, Sydney, 1993.

Green, H.M., *A History of Australian Literature, Pure and Applied*, vols 1 and 2, Angus and Robertson, Sydney, 1984.

Griffen-Foley, Bridget, *Sir Frank Packer: The Young Master*, HarperCollins, Sydney, 2000.

Harrison-Ford, ed., *Fighting Words*, Lothian, Melbourne, 1986.

Hodges, Harry, *Appendix to an Unwritten History*, Angus and Robertson, Sydney, 1949.

Johnston, Grahame, *Annals of Australian Literature*, Oxford University Press, Melbourne, 1970.

Keesing, Nancy, *Riding the Elephant*, Allen & Unwin, Sydney, 1988.

Kramer, Leonie, ed., *The Oxford History of Australian Literature*, Oxford University Press, Melbourne, 1981.

Lindsay, Norman, *Bohemians at the* Bulletin, Angus and Robertson, Sydney, 1973.

Lord, Mary, *Hal Porter: Man of Many Parts*, Random House, Sydney, 1993.

Marr, David, *Patrick White: A Life*, Random House, Sydney, 1990.

McVitty, Walter, *Authors & Illustrators of Australian Children's Books*, Hodder and Stoughton, Sydney, 1989.

Modjeska, Drusilla, *Exiles at Home*, Angus and Robertson, Sydney, 1981.

Munro, Craig, *Inky Stephensen: Wild Man of Letters*, University of Queensland Press, St Lucia, 1984.

Park, Ruth, *The Companion Guide to Sydney*, Collins, Sydney, 1973.

—— *A Fence Around the Cuckoo*, Viking, Melbourne, 1992.

—— *Fishing in the Styx*, Viking, Melbourne, 1993.

—— with D'Arcy Niland, *The Drums Go Bang!*, Angus and Robertson, Sydney, 1956.

Roe, Jill, ed., *My Congenials: Miles Franklin and Friends in Letters*, vols 1 and 2, Angus and Robertson, Sydney, 1993.

Rowley, Hazel, *Christina Stead: A Biography*, William Heinemann, Melbourne, 1993.

Starke, Ruth, *Writers, Readers and Rebels*, Wakefield Press, Adelaide, 1998.

Stewart, Douglas, *Norman Lindsay: A Personal Memoir*, Thomas Nelson, Melbourne, 1975.

—— *Springtime In Taranaki*, Angus and Robertson, Sydney, 1983.

—— *Writers of the* Bulletin, Australian Broadcasting Commission, Sydney, 1977.

Stewart, Meg, *Autobiography of My Mother*, Penguin, Melbourne, 1985.

Stone, Jean, *The Passionate Bibliophile*, Angus and Robertson, Sydney, 1988.

Throssell, Ric, *Wild Weeds and Wind Flowers: The Life and Letters of Katharine Susannah Prichard*, Angus and Robertson, Sydney, 1975.

Thwaite, Joy L., *The Importance of Being Eve Langley*, Angus and Robertson, Sydney, 1989.

Tyrrell, James R., *Old Books, Old Friends, Old Sydney*, Angus and Robertson, Sydney, 1987.

Wilde, Hooton, Andrews, eds, *The Oxford Companion to Australian Literature*, Oxford University Press, Melbourne, 1991.

Wilder, Ken, *The Company You Keep: A Publisher's Memoir*, State Library of NSW Press, Sydney, 1994.

Wilkes, G.A., *A Dictionary of Australian Colloquialisms*, Sydney University Press, Sydney, 1978.

Sound recordings
National Library of Australia
Beatrice Davis, George Ferguson, Colin Roderick, Douglas Stewart.

Interviews

Vincentia Anderson, Thea Astley, Anthony Barker, Lyle Blair, Alec Bolton, June Bonser, Peter and Doreen Bridges, John Broadbent, Charles Davis, Rosemary Dobson, Anne Dowey, Geoffrey Dutton, John Ferguson, Dorothy Fillingham, Elizabeth Fulton, Patrick Gallagher, Anne Godden, Harry Heseltine, Elva Hoy, Tom Hungerford, Barbara Ker Wilson, Christopher Koch, Leonie Kramer, Mary Lord, Margot Ludovici, Enid Moon, Frank Moorhouse, Geoff Morley, Nancy Phelan, Jack Radley, Leslie Rees, Elizabeth Riddell, Colin Roderick, Marilyn Stacy, Marley Stephen, Meg Stewart, Frank Thompson, Judy Wallace, Richard Walsh.

Written communication

Sue Ebury, Joan Fitzhardinge, Elisabeth Hughes, Ruth Park, Robert Sessions, Ivan Southall, Elizabeth Wood-Ellem, Patricia Wrightson.

Index